NH

T3-BSE-270

# PERSPECTIVES ON RESOURCE POLICY MODELING
## POLICY MODELING
### Energy and Minerals

# PERSPECTIVES ON RESOURCE POLICY MODELING
## Energy and Minerals

*Edited by*

RAPHAEL AMIT and MORDECAI AVRIEL
Technion—Israel Institute of Technology

BALLINGER PUBLISHING COMPANY
Cambridge, Massachusetts
A Subsidiary of Harper & Row, Publishers, Inc.

*333.79*
*P467*

Copyright © 1982 by Ballinger Publishing Company. All rights reserved. No part of this publication may be reproduced, stored in a retrieval system, or transmitted in any form or by any means, electronic, mechanical, photocopy, recording or otherwise, without the prior written consent of the publisher.

International Standard Book Number: 0-88410-837-6

Library of Congress Catalog Card Number: 81-12697

Printed in the United States of America


**Library of Congress Cataloging in Publication Data**
Main entry under title:

Perspectives on resource policy modeling, energy and minerals.
    Includes index.
    1. Energy policy–United States.  2. Conservation of natural resources–Government policy–United States.  3. Energy policy–United States–Decision making–Mathematical models.  4. Conservation of natural resources–United States–Decision making–Mathematical models.  I. Amit, Raphael.  II. Avriel, M.

| HD9502.U52P468 | 333.79'0973 | 81-12697 |
| ISBN 0-88410-837-6 | | AACR2 |

# Contents

[13008]

v

University Libraries
Carnegie Mellon University
Pittsburgh, Pennsylvania 15213

# List of Figures

# List of Tables

# PREFACE

*NA*

Energy- and mineral-modeling methodologies and applications have rapidly developed in recent years as the complexity of problems facing decisionmakers all over the world warranted more sophisticated decision tools, especially mathematical models. There is a great deal of similarity between policy decisions in the energy and the mineral sectors. In fact, the energy crisis of the mid-1970s was a combined result of policy decisions made by some of the countries that have the largest reserves of crude oil—one of the most important minerals in our world. The complexity of problems arising in energy and minerals is due to the fundamental role they play in our life— as an essential ingredient of a modern society—and their impact on the economy, the environment, and international relations.

Most modeling effort has been directed toward analyzing the interrelationship between energy or minerals and the economy. Several methodologies have been utilized for this purpose, the most notable being econometrics, input-output techniques, and process analysis. In econometrics, historical data are combined with economic theory to formulate sets of equations that quantitatively characterize the behavior and interaction between sectors of the economy. The input-output technique describes in a consistent way the transactions (in physical and monetary terms) between sectors of the economy, and in the process analysis approach, production processes are described through engineering relationships. Various combinations of these modeling techniques have been implemented to analyze the rather complex, continuously changing systems of energy or minerals and the implications of events and decisions on the economy as a whole and on its particular subsectors. This book includes a discussion of these methods, along with numerous examples of their applications in several countries.

Even though models are meant to be tools to aid decisionmakers in evaluating events or policies, potential model users are often hesitant in using models in their planning processes. Such an attitude is usually the result of a lack of proper communication between policymakers and model builders and, more generally, due to a lack of understanding of the role of models in the decisionmaking process. How decisionmakers and modelers visualize this process is a core question that should be addressed. An attempt has been made here to examine some aspects of this question and especially the extent and manner in which models can or should be utilized.

This volume contains lectures presented at the International Seminar on Resource Policy Modeling that was held in Herzlia, Israel, in December 1980. The seminar was organized by the editors of this book, themselves modelers in the energy and mineral areas. The seminar was attended by over fifty participants (model builders and decisionmakers) from Canada, France, Israel, and the United States. We would like to take this opportunity to thank the authors for their prompt and efficient help in the reviewing process and in the preparation of the final manuscripts.

We are deeply indebted to UNESCO for its financial support of the seminar and, in particular, to Mr. Sydney Passman, who was instrumental in arranging the grant. Special thanks are due to Mrs. Hemda Zinder, secretary general of the Israel Commission for UNESCO, for the generous financial support of the commission and for her active role in the success of the seminar. Many thanks are also due to the Israel Academy of Sciences and Humanities, IBM Israel, Technion—Israel Institute of Technology, and Yad Avi-Hayishuv for their sponsorship of the seminar. Professors Martin Greenberger, United States, and Edmundo Rofman, France, gave great assistance in the initiation of the seminar; and Solomon Berahas, Avi Breiner, and Reuven Karni of Technion provided assistance throughout its duration.

We are most grateful to Mrs. Nilly Schnapp for her outstanding administrative assistance in the organization and running of the seminar and to Dean Michael Rubinowitz, who made available to us resources of the Faculty of Industrial Engineering and Management of Technion.

Special thanks are also due to Mr. Steven Cramer and to Ms. Carol Franco, as well as to the rest of the Ballinger editorial staff for their behind the scenes help and guidance in the preparation of this book.

September 1981                                                    R. Amit
                                                                 M. Avriel

# INTRODUCTION

Methodological approaches to energy and mineral modeling, as well as their applications in assisting policy analysts and decisionmakers, are the focus of this volume. Four main areas are addressed—(1) A description and application of the main approaches to modeling energy-economy interactions (process analysis, econometric estimation, and input-output techniques) with examples from the United States, Canada, and Israel; (2) modeling the electricity sector, including demand estimation, pricing policies, and investment planning; (3) methods and applications of mineral supply models, including a discussion of mineral supply functions, resource depletion, costs of minerals, and the implications of government regulations; and (4) examination of the energy-related decisionmaking process, including a discussion of the role of models and modelers in policy formulation. These topics were discussed at the International Seminar on Resource Policy Modeling in Herzlia, Israel, in December 1980 and are organized into fourteen chapters that are briefly summarized in the following sections.

Chapter 1 (Jorgenson) presents an integrated dynamic general equilibrium model of energy-economy interactions in the United States. The model is based on process analysis, input-output, and econometric techniques. At the core of the model is a system of accounts for the private domestic sector of the U.S. economy, including interindustry transactions, primary inputs, and final demand. The industrial sectors are divided into five energy and four nonenergy sectors. This system of accounts is represented in the model

1

by an input-output table of coefficients. Whereas traditional input-output analysis assumes fixed coefficients, the coefficients in this model are determined by an econometric model that takes into account producer behavior for each industrial sector as a function of prices. Similarly, personal consumption coefficients are also determined by the econometric model as functions of prices and total personal consumption expenditures. The econometric model also determines a balance between the outputs of the energy- and non-energy-producing sectors and the deliveries to all industrial sectors and final demand.

The use of the dynamic general equilibrium model is illustrated in Chapter 1 by analyzing the impact on the U.S. economy of higher energy prices for the 1972–1976 period. The analysis is carried out by simulating two economic growth paths over the period. In the first simulation, actual values of world oil prices and other exogenous variables are employed to provide an estimate of the actual development of the U.S. economy. In the second simulation, energy prices are held fixed at their 1972 level. The differences in the model solutions of the two simulations indicate the impact of energy prices on both the quantity and the price aspects of the U.S. economy. The energy sector is represented by a process analysis type optimization model, in which eleven energy resource supplies are allocated to nineteen conversion processes to meet the demands for sixteen energy end products. The solution of the model is obtained by a linear program, whose dual solution provides a set of energy product and energy resource shadow prices. The process analysis model is well suited to analyze various aspects of introducing new energy technologies. In integrating the process analysis model with the econometric model, one can assess energy policy alternatives by receiving a detailed characterization of energy supply and conversion technologies, along with a complete representation of the economy. Chapter 1 concludes by analyzing a series of energy policy alternatives aimed at reducing energy use by varying degress of taxation and import tariffs.

In his nine-sector model, Jorgenson (Chapter 1) utilizes annual time series derived from conventional market data for estimating statistical cost functions that determine the I-O coefficients. Chapter 2 (Griffin) offers an alternative approach for long-run cost analysis—replacing actual data with data that are generated by simulating an engineering process model for alternative input prices as the basis for statistical cost function estimation. This data source, referred to as "pseudodata," allows for wide variations in relative input prices and for considering the effects of technological change as well as the effects of new government regulations. Despite these apparent advantages of the "pseudodata" approach to data generation, there are also potential limitations to this method. Specifically, the quality and detail of the engineering data contained in the process model are key to the success of this estimation method.

An economywide dynamic energy model, based on combined process analysis, input-output, and development planning approaches, is presented in Chapter 3 (Avriel, Breiner, and Karni). The OMER (Optimization Model for Energy Resources) model developed by the authors to study energy policy alternatives for Israel is described here, and three different future scenarios are analyzed. The OMER model uses process analysis to describe the various energy supply technologies available today and those that are planned for the future. This part of the model has a detailed electricity supply portion. Interindustry transactions are modeled by input-output type relations in which energy products (crude oil, distillates, coal, and so forth) and electricity are represented in true physical flows, whereas nonenergy products are expressed in fixed value monetary terms. Investments in the energy and nonenergy sectors of the economy are treated in a similar way. For the energy-producing sectors the investments are expressed in process analysis form, whereas investments in nonenergy sectors are represented by a capital coefficient matrix. Other portions of the model include income-dependent personal consumption, foreign trade, and labor force with time-dependent productivities. Altogether the combined model is solved by linear programming, in which discounted GDP, personal consumption, or some other measure of the standard of living is maximized. Since virtually all energy used in Israel today is oil based and the country has no domestic oil sources, the studies performed by the authors with the OMER model clearly indicate the need for diversifying primary energy sources to include coal, nuclear, hydro, solar, and other sources. The main difference between the scenarios is the assumed rate of increase in the world price of oil, coal, and uranium. These assumed rates have a strong impact on the possible growth of the Israeli economy and its structure.

Chapter 4 (Fuller, Schwartz, and Ziemba) describes a series of studies made with an economywide energy policy model for Canada. These studies focus on the possibilities for energy self-sufficiency and exports in the next half century. For the purpose of energy policy questions, Canada can be divided into two major regions—the East, which is the major energy-consuming region; and the West, which is the major supplier of energy. Lack of adequate transportation networks and the long distance between the two regions prevent, at present, a true energy self-sufficiency. The aim of the studies is to explore the possible limits of self-sufficiency under various supply constrained futures. The multiperiod energy model used for these studies is a combined process analysis type model of energy supply and econometric model of demand. The model determines output levels and endogenous energy prices in each period in the East and the West that balance supply and demand to maximize the discounted sum of consumers' plus producers' surplus. Assumptions used in the model contain limits on the fraction of oil demand in the East that can be met by oil from the West, introduction rates and dates of new technologies, limits on energy exports, and a two-price system of energy (domestic and international). Seven scenarios are developed and presented in the chapter, including low coal availability, a moratorium on new nuclear plants, unavailability of frontier oil and gas, and increased emphasis on energy conservation. The main conclusion is that Canada can become self-sufficient in the next decade and remain so for the rest of the planning horizon. This self-sufficiency can be attained with prices of domestic oil and gas well below current and projected world prices.

The next three chapters address modeling issues of the electricity sector. Taylor, Blattenberger, and Rennhack (Chapter 5) focus on the problems arising in building econometric demand models of a good or service, such as electricity, that is sold on a multipart (block) tariff—that is, the price of electricity varies with the quantity purchased, usually downwards. While in most empirical demand analysis, price is represented as a single parameter, since it is assumed that the individual consumer faces a price that is independent of the amount that is purchased, this can obviously not be assumed when a block tariff price structure exists. Taylor, Blattenberger, and Rennhack first review the implication of block tariffs for the theory of consumer choice. The main points here are that individual demand functions are discontinuous and may be multivalued. Also, the consumer's equilibrium cannot be derived analytically through solutions of the utility maximization problem. Since econometric analysis requires an analytic function, the above properties of individual demand functions need to be overcome. The authors discuss three approaches that require either the use of price variables that are constructed from rate schedules or the use of a simultaneous equation model in which the average price is assumed endogenous. The ways in which price variables are constructed and represented in an econometric equation are addressed and then illustrated with U.S. data. The empirical results for residential electricity consumption in the United States are quite similar for two alternative aggregation methods over consumers that are on the same schedule: The first method involves parameterizing the rate schedule in terms of total revenue as a function of quantity and then defining the marginal price as the slope of this function and the fixed charge as its intercept. The second method involves identifying a "typical" customer on the schedule and then defining the marginal price and the fixed charge in terms of the block that contains this customer.

Investment planning and pricing policy in the electricity sector are the subjects of Chapter 6 (Munasinghe). The author describes a modern methodology in which the optimal levels of investments and prices are determined, taking into account the relationship that exists between price and capacity levels. The factors considered in the author's analysis include the reliability of the system, short- and long-term marginal costs, outage costs, peak-load pricing, and capital indivisibilities. Prices and investment levels are determined by maximizing the net benefits of electricity consumption. In practice, however, more than a single objective function or criterion should be considered. The author describes an approach in which prices are set so that they are responsive to several objectives. A case study of optimizing the long-range electricity distribution plan of a Brazilian city, carried out by the author, concludes the chapter. The theoretical concepts and some details of the methodology presented in the chapter appear in the Appendixes.

Chapter 7 (Levin, Tishler, and Zahavi) preesents an engineering-economic model of electricity supply to determine the equilibrium price and quantity demanded of electrical energy over time, using a time step approach—by solving the problem as related one-year problems, with the equilibrium solution of a given year being the input to the following year. The core of the model is the one-step problem whose objective is to find the equilibrium solution for any given year in the future. The one-step model consists of a demand side and a supply side, integrated through a price mechanism to balance supply and demand. Analytical conditions are derived under which the equilibrium solution exists and is unique, and the sensitivity of the equilibrium solution to changes in the demand parameter is investigated. The model is relatively simple, and its flexibility enables decisionmakers to examine a variety of alternative economic and technological scenarios.

Methods and applications of mineral policy models are represented in this book by the chapters by Vogely; Barnett, van Muiswinkel, and Shechter; and Amit, Martin, and Naughton. Chapter 8 (Vogely) reviews a variety of issues related to mineral supply modeling. He starts by addressing the fundamental process of depletion, since in most supply-modeling efforts of mineral resources, it is assumed that the mineral stock is fixed and exhausted through time. Vogely concludes that the process of resource depletion is both an economic and a geological phenomenon. It is economic since any deposit will be abandoned when continued production is no longer profitable. The replacement of that depleted deposit depends both on geological occurrences of other deposits and on the economics of adding production capacity. Finally, the limit on further production is always an economic, not a geologic, phenomenon. Vogely then addresses the issue of adequacy of mineral resources to sustain economic growth. The problem here is whether or not quantities will be available at any given price level to meet resource requirements at that price level. Vogely argues that any projections of availability as a function of price through time for mineral resources is highly uncertain. Likewise, on the demand side, he argues that predicting the determining factors through time is impossible. Thus, he concludes that resource availability should be seen as a process, rather than as a point estimate and that strategies should be developed to address that process. Vogely then turns to a description of the worldwide distribution of reserves and the productive capacity of certain internationally traded materials, which arises from geologic and economic factors and which plays a major role in economic development. Realizing that supply modeling must be undertaken within the physical resource constraints, Vogely relates these limitations to problems of supply modeling. The fundamental structure of mineral supply functions is discussed, the characteristics of metals markets are presented, and many issues in modeling the supply of minerals are explored. The author concludes that supply modeling based upon cost is inhibited by the lack of fundamental knowledge of the first two stages of the production function—that is, the state of nature as incorporated in resource endowment and the modeling of the exploration function. Once a deposit is discovered and appraised, the entry of that deposit into the economic system as a source of supply much more closely parallels standard microeconomic theory, and so modeling problems at this stage do not create unusual difficulties.

Barnett, van Muiswinkel, and Shechter (Chapter 9) examine empirically the question of increasing economic scarcity of minerals and the underlying forces that affect mineral cost trends. Two main factors that may contribute to higher prices are identified—first, the physical endowments of mineral resources are fixed while demand grows resulting from economic growth causing reserves to be depleted; and second, the cheaper resources are utilized first. The authors have studied the price histories of minerals and measured world market prices. Their main argument is that from World War II until the early 1970s, the prices of minerals have generally declined relative to the overall price level in OECD-Europe. In the decade of the 1970s, following the rise in oil prices, the prices of the other fuel minerals and some of the nonfuel minerals have also risen. The effect of these price changes varies from country to country, with the developing countries being most powerfully affected.

Resource policy models can be useful tools for analyzing the impact of government regulations on the production and demand for a certain mineral resource. Amit, Martin, and Naughton (Chapter 10) present and test a methodology for measuring quantitatively the effects of legislative acts— some of which may conflict with each other—on coal production and prices. A quantitative analysis of the impact of two pieces of legislation on production and prices is provided. The implications of this technique on measuring the private sector cost associated with complying with government regulations are discussed. It is found that the cumulative cost of both regulations when analyzed together is greater than the cumulative cost of the individual regulations when analyzed separately.

The last four chapters deal with policy formulation, modelers, and the decisionmaking process. Aronofsky, Karni, and Marcuse (Chapter 11) focus on the more general problem of policymaking. Models employed for public policy analysis can usually provide answers to only a limited number of questions, with many important issues remaining unresolved. The authors address the question of formulating energy goals and policy alternatives. They first relate energy goals to more general societal goals on the one hand and to energy subgoals on the other, creating an energy goal hierarchy. Next, the concept of energy policy is defined and is related to energy goals and policy actions. Finally, the question of measuring the attainment of goals by the various policy actions is raised and discussed—that is, the structural aspects of the policymaking methodology (goals, actions, attributes, and the relationships between them) are combined into a general framework. The ideas of the methodology are illustrated by using the Israeli energy policy case.

Does the output of a model simulating the future reflect the personal views of the modeler? Are modelers different from other people in their projections of the future? Greenberger (Chapter 12) reports on an informal study on questioning energy modelers and a group of other persons, familiar with energy matters, on their projections concerning future oil prices. Greenberger concludes that modelers are not different from, say, executives of an oil company in this respect. Both groups think that oil prices will continue to increase in the future, and this prediction is also obtained from the models of the same modelers.

A critical appraisal of the role of models in the public policymaking process is presented in Chapter 13 (Bargur). The main theme is that there is an everwidening gap between the expectations of decisionmakers from policy models and the actual usefulness of these models for the decisionmakers. Bargur criticizes on the one hand decisionmakers, who expect more and more of models and then become disillusioned by the models' inability to provide answers to their specific questions, and on the other hand model builders, who are overconfident of the models' abilities to aid decisionmakers. The author continues his thesis by suggesting two types of exceptions in which models can be useful to the decisionmaker. The first type of exception is the so-called "comprehensive orientation" model, in which some large system (e.g., the macroeconomy) is modeled and the model produces "trend analysis" type results that are of a very general nature and do not provide "exact" predictions of a detailed nature. The second type of exception is the smaller, more specific problem-solving type model that can provide good predictions to very specific issues, limited in scope. Bargur claims that other combinations, such as using comprehensive models to obtain detailed predictions or using limited scope models to provide general orientations, are doomed to fail. The author aims to support his views, which are not necessarily shared by model builders or other decisionmakers, by analyzing the role of models in the Israeli energy policy area.

The book concludes (Chapter 14) with an abridged version of a panel discussion on the role of policy models in the decisionmaking process. The panel consisted of decisionmakers and model builders and attempted to analyze the issue mainly from the viewpoint of the personal experience of the panel members.

# 1 ECONOMETRIC AND PROCESS ANALYSIS MODELS FOR ENERGY POLICY ASSESSMENTS

*Dale W. Jorgenson*
*Frederic Eaton Abbe Professor of Economics*
*Harvard University*

1322
7230
2230
US

## INTRODUCTION

The assessment of alternative energy policies requires the analysis of the likely impacts of such policy measures as price controls, taxes to stimulate energy conservation in the private sector, government support to generate additional conventional energy supplies, and government-sponsored research and development programs directed toward providing new technology for energy production, conversion, and utilization. The evaluation of alternative energy policies must incorporate information from detailed engineering studies of specific technologies and must include the assessment of policy impacts on the structure of the energy sector and on the overall level and composition of economic activity.

Alternative models for energy policy assessment have been developed on the basis of both process analysis and econometrics. In the process analysis approach energy flows are described in physical terms. The description is not limited to a particular technology, but encompasses the entire system for the production and utilization of energy. In the econometric approach,

I am indebted to Dr. Kenneth C. Hoffman of Mathtech, Inc., and Dr. Edward A. Hudson of Dale W. Jorgenson Associates for material included in this chapter based on collaborative research reported more fully elsewhere. Financial support for the research has been provided by the National Science Foundation through Harvard University. Any remaining errors are the sole responsibility of the author.

the representation of technology is based on behavioral and technical responses of production patterns to alternative prices; a similar approach can be employed for the representation of consumer preferences. Flows of ecnomic activity, including energy flows, are described in terms of economic accounts in current and constant prices.

The process approach provides for the incorporation of information from detailed engineering studies, including studies of technologies that are under consideration for future implementation. This approach is well adapted to the description of the energy sector; however, the representation of aggregate economic activity by means of process analysis is infeasible. The econometric approach is well adapted to the description of aggregate economic activity in summary form and provides for the analysis of policy impacts on the overall level of economic activity and its distribution among industry groups or groups of consumers. However, this approach is infeasible for the study of technologies that are not already in use or for the study of consumer preferences for commodities not already in existence.

A satisfactory framework for the assessment of the full range of alternative energy policies requires an approach that encompasses both process analysis and econometrics. The usefulness of integrating these approaches to energy policy analysis is the fact that the output of the energy-producing industries is largely consumed by other industries rather than by final consumers such as households, governments, and the rest of the world. A natural focal point for the study of the impact of energy policy is the matrix of interindustry transactions, representing flows of commodities, including energy, among industrial sectors. For the energy sector, these transactions can be expressed in economic terms, in current and constant prices, to provide a link with econometric models. These energy sector transactions can also be expressed in physical terms, in British thermal units, to provide a link with process analysis models. Using both forms for the expression of energy flows, process analysis and econometric modeling can be combined.

The objective of this chapter is to present an approach to energy policy assessment based on the integration of econometric and process analysis models. In the following section, we present a dynamic general equilibrium model of the U.S. economy developed by Hudson and Jorgenson (1974a). We apply this model to an analysis of the impact of higher energy prices on the U.S. economy over the period 1972–76. In section three we present a process analysis model of the energy sector developed by Hoffman (1973) and his associates at Brookhaven National Laboratories. We then present a combined econometric and process model, incorporating features of the dynamic general equilibrium model of the U.S. economy and the process analysis model of the energy sector. In the final section, we employ the combined model to analyze the impact of alternative policies to reduce energy consumption in the United States.

## ECONOMETRIC INTERINDUSTRY MODEL

The first component of our model for the analysis of energy research, development, and demonstration policy is an econometric model of interindustry transactions, developed by Hudson and Jorgenson (1974a). This model is based on a system of accounts for the private domestic sector of the U.S. economy, including final demand, primary input, and interindustry transactions in current and constant prices. (The data are described in more detail in a report by Jack Faucett Associates 1973.) By means of this accounting system, we can trace the process of production for energy and nonenergy products from the purchase of primary inputs through all stages of intermediate processing to deliveries to final demand. The accounts in constant prices correspond to commodity flows in physical terms. For energy sectors (or industries), these flows can be measured in physical units such as tons of coal, barrels of petroleum, and thousands of cubic feet of natural gas or, alternatively, in energy units such as British termal units (btus). The accounts in current prices correspond to flows in financial terms and can be used to generate financial accounts for each industry group included in the model. For energy and nonenergy sectors the prices can be expressed as index numbers; for energy sectors the prices can also be given in terms of physical or energy units.

In our system of accounts, the private domestic sector of the U.S. economy is divided among nine industry groups, including five groups within the energy sector—coal mining, crude petroleum and natural gas, petroleum refining, electric utilities, and gas utilities. Our representation of the energy sector provides for an analysis of the impact of energy research, development, and demonstration policy on the industrial sectors directly affected by changes in energy technology. By incorporating final demand and four industry groups making up the nonenergy sector, we can assess the impact of changes in energy technology on the sectors that consume energy products. Our complete system of accounts is represented in diagrammatic form in Figure 1–1, which lists the nine industry groups included in the accounting system. The figure also lists three categories of primary inputs (capital services, labor services, and imports) and four categories of final demand (consumption, investment, government purchases, and exports).

**Figure 1-1.**    Interindustry Transactions in the Econometric Model.

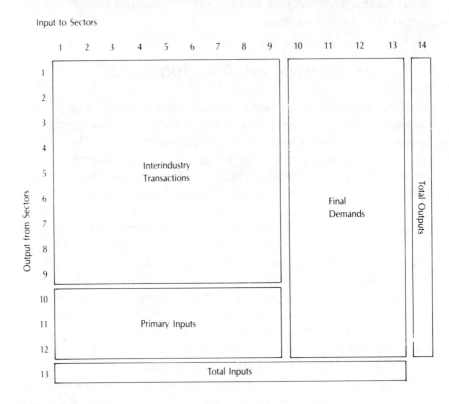

*Industry Sectors*

1.    Agriculture, nonfuel mining, and construction
2.    Manufacturing, excluding petroleum refining
3.    Transportation
4.    Communications, trade, and services
5.    Coal mining
6.    Crude petroleum and natural gas
7.    Petroleum refining
8.    Electric utilities
9.    Gas utilities

*Primary Inputs*

10.    Imports
11.    Capital services
12.    Labor services

*Final Demands*

10.    Personal consumption expenditures
11.    Gross private domestic investment
12.    Government purchases of goods and services
13.    Exports

In our system of accounts for interindustry transactions, each industry group purchases primary inputs and intermediate inputs produced in each of the nine industrial sectors. These purchases are represented as columns of the matrix of interindustry transactions in Figure 1-1. Intermediate inputs include five types of energy—coal, crude petroleum and natural gas, refined petroleum, refined natural gas, and electricity—and four types of nonenergy products. The output of each industry is distributed to final demand and to intermediate demand by each of the nine industrial sectors. These deliveries are represented as rows of the matrix of interindustry transactions in Figure 1-1. The rows corresponding to the five industries that make up the energy sector include deliveries of energy products to energy and nonenergy sectors and to final demand. Similarly, the rows corresponding to the four industries of the nonenergy sector include deliveries of nonenergy products.

## Econometric Model

Our econometric model of interindustry transactions (see Hudson and Jorgenson 1974a: 467–74) includes balance equations between supply and demand for the products of each of the nine industrial sectors included in the model. These balance equations state that the output of each sector in constant prices must be equal to deliveries of this output to all nine industrial sectors and to all four categories of final demand. For energy products the balance equations assure that for each form of energy, the energy units produced must be equal to the energy units consumed by all industrial groups and by final demand. Similarly, our econometric model includes balance equations stating that the output of each sector in current prices must be equal to the value of deliveries of this output to all nine industrial sectors and to final demand. These equations assure that differences between prices received by producers and prices paid by consumers reflect excise and sale taxes paid on the value of each product.

Our econometric model of interindustry transations includes models of producer behavior (Berndt and Jorgenson 1973; see also, Christensen, Jorgenson, and Lau 1973; Berndt and Wood 1976) for each industrial group included in the model. Producer behavior in each industrial sector can be characterized by a system of technical coefficients, giving primary and intermediate inputs per unit of output of the sector. The model of producer behavior gives the technical coefficients as functions of the prices of output and of primary and intermediate input. For each sector the technical coefficients as functions of the prices are generated from the price possibility frontier, giving the minimum price of output of the sector attainable for given prices of primary and intermediate inputs and for a given level of productivity of the sector. The minimum price of output depends on the technological possibilities for substitution among primary and intermediate inputs, including the substitution between energy and nonenergy inputs and the substitution among different forms of energy. The price possibility frontier for each sector provides a representation of the technology of that sector. This representation assures that the value of output of the sector is equal to the sum of the values of all primary and intermediate inputs into the sector.

Finally, our econometric model of interindustry transactions includes a model of consumer behavior (Jorgenson 1975; see also, Christensen, Jorgenson, and Lau 1975; Jorgenson and Lau 1975) that allocates personal consumption expenditures among the commodity groups included in final demand. Consumer behavior can be characterized by a system of quantities purchased per capita. The model of consumer behavior gives the quantities purchased as functions of total personal consumption expenditures per capita, prices of the products of the nine industrial sectors, and prices of capital services and noncompetitive imports. The quantities purchased as functions of total expenditure and the prices can be generated from the indirect utility function, giving the maximum level of utility attainable for given total expenditure and given prices. The maximum level of utility depends on the substitutability of alternative goods and services in consumption, so that the indirect utility function provides a representation of consumer preferences. This representation assures that the sum of the values of all quantities purchased is equal to total personal consumption expenditures.

Our econometric interindustry model is represented in diagrammatic form in Figure 1-2. Starting with prices of primary inputs—capital services, labor services, and imports—and levels of productivity in each of the nine industrial sectors, the prices of both energy and nonenergy products are determined by the nine price possibility frontiers. With prices of primary inputs and prices of energy and nonenergy products determined from our model of production, we can generate the matrix of technical coefficients, giving primary and intermediate inputs per unit of the output of each of the nine industrial sectors. Similarly, with total personal consumption expenditures, the prices of capital services and noncompetitive imports, and the prices of energy and nonenergy products, we can generate the quantities purchased per capita of the products of the nine industrial sectors, capital services, and noncompetitive imports. Given the level of population, we can convert these quantities per capita to quantities of personal consumption

**Figure 1–2.**   Flow Chart of the Econometric Model.

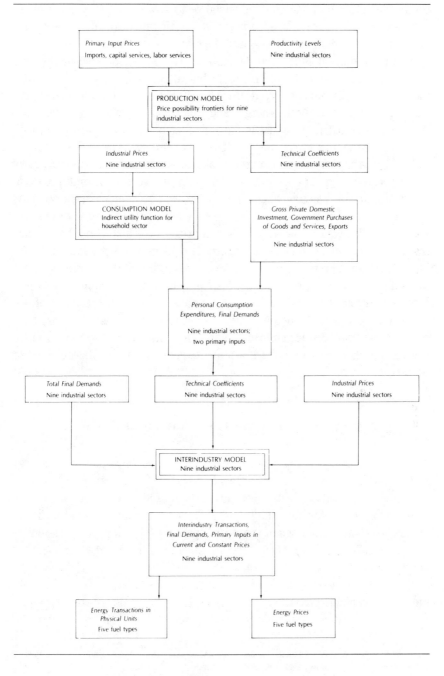

expenditures as a component of final demand. To obtain final demand for the output of each of the nine industrial sectors, we add personal consumption expenditures to gross private domestic investment, government purchases of goods and services, and exports.

From the quantities of final demand for the output of each of the nine industrial sectors and the matrix of technical coefficients, providing intermediate input per unit of output of each sector, we can determine the quantities of output of both energy and nonenergy sectors. We can also determine the distribution of the output of each sector between intermediate and final demand and the distribution of intermediate demand among intermediate inputs to each of the nine industrial sectors. The output of energy sectors and its distribution can be expressed in constant prices, in physical units such as tons of coal or barrels of petroleum, or in energy units such as btus. From the matrix of technical coefficients of primary input per unit of output, we can determine the quantities of primary input into each sector. Finally, given the nine industrial prices and the prices of primary inputs, we can express the flow of primary input, interindustry transactions, and final demand in current prices. We can generate the complete system of interindustry accounts in current and constant prices from the prices of primary inputs, the levels of productivity in each interindustry sector, total personal consumption expenditures, and the quantities of final demand for the output of each sector for investment, government purchases, and exports.[1]

## Energy Prices and the U.S. Economy, 1972–76

This section analyzes the impact on the U.S. economy of higher energy prices resulting from the establishment of the OPEC oil cartel in late 1973 and early 1974. 1972 is the last year of the "old" regime of energy prices and the starting point for our study. and 1976 is the termination point. These years correspond to periods of vigorous expansion following the recessions of 1970 and 1974. However, they differ drastically with regard to the level of energy prices.

The dynamic general equilibrium model described above was used to simulate two economic growth paths over the 1972–76 period. In the first simulation, actual values of the exogenous variables, including world oil prices.

---

1. Applications of the econometric model to policy analysis are given by Hudson and Jorgenson (1974 a,b,c; 1975 a,b) and Jorgenson and Wright (1975).

were employed as the basis for model solution. This simulation provides an estimate of the actual development of the U.S. economy between 1972 and 1976. In the second simulation, 1972 energy prices were employed over the whole 1972–76 period—that is, world oil prices were held at their 1972 real values. As world oil prices are the only set of exogenous variables to change between the two simulations, the differences in simulated economic activity can be attributed solely to the impact of the oil price increase.

The energy price increases and the associated changes in energy use have significant impacts on both the quantity and the price aspects of overall economic activity. The level of real GNP is reduced, or the rate of economic growth is slowed, as a result of the energy changes, while the structure of spending and production is also changed. The simulated level of real GNP for 1976 under actual energy prices conditions was 1.2 percent lower than its simulated level under 1972 energy prices. There are two broad sets of reasons for this decline, one centering on input productivity and one centering on capital. Producers can economize on energy by substituting other inputs for energy. This substitution is not perfect, so that productivity is adversely affected. Also, any additional input used as a substitute for energy must be taken from some other use, further reducing overall product potential.

A second result of the energy-induced changes is a reduction in the demand for capital services. The rise in energy prices leads to a decline in the rate of return on capital. This reduces the incentive for saving and investment, slowing the rate of capital formation. In addition, the energy price increase and the reduced level of real GNP lead to less saving and to a change in the allocation of income between consumption on the one hand and saving and investment on the other. This further slows the rate of capital formation. There is, then, a slowing of the rate of growth of productive capacity, with the result that the level of potential GNP is lower than would have been the case at lower energy prices. The combination of substitution and capacity expansion effects results in a reduction in 1976 real GNP estimated to be 1.2 percent.

The structure of economic activity, as well as the level of output, change as a result of the energy price increases: The pattern of relative prices is changed, with the more energy-intensive goods experiencing the largest price increases. These prices changes induce a shift in the pattern of final demand spending away from the now more expensive energy-intensive products. Similarly, the pattern of inputs into production is altered, with the role of energy being reduced. Since both the mix of final demand and the way in which output is made are adjusted away from energy, the composition of total output shifts away from energy and energy-intensive sectors. Thus, the energy content of each dollar of GNP is reduced.

Final demand patterns alter as a result of the energy price rises, partly in response to the price increases themselves and partly as a result of the associated reduction in income levels. The essence of the final demand changes is a movement away from energy-intensive and now more expensive, products. Table 1–1 shows the change in the pattern of final demand between

**Table 1–1.**   Composition of Final Demand and Input-Output Coefficients in 1976.

| | Simulated with 1972 Energy Prices | Simulated with 1976 Energy Prices |
|---|---|---|
| *Real Final Demand* | | |
| Agriculture, construction | 12.3 | 12.0 |
| Manufacturing | 32.4 | 32.2 |
| Transportation | 2.6 | 2.5 |
| Services, trade, communications | 48.8 | 49.9 |
| Energy | 3.9 | 3.4 |
| Total | 100.0 | 100.0 |
| *Input-Output Coefficients* | | |
| Agriculture | | |
| Capital | .2242 | .2222 |
| Labor | .2532 | .2591 |
| Energy | .0219 | .0204 |
| Materials | .5007 | .4983 |
| Manufacturing | | |
| Capital | .1059 | .1015 |
| Labor | .2822 | .2909 |
| Energy | .0215 | .0181 |
| Materials | .5904 | .5895 |
| Transportation | | |
| Capital | .1777 | .1743 |
| Labor | .4102 | .4135 |
| Energy | .0415 | .0380 |
| Materials | .3706 | .3742 |
| Services, trade, communications | | |
| Capital | .2962 | .2995 |
| Labor | .4262 | .4347 |
| Energy | .0176 | .0143 |
| Materials | .2599 | .2515 |

the high and low energy price simulations. This gives the allocation of real final demand—personal consumption expenditure, investment, government purchaes and exports—over the four nonenergy products and delivered energy. The principal change is the reduction in the relative importance of energy purchases.

The share of energy in total real final demand declines from 3.9 percent under low energy price conditions to 3.4 percent with higher energy prices. Purchases of transportation and of agriculture and construction show the next largest declines, while the share of manufacturing is reduced slightly. Purchases of services are increased, absorbing the expenditure directed away from each other type of output. The services share of total real final demand rises from 48.8 percent at the lower energy prices to 49.9 percent under the higher price conditions. In sum, final demand is redirected from energy to nonenergy products and, within the nonenergy group, is redirected to the purchase of services.

Producers respond to higher energy prices in a way analogous to the final demand. The motivation is to minimize unit costs in the face of the new price structure. The direction of adjustment is to economize on energy input: Given time to adjust, significant reductions in energy use are cost effective under a regime of high energy prices. This reduction in energy use is not costless; it is achieved by increases in the use of labor services, capital services, and other intermediate inputs. What is involved, therefore, is a redirection of input patterns away from energy, not a new reduction in input levels. The changes in input patterns can be represented by changes in input-output coefficients. These coefficients are given in Table 1–1 for four input categories—capital services, labor services, energy, and materials (all other intermediate inputs—into each nonenergy-producing sector. Two sets of coefficients are given for each sector, one of the simulated 1976 coefficeints, the other the coefficients simulated for 1976 on the basis of the 1972 energy prices.

The result of the adjustment from lower to the higher energy prices is that for every sector, the energy input coefficient is reduced. Thus, considerable energy savings are achieved in production activities. The greatest preportionate energy reductions are estimated to occur in services and in manufacturing, where the energy input coefficient is reduced about 15 percent. Agriculture, construction, and transportation obtain energy savings of half this magnitude. There are also considerable differences among the sectors as to how the other inputs are adjusted to compensate for reduced energy use. Labor input is increased in all sectors, and capital input is decreased in all sectors other than services. Manufacturing shows particularly noticeable adjustments:—The 16 percent reduction in the energy co-efficient is accompanied by a 4 percent reduction in the capital coefficient, with both of these reductions being offset by the 3 percent increase in labor intensity of production.

These changes in the structure of economic activity are significant. First, they imply that all aspects of the economy are affected by the energy changes, dispite the relatively small fraction that energy represents in total economic output. Thus, the relative sizes of the different sectors of the econ-omy are affected, as well as spending patterns and production patterns. In addition, the use of capital and labor inputs will be affected throughout the economy. Second, these structural changes have the effect of reducing the energy content of spending and of production. This means that under the higher energy prices, each dollar of GNP requires less  energy input.


## Reductions in Energy Use


In 1972, the United States used 72 quadrillion btu of primary energy input to sustain a real GNP of $1,171 billion in constant 1972 dollars (1972$). This corresponds to an energy-GNP ratio of 61.4 (million btu per 1972 $). In 1976, GNP had increased to $1,275 billion in constant dollars, but energy use had risen only to 73.7 quadrillion btu,[2]  giving a significantly reduced energy-GNP ratio. If the 1972 energy-GNP ratio still applied in 1976, the primary energy input required to sustain the actual 1976 GNP would have been 78.3 quadrillion btu. Further, if GNP had not been reduced by 1.2 per-cent as a result of the energy changes, the required energy input would have been 79.2 quadrillion btu. In these very aggregative terms, therefore, the changes in energy use patterns and economic structure induced by the rise in energy prices resulted in an annual energy reduction, by 1976, of 5.5 quadrillion btu.[3]

The nonenergy component of real final spending accounts for a larger proportion of total final spending in 1976 as a result of higher energy prices. This shift in itself implies that more energy will be absorbed in satisfying nonenergy final demand. Also, the composition of spending between the nonenergy types of goods and services is altered. Services absorb a greater

2. U.S. primary energy input in 1976 is estimated to be 73.7 quadrillion btu see Energy Information Administration 1978: II, xx.

3. The role of energy in the current recovery is also discussed in Jorgenson (1978). The impact of energy policy on future U.S. economic growth is considered in Hudson and Jorgenson (1978a).

part of this spending, while the other sectors decline in relative importance. Since services are the least energy-intensive type of production, this corresponds to a shift away from energy-intensive purchases. This shift works to reduce the energy content of final demand. These two types of adjustment work in opposite directions as far as energy use is concerned. The net change in the energy content of nonenergy final demand could therefore be either positive or negative.

The information needed to calculate the impact of the change in nonenergy final demand on energy utilization is presented in Table 1–2. This table determines the direct energy requirements for 1976 nonenergy final demand as well as the energy requirements of the same total spending allocated over commodities in the pattern associated with the 1972 energy prices. Under the higher energy prices, there is a reduced direct energy requirement for agricultrue and construction, manufacturing, and transportation. In contrast, spending on services is increased, and this additional energy demand is sufficient to offset the energy reduction in the other three sectors. The net effect is that the direct energy content of nonenergy final spending increases as a consequence of the higher energy prices. The increase is small, about $0.4 billion in constant dollars, but it does work to counter the energy reductions achieved by lower direct final purchases of energy.

The pattern of inputs into each production sector also changes as a result of the energy price increases; these changes have been analyzed above in terms of adjustments in input-output coefficients. This restructuring of inputs means that the energy content of any set of total sectoral outputs is reduced. The implications of this reduction for energy saving are developed in Table 1–2, which give the energy content of the 1976 gross sectoral outputs for input patterns simulated under the 1976 energy prices as well as the energy content of this output given the input patterns simulated on the basis of the 1972 energy prices. The change in energy content is the energy saving achieved by producing a given set of outputs in a less energy-intensive way. These energy savings are substantial, corresponding to $6.4 billion in constant 1972 dollars. The greatest energy savings are achieved in the manufacturing and the services sectors, reflecting their large size and the substantial reductions in unit energy requirements in these sectors.

The final type of energy saving is that due to a reduction in the overall level of economic activity. The rise in energy prices led to a reduction in 1976 real GNP, relative to its simulated level based on 1972 energy prices, of 1.2 percent. This reduction implies a decline of approximately 1.2 percent in energy use, even with no changes in economic structure. This yields an

**Table 1-2.** Change in Energy Input Due to Changes in Nonenergy Final Demand and Input Restructuring (real variables in 1972 $ billion).

| Change in Final Demand | Real Final Demand in Pattern for Prices 1976 | 1972 | Energy Input Coefficient for 1976 Based on 1972 Prices | Direct Energy Input for Spending in Pattern 1976 | 1972 | Change in Direct Energy Input |
|---|---|---|---|---|---|---|
| Agriculture, construction | 159.0 | 163.6 | .0219 | 3.48 | 3.58 | -0.10 |
| Manufacturing | 428.4 | 431.0 | .0215 | 9.21 | 9.27 | -0.06 |
| Transportation | 33.1 | 34.5 | .0415 | 1.37 | 1.43 | -0.06 |
| Services, trade, communications | 663.5 | 649.0 | .0176 | 11.68 | 11.42 | 0.26 |
| | | | | 25.75 | 25.70 | 0.04 |

| Input Restructuring | Total Output 1976 | Energy Input Coefficients for Energy Prices 1976 | 1972 | Energy Requirements with Coefficients 1976 | 1972 | Change in Energy Requirements |
|---|---|---|---|---|---|---|
| Agriculture, construction | 221 | .0204 | .0219 | 4.51 | 4.84 | -0.33 |
| Manufacturing | 719 | .0181 | .0215 | 13.01 | 15.46 | -2.45 |
| Transportation | 86 | .0380 | .0415 | 3.27 | 3.57 | -0.30 |
| Services, trade, communications | 1004 | .0143 | .0176 | 14.36 | 17.67 | -3.31 |
| | | | | 35.15 | 41.54 | -6.39 |

| Sources of Energy Saving in 1976 | Energy Reduction, Percent of Total | Energy Reduction, Quadrillion btu |
| --- | --- | --- |
| Changes in final demand | | |
| Reduction in energy purchases | 37.5 | 2.7 |
| Restructuring of nonenergy purchases | -2.5 | -0.2 |
| Total | 35 | 2.5 |
| Changes in inputs to production | | |
| Agriculture, construction | 2.1 | 0.1 |
| Manufacturing | 15.3 | 1.1 |
| Transportation | 1.9 | 0.1 |
| Services, trade, communications | 20.7 | 1.5 |
| Total | 40 | 2.8 |
| Reduction in economic activity | 25 | 1.8 |
| Total energy reduction | 100 | 7.1 |

estimate of $1.5 billion in constant dollars as the energy saved from reducing the scale of economic activity. Using the approximation that the three types of energy reduction sum to the total estimated 1976 energy saving of 5.5 quadrillion btu and that each constant dollar of energy purchases in equal to the same number of btu's, we can allocate the total energy saving over its source. The results are presented in Table 1–2.

Final demand changes account for 43 percent of the total saving, and all of this is due to redirection of final demand away from energy purchases and toward purchases of nonenergy goods and services. Changes in input patterns, as represented by the input-output coefficients, account for 46 percent of the total energy saving. Reductions in energy used in service types of activities are the greatest single source of saving, at 24 percent of the total, with energy savings in the manufacturing sector, at 18 percent of the total, also significant. Energy reduction in agriculture, construction, and transportation provides a much smaller volume of saving, about 5 percent of the total. Reduction in the scale of economic activity resulting from the higher energy prices yields the final 11 percent of energy saving. In terms of physical units of energy, the total saving of over 5 quadrillion btu is secured by a reduction of over 2 quads in final demand energy use, a reduction of 1 quad in manufacturing, a decline of 1 quad in services, and a decrease of less than 1 quad due to the reduced level of economic activity.

## Reduction in Capital Stock

The adjustments in spending and production patterns that reduce energy utilization relative to GNP also affect capital, labor, and other factors of production. Demand for capital is affected as a result of changes in the mix of final demand and of changes in the pattern of inputs into each sector. In addition, any effect of the energy changes on the level of real GNP will affect the overall level of demand for capital services as an input to production. Each of these three sources of change in demand for capital services is now examined, and the implications of the energy changes for investment and capacity growth are indicated.

The change in the composition of final demand will alter the demand for capital input. For example, a decline in the proportion of spending directed to energy and an increase in spending on services will result in a different overall level of demand for capital services, since the capital requirements of these two types of production are different. The magnitudes of these changes are calculated in Table 1–3, which presents the direct capital requirements of the simulated total 1976 real final demand when allocated over sectors in the 1976 patterns and when allocated over sectors in the patterns corresponding to the 1972 energy prices. As a result of the higher energy prices, spending is directed away from energy and goods and toward services. The capital content of each type of production is held constant at the levels given by the input-output coefficients corresponding to 1972 energy prices. Under these conditions, the change in final demand composition leads to an increase of $1.3 billion in constant 1972 dollars in the direct requirement of capital services input. The central reason for this increase is the shift of spending toward services, which are relatively capital intensive.

The demand for capital services also changes as a result of adjustments in the pattern of inputs to each producing sector. Specifically, the energy changes are accompanied by shifts in the capital input-output coefficients. In some sectors production becomes more capital intensive; in other sectors it becomes less. The overall change depends on the size of the shift in each sector and the magnitude of each sector. Estimates of the size of the overall change are presented in Table 1–3, which gives the input of capital services needed to sustain the simulated 1976 set of sector outputs under two sets of conditions—the 1976 input patterns and the input patterns simulated for 1976 based on 1972 energy prices. The difference in total demand for capital services, a reduction of $0.3 billion in constant 1972 dollars, is due to a change in methods of production. Under higher energy prices, manufacturing uses less capital services, while the services sector demands a higher input of capital. These are almost offsetting, leaving a small overall decline in demand for capital.

Also, the energy price increases lead to a reduction in the simulated 1976 real GNP below the level estimated on the basis of a continuation of 1972 energy prices. The 1976 real GNP was 1.2 percent less than the level estimated for lower prices. As an approximation, this corresponds to a 1.2 percent reduction in the demand for capital services input. In constant 1972 dollars, this results in a $5.8 billion reduction in demand for capital services, purely because the overall level of economic activity has been reduced.

The three types of changes in demand for capital services can now be brought together. Under the first order approximation that these components can be added to find the total change in capital demand, this gives the result that total demand for the input of capital services in 1976 is reduced by $4.8 billion in constant 1972 dollars due to the increase in energy prices. Capital services are the effective input services, or the implicit rental value, of capital stock. In any year, each dollar of capital stock provides about $0.14 of capital services. Therefore, this reduction in demand for

**Table 1–3.** Change in Capital Due to Changes in Final Demand and Input Restructuring (real variables in 1972 $ billion).

| Change in Final Demand | Real Final Demand in Pattern for Prices 1976 | 1972 | Capital Input Coefficient for 1976 Based on 1972 Prices | Direct Capital Input for Spending in Pattern 1976 | 1972 | Change in Direct Capital Input |
|---|---|---|---|---|---|---|
| Agriculture, construction | 159.0 | 163.6 | .2242 | 35.65 | 36.68 | −1.03 |
| Manufacturing | 428.4 | 431.0 | .1059 | 45.37 | 45.64 | −0.28 |
| Transportation | 33.1 | 34.5 | .1777 | 5.88 | 6.13 | −0.25 |
| Services, trade, communications | 663.5 | 649.0 | .2962 | 196.53 | 192.23 | 4.29 |
| Energy | 45.7 | 51.6 | .2396 | 10.95 | 12.36 | −1.41 |
| | 1329.7 | 1329.7 | | 294.38 | 293.04 | 1.33 |

| Input Restructuring | Total Output, 1976 | Capital Input Coefficients for Energy Prices 1976 | 1972 | Capital Requirements with Coefficients 1976 | 1972 | Change in Capital Requirements |
|---|---|---|---|---|---|---|
| Agriculture, construction | 221 | .2222 | .2242 | 49.11 | 49.55 | −0.44 |
| Manufacturing | 719 | .1015 | .1059 | 72.98 | 76.14 | −3.16 |
| Transportation | 86 | .1743 | .1777 | 14.99 | 15.28 | −0.29 |
| Services, trade, communications | 1004 | .2995 | .2962 | 300.70 | 297.38 | 3.32 |
| Energy | 128 | .2418 | .2396 | 30.95 | 30.67 | 0.28 |
| | | | | 468.73 | 469.02 | −0.29 |

| Sources of Reduction in Capital Stock in 1976 | Capital Reduction, Percent of Total | Capital Reduction, 1972 $ billion |
|---|---|---|
| Changes in final demand | -9.2 | -9.5 |
| Changes in inputs to production | | |
| Agriculture, construction | 3.0 | 3.1 |
| Manufacturing | 21.9 | 22.4 |
| Transportation | 2.0 | 2.0 |
| Services, trade, communications | -23.0 | -23.5 |
| Energy | -1.9 | -2.0 |
| Total | 2.0 | 2.1 |
| Reduction in economic activity | 107.2 | 110.7 |
| Total reduction in capital stock | 100.0 | 103.3 |

capital services corresponds to a reduction of $34 billion in constant dollars in the desired level of capital stock. The allocation of this reduction over its sources is given in Table 1–3. The principal sources of change in demand for capital are the restructuring of inputs into manufacturing, which has a $22.4 billion in constant dollars reduction in demand for capital stock; the restructuring of inputs into services, which increases demand for capital stock by $23.5 billion in constant dollars; and the decline in the level of economic activity, which reduces demand for capital stock by $41.1 billion in constant dollars.

These are significant changes in the demand for capital. The overall decrease in demand for capital stock will be reflected in investment levels being less than they would otherwise have been. If, for illustration, all the capital adjustment were made in 1976, investment would be $34 billion in constant dollars less than would normally be expected. When this is compared to the actual 1976 gross investment of $165 billion in constant dollars, it can be seen that the relative magnitude of the investment adjustment can be substantial.

## Increase in Employment

Demand for labor and employment is affected by the energy-induced adjustments through a restructuring of final demand spending, a restructuring of the pattern of inputs into production, and a reduction in the overall level of economic activity. Final demand is redirected, as a result of the higher energy prices, away from energy and energy-intensive products. The implications of this adjustment for labor demand are presented in Table 1–4. The 1976 total real final demand is allocated over sectors in two patterns, one based on the 1976 energy prices, the other based on the lower 1972 energy prices. The direct energy content of these demands is calculated using one set of input-output coefficients. The result of the rise in energy prices is a substantial increase in labor demand. This increase, $2.9 billion in constant 1972 dollars, reflects the shift of final demand toward services and away from energy and goods. Since service activities have a higher labor content than any of these other sectors, the result of the shift is an increase in the labor content of each dollar of real final demand.

A restructuring of input patterns occurs in the producing sectors of the economy. In each sector, increased labor input per unit of output results from the higher energy prices, so that the labor input for any given set of production outputs is increased. Table 1–4 presents the information to make an exact calculation of this change in labor demand. In each sector, the labor input coefficient increases, leading to additional labor demand, totaling $16.6 billion in constant 1972 dollars. The largest increases in labor demand occur in services and in manufacturing, although there is also a significant increase in the agriculture and construction sector.

These two structural shifts add substantially to the demand for labor. Together they amount to $19.5 billion in constant 1972 dollars or 2.64 percent of the total demand for labor at the lower energy prices. If there had been no change in real GNP as a result of higher energy prices, the adjustment to these higher prices would greatly stimulate the demand for labor. If all this increase were reflected in an increase in employment, it would imply a 2.6 percent reduction in the rate of unemployment as a result of higher energy prices. In the absence of an increase in energy prices, the rate of unemployment would have been 10.3 percent, rather than the actual rate of 7.7 percent. In fact, the increase in energy prices reduced the level of GNP. This decreases the demand for labor and works against the employment expansion resulting from higher energy prices.

The estimated real GNP impact of the higher energy prices in 1976 is a reduction of 1.2 percent. This reduces the demand for labor by approximately 1.2 percent. The overall labor impact of the higher energy prices, therefore, is an increase in effective demand of 1.4 percent. Even taking account of the recessionary impact of the higher energy prices, the price rises still lead to a significant expansion in labor demand and in employment.

This expansion is an increase of 1.3 million in the number of jobs. Table 1–4 shows the sources of this increase in employment. The principal source is the restructuring of the inputs into production as labor substitutes for energy input. In particular, there are large increases in employment in the manufacturing and services sectors. The change in final demand patterns adds slightly to labor demand, but this is more than offset by the effects of the reduced level of economic activity. All told, restructuring of inputs provides about 2 million more jobs, changed final demand patterns lead to 0.4 million jobs, and the decline in real GNP causes a loss of 1.1 million jobs.

The adjustments of spending and input patterns in response to higher energy prices leads to a substantial increase in the demand for labor. This increase in labor input is beneficial for employment, but it has an adverse effect on productivity. More labor input per unit of output is equivalent to less output per unit of labor input. These adjustments, therefore, lead to a reduction in the average gross productivity of labor. Specifically, the economic restructuring that occurs between the high and low energy price simulations leads to a 2.57 percent reduction in average labor productivity. To

**Table 1-4.** Change in Direct Labor Input Due to Changes in Final Demand and Input Restructuring (real variables in 1972 $ billion).

| Change in Final Demand | Real Final Demand in Pattern for Prices 1976 | 1972 | Labor Input Coefficient for 1976 Based on 1972 Prices: | Direct Labor Input for Spending in Pattern 1976 | 1972 | Change in Direct Labor Input |
|---|---|---|---|---|---|---|
| Agriculture, construction | 159.0 | 163.6 | .2532 | 40.26 | 41.42 | −1.16 |
| Manufacturing | 428.4 | 431.0 | .2822 | 120.89 | 121.63 | −0.73 |
| Transportation | 33.1 | 34.5 | .4102 | 13.58 | 14.15 | −0.57 |
| Services, trade, communications | 663.5 | 649.0 | .4262 | 282.78 | 276.60 | 6.18 |
| Energy | 45.7 | 51.6 | .1329 | 6.07 | 6.86 | −0.78 |
|  | 1329.7 | 1329.7 |  | 463.58 | 460.66 | 2.92 |

| Input Restructuring | Total Output 1976 | Labor Input Coefficients for Energy Prices 1976 | 1972 | Labor Requirements with Coefficients 1976 | 1972 | Change in Labor Requirements |
|---|---|---|---|---|---|---|
| Agriculture, construction | 221 | .2591 | .2532 | 57.26 | 55.96 | 1.30 |
| Manufacturing | 719 | .2909 | .2822 | 209.16 | 202.90 | 6.26 |
| Transportation | 86 | .4135 | .4102 | 35.56 | 35.28 | 0.28 |
| Services, trade, communications | 1004 | .4347 | .4262 | 436.44 | 427.90 | 8.54 |
| Energy | 128 | .1344 | .1329 | 17.20 | 17.01 | 0.19 |
|  |  |  |  | 755.62 | 739.05 |  |

| Sources of Reduction in Employment in 1976 | Employment Reduction, Percent of Total | Employment Reduction, Millions of Jobs |
|---|---|---|
| Changes in final demand | −71.1 | 0.3 |
| Changes in inputs to production | | |
| Agriculture, construction | −31.6 | 0.2 |
| Manufacturing | −152.3 | 0.8 |
| Transportation | −6.8 | 0.0 |
| Services, trade, communications | −207.8 | 1.0 |
| Energy | −4.6 | 0.0 |
| Total | −403.1 | 2.0 |
| Reduction in economic activity | 574.2 | −2.8 |
| Total increase in employment | 100.0 | −0.5 |

place this change in perspective, it can be noted that the average annual rate of labor productivity increase between 1950 and 1970 was 1.44 percent. The reduction of 2.57 percent corresponds to the loss of two years of productivity improvement.

The decline in productivity growth implies that the rate of growth in real wages will not be as rapid as would otherwise have occurred. To the extent that real wages outstrip the slower growth of productivity, unit labor costs will increase, and inflation will be accelerated. Lower productivity leads to slower real growth, to slower growth of real wages, and to more rapid inflation. It should be noted that these are one-time effects rather than permanent trends. Once the economy has adjusted to the new labor and productivity conditions, there will be no further energy-induced pressures for further changes.

## INTEGRATION OF ENERGY POLICY MODELS

The second component of our model for the analysis of energy policy is a process analysis model of the energy sector, developed at the Brookhaven National Laboratory (see Hoffman 1973; Cherniavsky 1974). This model is based on the reference energy system description (see Beller 1975) of the U.S. energy system, which provides a complete physical description of the energy flows and conversion efficiencies from extraction of primary energy sources through refining and various stages of conversion from one energy form to another and through transportation, distribution, and storage of energy. The reference energy system provides the format and structure for the Brookhaven Energy System Optimization Model (BESOM). BESOM, in turn, is coupled to a 110-sector fixed coefficient input-output model used as the framework for disaggregating energy product and final demand from the econometric model for treatment in the energy optimization model.

In the Reference Energy System, energy supplies such as nuclear fuels, fossil fuels, hydropower, and so on may be allocated to energy demands defined on a functional basis such as space heating, process heat, transportation, and so on. Thus, the characteristics of utilizing technologies, which are important in conservation and fuel substitution, are included at the same level of detail as supply technologies. The assignment of supplies to demands depends on the energy technologies that are available and on the losses of energy associated with each technology and with transportation, distribution, and storage and may be determined by a judgemental or optimization approach. Conversion losses are represented by the efficiency of each conversion process in physical terms. In the Reference Energy System all energy flows are measured in British thermal units.

In the Reference Energy System, energy supplies and demands are linked by energy conversion processes, such as steam generation of electricity from coal. This process converts a primary energy supply, coal, into an intermediate form of energy, electricity. Electricity can be used to satisfy demands for a variety of energy products, such as base, intermediate, and peak load electricity. For each process, we can specify the efficiency of conversion of primary energy supplies into intermediate forms of energy and the efficiency of conversion of the intermediate forms into final energy products. For the coal-steam-electric process, the conversion loss from the primary to the intermediate form of energy is associated with the generation of electricity. Similarly, the conversion loss from intermediate to final form of energy is associated with transmission and distribution losses for electric energy and the conversion efficiency of the end use device. The supply efficiency for a given energy source is defined as the product of the supply efficiencies on a path from the primary resource to the intermediate form of energy. Similarly, the demand efficiency is defined as the product of the demand efficiencies on a path from the intermediate form to the final energy product.

## Process Analysis Model

The Brookhaven Energy System Optimization Model (BESOM) is based on the allocation of energy supplies to energy demands to minimize cost. The minimization of cost can be formulated as a linear programming problem of the transportation type. Sources in the transportation problem can be identified with energy supplies; in the optimization model there are eleven types of energy supplies, including underground and strip-mined coal; domestic shale; and imported oil, domestic and imported natural gas; and hydro, nuclear, geothermal, and solar energy. Uses in the transportation problem can be identified with energy demands, including base, intermediate, and peak load electricity; low, intermediate, and high temperature thermal; ore reduction; petrochemicals; space heat, air conditioning, and water heat; and air, truck and bus, rail, and automobile transportation. Energy storage and synthetic fuels, including hydrogen, are also incorporated in the model. The energy sector optimization model is represented in diagrammatic form in Figure 1–3. The energy supplies and demands are listed in this figure.

**Figure 1–3.**    Interindustry Transactions in the Optimization Model.

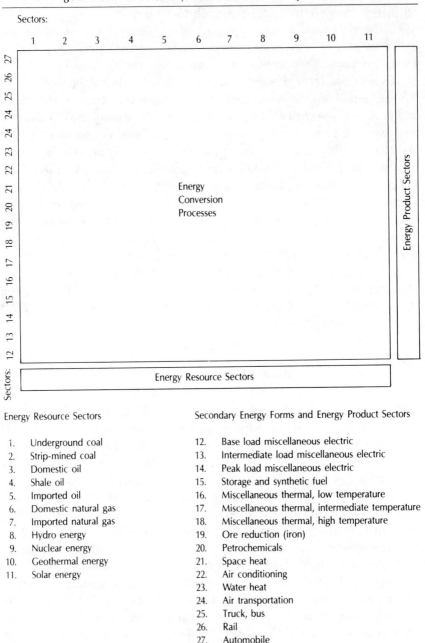

Energy Resource Sectors

1. Underground coal
2. Strip-mined coal
3. Domestic oil
4. Shale oil
5. Imported oil
6. Domestic natural gas
7. Imported natural gas
8. Hydro energy
9. Nuclear energy
10. Geothermal energy
11. Solar energy

Secondary Energy Forms and Energy Product Sectors

12. Base load miscellaneous electric
13. Intermediate load miscellaneous electric
14. Peak load miscellaneous electric
15. Storage and synthetic fuel
16. Miscellaneous thermal, low temperature
17. Miscellaneous thermal, intermediate temperature
18. Miscellaneous thermal, high temperature
19. Ore reduction (iron)
20. Petrochemicals
21. Space heat
22. Air conditioning
23. Water heat
24. Air transportation
25. Truck, bus
26. Rail
27. Automobile

In BESOM each energy supply-demand combination is associated with costs of extraction, refining and conversion, transportation and storage, and final utilization.[4] Costs per unit of operation of an energy conversion process include both capital costs and operating costs. Capital costs are converted into annual form and are conceptually equivalent to the capital service prices that enter into our econometric model of interindustry transactions. The model includes constraints (Cherniavsky 1974: 9–18) on the levels of energy conversion processes that assure that available energy supplies are not exceeded and that energy demands are met. The optimization model has been linked with the 110-sector interindustry transactions table developed for energy analysis at the University of Illinois.[5] The purpose of this linkage is to allocate fuel use represented in the econometric interindustry model with energy product demands represented in the optimization model.

To implement the energy sector optimization model, we choose a set of energy conversion levels that minimizes the cost of satisfying energy product demands from energy resource supplies. The dual to this linear programming problem is to maximize the value of energy products less the value of primary energy supplies by choosing a set of energy product and energy resource shadow prices. These shadow prices assure that the value of the output of each conversion process in actual use is equal to the value of input, including the input cost of primary energy supplies and any scarcity shadow prices and costs of extraction, conversion, and transportation, just as in our econometric model of interindustry transactions. Any energy resource with a positive price is fully utilized; similarly, the demand for any energy product with a positive price is exactly satisfied. For energy products and resources with positive shadow prices, supplies and demands are balanced in both physical terms and in current prices, as in our econometric model of interindustry transactions.

The optimization model for the energy sector is represented in diagrammatic form in Figure 1–4. Given the energy resource supplies, the energy product demands, and the unit costs associated with energy conversion processes, the energy conversion levels for the nineteen energy conversion processes are determined by the linear programming model. In addition, the

---

4. The objective function of the optimization model is described by Cherniavsky (1974: esp. 18–23).

5. Interindustry accounts for the year 1967 have been compiled in an appropriate format by Bullard and Herendeen (1973 a,b). The corresponding interindustry model has been linked to the Brookhaven Energy System Optimization Model by Hoffman et al. (1974) and by Behling et al. (1975). Energy flows for six years have been compiled for the Federal Energy Administration by Jack Faucett Associates (1975).

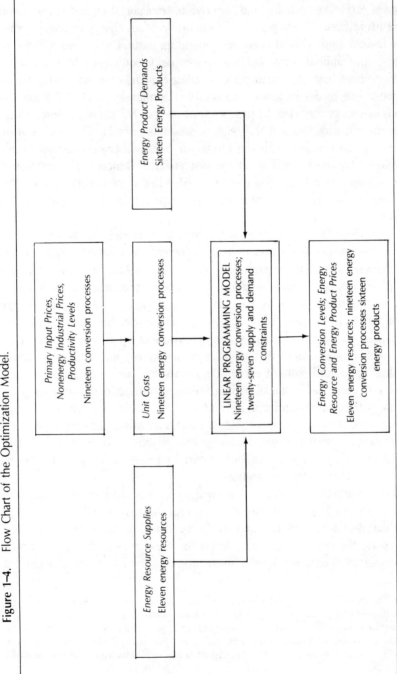

**Figure 1–4.**   Flow Chart of the Optimization Model.

model determines the shadow prices associated with energy products and energy resources. The assignment of energy supplies to energy demands through energy conversion processes can be represented by means of the Reference Energy System. The supply efficiency for each energy resource and the demand efficiency for each energy product is determined by the linear programming model. The Reference Energy System format can be used to provide a complete description of the energy sector in physical terms. Given the prices of energy products and resources and the costs associated with energy conversion processes, BESOM also provides a complete description of the energy sector in financial terms. We can generate the resultant energy system scenario in the format of the Reference Energy System in both physical and financial terms from the costs of energy conversion processes, the availability of energy resources, the requirements for energy products, and any additional constraints associated with conversion capacities and environmental restrictions.

In appriasing alternative energy research, development, and demonstration policies, we first associate with each policy the resulting technology for the energy sector; changes in energy policy are associated with changes in energy technology.[6] We can introduce the corresponding changes in energy technology into the baseline Reference Energy System in two ways. First, the introduction of new technologies provides new energy conversion processes in addition to those that already exist. Accelerated research, development, and demonstration programs may make it possible to accelerate the introduction of new technologies. Second, the improvement of existing technologies may increase the efficiency of energy conversion or may reduce the costs of extraction, conversion, or transportation. More extensive research, development, and demonstration may speed the increase in efficiency or the reduction in cost. The introduction of new energy technology or the improvement of existing technology may reduce the costs associated with meeting given demands for energy products from given energy resource supplies. For any change in technology we can assess the effects on the energy sector in both physical and financial terms, using the energy sector optimization model. We can also assess the environmental impact of the changes, using the environmental impact associated with alternative energy conversion processes.

6. Methodology for application of the optimization model for assessment of alternative energy research, development, and demonstration policies is described by Hoffman and Cherniavsky (1974) and Cherniavsky (1975). This methodology was applied in a series of twelve scenarios for 1985 and 2000 in *A National Plan for Energy Research, Development, and Demonstration* (ERDA 1975).

## Model Integration

Although both components of our energy policy model can be used to generate a description of the energy sector in physical and financial terms, the energy sector optimization model provides a far more detailed characterization of technology and permits the analysis of the effects of introducing new technologies. The econometric model also provides a description of the nonenergy sector and generates a complete description of the U.S. economy, including flows of primary input, interindustry transactions, and final demand in current and constant prices. The energy sector optimization model is especially well suited to the assessment of the impacts of alternative research, development, and demonstration policies on the energy sector. The econometric interindustry model is well suited to the assessment of the impact of these policies on the economy as a whole. By integrating the two models we can combine the detailed characterization of technology available from the energy sector optimization model with the complete representation of the economy, including energy and nonenergy sectors, available from the econometric interindustry model. The integrated model is based on an expanded system of interindustry accounts for the private domestic sector of the U.S. economy.

In our expanded system of interindustry accounts, the energy sector is divided into energy resource sectors, energy conversion processes, and energy product sectors. The remaining components of our original system of interindustry accounts — interindustry transactions in nonenergy products, primary inputs, and final demands — are also included in the expanded system. The expanded system of interindustry accounts is presented in diagrammatic form in Figure 1–5. A complete list of the sectors included in this system of accounts is also given in Figure 1–5. Deliveries from energy resource sectors to energy conversion processes and from conversion processes to energy product sectors are represented as energy flows in the same way as in the Reference Energy System. Deliveries from energy product sectors to nonenergy industry sectors and to final demand are represented as energy flows in the same way as in our original system of interindustry accounts. Deliveries from each energy sector in the original system are allocated first to conversion activities and then the output of these conversion activities are allocated to a detailed list of energy products in the expanded system. Finally, deliveries of nonenergy products and primary inputs to the five industry groups comprising the energy sector in the original system are allocated among energy product, energy conversion, and energy resource sectors in the expanded system. Energy flows are given in physical terms; nonenergy flows are given in constant dollars. Corresponding to a given set of energy product and resource prices and prices for nonenergy products and primary inputs, our system of interindustry accounts can also be represented in current prices.

The integrated model incorporates an interindustry model with final demands, technical coefficients, and prices generated by components of the econometric interindustry model and the energy sector optimization model. This expanded interindustry model can be used to generate a complete system of interindustry accounts in current and constant prices, as in Figure 1–6. The levels of energy resources utilized and energy products delivered in the expanded interindustry model correspond to energy resource supplies and energy product demands in the energy sector optimization model. From the prices of primary inputs, the prices of nonenergy industrial products, and the productivity levels for each of the energy conversion processes, we can generate the unit costs associated with each conversion process.[7] Given the unit costs and the energy demands and supplies, the energy sector optimization model generates cost-minimizing levels for the energy conversion processes and value-maximizing prices associated with the energy demands and supplies in the same way as before. The integrated model incorporates the complete energy sector optimization model. In addition to the conversion levels and energy prices, the energy sector optimization model generates technical coefficients for the energy resource, energy conversion, and energy product sectors of the expanded interindustry model.[8]

We continue with the description of our energy policy model by observing that the dual solution of the energy sector optimization model also determines the prices of each of the five fuel types entering each sector. From these prices, the prices of primary inputs, and the productivity levels of the four nonenergy industrial sectors, we can generate the prices of nonenergy products from the four price possibiltiy frontiers for the nonenergy industrial sectors. From energy and nonenergy prices and the prices of primary inputs, we can generate the technical coefficients for the nonenergy industrial sectors of the expended interindustry model. Given these same prices, we can employ the consumption model of our

7. This link between prices and costs has not been programmed.
8. At present, fixed coefficients are used to relate nonenergy inputs and energy resource and conversion processes. The optimization model is used to generate the resource into energy conversion coefficients and the energy conversion into energy product coefficients.

**Figure 1–5.**    Interindustry Transactions in the Integrated Model.

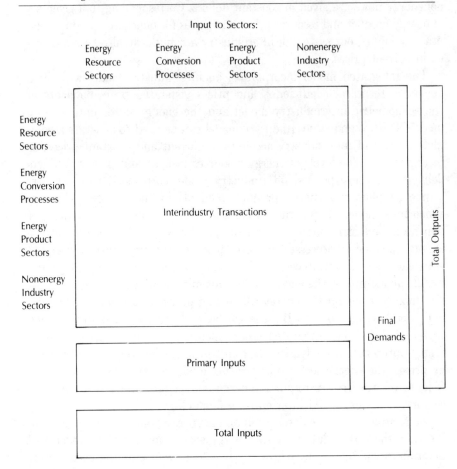

Energy Resource Sectors

1.  Underground coal
2.  Strip-mined coal
3.  Domestic oil
4.  Shale oil
5.  Imported oil
6.  Domestic natural gas
7.  Imported natural gas
8.  Hydro energy
9.  Nuclear energy
10. Geothermal energy
11. Solar energy

Energy Conversion Processes

12. Coal-steam-electric
13. Coal-steam combined cycle
14. Oil-steam-electric
15. Oil-steam combined cycle
16. Gas turbines
17. Gas-steam-electric
18. Total energy systems
19. LWR electric
20. LMFBR electric
21. HTGR electric
22. Hydro electric
23. Geothermal electric
24. Solar electric
25. Pumped storage
26. Synthetic gas from oil
27. Synthetic gas from coal
28. Electrolytic hydrogen
29. Methanol
30. Hydrogen from coal

Secondary Energy Forms and Energy Product Sectors

31. Base load miscellaneous electric
32. Intermediate load miscellaneous electric
33. Peak load miscellaneous electric
34. Storage and synthetic fuel
35. Miscellaneous thermal, low temperature
36. Miscellaneous thermal, intermediate temperature
37. Miscellaneous thermal, high temperature
38. Ore reduction (iron)
39. Petrochemicals

40. Space heat
41. Air conditioning
42. Water heat
43. Air transportation
44. Truck, bus
45. Rail
46. Automobile

Nonenergy Industry Sectors.

47. Agriculture, nonfuel mining, and construction
48. Manufacturing, excluding petroleum refining
49. Transportation
50. Communications, trade, and services

Primary Inputs

51. Imports
52. Capital services
53. Labor services

Final Demands

54. Personal consumption expenditures
55. Gross private domestic investment
56. Government purchases of goods and services
57. Exports

**Figure 1–6.**    Flow Chart of the Integrated Model.

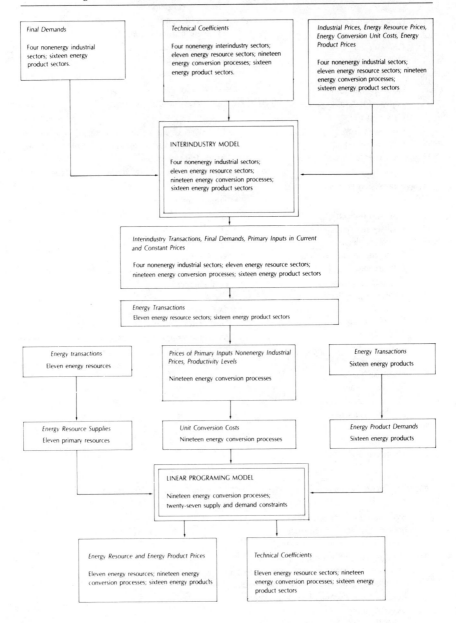

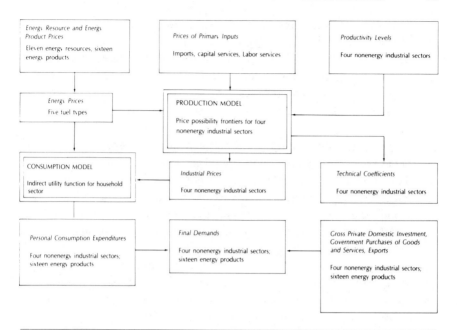

econometric interindustry model to generate the allocation of personal consumption expenditures; the energy products determined in the consumption model must be allocated among energy products in the energy sector optimization model to determine the personal consumption component of final demand in the expanded interindustry model. The remaining components of final demand—investment, government purchases, and exports—are given exogenously, as before.

The expanded interindustry model includes technical coefficients for the energy sector from the energy sector optimization model; technical coefficients for the nonenergy sector from the production models for the four nonenergy industrial sectors from the econometric interindustry model; and final demands for energy and nonenergy products from the econometric interindustry model, allocated among the energy products of the energy sector optimization model. The expanded interindustry model assures that supplies and demands are balanced for energy resources, energy conversion processes, energy products, and nonenergy products. A solution of the integrated model consists of a solution of the expanded interindustry model, for which the following conditions hold:

1.  The energy conversion levels minimize cost for the corresponding levels of energy demands and supplies and for the corresponding unit costs of the energy conversion processes.

2.  The prices of energy products and energy resources maximize the value of the products less the value of the resources.
3.  The prices of the five fuel types in the econometric interindustry model are generated by dual solution of the linear programming (LP) model.
4.  The prices of the four nonenergy products are consistent with the energy product and fuel prices and the exogenously given prices of primary inputs.
5.  The unit costs of the energy conversion processes are consistent with nonenergy product prices and the given prices of primary inputs.
6.  The technical coefficients for the energy sectors are those associated with the cost-minimizing solutions of the energy sector optimization model; the technical coefficients for the nonenergy sectors are those associated with the prices for primary inputs, the four nonenergy products, and the five fuel types.
7.  The final demands for energy and nonenergy products are those associated with the prices for these products. Under these conditions the value of the output of each sector of the expanded interindustry model is equal to the value of the input of the sector.

## THE ECONOMIC IMPACT OF POLICIES TO REDUCE U.S. ENERGY GROWTH

The purpose of this section is to quantify the impact of alternative energy policies on future energy prices, energy utilization, and economic growth in the United States. Growth in energy consumption has become an important issue in U.S. economic policy as a result of the establishment of an effective international petroleum cartel by the Organization of Petroleum Exporting Countries (OPEC). The OPEC cartel has succeeded in raising world petroleum prices fourfold since 1973. This has resulted in rapid increases in the real price of delivered energy in the United States, which rose 7 percent annually between 1973 and 1977. To put these price increases in historical perspective, it can be noted that from 1950 to 1973 the real price of delivered energy in the United States declined at the rate of 1.8 percent per year.

Since 1954, the Federal Energy Regulatory Commission has maintained a system of wellhead price controls for natural gas entering interstate commerce. These controls have maintained prices below market clearing levels and have necessitated the development of a system for the quantitative allocation of interstate natural gas. A similar situation has developed in the petroleum market. The U.S. government responded to the increase in world petroleum prices beginning in 1973 with a system of controls on domestic crude oil prices and on prices of petroleum products. During 1979, the Carter administration announced plans for gradual decontrol of prices for both natural gas and petroleum.

## Alternative Energy Policies

The starting point for our analysis of the impact of alternative energy policies is a base case projection of future energy and economic growth with no change in energy policy. We assume that any quantity of petroleum imports is available at the world price, where the world price of petroleum rises at a rate of 1 percent per annum relative to the rate of growth of the U.S. GNP price deflator until 1990 and 2 percent annually, in real terms, thereafter. The annual rate of growth of real GNP is projected to average 3.2 percent from 1977 to 2000. This growth is considerably slower than the average annual growth rate of 3.8 percent between 1950 and 1973. The decline is partly due to a reduction in population growth and partly due to a reduction in productivity growth resulting from higher energy prices. Primary energy input is projected to rise from 76 quadrillion btu in 1977 to 139 quadrillion btu in 2000, an average annual growth rate of 2.6 percent. This growth is also slower than that experienced in the past: The average rate of growth of primary energy input between 1950 and 1973 was 3.2 percent per annum. Part of the reduction is due to decreased economic growth and part is caused by the continuing rise in real energy prices.

The increase in the relative price of petroleum over time leads to a steady decline in the relative importance of petroleum in total energy use. Natural gas is also projected to decline in relative importance, due to supply constraints and price increases. Coal and nuclear sources sustain much of the growth in energy use; both direct use of coal and the use of electricity grow relatively rapidly. Imported petroleum accounts for approximately half of all petroleum use in 1977, while in the base case projection this share rises to almost 60 percent by 2000. The base case projections imply continued reliance on imports for a substantial fraction of energy supply. The reduction of import dependence, in order to reduce the associated economic and political risks, is an important objective underlying U.S. energy policy proposals. To analyze such policies and their energy and economic effects, we consider the following set of policy packages:

Policy 1:    Taxes are imposed on U.S. petroleum production to bring domestic petroleum prices to world levels; natural gas prices are
increased, but price controls are retained; and energy conservation is stimulated by taxes on use of oil and gas in industry,
restriction of oil and gas use by electric utilities, subsidies for
insulation of structures, and mandatory performance standards
for energy-using appliances.

Policy 2:    The measures included in Policy 1 are combined with tariffs on
imported oil (rising to $4.50 per barrel in 1985 and to $7 per
barrel in 2000) and with corresponding taxes on natural gas.

Policy 3:    Policy 2 is combined with excise taxes on delivered energy sufficient to reduce total primary energy input in 2000 to 90 quadrillion btu.

Policy 4:    Policy 3 is combined with excise taxes on delivered energy sufficient to reduce total primary input in 2000 to 70 quadrillion btu.

## Adjustments in the Price Structure

The immediate point of impact of energy policy measures is in the structure
of relative prices: Energy becomes more expensive relative to other goods
and services. In the attempt to allocate purchases so as to minimize production costs, producers reduce energy use, moving toward less energy-intensive
inputs and processes. Similarly, in the attempt to derive maximum value
from their consumption budgets, households redirect their expenditure patterns to economize on the now expensive energy and energy-intensive goods
and services. Thus, higher prices for energy and for energy intensive products lead to reductions in energy use and to slower growth in energy consumption. In addition, the nonprice energy conservation measures contained
in the Policy 1 package add considerable further pressure to the shift toward less intensive energy use.

The price adjustments commence with the relative prices of inputs. Table
1–5 shows these changes for the simulations for 2000. The changes in capital, labor, materials, and energy input prices feed through the production
structure to alter the whole pattern of relative prices of produced goods and
services. The price of capital services is taken as the numeraire in the model
system, so the observed variation in prices is for other prices to adjust relative to the prices of capital services. The variation involves an increase in
the price of energy, an increase in the price of intermediate materials, and a
decrease in the price of labor services.

**Table 1–5.**    Adjustments in Input and Output Prices in 2000.

|  | Policy 1 | Policy 2 | Policy 3 | Policy 4 |
|---|---|---|---|---|
| Input Prices, Percent Change from Base Case | | | | |
| Capital | — | — | — | — |
| Labor | −0.68 | −2.04 | −5.43 | −9.90 |
| Energy | 15.73 | 29.74 | 108.24 | 217.01 |
| Intermediate materials | 0.24 | 0.80 | 1.12 | 2.61 |
| Output Prices, Percent Change from Base Case | | | | |
| Agriculture, Nonfuel mining, construction | 1.07 | 1.31 | 2.29 | 5.54 |
| Manufacturing | 0.08 | −0.23 | 1.14 | 5.91 |
| Commercial transportation | 3.11 | 4.57 | 7.83 | 13.38 |
| Services, trade, communications | −0.26 | −0.87 | 0.56 | 2.24 |
| Energy, actual prices[a] | 0.19 | 10.75 | 87.71 | 187.33 |
| Energy, effective costs[b] | 15.73 | 29.74 | 108.24 | 217.01 |

[a] Actual energy prices refer to the average dollar cost of delivered energy in terms of dollars per btu.

[b] Effective energy costs refer to the average cost of energy services to energy purchasers, allowing for both price and nonprice conservation measures and calculated using a fixed weight quantity index.

The rise in energy prices directly reflects taxes and other policy measures. Two measures of the energy price increase are given. The first, referring to actual energy prices, relates to dollar prices paid for the purchase of energy. These increases, relative to the base case, by 0.2 percent for Policy 1 and by 187 percent for Policy 4. However, the effective cost of energy rises by more than this, due to the effect of nonprice policy measures. Nonprice regulations that require the use of more capital equipment or of different production processes increase average costs of production. The estimate of these additional costs, together with the direct price increases, is given by the second measure, effective energy cost. For Policy 1, this overall measure of energy cost is 16 percent above the base case; for Policy 4 it is 217 percent higher. Thus, both price and nonprice measures contribute significantly to the pressure to reduce consumption of energy.

Labor prices show a relative decline. This means that labor prices under the policy simulations show a less rapid growth over the forecast period than under base case conditions. The reason for this slower growth lies in the employment constraint imposed on the simulations: The rate of unemployment is constrained to be the same as in the base case. As the energy measures lead to a reduction in the level of economic activity, the demand for labor is reduced. This reduction can be more than enough to offset the additional labor use due to energy-labor substitution. A relative reduction in labor prices is required in order to stimulate labor use. Thus, labor prices in Policy 2 are 2 percent less than in the base case, and they are 10 percent less in Policy 4. Finally, the prices of intermediate materials show a small increase as a result of the policy measures. This is due to the effect of higher energy costs, which raise production costs for these materials to an extent greater than the cost reduction following the decline in labor prices.

These changes in input prices lead to adjustments in the level and pattern of output prices. The overall level of output prices is increased. However, since energy represents, compared to capital, labor, and materials inputs, only a small component of total production costs in most industries, the higher energy prices lead to relatively small increases in average output prices. The pattern of relative prices is more substantially altered. Energy prices rise significantly, in Policy 3, for example, by 88 percent in terms of dollars per btu and by 108 percent in terms of effective costs to purchasers. Other output prices change by smaller proportions: In Policy 3, transportation prices rise by 8 percent; agriculture, nonfuel mining, and construction prices by 2.3 percent; and manufacturing prices by 1.1 percent

The pattern of price changes is closely related to the mix of inputs used in each sector. Energy output, of course, is highly energy intensive, and it shows a substantial price increase. Commercial transportation is the next most energy-intensive sector, and its price also rises significantly. Agriculture, nonfuel mining, and construction and manufacturing are less energy intensive and show smaller price increases. Services, trade, and communications is the least energy-intensive sector and is also relatively labor intensive, so that these prices either decline or show only a small increase. The pattern of changes in prices and effective costs alters to make energy-intensive goods and services relatively expensive. Together with the associated nonprice measures, this is the force motivating producers and consumers to redirect their expenditure patterns and to use less energy in production and consumption activities.

## Changes in the Pattern of Final Demand

Final demand expenditure is a critical determinant of the overall level and composition of activity in the economy. Final demand—personal consumption expenditure, private investment, government purchases, and exports—dictates what is produced in the economy. Changes in final demand are therefore important in securing reductions in the energy intensity of economic activity. Reduction in final demand purchases of energy result directly in energy saving. Also, reductions in final demand purchases of energy-intensive goods permit less energy to be used in production activities and so accentuate the overall saving in energy. Both these types of expenditure adjustments—less energy purchases and less use of energy-intensive products—are induced by the restructuring of output prices.

Table 1–6 summarizes the changes in final demand spending resulting from various energy policy measures. The broad pattern of spending is similar under all policies, with services absorbing a little more than half and manufacturing about one-third of total real final demand. However, there are some significant shifts in final spending induced by the price and nonprice energy policy measures.

The changes in the price structure and the other energy conservation measures results in a substantial adjustment in real final demand. The overall level of real final demand is reduced; this in itself results in a significant reduction in energy use. This energy saving is compounded by a redirection of spending patterns away from energy and energy-intensive goods and services. Nonenergy-intensive output, particularly services, becomes relatively more important within the pattern of final spending. Final demand for energy shows the most substantial reduction: It is reduced by 13 percent below the base case under Policy 1.

## Changes in Production Patterns

The patterns of inputs into each production sector also change in response to the energy policy measures. Higher energy prices create an incentive for producers to alter input patterns away from energy and thereby reduce production costs. The nonprice direct regulations concerning energy use provide additional pressure to reduce energy purchases. Also, the changes in labor prices and prices of other intermediate inputs provide incentives for further adjustments in the mix of inputs and processes. The net result

**Table 1–6.**   Final Demand Patterns in 2000.

| | Base case | Policy 1 | Policy 2 | Policy 3 | Policy 4 |
|---|---|---|---|---|---|
| Composition of Real Final Demand | | | | | |
| Agriculture, nonfuel mining, construction | 8.38 | 8.30 | 8.22 | 8.13 | 8.06 |
| Manufacturing | 30.48 | 30.48 | 30.45 | 30.30 | 30.02 |
| Commercial transportation | 3.64 | 3.48 | 3.36 | 3.30 | 3.21 |
| Services, trade, communications | 54.08 | 54.70 | 55.15 | 55.91 | 56.94 |
| Energy | 3.43 | 3.04 | 2.82 | 2.36 | 1.77 |
| Total | 100.00 | 100.00 | 100.00 | 100.00 | 100.00 |
| Real Final Demand, Percent Change from Base Case | | | | | |
| Agriculture, nonfuel mining, construction | | −3.1 | −5.6 | −10.6 | −15.9 |
| Manufacturing | | −1.9 | −3.9 | −8.4 | −13.9 |
| Commercial transportation | | −6.2 | −11.0 | −16.6 | −22.8 |
| Services, trades, communications | | −0.8 | −1.9 | −4.7 | −8.0 |
| Energy | | −13.1 | −20.9 | −36.5 | −54.9 |
| Total | | −2.0 | −3.9 | −7.9 | −12.6 |

of these pressures is to induce—or to force—producers to adjust their purchase patterns, economizing on energy use by changed production practices and processes, and to place greater reliance on nonenergy inputs. Thus, not only is energy input reduced, but the entire pattern of inputs into each sector is changed. The estimated changes in input patterns are shown in Table 1–7, which gives the aggregate input-output coefficients for each of the major nonenergy-producing sectors—agriculture, nonfuel mining, and construction; manufacturing; commercial transportation; and services, trade, and communications. These coefficients measure the proportion of the total real input into the sector that is of the specified form, whether capital services, labor services, energy, or intermediate materials.

**Table 1-7.**   Input Patterns in Nonenergy Production, 2000 (input-output coefficients for aggregate input categories).

|  | Base Case | Policy 1 | Policy 2 | Policy 3 | Policy 4 |
|---|---|---|---|---|---|
| Agriculture |  |  |  |  |  |
| Capital | .1946 | .1938 | .1932 | .1921 | .1900 |
| Labor | .2542 | .2575 | .2598 | .2661 | .2722 |
| Energy | .0242 | .0232 | .0225 | .0200 | .0176 |
| Materials | .5271 | .5255 | .5245 | .5218 | .5193 |
| Manufacturing |  |  |  |  |  |
| Capital | .1194 | .1176 | .1161 | .1143 | .1131 |
| Labor | .2815 | .2845 | .2881 | .2963 | .3046 |
| Energy | .0235 | .0231 | .0226 | .0193 | .0179 |
| Materials | .5756 | .5748 | .5732 | .5701 | .5644 |
| Transportation |  |  |  |  |  |
| Capital | .1971 | .1956 | .1939 | .1920 | .1888 |
| Labor | .4016 | .4031 | .4049 | .4076 | .4100 |
| Energy | .0384 | .0373 | .0361 | .0327 | .0298 |
| Materials | .3629 | .3640 | .3651 | .3677 | .3714 |
| Services |  |  |  |  |  |
| Capital | .3389 | .3405 | .3418 | .3456 | .3493 |
| Labor | .3526 | .3585 | .3627 | .3738 | .3864 |
| Energy | .0186 | .0180 | .0175 | .0151 | .0131 |
| Materials | .2899 | .2830 | .2780 | .2655 | .2512 |

The unit input requirement of energy into agriculture, nonfuel mining, and construction is reduced by 4 percent in Policy 1 and by up to 27 percent in Policy 4. Energy and capital show a complementary relationship in this sector; when energy prices increase, the use of capital input is reduced. Therefore, capital input is reduced as part of the adjustment process, although this change is not large. The reduction in energy and capital inputs must be compensated by an increase in other inputs. Labor is the key input that provides this compensating increase. The input-output coefficient of labor rised from 0.2542 in the base case to 0.2722 in Policy 4, a sufficient rise to offset the move away from energy, capital, and materials. Finally, the input of intermediate materials is reduced slightly as part of the adjustment process.

The manufacturing sector follows a similar pattern of adjustments between inputs. The use of energy per unit of output is significantly reduced.Also, energy and capital show a strong complementary relationship.

This means that a reduction in capital input is associated with the higher energy costs and with reduced energy input. In contrast, labor is a substitute for both capital and energy. Consequently, the more expensive energy and capital input mix is partially replaced by the now relatively less expensive input of labor services. Input of intermediate materials declines slightly. Overall, energy saving in manufacturing is achieved by a reduction in energy and capital use, accompanied by an increase in labor input.

The nature of the energy-capital link can be complex. Some types of capital have a direct complementary relationship with energy in that the more capital used, the more energy input is required. This is true for many types of motive power uses of energy and capital and for some types of process uses. In other instances, however, there is a substitution relationship between capital and energy, whereby energy can be saved by the use of more capital equipment. For example, energy required per unit of output can often be reduced by the use of more sophisticated and more expensive capital. However, even this energy-capital substitution relationship is consistent with an overall appearance of complementarity between energy and capital. The reason for this operates through a separate input, labor, which is typically a substitute for both capital and energy. A rise in the price of energy gives rise to the following adjustments: Energy use is reduced; capital input tends to be increased (energy-capital substitutability); labor input is increased (energy-labor substitutability); and capital input tends to be decreased (labor-capital substitutability).

There are pressures to reduce and to increase capital use. In manufacturing, the net result is that a reduction in capital use accompanies the reduction in energy input. Transportation shows a substantial decline in energy intensity as a result of the policy measures: For example, the input coefficient for energy falls from 0.038 to 0.036, an 11 percent decline, between the base case and Policy 2. Complementarity between energy and capital leads to a reduction in the input of capital services; the capital input coefficient rises by 2 percent for Policy 2. Both labor and intermediate materials can substitute for energy and capital in transportation, and the coefficients for these inputs in Policy 2 rise by 0.8 percent and 0.6 percent, respectively.

The services, trade, and communications sector responds somewhat differently from the other nonenergy-producing sectors. The extent of the energy reduction, 6 percent in Policy 2, is comparable to that achieved in the other sectors, but the manner in which this reduction is achieved is different. The principal difference is in the role of capital. In services, the relationship between energy and capital is one of substitutability: Higher energy costs and reduced energy input are associated with greater use of capital services. The reduction in energy input is, in part, secured by an increase in capital input. A central reason for the different energy-capital relationship in this sector lies in the type of use made of energy. In services, a great deal of energy is used for space heating and for air conditioning. Reduction in this use of energy can be achieved through improved design and insulation of structure and more sophisticated heating and cooling equipment. Each of these changes uses additional capital. In Policy 2, for example, the reduction in the energy input coefficient is associated with a 0.9 percent increase in the capital input coefficient. Labor also can be substituted for energy; in fact, the degree of substitution is greater than that between energy and capital, and the labor input coefficient is increased by 2.9 percent. The final set of inputs, nonenergy intermediate goods, are reduced substantially, the input coefficient in Policy 2 being 4 percent less than in the base case. In sum, the input restructuring in services is to move away from the energy and other produced inputs toward capital and labor inputs.

The economy-wide pattern of capital, labor, energy, and materials inputs is determined jointly by the pattern of these inputs in each sector and by the relative size of each sector in the economy. Higher energy prices and nonprice restrictions on energy use result in a restructuring of input patterns away from energy, away from capital (except in services), and toward labor. In addition, the sectoral composition of output shifts away from energy, transportation, and agriculture and toward services. The overall effect of these changes is to substantially reduce the overall energy intensity of production: The average labor intensity increases, and the average capital intensity shows a very small increase.

## Dynamic Adjustments Through Investment

The above analysis has focused on adjustments to spending and input patterns that were essentially substitution responses to changes in relative prices. These are the principal means by which the economy adjusts to a less energy-intensive structure. However, another very significant—and related—set of effects is through investment and the capital stock. Higher energy prices lead to a reduction in capital income and to a reduced rate of return on capital. Part of this reduction in the rate of return is related to the energy-capital complementarity observed in some sectors. Additional investment in energy-conserving capital, particularly where it is forced by direct regulation and mandatory performance standards, can have low total productivity and can accentuate the decline in yield on capital. Lower rates of return lead directly to reduced saving and investment in the private economy. In addition, the income reductions due to the substitution adjustments considered above lead to further cutbacks in the volume of private saving and investment. Thus, private investment is reduced below base case levels. This results directly in a slowing of the rate of growth of capital stock. In fact, the growth paths of capital stock under the energy policy measures are projected to be permanently below the base case growth path.

The significance of these reductions in investment and the capital stock is that one of the principal inputs into production, capital services, is reduced. Reduced investment and capital means that the productive capacity of the economy is reduced throughout the forecast period. Further, this lowering of productive potential, compared to base case level, becomes progressively greater over time. This capital reduction or dynamic effect is a fundamental mechanism through which the shift to a less energy-intensive configuration of spending and production can lead to slower growth and can impose output and income loss on the economy.

The magnitudes of the investment and capital effects are shown in Table 1–8. Investment rises over time under the energy policies as well as in the base case, but the rate of growth of investment is less under the policy measures; the level of real investment in each year is less than in the base case. The relative reduction in investment levels is not large—by 2000 it is 1.6 percent for Policy 1 and 4.9 percent for Policy 2—but the cumulative impact on the level of capital stock is significant. Under Policy 2 conditions, the level of capital stock in 1990 is 1.3 percent below the base case, and by 2000 it is 3 percent below. This slowing in the rate of growth of capital directly implies that the productive potential of the economy grows less rapidly than in the base case.

## Aggregate Economic Cost of Energy Reductions

Two types of adjustment of the economy to changes in energy conditions have been analyzed. The first involves the restructuring of production and

**Table 1–8.**    Investment, Capital Stock, and GNP Effects of Energy Policies.

|  | 1985 | 1990 | 2000 |
|---|---|---|---|
| Investment: Percent Change from Base Case | | | |
| Policy 1 | −0.4 | −1.0 | −1.6 |
| Policy 2 | −1.4 | −3.0 | −4.9 |
| Policy 3 | −1.8 | −5.2 | −10.5 |
| Policy 4 | −2.4 | −6.7 | −16.3 |
| Capital Stock: Percent Change from Base Case | | | |
| Policy 1 | −0.17 | −0.47 | −1.17 |
| Policy 2 | −0.49 | −1.27 | −3.03 |
| Policy 3 | −0.63 | −1.85 | −7.00 |
| Policy 4 | −0.81 | −2.40 | −10.75 |
| Change in Real GNP from Base Case (1972 $ billion) | | | |
| Policy 1 | −10.6 | −24.0 | −41.9 |
| Policy 2 | −29.9 | −53.5 | −86.8 |
| Policy 3 | −36.9 | −79.6 | −197.1 |
| Policy 4 | −48.4 | −107.3 | −324.7 |
| Change in Real GNP from Base Case (percent) | | | |
| Policy 1 | −0.60 | −1.18 | −1.54 |
| Policy 2 | −1.69 | −2.64 | −3.19 |
| Policy 3 | −2.08 | −3.91 | −7.24 |
| Policy 4 | −2.73 | −5.27 | −11.93 |
| Growth in Real GNP (average percent per annum) | | | |
| Base Case | 3.65 | 2.82 | 2.94 |
| Policy 1 | 3.58 | 2.70 | 2.90 |
| Policy 2 | 3.43 | 2.63 | 2.88 |
| Policy 3 | 3.38 | 2.44 | 2.58 |
| Policy 4 | 3.30 | 2.28 | 2.19 |

spending patterns away from energy and energy-intensive inputs and production. The second adjustment operates through changes in savings and investment and results in a slower growth of capital and aggregate productive capacity. Both of these adjustment mechanisms impose costs on the economy. From an aggregate point of view, these costs take the form of a reduction in the volume of final output that can be obtained from the economy, compared to that possible under base case conditions. This economic cost arises from both the substitution or restructuring and the dynamic or capital types of adjustment.[9]

The substitution of labor, capital, and nonenergy goods and services for energy input into production is not perfect; some output is lost as a result of the restructuring. In other words, additional labor and other inputs can help to compensate for less energy input, but some reduction in net output is still probable. Also, additional labor and other inputs used to replace energy must be obtained from other uses, thus reducing the total volume of potential output. These same adjustments can be viewed in terms of factor productivities. The process of reducing intensity of energy use involves increasing the intensity of labor use and, in some cases, capital use. The input-output coefficients for labor and, in an aggregate sense, capital increase. Thus, more labor and capital are used per unit of output. This is equivalent to saying that the productivities of labor and of capital are reduced as a result of the energy adjustments. At any time that these inputs are limited in supply, reduction in their productivities translated directly into a reduction in the potential output of the economy. Real GNP declines, or its growth rate slows, as a result of the substitution away from energy input into production.

The dynamic costs of energy reduction follow in part from these substitution costs and in part from separate mechanisms. The reduction in output and income as a result of the substitution processes leads directly to a reduction in the aggregate level of saving and investment. In addition, the rate of return on capital can fall as a result of the higher energy prices and the greater input of capital per unit of output in the economy as a whole. A decline in rates of return leads to further reductions in saving and investment. Therefore, capital growth under the energy policies is lower than in the base case. This corresponds directly to a slowing of the growth of the productive capacity. At any given time, this involves a lower real GNP than under base case conditions, compounding the economic cost caused by the substitution process.

The magnitudes of the economic costs of restrictive energy policies are shown in Table 1–8 in terms of real GNP. For each of the four policy packages, real GNP is less than in the base case. Further, the reduction is larger, the more restrictive the policy measures. Also, the reduction under each pol-

---

9. A detailed analysis of the reduction in productivity, capital, and real GNP resulting from higher energy prices (in this case the 1973 and subsequent rises in world oil prices) is given in Hudson and Jorgenson (1978b).

icy becomes larger over time in both absolute and relative magnitude. For Policy 1, the economic cost in 1985 is 0.6 percent of real GNP, while in 2000 the cost rises to 1.5 percent of GNP. Under Policy 4 the cost is 2.7 percent of GNP in 1985, rising to 11.9 percent in 2000. Economic growth is reduced under each policy, but positive growth continues in all cases. For example, Policy 1 reduces the annual rate of economic growth by about 0.1 percent. These economic costs are substantial. One way to calculate the overall cost is to find the present value of the real GNP loss over the entire 1977 to 2000 period. These present values (as at 1977, using a 5 percent discount rate) are $148 billion for Policy 1, $350 billion for Policy 2, $615 billion for Policy 3, and $919 billion for Policy 4, all in 1972 dollars. To place these in perspective, it can be noted that U.S. real GNP in 1977 was about $1,330 billion (1972 $). Thus, although energy reductions can be achieved, they do involve a substantial real cost in loss of potential income and output.

The GNP loss from energy policies can be separated into a part resulting from the substitution cost and a part resulting from the dynamic or capital cost. This separation is only approximate, since both costs arise from interdependent adjustment processes, but it does indicate the relative magnitudes of these two cost components. The GNP loss resulting from reduced input is calculated by using a result from the macroeconomic theory of growth, which states that if factor inputs are paid at rates equal to the value of their marginal products, a 1 percent change in capital input leads to a $S_k$ percent change in real GNP, where $S_k$ is the share of capital income in national income. This income share in the projections is approximately 0.35. The relative GNP loss arising from the dynamic adjustment mechanism is indicated by 0.35 multiplied by the percentage reduction in capital stock relative to the base case. The remaining GNP loss is attributed to the substitution effects moving towards less energy-intensive input patterns.

Table 1–9 shows the separation of real GNP loss into substitution and dynamic effects. The greater part of the loss arises from the substitution effect. Thus, in Policy 2 in 1985, the 1.69 percent real GNP reduction comprises a 1.54 percent decline due to substitution effects and a 0.15 percent decline due to dynamic effects—that is over 90 percent of the reduction is due to substitution effects. Over time, however, the dynamic effect becomes more important. By 2000, for the 3.19 percent GNP reduction in Policy 2, 2.28 percent of the loss is now due to substitution effects. The cumulative and durable nature of capital means that the relative importance of the dynamic changes further increase in the more distant future.

Table 1–9.    Substitution and Dynamic Effects in GNP Reduction.

|  | 1985 | 1990 | 2000 |
|---|---|---|---|
| Change in Real GNP (percent change from base case) | | | |
| Policy 1 | −0.60 | −1.18 | −1.54 |
| Policy 2 | −1.69 | −2.64 | −3.19 |
| Policy 3 | −2.08 | −3.91 | −7.24 |
| Policy 4 | −2.73 | −5.27 | −11.93 |
| Dynamic Effect: Change in Real GNP due to Capital Reduction (percent) | | | |
| Policy 1 | −0.05 | −0.14 | −0.35 |
| Policy 2 | −0.15 | −0.38 | −0.91 |
| Policy 3 | −0.19 | −0.56 | −0.10 |
| Policy 4 | −0.24 | −0.72 | −3.23 |
| Change in Real GNP due to Substitution Effects (percent) | | | |
| Policy 1 | −0.55 | −1.04 | −1.19 |
| Policy 2 | −1.54 | −2.26 | −2.28 |
| Policy 3 | −1.89 | −3.35 | −5.14 |
| Policy 4 | −2.49 | −4.55 | −8.70 |
| Proportion of Real GNP Change due to Substitution Effects (percent) | | | |
| Policy 1 | 92 | 88 | 77 |
| Policy 2 | 91 | 86 | 71 |
| Policy 3 | 91 | 86 | 71 |
| Policy 4 | 91 | 86 | 73 |
| Aggregate Relationship between Energy Input and Real GNP (ratio of percentage change in real GNP to percentage change in primary energy input, changes relative to the base case). | | | |
| Policy 1 | 0.18 | 0.18 | 0.18 |
| Policy 2 | 0.19 | 0.19 | 0.20 |
| Policy 3 | 0.19 | 0.20 | 0.21 |
| Policy 4 | 0.20 | 0.21 | 0.24 |

## Summary and Conclusion

Analysis of each of the four energy packages suggests that substantial reductions relative to the base case can be achieved in the volume of energy use. These reductions occur as a result of adjustments in the pattern of energy use and in the structure of economic activity. However, a consequence of these adjustments is a reduction in the level of real GNP relative to the base case. For example, real GNP in 2000 for Policy 2 is predicted to be 3.2 percent or $87 billion (1972$) below the base case, while the loss in real GNP in Policy 4 is 11.9 percent or $325 billion (1972$). Alternatively, the effects may be viewed in terms of growth rates: The growth of energy use can be slowed, but at the cost of some decrease in the rate of aggregate economic growth. For example, the policies can reduce average annual real GNP growth rates by up to 0.7 percent. Thus, a significant economic effect and economic cost may be predicted as a result of energy conservation policies.

However, a significant result of the analysis is that the economic impact as measured by the loss in real GNP is relatively less than the reduction in energy use. Adjustments in the pattern of energy use and of economic activity permit the energy intensity of spending and production to be reduced. This reduces the average energy content of each dollar of economic activity. Conversely, it means that the decline in real GNP caused by energy policy is less than the proportionate decline in energy use. Table 1–9 summarized the relationship between the decline in real GNP and the reduction in energy input. On average, each percentage point reduction in energy input leads to only a 0.2 percent reduction in real GNP. Thus, in Policy 2 in 2000, for example, the 16 percent reduction in energy input is associated with a 15 percent improvement in the aggregate economic efficiency of energy use and so requires only a 3 percent reduction in the total output of the economy. The relative economic cost of energy reduction becomes greater as the strength of the policy measures increases, since energy saving becomes progressively more difficult and costly. Also, the relative cost increases over time, due to the investment and capital reductions caused by restrictive energy policies.

This chapter has focused on the economic adjustment mechanisms that provide the flexibility in energy use underlying the result that energy reductions can be achieved with less than proportionate reductions in the level of growth of economic output. In particular, two features of this energy-economy relationship have been analyzed. The first covers the nature of the adjustment mechanisms and the reasons for partial rather than total flexibility in the relationship between energy input and economic output. The second covers the reasons for the variation in this relationship, particularly the increasing economic impact over time of energy reductions.

Our empirical finding that there is a reasonable degree of flexibility in the energy-economy relationship is highly significant. From a policy point of view, it suggests that it is possible to implement energy policies designed to restrict energy growth without having to suffer comparably large economic costs in terms of reduced GNP and slower economic growth. This makes it possible to contemplate restrictive energy policies designed to reduce petroleum imports. At the same time, there is an economic cost associated with such policies. Only if policymakers judge this cost to be less than the benefits obtained from promoting energy-related objectives are the measures justified. From a forecasting point of view, the finding provides important information for assessing the likely economic impacts of increases in energy prices, whether due to government policy, to increasing relative scarcity of resources, or to external influences.

## REFERENCES

Behling, D.J.; R. Dullien; and E.A. Hudson. 1976, *The Relationship of Energy Growth to Economic Growth Under Alternative Energy Policies.* Upton, New York: Brookhaven National Laboratory, March.

Behling, D.J.; W. Marcuse; M. Swift; and R.C. Tessman. 1975. *A Two-Level Iterative Model for Estimating Inter-Fuel Substitution Effects.* BNL 19863. Upton, New York: Brookhaven National Laboratory.

Beller, M., ed. 1975. *Sourcebook for Energy Assessment.* BNL 50483. Upton, New York: Brookhaven National Laboratory.

Bernanke, B., and D.W. Jorgenson. 1975. "The Integration of Energy Policy Models," *Computers and Operations Research* 2, no. 3 (September). 225–249.

Berndt, E.R., and D.W. Jorgenson. 1973, "Production Structure," In D.W. Jorgenson et al., *U.S. Energy Resources and Economic Growth,* Ch. 3. Final Report to the Energy Policy Project, Washington, D.C.

Berndt, E.R., and D.O Wood. 1976, "Technology, Prices, and the Derived Demand for Energy," *Review of Economics and Statistics* 58, no. 1 (February): 1–10.

Bullard, C.W., and R.A. Herendeen. 1973a. *Energy Cost of Consumption Decisions.* Document 135, Center for Advanced Computation. Urbana: University of Illinois at Urbana-Champaign.

_____. 1973b. *Energy Cost of Consumer Goods 1963/67.* Document 140, Center for Advanced Computation. Urbana: University of Illinois at Urbana-Champaign.

Cherniavsky, E.A. 1974. *Brookhaven Energy System Optimization Model,* BNL 19569, Upton, New York: Brookhaven National Laboratory.

_____. 1975. *Linear Programming and Technology Assessment.* BNL 20053. Upton, New York: Brookhaven National Laboratory.

Christensen, L.R.; D.W. Jorgenson; and L.J. Lau. 1973. "Transcendental Logarithmic Production Frontiers." *Review of Economics and Statistics* 55, no. 1 (February): 28–45.

———. 1975. "Transcendental Logarithmic Utility Functions." *American Economic Review* 65, no. 3 (June): 367–83.

Dullien, R., ed. 1976. *User's Guide to the DRI Long-Term Interindustry Transactions Model*. Interim Report to the U.S. Department of the Interior. Washington, D.C.

Energy Information Administration. 1978. *Annual Report to Congress*. Washington, D.C.: U.S. Department of Energy, April.

Energy Research and Development Administration. 1976. *A National Plan for Energy Research, Development, and Demonstration: Creating Energy Choices for the Future*. ERDA 76-1. Washington, D.C.

Federal Energy Administration. 1976. *1976 National Energy Outlook*. Washington, D.C.

Hoffman, K.C. 1973. "A Unified Framework for Energy System Planning." In M.F. Searl, ed., *Energy Modeling*. Washington, D.C.: Resources for the Future.

Hoffman, K.C., and E.A. Cherniavsky. 1974, *Interfuel Substitution and Technological Change*. BNL 18919. Upton, New York: Brookhaven National Laboratory.

Hoffman, K.C.; P.F. Palmedo; W. Marcuse; and M.D. Goldman. 1974. *Coupled Energy Systems–Economic Models*. BNL 19293. Upton, New York; Brookhaven National Laboratory.

Hogan, W.W. 1977. "Capital Energy Complementarity in Aggregate Energy-Economic Analysis." Energy Modeling Forum, Institute for Energy Studies, Stanford University, September.

Hudson, E.A., and D.W. Jorgenson. 1973. "Interindustry Transactions." In D.W. Jorgenson et al., *Energy Resources and Economic Growth*, Ch. 5. Final Report to the Energy Policy Project. Washington, D.C.

———. 1974a. "U.S. Energy Policy and Economic Growth, 1975–2000." *Bell Journal of Economics and Management Science* 5, no. 2 (Autumn): 461–514.

———. 1974. "Tax Policy and Energy Use." In Committee on Finance, United States Senate, *Fiscal Policy and the Energy Crisis,* pp. 1681–94. 93rd Cong. 1st and 2nd sess.

———. 1974. "Economic Analysis of Alternative Energy Growth Patterns." Report to the Energy Policy Project, Ford Foundation. In David Freeman et al., *A Time to Choose,* pp. 493–511. Cambridge, Massachusetts: Ballinger.

———. 1977. *The Long Term Interindustry Transactions Model: A Simulation Model for Energy and Economic Analysis*. Final Report to the Applied Economics Division, Federal Preparedness Agency, General Services Administration, September.

———. 1978a. "Energy Policy and U.S. Economic Growth." *American Economic Review* 68, no. 2 (May):118–123.

———. 1978b. "Energy Prices and the U.S. Economy, 1972–1976." *Natural Resources Journal* 18 no. 4. (October):209–220.

Jack Faucett Associates. 1973. *Data Development for the Input-Output Energy Model*. Final Report to the Energy Policy Project. Washington, D.C.

_____. 1975. *Historical Energy Flow Accounts.* Final Report to the Federal Energy Administration. Washington, D.C.

Jorgenson, D.W. 1975, "Consumer Demand for Energy." W.D. Nordhaus, ed., *In Proceedings of the Workshop on Energy Demand,* pp. 765–802. Laxenburg, Austria: IIASA.

_____. 1978." The Role of Energy in the U.S. Economy." *National Tax Journal* 31, no. 3 (September): 209–220.

Jorgenson, D.W., and E.A. Hudson. 1975a. "Tax Policy and Energy Conservation." in D.W. Jorgenson, ed., *Econometric Studies of U.S. Energy Policy.* Amsterdam: North-Holland.

_____. 1975b. "Projections of U.S. Economic Growth and Energy Demand." Report to the Edison Electric Institute, September. Published in condensed form in R.W. Greenleaf, ed., *Structural Change and Current Problems Facing Regulated Public Utilities,* pp. 75–128. Indianapolis: Graduate School of Business, Indiana University.

Jorgenson, D.W., and L.J. Lau. 1975. "The Structure of Consumer Preferences," *Annals of Social and Economic Measurement* 4, no. 1 (January): 49–101.

Jorgenson, D.W., and B.D. Wright. 1975. "The Impact of Alternative Policies to Reduct Oil Imports." Report to the Office of the Secretary, U.S. Department of the Treasury. *Data Resources Review* 4, no. 6 (June).

Marcuse, W.; L. Bodin; E.A. Cherniavsky; and Y. Sanborn. 1975. *A Dynamic Time Dependent Model for the Analysis of Alternative Energy Policies,* BNL 19406, Upton, New York: Brookhaven National Laboratory.

7230
1323

# 2 PSEUDODATA
# A Synthesis of Econometric and
# Process Modeling Methodologies

James M. Griffin
*Department of Economics*
*University of Houston*

## INTRODUCTION

The simultaneous development of generalized cost functions together with the emergence of energy policy concerns has opened a number of interesting avenues for empirical investigation. With the recognition that energy markets require substantial periods for adjustment, macroeconometric models with input-output detail have been developed to forecast to the year 2000. Policy simulation analysis is possible with E. A. Hudson and D. W. Jorgenson's (1974) nine-sector growth model, as well as with Ross Preston's (1972) Wharton Annual Model, which has sixty-three-industry detail. In both models, annual time series are used to estimate cost functions, which assure that the input-output coefficients are price responsive. Implicit in this work is the assumption that techniques used in short-run analysis are appropriate for long-range analysis as well. Particularly, we note the deficiencies of time series data in (1) exhibiting sufficient relative price variation, (2) eliciting long-run equilibria, (3) incorporating the effects of technological change, and (4) including the effects of future environmental controls.

The purpose of this chapter is to examine how a statistical cost function estimated from an unconventional data source offers an alternative to existing long-run cost analysis. The data source, which L. R. Klein has dubbed

The author acknowledges his extensive use of materials drawn from Griffin (1979)

"pseudodata," is merely the cost-minimizing inputs generated by an engineering process analysis model for alternative input prices. Each model solution yields the corresponding input levels and total costs for a given set of input prices. Data generated by the process model replace conventional market data as the basis for statistical cost function estimation. The resulting statistical cost function serves as a type of single equation, reduced form description of the technological structure embodied in the multiequation process model. In this exercise, the process analysis model is a 298-equation linear programming model with 638 activities describing the iron and steel industry.

The statistical cost function estimated from pseudodata has important advantages relative both to a cost function estimated from conventional data and to the direct use of the process model. Unlike conventional data, relative input prices can be varied widely, thereby avoiding multicollinearity and enabling the estimation of cost functions with many input prices. The pseudodata statistical cost function offers the capability to describe new environmental controls and new technologies, both of which are likely to be critical for long-range simulation exercises.

The pseudodata statistical cost function also offers several important advantages relative to direct use of the process model. First, since process models are typically described through a linear programming framework, the production surface is continuous, but nondifferentiable. Alternatively, the statistical cost function offers a differentiable approximation to the nondifferentiable engineering technology, thereby enabling the calculation of substitution elasticities and price elasticities. In principle, the process model could directly provide input-output coefficients. However, it would require repetitive solutions of the process model for each iteration of the macro model.[1] The statistical cost function offers a much cheaper alternative, since once the fixed cost of pseudodata generation is incurred, the variable cost of calculating input-output coefficients from the cost function is trivial. By Shephard's lemma the partial derivatives of the unit cost function with respect to the input prices yield the input-output coefficients.

Section two describes the iron and steel process model developed by Russell and Vaughan (1976) at Resources for the Future and the method of pseudodata generation. After reading section two, the reader unfamiliar with process models can then judge the strengths and weaknesses of pseudodata relative to conventional data. Section three provides such a

---

1. In just one simulation to the year 2000, this would involve one hundred separate solutions to the industry process model, assuming five iterations are required for convergence each year.

comparison and elaboration of the points raised in the introduction. In the fourth section the translog cost function is described along with its properties. Section five presents the statistical cost function and empirical tests. In the sixth section the various substitution elasticities are examined for their implications about an energy aggregate and the nature of the production technology. Section seven considers how the pseudodata statistical cost function can be used to model the input-output coefficients for long-run policy simulation analysis. Section eight recapitulates the major findings.

## PSEUDODATA GENERATION FROM A PROCESS MODEL

The major constraint to the general application of pseudodata for statistical cost estimation is the availability of high quality engineering process models. Several private engineering consulting firms have eveloped such models, but they are not easily accessible for academic research. Work at Resources for the Future under the direction of Clifford Russell is helping to relax this constraint. In 1973 RFF developed a petroleum-refining model (see Russell 1973), and most recently Russell and William Vaughan (1976) have developed an iron and steel model. This latter model serves as the basis for the exercises here.

The iron and steel model contains an engineering description of all the major operations—discharges of air and water pollution, pollution control equipment, and the latest steel-making technology—all of which make it particularly appropriate for the application here. The technology, which is posited to exhibit constant returns to scale, is described through a standard linear programming framework with linear constraints. As noted earlier, the model is relatively large, as it contains 298 rows (equations) and 638 columns or process activities to be chosen from. The Russell and Vaughan model was designed to consider policy questions regarding alternative pollution strategies; therefore, the model provided detailed information on water pollution discharges of heat, BOD (biochemical oxygen demand), toxics (cyanide and phenols), ammonia, and suspended solids. The model also describes the available cleanup technology to reduce these water pollutants. Similarly, with respect to air pollution, the model measures $SO_2$ and particulate emissions and includes the corresponding cleanup technologies, such as electrostatic precipitators, stack gas scrubbers, and the option of purchasing low sulphur fuels.

The modifications to the process models required for generation of the pseudodata were minimal. First, since the analysis is long run, all capacity constraints were relaxed so that only optimal capacity configurations are solved for. Next, input prices were rescaled to approximate 1974 prices, as we used this set as our base case around which the translog cost function provides a local approximation. Also, the product mix was set to approximate recent requirements.

The iron and steel process model is described through a straightforward linear programming (LP) problem of minimizing costs of producing 2,000 tons of the appropriate product mix as follows:

$$\min P_z X_z \qquad\qquad z = 1, \ldots, T$$

subject to

$$A\ X_z \le\ _b \tag{2.1}$$

where $P_z$ is an $n \times 1$ vector of unit input prices, and $X_z$ is an $n \times 1$ vector of process activity levels. $A$ is the $m \times n$ matrix of technical coefficients based on engineering data. The vector $b$ is the $m \times 1$ right-hand side constraint vector where the $b_j$th element constrains output of the fixed product mix to be $\ge 2{,}000$. In order to restrict the number of inputs for statistical cost analysis, we aggregate to seven inputs that include operating cost inputs, capital, electricity, coal, natural gas (including fuel oil), iron ore (including pellets), and scrap steel. Operating cost inputs consist primarily of labor, although minor inputs of limestone and the like are included. Even the individual fuels involved some aggregation, as the model allows for the purchase of fuels of differing sulphur content. This level of aggregation captures all of the major inputs (capital, operating inputs, iron ore, and scrap) and the various fuels.

Initially the base case solution for 1974 prices and environmental constraints must be calculated. Using 1974 prices, equation (2.1) was solved assuming no constraints on air or water pollution. After obtaining the uncontrolled pollution levels, the pollution constraints in the $b$ vector were set at 50 percent of the levels that would occur in the absence of environmental regulations, and the model was solved for the base case set of inputs $X_1$.

The second-order local approximation of the translog function provides a rationale for varying each price sequentially, while holding all others constant. Each price was varied by the following multiple ($\Theta$), while holding other prices at 1974 levels:

$$
\theta = \begin{matrix} 2.0 \\ 1.25 \\ 1.1 \\ 0.905 \\ 0.8 \\ 0.5 \end{matrix} \tag{2.2}
$$

Each input is varied from a level of 50 percent below to 100 percent above 1974 prices, while holding constant all other prices. Applying this procedure for each price yields six observations per input price times the seven prices, or forty-two observations plus the base case solution. An additional eight observations were obtained by simulating the model for four alternative air control levels and for four alternative water control levels.[2] Therefore, $T$ in equation (2.1) is 51. As shown subsequently, the cost shares from the translog cost function are linear in the logarithms of prices, thereby justifying the sequential variation of input prices. The local approximation nature of the translog function suggests that prices be restricted to a reasonable range about the point of approximation. The choice in equation (2.2) restricts most of the observations to the price range of $\pm 25$ percent. The additional points $0.5P$ and $2P$ are added to provide some ability to explain the wide relative price variations possible in long-range exercises.

## A COMPARISON OF TIME SERIES AND PSEUDODATA

Statistical cost functions estimated from annual time series data for the postwar period have served as the basis for modeling input-output coefficient change as well as for much of the work on energy and interfuel substitution analysis. Theoretical arguments against the use of time series data to estimate statistical cost functions are by no means new. The objections here to time-series-estimated cost relationships for long-range analysis do not rest on the standard concerns with simultaneous equation bias, specification error, aggregation bias, and the like (see Walters 1963; Johnston 1960). The primary objections center on the ability of such relationships to describe the long-run production structure, which is affected by new technologies and environmental constraints.

2. Recall that in the base case, pollution discharges are set at 50 percent the uncontrolled levels. Subsequent solutions were made for 100, 75, and 25 percent and for the minimum percentage of the uncontrolled emission level.

First, it must be recognized that irrespective of the data, a statistical cost function can offer at best only a local rather than a global approximation to the technology. The relevant question hinges on whether pseudodata offer a better local approximation than time series data. Time series data suffer from two weaknesses in this regard. First, relative prices may exhibit considerable multicollinearity, thereby preventing the estimation of the underlying structural parameters. This problem is particularly acute if we wish to elicit interfuel substitution effects and substitution between energy and nonenergy inputs with annual postwar U.S. data. Second, time series observations are unlikely to represent long-run equilibria. Hudson and Jorgenson (1974) implicitly assume an instantaneous (one-year) adjustment. One can legitimately question whether the restrictive nature of the assumed lag obfuscates the measurement of the long-run equilibrium responses. In contrast, the method by which the pseudodata are generated in equation (2.2) completely avoids the multicollinearity problem as the price variation is orthogonal. In addition, the solution to equation (2.1) by necessity provides long-run cost-minimizing equilibria.

Both new technology and environmental policies are likely to be critical factors in long-range simulation exercises, and yet they are typically not reflected in historical time series. The time series treatment of technological change is frequently cast in terms of Hicks neutral or some type of biased technical change for lack of data on specific process advancements. Either treatment of pollution controls is completely omitted due to its unimportance over the sample period or a dummy pollution control variable or ad hoc constant adjustment is introduced. These approaches bear little relationship to industry level developments. For example, technological change over the next twenty-five years in iron and steel making is likely to result in the widespread adoption of continuous casting plants and the reliance on iron ore pellets. Air pollution regulations involving sulphur dioxide ($SO_2$) emissions will have an impact on the sulphur content of the coal burned and the relative mix of electric arc to basic oxygen furnaces. Water pollution controls include the elimination of waste organics and inorganics as well as heat discharge controls—all of which will affect the production costs and process configuration. As illustrated in the previous section, it is possible to introduce environmental controls explicitly into the statistical cost function via the pseudodata, since the process model explicitly describes these alternatives. New technologies can also be introduced in an analogous manner.

From the preceding comparison, the reader might be inclined to conclude that pseudodata should completely supplant time series analysis whenever possible. While pseudodata offer distinct advantages for testing aggregates and for long-range forecasting and simulation exercises, they are not likely to displace time series data for short-range forecasting. Despite problems of simultaneous equation bias and measurement error, time series estimates of short-run responses are likely to exhibit less error than those based on pseudodata. Pseudodata are subject to both measurement error and a behavioral error. Measurement error is introduced because the observed technology matrix, $A$ in equation (2.1), differs from the technically correct matrix $A^*$. The engineering data implicit in $A$ are collected from a variety of sources and are in many cases estimates. Behavioral error arises because even if $A$ were free of measurement error $(A = A^*)$, observed behavior may differ from the frictionless type of cost minimization posited here. In contrast, statistical cost functions based on time series data do not rely as extensively on the cost minimization assumptions. Persistent errors in cost minimization become implicit in the time-series-dependent cost function via market data.

## THE TRANSLOG COST FUNCTION

Since the development of the translogarithmic function by Christensen, Jorgenson, and Lau (1973), applications of it have spread rapidly to its use in production functions, cost functions, and profit functions. Recent cost function applications include those by Hudson and Jorgenson (1974), Berndt and Wood (1975), and Humphrey and Moroney (1975). The translog is one of a group of functional forms that place no a priori restrictions on the substitution elasticities. We arbitrarily choose the translog function. Since in the iron and steel application there are seven inputs, we write the translog cost function as follows:

$$
\begin{aligned}
\ln C = \ln \alpha_o + \ln Q &+ \sum_{i=1}^{7} \alpha_i \ln P_i + \sum_{k=1}^{4} \gamma_k \ln D_k^{*A} + \sum_{k=1}^{4} \delta_k \ln D_k^{*W} \\
&+ \frac{1}{2} \sum_{i=1}^{7} \sum_{j=1}^{7} b_{ij} \ln P_i \ln P_j + \frac{1}{2} \sum_{k=1}^{4} \sum_{j=1}^{7} \gamma_{jk} \ln D_k^{A} \ln P_j \\
&+ \frac{1}{2} \sum_{k=1}^{4} \sum_{j=1}^{7} \delta_{jk} \ln D_k^{W} \ln P_j + \frac{1}{2} \sum_{k=1}^{4} \sum_{l=1}^{4} \psi_{kl} \ln D_k^{W} \ln D_l^{A}
\end{aligned}
\tag{2.3}
$$

where $C$ is total costs, $Q$ is output, $P_i$ refers to input prices, and $D_k^{W}$ and $D_k^{A}$ refer to water and air pollution dummy variables, respectively. The translog cost function in equation (2.3) differs somewhat in formulation from other applications. Implicit in equation (2.3) is the assumption of constant returns to scale, which is consistent with the linear programming description of the industry technology. The independent variables, $\ln D^A{}_l$ and $\ln D^W$, equal 1 or 0 depending on whether a given set of water pollution ($D^W$) or air pollution ($D^A$) controls are in effect.

If we differentiate equation (2.3) with respect to each price and invoke Shephard's lemma, the seven cost share formulas ($S_i$), which form the basis for statistical examination, are obtained:

$$S_i \equiv \frac{X_i P_i}{C} = \frac{\partial C}{\partial P_i} \frac{P_i}{C} = \frac{\partial \ln C}{\partial \ln P_i}$$

$$= \alpha_i + \sum_{j=1}^{7} \beta_{ij} \ln P_j + \sum_{k=1}^{4} \gamma_{ik} \ln D^A{}_k$$

$$+ \sum_{k=1}^{4} \delta_{ik} \ln D^W{}_k \quad k = 1,\ldots,7 \tag{2.4}$$

The value shares $S_i$ sum to unity because $C = \sum_{i=1}^{7} P_i X_i$

In the estimation of the cost share equations in (2.4), we make use of certain theoretical properties that reduce the number of coefficients to be estimated. By assumption the symmetry conditions are

$$\beta_{ij} = \beta_{ji} \qquad \begin{matrix} i,j = 1,\ldots,7 \\ i \neq j \end{matrix} \tag{2.5}$$

As a consequence of the cost shares summing to unity, it follows that

$$\sum_{i=1}^{7} \beta_{ij} = 0 \quad \sum_{i=1}^{7} \gamma_{ik} = 0 \quad \sum_{i=1}^{7} \delta_{ik} = 0 \quad \begin{matrix} j = 1,\ldots,7 \\ k = 1,\ldots,4 \end{matrix} \tag{2.6}$$

and

$$\sum_{i=1}^{7} \alpha_i = 1 \tag{2.7}$$

These are generally referred to as equality conditions. Symmetry combined with the quality conditions assures linear homogeneity in prices.

In addition to the constraints on the parameters of the translog, other conditions must also be tested because the translog function need not be well behaved for all input prices. For the cost function to be well behaved, an increase in an input price increases cost; by equation (2.4), this requires positive cost shares. This test is referred to as either positivity or monotonicity. In addition, if the cost function is well behaved, it must be concave in input prices, which requires that the Hessian matrix be negative semidefinite at the point of approximation. The elasticities of substitution are calculated in the translog cost function framework as

$$\sigma_{ii} = \frac{\beta_{ii} + S^2_i - S_i}{S^2_i} \qquad i = 1,\ldots,7$$

$$\sigma_{ij} = \frac{\beta_{ij} + S_i S_j}{S_i S_j} \qquad \begin{array}{l} i,j = 1,\ldots,7 \\ i \neq j. \end{array} \qquad (2.8)$$

Unlike more restrictive forms such as the Cobb-Douglas or CES, the $\sigma_{ij}$'s vary between inputs with $\sigma_{ij} > 0$ implying substitutes and $\sigma_{ij} < 0$ implying complements. The own and cross-price elasticities of demand can be calculated from the $\beta_{ij}$ parameters and the cost shares:

$$E_{ii} = \frac{\partial \ln X_i}{\partial \ln P_i} = \frac{\beta_{ii} + S^2_i - S_i}{S_i} = S_i \sigma_{ii} \qquad i = 1,\ldots,7$$

$$E_{ij} = \frac{\partial \ln X_i}{\partial \ln P_j} = \frac{\beta_{ij} + S_i S_j}{S_i} = S_j \sigma_{ij} \qquad \begin{array}{l} i,j = 1,\ldots,7 \\ i \neq j. \end{array} \qquad 2.9$$

Furthermore, if linear homogeneity is satisfied, the sum of own and cross-price elasticities equals zero.

## STATISTICAL COST FUNCTION ESTIMATION

For estimation purposes, we posit normally distributed additive disturbances $\varepsilon_i (i = 1,\ldots,7)$, which are to be affixed to the cost share equations. They are assumed to be normally distributed with mean zero and the following variance-covariance structure:

$$E(\varepsilon_{it}, \varepsilon_{jt}') = \begin{cases} \Omega & \text{if } t = t' \\ 0 & \text{if } t \neq t' \end{cases} \qquad (2.10)$$

where

$$\Omega = \begin{matrix} \sigma 11 \ldots \sigma 17 \\ \vdots \quad \vdots \\ \sigma 17 \ldots \sigma 77 \end{matrix}$$

The additive disturbances in equation (2.10), which are affixed to the cost shares in equation (2.4), arise due to omitted higher order price and environmental terms in the translog approximation in equation (2.3). Pseudodata do give rise to an added estimation difficulty because of the piecewise linear nature of the production surface. An intriguing type of local bias exists at the points of nondifferentiability. The extent of local bias depends on the frequency of basis changes in the process model; the more frequent the basic changes, the smaller the local bias and the closer the approximation to a differentiable technology.

In order to obtain asymptotically efficient estimators, the nonzero covariance among the cost shares for any particular observation must be taken into account. We utilize the iterative Zellner efficient (IZEF) estimation procedure, which yields maximum likelihood estimators. Since the parameters of the full system are determined by only $j - 1$ equations, cost share $S_7$ is omitted. The IZEF estimators are invariant, however, to the equation omitted.

First, the set of equations in (2.4) is estimated with the equality and symmetry conditions imposed. These results indicated that the first three dummy variables for air and water controls at 0, 25, and 75 percent reductions were small and nonsignificant. Only $\delta_{i4}$ and $\gamma_{i4}$ for the maximum removal case (95 percent for water and 82 percent for air) were significant. The results of those value share equations for a model omitting $\delta_{i1}$, $\delta_{i2}$ and $\delta_{i3}$, and $\gamma_{i1}$, $\gamma_{i2}$, $\gamma_{i3}$ are shown in Table 2–1. Given in parentheses below each directly estimated coefficient is the asymptotic standard error of the parameter estimate. We recall from equation (2.8) that $\beta_{ij} = 0$ implies a Cobb-Douglas relationship between inputs $i$ and $j$. From inspection, we note that a large number of the coefficients are statistically different from zero, so the added generality of the translog function appears worthwhile.[3] A critical question in the use of a statistical cost function to approximate a process model's technological structure is the accuracy of the approximation. The $R^2$ for the cost share equations indicate, with the exception of operating

---

3 To illustrate the "flexibility" of the translog's production structure, Berndt and Wood's (1975) translog study showed the capital-energy substitution elasticity ($\sigma_{KE}$ of $-3.2$, indicating strong complementarity. Using a three factor, K,L,E, model, Griffin and Gregory's (1976) translog study found $\sigma_{KE} = 1$, indicating capital and energy are substitutes.

**Table 2-1.** Translog Estimates of Cost Share Equations (symmetry and equality imposed).

| | $\alpha_i$ | $\gamma_{14}$ | $\delta_{14}$ | $\beta_{.1}$ | $\beta_{.2}$ | $\beta_{.3}$ | $\beta_{.4}$ | $\beta_{.5}$ | $\beta_{.6}$ | $\beta_{.7}$ | $R^2$ | S.E. |
|---|---|---|---|---|---|---|---|---|---|---|---|---|
| $\beta1$ | 0.305 (0.005)[a] | −0.042 (0.037) | −0.037 (0.034) | 0.095 (0.026) | −0.104 (0.006) | −0.024 (0.007) | 0.003 (0.007) | −0.006 (0.002) | 0.010 (0.016) | 0.026 | 0.202 | 0.031 |
| $\beta2$ | 0.361 (0.001) | −0.065 (0.010) | −0.057 (0.010) | | 0.179 (0.004) | 0.008 (0.003) | −0.043 (0.003) | 0.006 (0.001) | −0.089 (0.006) | 0.043 | 0.932 | 0.009 |
| $\beta3$ | 0.031 (0.001) | 0.024 (0.010) | 0.025 (0.010) | | | 0.013 (0.004) | 0.015 (0.003) | −0.001 (0.002) | 0.033 (0.006) | −0.044 | 0.585 | 0.009 |
| $\beta4$ | 0.050 (0.001) | −0.037 (0.010) | −0.037 (0.010) | | | | 0.021 (0.003) | 0.003 (0.002) | −0.053 (0.006) | 0.054 | 0.726 | 0.003 |
| $\beta5$ | 0.003 (0.0003) | 0.019 (0.003) | 0.018 (0.003) | | | | | 0.002 (0.001) | 0.011 (0.002) | −0.015 | 0.721 | 0.003 |
| $\beta6$ | 0.109 (0.003) | −0.084 (0.022) | −0.083 (0.022) | | | | | | −0.034 (0.014) | 0.122 | 0.637 | 0.022 |
| $\beta7$ | 0.141 | 0.185 | 0.172 | | | | | | | −0.186 | | |

Notes: Identification of inputs:
1. Operating inputs  5. Natural gas
2. Capital             6. Iron ore pellets
3. Electricity         7. Scrap
4. Coal

[a]Asymptotic standard error of parameter estimates.

costs ($S_1$), a fairly close approximation. This is particularly true in terms of the standard errors of each equation.

A legitimate concern of the use of a smooth differentiable functional form to approximate a continuous but nondifferentiable technology is the overall sample fit. Therefore, using the parameters in Table 2–1, we estimated equation (2.3), the total cost function. $R^2$ was 0.83, and the standard error was only 0.008.

As noted earlier, there are a number of formal tests besides sample fit for the adequacy of the translog approximation. First, a test for symmetry, which is equivalent to a test for linear homogeneity in prices, is performed. Symmetry is tested for by using the conventional $F$ test. We calculate the difference in the weighted sum of squared residuals divided by the change in degrees of freedom. This ratio is then divided by the ratios of the weighted sum of squared residuals of the unconstrained estimates to the degrees of freedom. These tests revealed that symmetry cannot be rejected.[4] The test for positivity is particularly useful for forecasting purposes as it elicits the sample range over which the translog approximation breaks down. Positivity was checked for each of the fifty-one observations for each of the seven cost shares. This revealed five out of a possible three-hundred fifty-seven violations.[5] Moreover, four of these five violations occurred for price variations of 0.5 or $2P$. Thus, over the most likely range of future relative price variations, the translog is well behaved and offers a surprisingly robust "local approximation" for the iron and steel industry. A final test is for concavity in input prices. The Hessian matrix was evaluated for the base case and was found to be negative semidefinite. In sum, the translog representation appears quite suitable.

## SUBSTITUTION AND PRICE ELASTICITIES

An important capability of the preceding statistical cost function is that substitution and price elasticities can be easily obtained. These elasticities are a prerequisite for a variety of micropolicy and methodological investigations. As noted earlier, the nondifferentiable nature of the process model technology prevents direct calculation of such elasticities, yet the statistical cost function approximation overcomes this problem.

---

4. $F_{(21,246)} = 1.07$ where $F^*_{.01} (21,246) = 1.9$

5. All seven violations occurred for natural gas at the following price vectors: $2P_1$, $0.5P_2$, $0.5P_7$, $1.25 P_8$, $2P_8$. The smallest cost share was $-0.007$.

Estimates of substitution and price elasticities are extremely valuable results in themselves, as they can be readily applied to energy policy questions. Table 2–3 gives the corresponding price elasticities based on equation (2.9), evaluated for base case relative prices. In looking at the substitution elasticities in Table 2–2, we observed that in the long run, the production technology is extremely flexible, as most of the substitution elasticities exceed the commonly assumed value of unity.

In view of the importance of energy and our concern with estimating interfuel substitution responses involving energy, we note that strong interfuel substitution forces are at work between coal and the other energy forms. A possible complementarity relationship exists between electricity and natural gas. Nevertheless, complementarity may be reasonable here because cheaper electricity prices favor the electric arc furnace, which uses 100 percent scrap and no hot iron. In turn, this reduces the requirement for hot iron and coke. The reduction in coke production reduces by-product coke oven gas that is used in downstream processing for process heat; therefore, natural gas must be purchased instead. The substitution elasticities translate into inelastic, but statistically significant, own price response for fuels. The cross-price elasticities among fuels tend to be less than unity, but nevertheless nontrivial.

The results of Table 2–2 offer important insights into the commonly made assumption of the existence of an energy aggregate. To the extent that

**Table 2–2.** Partial Elasticities of Substitution ($\sigma_{ij}$).

| | Operating Inputs | Capital | Electricity | Coal | Natural Gas | Ore and Pellets | Scrap |
|---|---|---|---|---|---|---|---|
| Operating Inputs | −1.28 | 0.06 | −2.05 | 1.18 | −7.56 | 1.28 | 1.68 |
| | (0.28) | (0.06) | (0.90) | (0.42) | (3.33) | (0.44) | |
| Capital | | −0.39 | 1.88 | −1.15 | 7.67 | −1.00 | 1.89 |
| | | (0.03) | (0.31) | (0.14) | (1.41) | (0.14) | |
| Electricity | | | −18.67 | 11.43 | −13.83 | 11.49 | −12.18 |
| | | | (5.91) | (2.06) | (24.9) | (2.0) | |
| Coal | | | | −10.44 | 25.98 | 7.05 | 8.73 |
| | | | | (0.94) | (8.4) | (0.90) | |
| Natural Gas | | | | | −131.4 | 38.4 | −46.1 |
| | | | | | (190.0) | (6.9) | |
| Ore and Pellets | | | | | | −9.54 | 8.77 |
| | | | | | | (1.01) | |
| Scrap | | | | | | | −17.89 |

Table 2-3.   Own and Cross-Price Elasticities of Demand ($E_{ij}$).

| | Operating Inputs | Capital | Electricity | Coal | Natural Gas | Ore and Pellets | Scrap |
|---|---|---|---|---|---|---|---|
| Operating Inputs | −0.39 | 0.02 | −0.05 | 0.06 | −0.02 | 0.16 | 0.22 |
| | (0.09) | (0.02) | (0.02) | (0.02) | (0.01) | (0.05) | |
| Capital | 0.02 | −0.14 | 0.05 | −0.06 | 0.02 | −0.12 | 0.24 |
| | (0.02) | (0.01) | (0.01) | (0.01) | (0.00) | (0.02) | |
| Electricity | −0.62 | 0.69 | 0.49 | 0.62 | −0.03 | 1.39 | −1.57 |
| | (0.27) | (0.11) | (0.15) | (0.11) | (0.06) | (0.24) | |
| Coal | 0.36 | −0.42 | 0.30 | −0.57 | 0.06 | −0.85 | 1.12 |
| | (0.13) | (0.05) | (0.05) | (0.05) | (0.02) | (0.11) | |
| Natural Gas | −2.27 | 2.81 | 0.36 | 1.42 | −0.33 | 4.65 | −5.95 |
| | (1.00) | (0.52) | (0.64) | (0.46) | (0.48) | (0.84) | |
| Ore and Pellets | 0.38 | −0.37 | 0.30 | −0.38 | 0.10 | −1.16 | 1.13 |
| | (0.13) | (0.05) | (0.05) | (0.05) | (0.02) | (0.12) | |
| Scrap | 0.51 | 0.69 | −0.32 | 0.48 | −0.11 | 1.06 | −2.30 |

[a]Estimated standard errors in parentheses.

a nonenergy input such as capital exhibits a substitute relationship with respect to electricity and natural gas and a complementary one with respect to coal, it follows that the concept of an energy aggregate is incompatible with the underlying production structure.

## APPLICATIONS FOR LONG-RANGE ANALYSIS

In this section we explore the potential of the pseudodata statistical cost function as a long-range simulation tool. The statistical cost function offers important advantages in allowing a more disaggregated analysis of the production structure as well as a vehicle for introducing environmental and technological changes. The advantages of a more disaggregated cost function for tax policy analysis should be apparent from the substitution and price elasticities in the previous section. Therefore, attention here is focused on the potential for dealing with environmental and technological changes in a more exact manner.

Statistical cost functions are particularly useful devices as a procedure for modeling changes in input-output coefficients. By Shephard's lemma, partial differentiation of the unit cost function with respect to the $i$th price yields the desired long-run, input-output coefficient $(\alpha_i^{LR})$. The long-run nature of the statistical cost function poses a problem in dynamic analysis, since at any given time, a multiplicity of competing processes is observed, rather than the one set consistent with long-run cost minimization. In effect, the short-run equilibria differ from long-run equilibria, since the capital stock cannot be adjusted instantaneously. Some method is needed to distinguish between short- and long-run equilibria and the capital adjustment process between the two. Perhaps the most tractable procedure is to posit a dynamic demand formulation where changes in the observed input-output coefficients $(\alpha_i)$ depend on the difference between the actual and desired long-run coefficients $(\alpha_i^{LR})$.

$$\Delta\alpha_i = \lambda(\alpha_i^{LR} - \alpha_{i-1}) \qquad \begin{array}{l} i = 1,\ldots,n \text{ inputs} \\ 0 < \lambda \le 1 \end{array} \qquad (2.11)$$

The adjustment rate $\lambda$ can be determined empirically. The desired long-run coefficients $\alpha_i^{LR}$ can be calculated over some historical sample period from equation (2.4). Time series observations for the actual coefficients $(\alpha_i)$ are known. Thus, time series data would be introduced at this point to model the adjustment rate between long-run equilibria.

In subsequent research by Finan and Griffin (1978), this approach has been illustrated for the electric utility industry, comparing this technique for modeling input-output coefficients with time series approaches such as the Hudson-Jorgenson model on the Wharton Annual Model (Preston 1975). This exercise revealed the strength of pseudodata, particularly in modeling responses to factors not fully captured in historical time series data such as the effects of fuel and capital prices on nuclear fuel expansion.

Having seen how the long-run coefficients can be related to short-run responses, we turn to the critical question of how environmental and technological changes can be introduced in $\alpha_i^{LR}$. Process models offer the only method by which well-defined environmental or technological changes can be assessed, since the technology is implicit in the $A$ matrix, and environmental constraints enter through prices or the materials balance constraints in the $b$ vector. Under pollution taxes, a separate price or tax is entered directly in the cost function for that pollutant, just as it would have a nonzero price in the $P$ vector of the process model.

In the case of environmental standards, which is the case considered here, dummy variables may offer a simple, inexpensive method of treating environmental standards if the second-order local approximation of the translog function is adequate over the sample range. Acceptance of the formulations in equation (2.3) leads to additive dummy pollution variables in equation (2.4), implying that the $\alpha$ and $\beta$ coefficients are not affected by the type of pollution constraint. If valid, the full grid of pseudodata need not be reestimated for a different level of environmental controls. The more computationally involved procedure is to estimate a separate cost function for each set of environmental controls. It does, however, avoid the overly restrictive assumption of equation (2.3), whereby environmental controls enter through dummy variables. In the application here, the former approach is illustrated, leaving it to further research to determine which of the two approaches is superior.

Table 2–4 contrasts the two extremes of zero and maximum controls on both air and water pollutants, as they have an impact on the input-output coefficients and the level of production costs. Assuming 1974 relative prices and using equation (2.4), we determine the input-output coefficients that exhibit significant change at maximum air and water pollution standards. In order to determine the effects on total costs, the $v^*$ and $\sigma^*$ coefficients in equation (2.3) are necessary. A complete relaxation of air pollution standards results in 0.6 percent cost decrease, while the maximum cleanup involves an 8.7 percent increase. In the case of water standards, maximum cleanup increases production costs by 7.1 percent relative to the uncontrolled case.

Table 2–4.    Comparison of Input-Output Coefficients Under Alternative Pollution Control Systems.[a]

| | Air Pollution Controls | | Water Pollution Controls | |
|---|---|---|---|---|
| | No restrictions | Maximum abatement | No restrictions | Maximum abatement |
| Inputs | | | | |
| Operating inputs | 0.305 | 0.263 | 0.305 | 0.268 |
| Capital | 0.361 | 0.297 | 0.361 | 0.304 |
| Electricity | 0.031 | 0.055 | 0.031 | 0.056 |
| Coal | 0.050 | 0.013 | 0.050 | 0.013 |
| Natural gas | 0.003 | 0.022 | 0.003 | 0.021 |
| Iron ore | 0.109 | 0.025 | 0.109 | 0.026 |
| Scrap | 0.141 | 0.326 | 0.141 | 0.313 |
| Unit production cost (1974 base = 1.0) | 0.994 | 1.087 | 0.995 | 1.066 |

[a]Assumes 1974 relative prices.

The new effects of technology can also be approximated in an analogous manner. Entering $ln\ T_o$ as a technology dummy in equation (2.3) yields the following set of input-output coefficients:

$$\alpha_i^{LR} = \frac{X_i}{Q} = \frac{P_Q}{P_i}\ [\alpha_i + \Sigma_j\beta_{ij}\ ln\ P_j + \gamma_{i4}\ ln\ D^A_4$$
$$+\ \delta_{i4}ln\ D^W_4 + \phi_i\ ln\ To] \qquad i = 1,\ldots,7 \quad (2.12)$$

Put another way, the effect of the new technology is simply

$$\Delta\alpha_i^{LR} = \frac{P_Q}{P_i}\ \phi_i. \tag{2.13}$$

Both $P_i$ and $P_Q$ are known, and $\phi_i$ can be thought of as merely a constant adjustment to the $i$th cost share, obtained by solving the LP model once for the cost-minimizing cost shares under the new technology. $\phi_i$ is the difference between the new cost share, $S_i^{new}$ and the old cost share $S_i^{old}$. The change in unit costs can be taken directly from the LP solution as well.

As an example, we ask what the coefficients would look like if within process improvements in hot iron production had not occurred. Over the last two decades, there has been a significant real reduction in both the coke and the capital necessary to produce a ton of hot iron. These improvements limited the incursion of the electric arc process, which in recent years has stabilized at about 20 percent of steel capacity. The $A$ matrix in equation (2.1) was modified to require 12 percent more coke per ton of iron output and 12 percent higher capital costs. The process model was solved for the less efficient technology, and the changes in the cost shares were calculated, thereby yielding the $\phi_i$ coefficients. The effect on total costs was also determined analogously. Table 2–5 gives comparisons of the input-output coefficients and unit production costs and shows that despite the tendency to reduce coal input due to higher coke efficiency, coal input actually increased due to the overall economic improvement of the hot iron method of producing steel. Similarly, because of the substitution of hot iron for scrap, the input of capital is only slightly reduced.

The effect of this technological improvement also helped substantially reduce the needs for natural gas, since coke oven gas is a by-product of the coking process. The pseudodata statistical cost function provides a rich framework for long-range simulation exercises. Price and substitution elasticities are of direct use for a variety of policy questions. Perhaps of more importance is the capability to deal with environmental and technological changes in a more explicit manner. The previous section illustrated how the

**Table 2–5.**    Comparison of Input-Output Coefficients Under Alternative Technologies.[a]

| | Lower Coke-Capital Requirements | Higher Coke-Capital Requirements |
|---|---|---|
| Inputs | | |
| Operating inputs | 0.305 | 0.307 |
| Capital | 0.361 | 0.348 |
| Electricity | 0.031 | 0.053 |
| Coal | 0.050 | 0.031 |
| Natural gas | 0.003 | 0.015 |
| Iron ore | 0.109 | 0.085 |
| Scrap | 0.141 | 0.162 |
| Unit production cost (1974 base = 1.0) | 1.0 | 1.001 |

[a]Assumes 1974 relative prices.

explicit representation of these phenomena could be linked to the statistical cost function via the pseudodata. These examples seem sufficiently strong to cause long-range model builders to rethink the merits of conventional methodology.

## SUMMARY

While we feel that the pseudodata statistical cost function offers a marked advance, it is subject to certain limitations. Specifically, it is not being advocated as a short-run forecasting device. In the short run, measurement errors in the process model, approximation errors in the statistical cost function, and differences between short- and long-run equilibria are likely to dominate the errors associated with time series data. Even in long-run analysis, the success of the pseudodata approach rests on several factors. First and foremost is the quality and detail of the engineering data embedded in the process model. Moreover, economists are ill equipped to judge such technical characteristics. A second potential problem area lies with the ability of the translog, or any of the other "generalized" functional forms, to approximate closely the production surface over a sufficiently wide price range for policy analysis. The results for iron and steel are quite pleasing in this regard, but this degree of approximation need not be exhibited for all production surfaces.

## REFERENCES

Berndt, E.R., and L.R. Christensen. 1973. "The Translog Function and the Substitution of Equipment, Structures, and Labor in U.S. Manufacturing 1929–68." *Journal of Econometrics* I (Spring): 81–114.

Berndt, E.R., and D.O. Wood. 1975. "Technology, Prices, and the Derived Demand for Energy." *Review of Economics and Statistics* LVII 1973.: 259–68.

Christensen, L.R.; D.W. Jorgenson; and L.J. Lau. 1973. "Transcendental Logarithmic Production Frontiers." *Review of Economics and Statistics* LV (February): 28–45.

Federal Energy Administration, *Monthly Energy Review*, September 1977.

Finan, W.F., and Griffin, J.M.. 1978. "A Post Arab Oil Embargo Comparison of Alternative I-O Coefficient Modelling Techniques." *Resources and Energy* 1 (Fall): 315–24.

Griffin, J.M. 1979. "Statistical Cost Analysis Revisited." *Quarterly Journal of Economics* 93 (February): 1976. 107–28.

Griffin, J.M., and Paul Gregory. 1976. "An intercountry translog model of energy substitution responses." *American Economic Review* 66, no. 5 (December): 845–57.

Hudson, E.A., and D.W. Jorgenson. 1974. "U.S. Energy Policy and Economic Growth 1975-2000." *Bell Journal* V (Fall): 461–514.

Humphrey, D.B., and J.R. Moroney. 1975. "Substitution among Capital, Labor, and Natural Resource Products in American Manufacturing." *Journal of Political Economy* LXXXIII (February): 57–82.

Johnston, J. 1960. *Statistical Cost Analysis*. New York: McGraw-Hill.

Preston, Ross. 1975. "The Wharton Long Term Model: Input-Output Within the Context of a Macro Forecasting Model." *International Economic Review* XVI (February): 3–19.

―――. 1972. *The Wharton Annual and Industry Forecasting Model*. Philadelphia: Economics Research Unit, University of Pennsylvania.

Russell, C.S. 1973. *Residuals Management in Industry: A Case Study of Petroleum Refining*. Baltimore: Johns Hopkins Press.

Russell, C.S., and W. J. Vaughan. 1976. *Steel Production: Processes, Products, and Residuals*. Baltimore: Johns Hopkins Press.

Shephard, R.W. 1953. *Cost and Production Functions*. Princeton: Princeton University Press.

Walters, A.A. 1963. "Production and Cost Functions: An Econometric Survey." *Econometrica* XXXI (April): 1–66.

7230 ᵛ
1322
↑

# 3 ENERGY-ECONOMIC PLANNING IN ISRAEL
## The OMER Study

*Mordecai Avriel, Avishai Breiner,
and Reuven Karni
Energy Planning and Policy Research Group
Faculty of Industrial Engineering and Management
Technion - Israel Institute of Technology*

## INTRODUCTION

The adjustment of a national economy to exogenous changes is a slow process. Most nations of the world presently experience such a process, caused by the sharp increases in the price of oil and by uncertainties about its availability in the coming decades. The Israeli economy, based in the past almost entirely on imported oil, is especially vulnerable to world oil market conditions. The transition period for the necessary structural changes in the energy supply sectors, as well as in the energy-consuming ones, to decrease Israel's dependence on foreign oil is estimated to be twenty-five to thirty years. The OMER (Optimization Models for Energy Resources) study, initially sponsored by the National Council of Research and Development and subsequently by the Ministry of Energy and Infrastructure, is an attempt to provide decisionmakers with a consistent framework for planning the energy supply sectors—and their interactions with the national economy—during the transition (or a longer) period. This study is centered around the OMER model—a comprehensive energy-economic model—that can be used to explore the implications of both short- and long-range energy-related decisions and scenarios.

In the following sections, a nonmathematical description of the model is presented, and its use is illustrated by three sample scenarios. In these sce-

Research for this chapter was sponsored by the Israeli Ministry of Energy and Infrastructure.

narios a planning horizon extending to the end of the century was chosen. The difference between the scenarios is in the assumptions on the future price of imported oil.

## OUTLINE OF METHODOLOGY

Generally speaking, the OMER model is an intertemporal multisector development-planning model in which the energy supply sectors are treated in a special way. A description of an earlier version can be found in Avriel et al. (1978). The first model of this kind was developed by G. B. Dantzig and co-workers (see, for example, Dantzig 1976). Whereas the interindustrial relations of the energy-consuming sectors and the final demand requirements are modeled in the traditional input-output format, the supply of energy is represented by a process analysis type submodel. This approach allows for a more detailed planning of Israel's oil refineries and electric-power-generating system. Other features of the model include personal consumption capturing income effects; endogenous sector-by-sector import and export activities subject to trade balance constraints; a detailed capital formation module, including alternative refining and electricity generation processes; and the modeling of labor force inputs by skill groups.

In the usual mode of operation, the planning horizon of the model spans a multiple of five-year periods such that the first period is centered around the year for which the last input-output tables are available (currently the 1975–76 fiscal year). Special terminal conditions are imposed to incorporate assumptions on the posthorizon period in order to reduce the errors that would otherwise appear (mainly in the last periods) due to truncating an essentially infinite horizon model to a finite horizon one.

The complete model is formulated as a linear program with an appropriate objective function. In most runs of the model, discounted GDP is maximized, but various alternatives can also be accommodated. The generation of the model matrix is carried out by the MAGEN software package (by courtesy of Haverly Systems Inc.), and the linear program is solved by the MPSX package of IBM.

## MODEL DESCRIPTION

The OMER model consists of the following major portions, which are described below:

- Energy supply sectors,
- Industrial (nonenergy) sectors of the economy,
- Personal consumption and public services,
- Investments in the energy and nonenergy sectors,
- Foreign trade, and
- Labor force.

## Petroleum Supply

The first submodel of energy supply is a process analysis type representation of petroleum-related activities. It includes domestic oil and gas exploration and production, oil imports and exports, and distilling and cracking processes. Since the proven oil and gas reserves of the country are very small, imported oil plays a dominant role in Israel's energy economy. One of the major changes occurring in the structure of the energy supply sectors is a shift from an almost totally oil-based energy economy toward a more balanced one. This is a trend that will certainly continue in the next decades. The first step in this direction is the introduction of coal as a primary energy source, mainly for electricity generation. Consequently, domestic refineries will have to readjust their product mix to reflect a relatively lower demand for heavy fuel oil. The model recognizes the changing oil picture by the possibility of selecting various types of crude and distillate imports and by modifying refinery outputs through the addition of cracking units. A schematic representation of the oil and gas submodel is presented in Figure 3–1.

Domestic oil and gas exploration activities are presently very limited due to lack of investors. In view of the discouraging results of exploration activities in the past, the model does not include a detailed domestic exploration and production submodule. The model user can, however, set the future levels of domestic oil and gas production to arbitrary values, reflecting his views on the prospects of finding oil and gas in Israel.

Import and export of crudes and distillates are explicitly modeled, and their quantities are endogenously determined. Since the OMER model is not intended to plan these activities at an operational level, only two types of imported crudes are considered—a light (34 API) and a heavy (24 API) crude, whose prices are exogenously given. Seven types of distillates are included in the model—liquefied petroleum gas (LPG), gasoline, kerosene, diesel fuel, light fuel oil, heavy fuel oil, and residuals. These distillates are

Figure 3–1.    Oil and Gas Submodel.

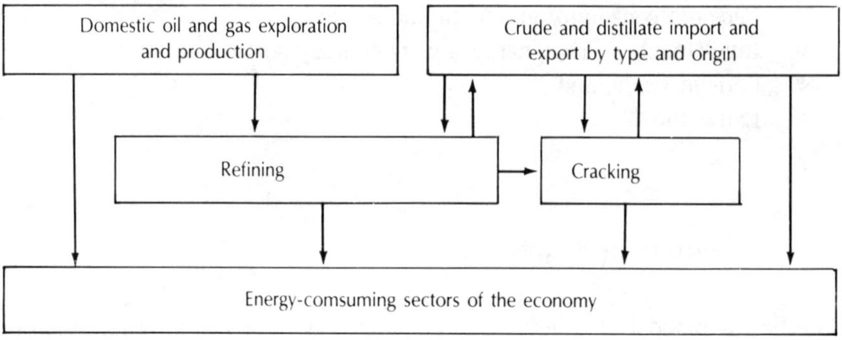

supplied to the economy either by direct import or by refining crude oil in domestic refineries. The processing activities of the refineries are represented in the model by specifying the range of yields of the distillates that can be obtained from the crudes. By exports of certain distillates, a proper balance between supply and domestic demand is achieved. Because of the anticipated shift toward higher demands for light fractions and considerably lower demands for heavy fractions, even though the total demand for petroleum products will not change drastically, cracking activities will be increasingly needed. The model, therefore, explicitly considers catalytic cracking and can determine the development of this activity within the refinery's structure.

## Electricity Production and Distribution

The second energy supply submodel describes the electricity production and distribution system. This is a model for optimal electricity generation and for expansion of the existing power system. Currently operating power plants, those under construction, and potential new plants of various types are explicitly modeled. Whereas in the traditional input-output format electricity, like any other sector of the economy, is represented by a single column and a single row, in OMER electricity supply is modeled by a process analysis type submodel. The purpose of such a detailed submodel is to include different types of electricity-generating technologies and capacities so that the model can find the best combination of generating units to supply the demand for electricity over time. Simultaneously, the model finds the levels and timing of investment and installation of new units. The electricity submodel also reflects the relationship between average and instantaneous power demands from which the required installed capacity is determined. In addition to various possible types of power generation, the activities of transmission and distribution are also represented as separate sectors. A schematic diagram of the electricity submodel is given in Figure 3–2.

Whereas the activity levels of the energy-consuming sectors of the economy endogenously determine the average annual power load, an exogenously imposed load duration curve (LDC), in which instantaneous load is expressed relative to the average load, is included in the model so that the required installed capacity of the various generating units is also determined. The nonlinear LDC is approximated in the model by four rectangles (representing base, intermediate, high, and peak load levels, respectively), similar to the approach used in Beglari and Laughton (1973). The main parameters of the discrete LDC used in the model are given in Table 3–1.

Installation of new power plants is preceded by an investment period whose length varies according to the type of unit. The model recognizes these lead times and allocates the necessary investments over time for new generating units. Table 3–2 lists the types of existing and future power plants considered in the model. Note that the building of new oil-fired units is not allowed in the model except in those cases where construction has already begun.

Figure 3–2.    Electricity Submodel.

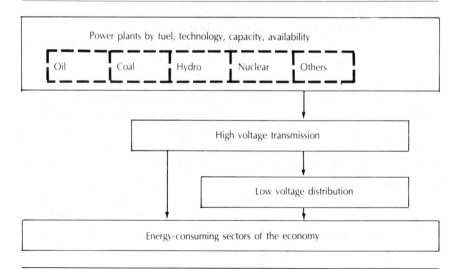

**Table 3–1.**    Discrete Load Duration Curve.

| Load Level | Percent of Average Load[a] | Duration (hours) |
|---|---|---|
| Base | 71.3 | 8760 |
| Intermediate | 89.3 | 7050 |
| High | 120.1 | 3950 |
| Peak | 148.6 | 100 |

[a]Average Load $= \dfrac{\text{Annual demand for electricity (kWh)}}{8760}$

It is worthwhile to mention here that the model derives the levels of energy supply and demand endogenously, by the simultaneous solution of the petroleum and electricity submodels, together with the other portions of the model as a single large-scale linear program.

## Energy-Consuming Sectors

The energy-consuming sectors of the economy comprise the industrial (nonenergy) sectors and final demands. The industrial sectors are represented in the model by means of a Leontieff type input-output matrix. Energy inputs for the industrial sectors are expressed in physical (toe or kWh) units per unit sectorial output. The level and map of aggregation of the industrial sectors are determined by the energy intensity of the sectors, the type of output goods produced, and the desired size of the input-output matrix from a computational viewpoint. The nonenergy industries are presently aggregated into fifteen sectors, as shown in Table 3–3.

Substitution possibilities between alternative technologies can be represented in OMER by introducing additional columns for those industries that consider technological changes. For example, a study is currently being made with the aid of the model to assess the impact of converting some large heavy chemicals and cement plants to the use of coal as the primary source of nonelectric energy, instead of oil-based products. Other changes in inputs, such as those reflecting energy conservation, can also be exogenously introduced by appropriately modifying the input-output coefficients.

Disaggregating the energy-consuming industries to a detail of approximately fifteen sectors was necessary in order to forecast trends in the economy with respect to sectoral outputs, primary energy (electric and

**Table 3–2.** Characteristics of Electric Power Plants.

| Type | Nominal Capacity (MW) | Investment period (years) |
|---|---|---|
| Oil-fired (to 75 MW) | 590[a] | — |
| Oil-fired (over 75 MW) | 1450[a] | — |
| Gas turbines | 350[a] | 1 |
| Coal-fired (type 1) | 4 × 350 | 9 |
| Coal-fired (type 2) | 2 × 550 | 7 |
| Nuclear (type 1) | 1 × 950 | 12 |
| Nuclear (type 2) | 2 × 950 | 13 |
| Hydroelectric | 1 × 100 | 4 |

[a]Total installed capacity at present.

**Table 3–3.** Nonenergy Industrial Sectors in OMER.

| Industrial Sector | Share in Total Nonenergy Output[a] (percent–IS/IS) | Energy Share in Sector Output[b] (percent–IS/IS) | Energy Intensity of Output[c] (TOE/$10^3$ IS(10/1980)) |
|---|---|---|---|
| Water | 0.7 | 31.4 | 0.3045 |
| Chemical, plastics | 5.0 | 5.6 | 0.0429 |
| Mining, glass, cement | 2.8 | 11.9 | 0.1488 |
| Metals, metal products | 5.8 | 2.1 | 0.0159 |
| Machinery, equipment | 8.1 | 1.6 | 0.0057 |
| Textiles | 5.6 | 3.4 | 0.0163 |
| Wood, paper, print | 4.4 | 2.4 | 0.0191 |
| Agriculture | 7.6 | 5.3 | 0.0138 |
| Food, beverages, tobacco | 10.0 | 4.4 | 0.0163 |
| Diamonds | 3.6 | 0.1 | 0.0008 |
| Road transport | 4.3 | 13.7 | 0.0974 |
| Sea and air transport, communications | 6.5 | 10.6 | 0.0432 |
| Construction | 12.5 | 3.8 | 0.0093 |
| Services | 15.0 | 1.6 | 0.0057 |
| Trade | 8.1 | 2.1 | 0.0081 |

[a]According to 1975–76 output levels.
[b]Based on total input-output coefficients of primary energy sources.
[c]Based on direct input-output coefficients of electric and nonelectric energy.

nonelectric) usage, and foreign trade in the energy and nonenergy sectors. In addition, there are several sectors in the economy that operate near a saturation point such that past growth rates are unlikely to continue in the future. For such sectors, constraints are imposed on future levels of activity—as, for example, that the availability of fresh water via existing technologies will be a limiting factor in the future development of intensive agriculture in Israel.

Similarly, an often neglected factor in aggregated economic forecasts is the labor input to economic activity. Full employment conditions prevailed in Israel during the last years when the economy was rapidly expanding, accompanied by a remarkable growth in labor productivity. Slower projected growth in the size of the labor force and in productivity gains indicate that manpower constitutes a significant constraint on economic growth. Experiments with the OMER model have fully verified this assumption, and in fact, the model is very sensitive to the size of the labor force. Further experiments involved dividing the labor force into five skill groups—(1) professionals and managers, (2) office workers, (3) agricultural workers, (4) skilled industrial workers, (5) service and unskilled workers—and allowing some measure of migration over time among these groups.

In this form of the model, for each industrial sector the man-hours of the various skill groups required for a unit output are represented in the model as labor coefficients. These coefficients change from period to period due to sectorial change in productivity. The total man-hours available in each period is determined by an assumed growth rate of the population, the participation rate in the labor force, and a projected shift between the skill groups reflecting demographic and educational patterns. Results of these experiments showed that lack of properly trained manpower can be a serious constraint on the growth of certain industrial sectors.

## Final Demands

Personal consumption of energy and nonenergy goods and services is modeled on a sector-by-sector basis. The relative consumption level of goods changes with personal income. Empirical evidence suggests that personal consumption follows a "linear expenditure" pattern—that is, the consumption level of goods and services is a linear function of the aggregate level of personal expenditure. Fixed proportions of consumption by the public sector are assumed in the model. The aggregate public expenditure is either exogenously given (with a predetermined path of growth over the planning horizon), or it is linked to some other activity in the model.

The investment submodel of OMER deals with the replacement of old production facilities and the expansion of output capacities of all (energy and nonenergy) industrial sectors. Investments are among the most important intertemporal links of the model. In each period an endogenously determined portion of the industrial output is allocated to investment (capital formation) in the energy and nonenergy sectors of the economy. The distribution of the total investments between the sectors is also endogenous. An important element of the investment submodel is a capital coefficient matrix that represents the sector-by-sector amounts of goods and services needed for building a unit capacity in each sector. An even more detailed capital coefficient matrix is used for the energy supply sectors, where for each energy supply technology a different capital coefficient vector is computed. Other modeling features worth mentioning here include sectorial representation of production facility lifetimes, geometric depreciation rates, and maturity lags of new facilities built. For the energy supply sectors, these data refer to individual technologies.

### Foreign Trade

Foreign trade activities are modeled on a sector-by-sector basis. There are two types of imports in the model: First are noncompetitive (essential) imported goods and services for which there is no domestic counterpart and that are needed for the economic activities of the industrial sectors or final demands. These imports are modeled as fixed inputs, and consequently, the levels of noncompetitive imports are proportional to the levels of activity of the domestic sectors. The other type of imports are the competitive (nonessential) imports that are substitutable by domestic goods and services. The optimal levels of competitive imports, subject to a trade balance constraint, are determined by the model in order to obtain a better balanced bill of goods for final demands. Exports are treated in the model analogously to competitive imports. The level of exports is also determined endogenously. For competitive imports and exports of certain sectors, quantity limits are imposed to reflect realistic limitations related to world trade conditions. Essential and competitive imports and exports are linked by a trade balance constraint, representing the requirement that in each period, total imports cannot exceed total exports by more than some predetermined trade deficit. The exogenously given values of trade deficit over time are one of the key parameters in the model by which the projected future growth of the economy can be varied. It can be easily demonstrated that forecasts on general economic development in Israel and on the energy sector in particular that do not take into account foreign trade balance relations in some form can produce unrealistic and misleading results. Since Israel will continue to rely on imports in the foreseeable future, the explicit inclusion of foreign trade in OMER was essential in order to obtain a consistent projection of the future state of the economy.

## Objective Function

The objective function used in the linear programming solution of the OMER model can be exogenously chosen by the user of the model. The most often used expression in multiperiod scenarios is maximizing discounted gross national product, consisting of the sum of private and public consumption, investment (capital formation), and exports, less imports. The discounting is carried out for each period of the planning horizon and in a lumped fashion for the posthorizon value of GNP, similar to the approach in Manne (1974). Other possible forms of objective function can be maximizing private consumption, minimizing trade balance deficits or unemployment, or any other combination of the model variables.

## Control Mechanisms

Finite horizon multisector multiperiod models, such as the OMER model, must have appropriate initial and terminal conditions in order to obtain meaningful results. In the usual mode of operation, the first period in OMER is chosen such that relevant macroeconomic and energy-related data for its midperiod "base year" are known at the time of running the model. These data, such as installed energy production facilities and those under construction, nonenergy industrial capacities, population and labor force figures, foreign trade deficit, and the like, are used as initial conditions for the model. Similarly, the model must be provided with appropriate end conditions in order to ensure that it does not return results as if the whole economy would terminate its existence at the end of the planning horizon. The terminal conditions in the OMER model assume that production capacities of all sectors of the economy grow at an asymptotic rate during all periods subsequent to the last period of the planning horizon.

In addition to terminal conditions, some other control measures are sometimes needed for a "smooth" operation of the model. When the GDP is employed as the objective function, there exists the likelihood that investment may be preferred to private consumption, leading to the creation of a large unused production capacity. In order to prevent this phenomenon, constraints that limit unused capacity to a certain fraction of the nominal production capacity can be imposed if necessary. Furthermore, constraints that limit the rate of change of production levels from one period to the next may be needed for certain industrial sectors.

A summary view of the model is presented in Table 3–4. A large effort is required to develop and operate a model of the size of OMER, involving formulation of the model structure, extensive data collection and manipulation, and substantial computing and software resources. In the authors' opinion, this effort is justified in view of the model's performance, its great flexibility, and the ability to draw both general and detailed conclusions from the model outputs. In every model, there are exogenous and endogenous variables—that is, parameters having assumed values and variables computed by the model, respectively. The larger the model, the more the assumptions about the real world, outside the system to be modeled, can be explicitly incorporated and changed if necessary. The model builder can this way challenge the decisionmaker (the user of the model) to quantify his assumptions about the outside world. Moreover, the larger the model, the more of these parameters may be made into endogenous variables.

Detailed models involving portions of the economy are usually more consistent with the whole economy than simpler or more aggregated ones, and trends indicated by the detailed model can be better understood by examining the behavior of all the sectors in the model. The frequently observed lack of consistency in a highly aggregated model is due to the ignoring of possible constraints and saturation effects acting upon the system being modeled. These effects can usually become apparent only if the model is sufficiently detailed. Finally, a detailed model such as the OMER model is so flexible that hundreds of different meaningful scenarios, testing hypotheses, and trends can be run without much added effort on the part of the modeler or the decisionmaker.

## SCENARIO OUTPUTS

The OMER model can therefore provide policymakers with valuable information on the development of the Israeli economy, together with a detailed

**Table 3–4.**   Summary of OMER Characteristics.

1. *General*
   | | |
   |---|---|
   | Planning horizon | 1972–2002 |
   | Number of Periods | 6 |
   | Period length (years) | 5 |
   | Number of nonenergy industrial sectors | 15 |

2. *Structure*
   | | |
   |---|---|
   | Nonenergy industrial sector definition | by 1975–76 input-output tables |
   | Investment in nonenergy industrial sectors | by capital coefficient matrix |
   | Initial production capacities | 1975–76 levels |

3. *Refining submodel*
   | | |
   |---|---|
   | Crudes | light and heavy |
   | Number of distillates | 7 |
   | Refining limits | preset for each crude |
   | Cracking | included |
   | Investment in refining and cracking | by capital coefficient matrix |
   | Import-export of distillates | included |

4. *Electricity submodel*
   | | |
   |---|---|
   | Components | generation, transmission, distribution |
   | Power plants | oil-fired, coal-fired, nuclear, gas turbines, hydroelectric |
   | Load duration curve | base, intermediate, high, peak |
   | Investment in electricity generation | by capital coefficient matrix (processwise) |

5. *Labor force*
   | | |
   |---|---|
   | Number of skill groups | 5 |
   | Migration between sectors | allowed |
   | Migration between skill groups | limited |
   | Productivity changes | by sector |

6. *Final uses*
   | | |
   |---|---|
   | Private consumption composition | by linear expenditure |
   | Aggregate public consumption | set by user |
   | Public consumption composition | fixed |

7. *Foreign trade*
   | | |
   |---|---|
   | Competitive-noncompetitive imports | by sector |
   | Exports | by sector |
   | Export-import limits | imposed on some sectors |
   | Export-import unit prices | set by user |
   | Trade balance deficit | set by user |

**Table 3-4.**    Continued

8. *Control system*
| | |
|---|---|
| Terminal condition | posthorizon asymptotic growth rate |
| Unused production capacities | can be imposed |
| Production level changes | can be imposed |

9. *Objective function*
| | |
|---|---|
| Type | user specified |

10. *Problem size (typical run)*
| | |
|---|---|
| Number of variables per period | 203 |
| Total number of variables | 1,218 |
| Number of constraints per period | 130 |
| Terminal conditions, miscellaneous | 80 |
| Total number of constraints | 800 |

planning strategy of the energy supply sectors. Such information is obtained by running various scenarios—that is, by making various assumptions on the exogenous parameters of the model. This is the most common approach among policy analysts to account for future uncertainties. In the rest of this chapter, typical output results of the model for three scenarios are presented. The main difference between the scenarios is the assumed rate of increase in future prices of imported oil. The base price case (B) scenario assumes an annual increase (in real terms) of 5 percent in the price of imported crude oil and distillates; the more pessimistic high price case (H) scenario assumes a higher annual increase of 8 percent; an optimistic low price case (L) assumes a lower annual increase of 2 percent. The key assumptions and data for the scenarios are summarized in Table 3-5.

The planning horizon of these scenarios corresponds to that of the Israeli Ministry of Energy with regard to policy alternatives in the energy supply area. Population estimates are based on natural growth and a net annual immigration of 10,000 persons. The terminal conditions are based on the assumption that the next two decades represent a transition period from an economy based entirely on relatively inexpensive and abundant oil supplies to an economy in which the primary energy resources are significantly more expensive and are diversified, encompassing oil, coal, nuclear, hydro, solar, and other alternative sources. Toward the end of the century the sectorial composition of the economy can achieve an optimal pattern and continue to grow at some uniform rate.

**Table 3–5.**    Key Input Assumptions for OMER Scenarios.

Planning horizon: 1972–2002 (six periods, five years each)
First period base year: 1975
Population: Assumption "B" of the Central Bureau of Statistics

| Year | 1975 | 1980 | 1985 | 1990 | 1995 | 2000 |
|---|---|---|---|---|---|---|
| Population (thousands) | 3,493 | 3,912 | 4,349 | 4,797 | 5,268 | 5,757 |

Labor force: 33.2 percent of population
Labor force productivity growth: Exponential growth (for each sector the
    growth rates are 1970–79 average)
Total public sector consumption: 4 percent annual growth
Defense imports: 2 percent annual growth
Foreign trade deficit: 2 percent annual growth until 1985 (then constant)
Annual price escalation of imported fuels (percent):

| Fuel | Low Price (L) | Base Price (B) | High Price (H) |
|---|---|---|---|
| Crude oil | 2 | 5 | 8 |
| Coal | 2 | 3 | 4 |
| Nuclear fuel | 2 | 3 | 4 |

Terminal conditions: 4 percent annual growth in the posthorizon era for the
    low and base price scenarios; 2.5 percent annual growth for the high price
    scenario
Water resources: Limited to 2,300 million m³ by the end of the century
Electricity generation: Load duration curve by 1975–76 proportions
Electricity investments: First coal-fired power plant not before 1980;
                        first nuclear power plant not before 1995;
                        first hydroelectric power plant not before 1984
Oil refining: Cracking capacity growth not greater than 750,000 tons per
    period (current cracking capacity)
Petroleum product prices: Fixed percentage of crude oil price

## Macroeconomic and Energy-Related Results

A short summary of some macroeconomic output figures of the model in the three sample scenarios is presented in Table 3–6. It can be seen that the price of imported oil plays an important role in the national economy. The increasing relative share of the cost of energy imports in the GDP is also shown in Figure 3–3. The effect of energy prices on GDP, personal consumption, and investments is clearly demonstrated in Table 3–6. The adjustment

**Table 3-6.**  Macroeconomic Results of Scenario Runs.

| Macroeconomic Indicators | Base Price 1980 | Base Price 2000 | High Price 2000 | Low Price 2000 |
|---|---|---|---|---|
| Gross domestic product (IS end of 1980) | $145 \cdot 10^9$ | $410 \cdot 10^9$ | $337 \cdot 10^9$ | $450 \cdot 10^9$ |
| GDP growth rate (%/yr) | – | 5.3 | 4.4 | 5.7 |
| Per capita personal consumption (IS end of 1980) | $21.7 \cdot 10^3$ | $45.6 \cdot 10^3$ | $33.1 \cdot 10^3$ | $53.5 \cdot 10^3$ |
| Per capita personal consumption growth rate (%/yr) | – | 3.8 | 2.1 | 4.6 |
| Investments (private capital formation)(IS end of 1980) | $39.7 \cdot 10^9$ | $85.9 \cdot 10^9$ | $77.4 \cdot 10^9$ | $92.9 \cdot 10^9$ |
| Investments growth rate (%/yr) | – | 3.9 | 3.4 | 4.3 |
| Domestic energy consumption ($10^3$ toe) | 8,200 | 20,900 | 18,600 | 22,900 |
| Domestic energy consumption growth rate (%/yr) | – | 4.8 | 4.2 | 5.3 |
| Electricity generation ($10^6$ kWh) | 12,500 | 32,400 | 31,500 | 34,400 |
| Electricity generation growth rate (%/yr) | – | 4.9 | 4.7 | 5.2 |
| Electricity share in domestic energy consumption (%) | 36.4 | 37.2 | 40.6 | 36.1 |
| Energy input cost (1980 $/yr) | $2.32 \cdot 10^9$ | $10.93 \cdot 10^9$ | $15.43 \cdot 10^9$ | $7.20 \cdot 10^9$ |
| Energy import share in GDP (%)[a] | 12.0 | 20.0 | 34.3 | 12.0 |

[a]Based on U.S.$ 1 = 7.5 Israeli Shekel and $285/ton crude.

of the economy to increasing energy prices is shown in Figure 3–4. The share of high energy-intensive sectors in the total industrial output decreases throughout the planning horizon, accompanied by a significant increase in the share of low energy-intensive sectors. For in-depth studies, OMER can also provide detailed sectorial projections, changes in personal consumption patterns, employment figures, foreign trade levels, and so forth in a structurally consistent macroeconomic framework.

Turning to the question of energy supply and demand, Figures 3–5 and 3–6 show total primary energy consumption and its composition throughout the planning horizon. According to the model projection, domestic energy consumption in Israel in 2000 will reach 20.9 million tons of oil equivalent in

Figure 3-3.    Energy Import as a Percentage of GDP.

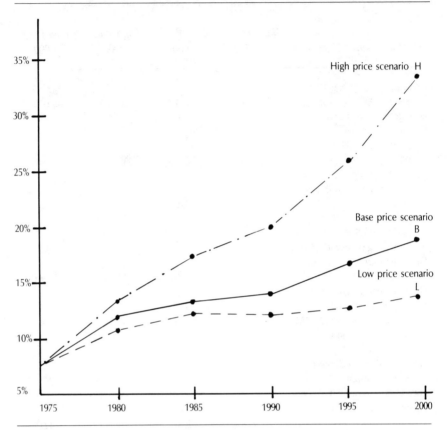

the base case, 18.6 million tons in the high price case, and 22.9 million tons in the low price case. These quantities represent respective increases of 150, 126, and 180 percent over the present level of consumption. Consumption of oil-based energy, however, will only increase by 46 percent in the base case and will remain unchanged in the high price case. Whereas almost 100 percent of all energy consumed at present is oil based, in 1997 this share will decrease to 50–70 percent. The proportion of energy consumed as electricity will rise slightly from today's 34 percent to 37 percent in the base price case and to 40 percent in the high price case. These proportions are somewhat higher than those encountered elsewhere (except for countries having an extensive hydroelectric base).

It should be mentioned here that in these scenarios coal is an alternative source to oil in generating electricity, but no substitution of oil by coal in

**Figure 3–4.**    Relative Nonenergy Industrial Output in Base Case.

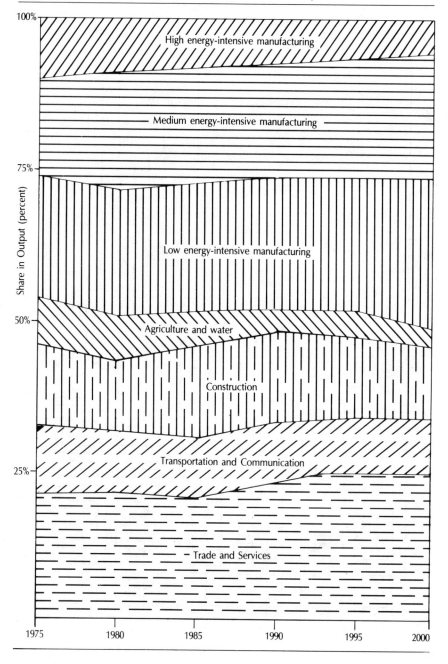

**Figure 3–5.**     Energy Consumption and Electricity Share

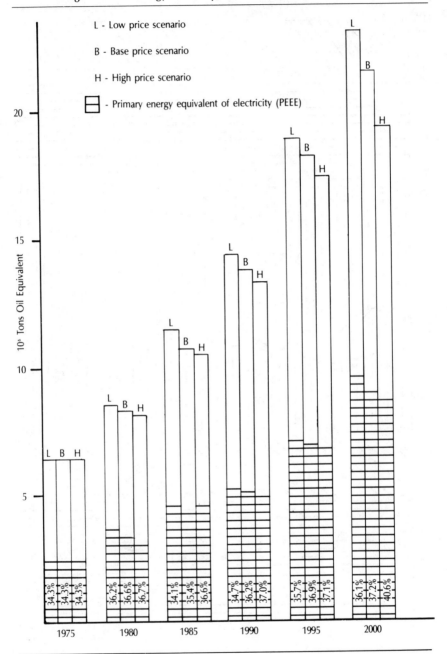

**Figure 3–6.**    Energy Consumption by Primary Sources in Base Case.

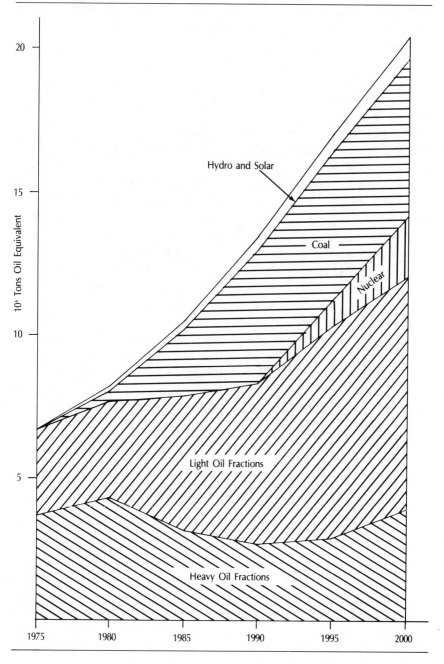

other uses, such as synthetic fuels or direct industrial heat, is allowed. Similarly, these sample scenarios do not consider the possible Mediterranean–Dead Sea canal, which would increase the share of hydroelectric power generation.

### Planning the Electricity Sector

Estimates of macroeconomic parameters and total future energy requirements as described above are calculated by the OMER model in parallel with a detailed planning of the energy sector. The planning of electricity generation and demand throughout the horizon is described below. Figure 3–7 illustrates the range of future electricity demand that corresponds to the three scenarios discussed in this chapter. Electricity consumption in all cases is not significantly different. The reason is that in these scenarios, the model is looking for those solutions in which alternative sources can replace imported oil as a primary energy source. The most efficient way to accomplish this goal is to base every future expansion of the power generation system on coal and nuclear energy and to replace the currently operating oil-fired power plants by new ones that use alternative fuels. This trend is clearly illustrated in Figure 3–8. Electrical energy consumption, represented by the area under the load duration curve, is supplied totally by oil-fired power plants in 1980. By 1990 coal will replace oil in generating base load electricity, and a small hydroelectric plant will be used to support peak demand. The phasing out of oil-fired power plants (except gas turbines) and the introduction of nuclear energy will be completed by the end of the century.

Whereas a wide range of fuel substitution possibilities exists in the electricity supply technologies represented in the model, substitution possibilities in the demand side are yet to be incorporated in OMER. The need for such substitution of, say, electric-nonelectric energy is clearly demonstrated by the scenarios presented in this chapter. It is reasonable to assert that the ratio of energy for electricity production to the total energy requirements of the economy will in reality be higher than the projected value in these scenarios. The reason is that electricity generated by fuels other than oil can substitute to some extent for the presently oil-based nonelectric energy requirements. Concerning installed electricity-generating capacities, independent studies performed in Israel show projections close to those of the OMER study, as given in Table 3–7. If the demand for electricity will in reality exceed the values predicted by the model, oil-fired power plants will

**Figure 3–7.**    Electricity Consumption.

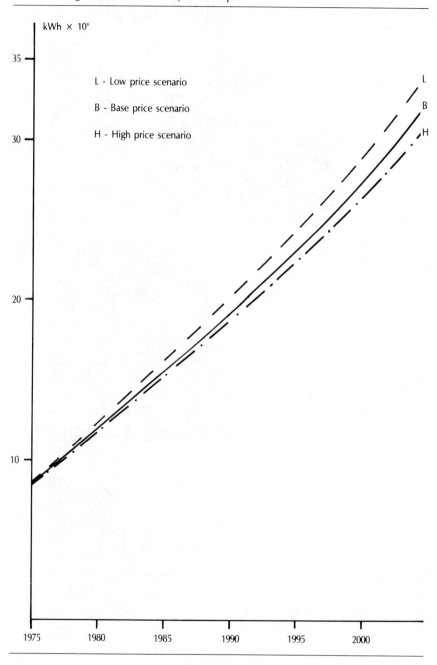

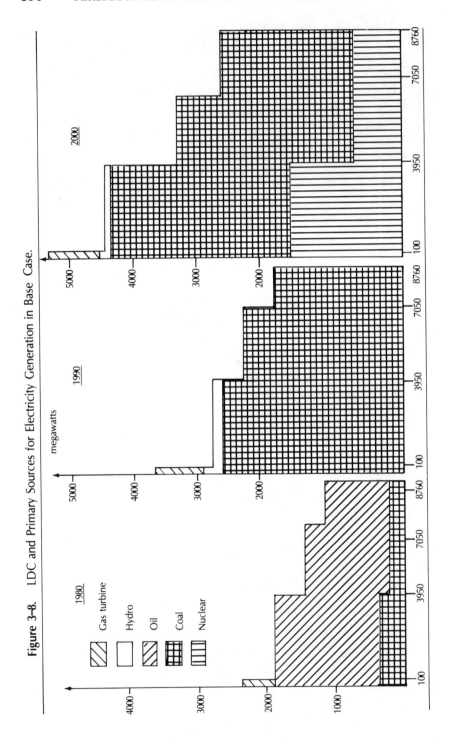

Figure 3-8.    LDC and Primary Sources for Electricity Generation in Base Case.

Table 3–7.   Installed Capacity and Its Utilization in 2000.

| Technology | Base Price Case | | | High Price Case | | | Low Price Case | | |
|---|---|---|---|---|---|---|---|---|---|
| | Installed Capacity (10³ kW) | Generation (10⁶ kWh) | Capacity factor (percent) | Installed capacity (10³ kW) | Generation (10⁶ kWh) | Capacity factor (percent) | Installed capacity (10³ kW) | Generation (10⁶ kWh) | Capacity factor (percent) |
| Gas turbines | 970 | 100 | 1.2 | 940 | 95 | 1.2 | 1,035 | 110 | 1.2 |
| Hydro | 200 | 400 | 23 | 200 | 400 | 23 | 200 | 400 | 23 |
| Oil-fired | 1,600 | – | 0 | 1,600 | – | 0 | 1,600 | – | 0 |
| Coal-fired | 3,500 | 22,900 | 74.7 | 3,350 | 22,005 | 75 | 3,800 | 24,890 | 74.7 |
| Nuclear | 1,520 | 9,000 | 67.6 | 1,520 | 9,000 | 67.6 | 1,520 | 9,000 | 67.6 |
| Total | 7,790 | 32,400 | 47.5 | 7,610 | 31,500 | 47.3 | 8,155 | 34,400 | 48.2 |

inevitably be needed to support the other components of the generating system.

## The Oil Industry

The changes in the fuel mix for electricity generation have far-reaching consequences for the oil industry. The most important projected development concerns changes in the distillate mix, as illustrated in Figure 3–9. It can be seen that the share of fuel oil (mainly used for electricity generation) will decline from its present level of 52 percent to about 26 percent by 2000. This decline in the refinery output mix will be balanced by a corresponding increase in the share of light fractions. The changing demand for oil products in the coming decades can be supplied by the industry by means of adjusting the quantity and types of imported oil, by increasing and modifying refinery (especially cracking) capabilities, and by more extensive foreign trade activities of refinery products.

## CONCLUSIONS

The above results illustrate a portion of the ongoing OMER study on the development of the Israeli economy as it faces a changing energy picture throughout the rest of this century. These years represent a transition period from an economy based entirely on imported oil to one in which primary energy sources are more diversified. It is shown that in both scenarios presented, macroeconomic indicators such as GDP, personal consumption, or investments will grow at a slower rate than in the last thirty years. The lower rate of growth is more profoundly demonstrated if an 8 percent annual increase in the price of oil is assumed. The rising cost of oil imports will more than ever force the accelearated development of the exporting sectors of the economy. At the same time, the share of energy-intensive sectors in the industrial output will have to decrease.

The study also deals with a detailed planning of the energy supply sectors and in particular the electricity and oil industries. Throughout the planning horizon coal-fired power plants, subsequently supported by nuclear power plants, will generate base load electricity. Consequently, oil-fired power plants will be phased out, causing a major change in the demand for refinery products. This change involves a considerable decrease in the share

**Figure 3–9.**    Refinery Product Mix in Base Case.

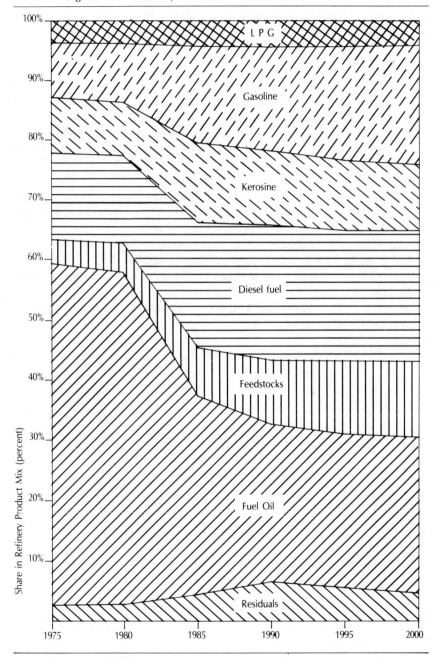

of the heavy fractions, resulting in necessary adjustments in the refineries and in foreign oil trade policies.

## REFERENCES

Avriel, M.; A. Breiner; D. Marmur; and A. Melnik. 1978. "A Mathematical Model for Assessing Energy-Economic Options on a National Level." In P. Adulbhan and N. Sharif, eds., *Proceedings of the International Conference on Systems Modelling in Developing Countries*, pp. 183–99. Bangkok, Thailand: Asian Institute of Technology.

Beglari, F., and M. A. Laughton. 1973. "Model Building with Particular Reference to Power System Planning: The Improved Z-Substitutes Method." In *Energy Modelling,* A Special *Energy Policy* Publication, pp. 57–69. Guilford, United Kingdom: IPC Science and Technology Press.

Dantzig, G. B. 1976. "A PILOT Linear Programming Model for Assessing Physical Impact on the Economy of a Changing Energy Picture." in *IIASA Conference '76,* 2, 183–200. Laxenburg, Austria: International Institute for Applied Systems Analysis.

Manne, A. S. 1974. "Multi-Sector Models for Development Planning." *Journal of Development Economics* 1: 43–69.

109-47

# 4 ENERGY SELF-SUFFICIENCY AND EXPORT POSSIBILITIES FOR CANADA: 1980–2030

7230

J. D. Fuller
Department of Management Science
University of Waterloo
S. L. Schwartz
Management Science Department
University of British Columbia
W. T. Ziemba
Management Science Department
University of British Columbia

## INTRODUCTION: THE CANADIAN ENERGY SCENE

In this chapter we analyze several possible energy futures for Canada during the period 1980–2030 to investigate the possibility of achieving and maintaining energy self-sufficiency and the potential for energy resource exports. In this section we provide a background to the Canadian energy situation, including geographical layout, historical demand, supply sources, trade, and institutional aspects. The main features of the model used for the analysis are described in section two. In section three we describe the basic input data used for the base case and six other scenarios that focus on the possible effects of low coal availability, a prohibition against new nuclear development, the unavailability of frontier oil and gas, and an increased emphasis on energy conservation. The results of the seven scenarios are analyzed in the fourth section; key information is provided in figures and tables. Section five concludes the chapter with a summary of the major findings and their policy implications.

Without implicating them, we would like to thank the Department of Energy Mines and Resources and Imperial Oil for financial support; E. R. Berndt, G. Griffiths, J. F. Helliwell, A. S. Manne, A. Meisen, J. Rowse, and H. Wynne-Edwards for helpful discussions related to this work; and Debbie Janson for research assistance.

109

An important consideration essential to an understanding of Canadian energy issues is the physical and geographic nature of the country. Figure 4–1 contains a map of Canada on which some of the major energy resources are displayed. Below the map is a distribution of population, which provides a rough proxy for energy demands. The country is sparsely populated, with the majority of the populace living close to the U.S. border. This narrow, striplike phenomenon results in a substantial effect of the transportation systems on the energy and overall economy. The bulk of the population and industry are located in the East, while the main hydrocarbon resources are located in the West. Thus, despite substantial excesses of energy supplies in the West and shortages in the East, transportation costs and lack of transportation networks yield the phenomenon of Western exports and Eastern imports that provide a net balance of exports (see Figure 4–2). Hydroelectric power is readily available in substantial quantities in both regions. The country has the second greatest land mass and is about 8,000 kilometers from east to west and nearly 5,000 kilometers from north to south. The distance to bring Arctic oil and gas to southern Alberta is as great as the distance to pipe Albertan oil and gas to major consuming areas such as Toronto.

For many energy issues the country can be conveniently divided in half—at, say, the Manitoba-Ontario border[1] —the East then being the major energy consumer and industrial sector and the West the major supplier of energy. Figures 4–3 and 4–4 give the total energy use in 1978 by region in the East (Atlantic, Quebec, and Ontario) and West (Prairies and British Columbia–Yukon) by use (industrial, transportation, and so forth) and by fuel (coal, oil, and the like). There are substantial energy use differences within and between sectors. Energy moved in interregional trade must go vast distances through rough terrain including arctic tundra, mountains, and so forth. Much transportation infrastructure will need to be built over the coming decades if Canada is to become truly self-sufficient as opposed to having net self-sufficiency.

Canada has the dubious distinction of being the highest per capita user of energy among major nations of the world. In tons of oil equivalent, Canada used 5.4 per capita in 1960 and 8.7 in 1977. This was 50 percent more than Sweden, another northern country; twice that of Germany; and about three times that of Japan (Bank of Montreal 1980). This enormous energy

---

1. In the analysis and model that follow we have utilized this traditional split. It may be noted, however, that Manitoba is a net energy supplier, although this excess is slight in comparison to the total energy supply-demand of the country.

**Figure 4–1.** Some Major Primary Energy Supplies in Canada.

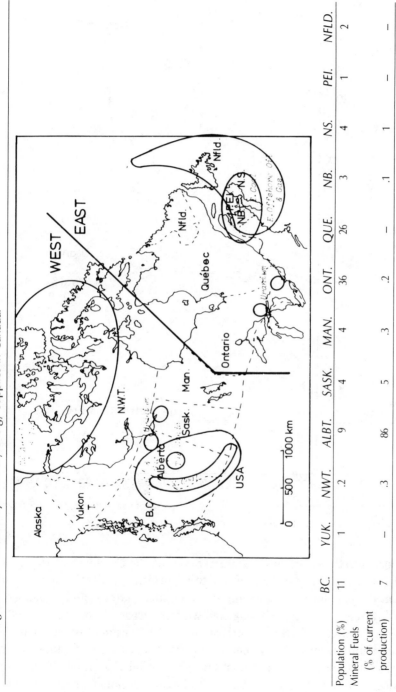

| | BC. | YUK. | NWT. | ALBT. | SASK. | MAN. | ONT. | QUE. | NB. | NS. | PEI. | NFLD. |
|---|---|---|---|---|---|---|---|---|---|---|---|---|
| Population (%) | 11 | 1 | .2 | 9 | 4 | 4 | 36 | 26 | 3 | 4 | 1 | 2 |
| Mineral Fuels (% of current production) | 7 | – | .3 | 86 | 5 | .3 | .2 | – | .1 | 1 | – | – |

Figure 4–2.    Net Trade in Energy Resources and Net Balance, 1966–80.

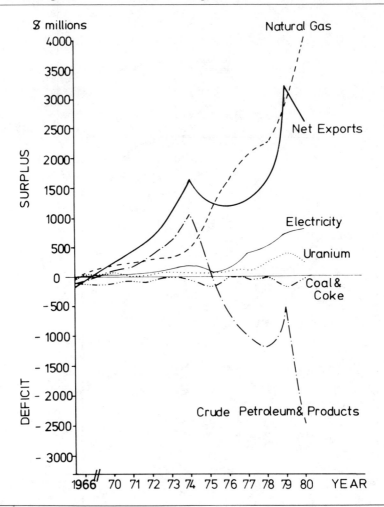

Source: Statistics Canada and Energy Mines and Resources (1980).

appetite reflects the basic characteristics of the Canadian energy econo-my—a large energy utilization for transportation, reflecting a small, dis-persed population; substantial domestic, farm, and commercial utilization, reflecting the long cold winters; urbanization; the rise of the service sector; and North American heavy utilization of energy, based on past habits formed during periods of cheap and readily available energy supplies. Canada's current domestic price of oil is about half the world price. Heavy industry use also reflects the development of a resource-

Figure 4–3.    Total Energy Use, 1978.

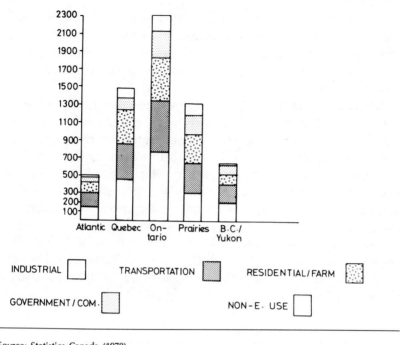

Source: Statistics Canada (1978).

Figure 4–4.    Net Domestic Consumption, 1978.

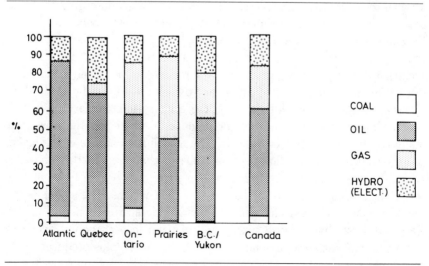

Source: Statistics Canada (1978).

based economy, further intensified by the availability of cheap hydroelectric power.

The "historic fuel" shares are presented in Figure 4–5. The relatively
large share (about 23 percent) of hydro is in contrast to the United States,
where hydro is only about 4 percent of total energy. Since 1950 there has
been a substitution of oil and gas for coal and a modest nuclear development in the East.

Canada is also rich in primary energy resources such as oil, coal, gas, and
uranium, as well as the vast tar sands, which are currently in their early
stages of development. Despite these resources, the country is a net import-
er of petroleum supplies. An ongoing debate concerning the resource rent
splits among the federal and provincial governments and the major energy
companies revolves around the possibility of achieving self-sufficiency in all
energy forms while maintaining domestic energy prices below current and
anticipated world levels. Further background concerning the Canadian energy scene may be found in Energy Mines and Resources (1978, 1980); Fuller,
Schwartz, and Ziemba (1982); Helliwell (1979); Helliwell and McRae (1981);
Scarfe (1981); Ziemba, Schwartz, and Koenigsberg (1980); and Ziemba and
Schwartz (1980).

## A LONG-TERM ENERGY POLICY MODEL FOR CANADA

To analyze alternative possible energy futures for Canada during the next
half century we have used Fuller's (1980) dynamic energy policy model for
Canada, which relates the major supply options to end use demands via a
process model of interfuel substitution, transmission, and distribution.
Figures 4–6, 4–7, and 4–8 give a schematic representation of the model. Figure 4–6 shows the balancing of supply and demand in a typical period, while
Figures 4–7 and 4–8 provide detail on the primary to secondary to output
energy flows in the West (the major producing sector) and the East (the
major consuming sector), respectively. The modeling technique of the linear
process model of energy flows is analogous to that used in Brookhaven's
BESOM model of the United States economy (see, e.g., Kydes, 1980), adapted for the special situations in the two Canadian regions. The model determines output levels and endogeneous energy prices in each period in the
East and West that balance supply and demand in each period over the
horizon to maximize the discounted sum of consumers' plus producers' surplus. Since our primary concern is in the transitional period up to 2030, the

Figure 4–5.    Canadian Fuel Shares, 1950–79.

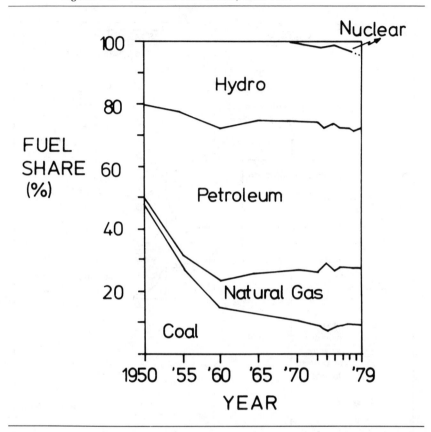

Source: Statistics Canada.

post-2030 economy is assumed to be in a form of steady state; Grinold's (1980) dual equilibrium method[2] is used to represent this era. The model has six periods—1980–85, 1985–90, 1990–2000, 2000–10, 2010–20, and 2020–30—plus the posthorizon period. (In the figures that follow, values are plotted at period midpoints such as 1988 or 2025; monetary values are always in constant 1980 Canadian dollars.)

Economywide demand for end use energy services is represented by econometric demand equations for East and West for the sectors—industrial;

2. The essential assumption is that real prices are constant after 2030 (i.e., all dual variables and output energy prices are constant if they are expressed in real as opposed to nominal terms).

Figure 4–6.    Schematic Diagram of Model in Each Period.

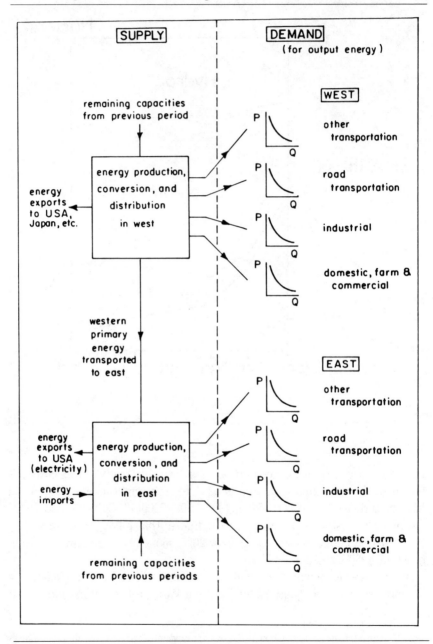

Figure 4-7. Energy Flows in Western Canada.

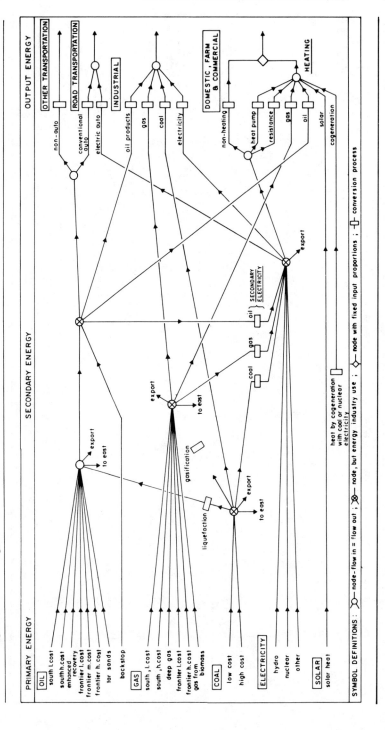

Figure 4–8.    Energy Flows in Eastern Canada.

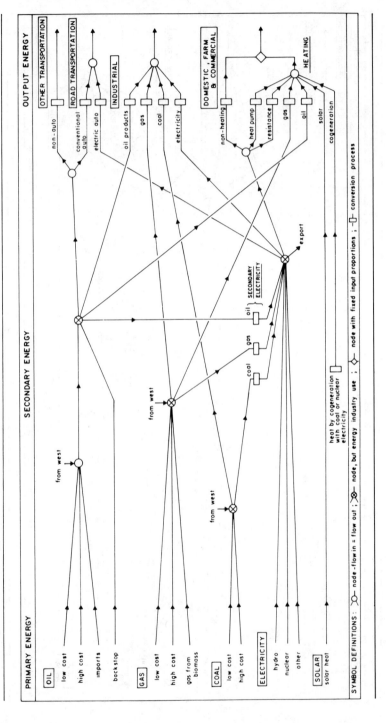

domestic, farm, and commercial (mostly heating); road transportation; and other transportation. The demands are for the services—such as heating, transportation, and the like—and may be met by various combinations of inputs such as secondary energy and capital. The use of output energy in the demand functions allows a process representation of present and possible future devices for supplying the services represented by output energy. In this way, the secondary energy fuel shares may be determined endogenously, with explicit consideration of future technologies that will use secondary energy.

The demand equations are adapted from those estimated by Sahi (1979, 1980) and by Sahi and Erdmann (1980) for the Department of Energy, Mines, and Resources and by Dewees, Hyndman, and Waverman (1975) for road transportation. Long-term versions of the demand equations have been used because

1. The model has 5- and 10-year periods, but typical adjustment times range from 4.6 years to 7.3 years for 90 percent of the adjustment to be made; and
2. The linear process model of energy supply incorporates lag effects by forcing the continued use of established capacity of many energy supply and end use technologies for specified lifetimes.

The final demand equations used in the model are displayed in Table 4–1; see Fuller (1980: Appendix A) for a full discussion of their derivation and implications.

Table 4–1.  Output Demand Equations Used in the Model in a Given Period.

| Sector | Equation |
|---|---|
| 1. Domestic, farm, and commercial | $DFC_i = D_i pop_i (ipc_i)^{.71} P_{Di}^{-.81}$ |
| 2. Industrial | $IND_i = I_i rdp_i (cor_i)^{.667} P_{Ii}^{-.48}$ |
| 3. Road transportation | $RTR_i = R_i pop_i (ipc_i)^{.8} P_{Ri}^{-.36}$ |
| 4. Other transportation | $OTR_i = O_i rdp_i P_{oi}^{-.36}$ |

Notes: $DFC_i$, $IND_i$, $RTR_i$, and $OTR_i$ are the output demands in the various sectors; $D_i$, $I_i$, $R_i$, and $O_i$ are regional constants; $pop_i$, $ipc_i$, $rdp_i$, and $cor_i$ are indexes (1973 = 1) of population, disposable income per capita, real domestic product, and capital-output ratio (i.e., manufacturing capital stock divided by industrial output), respectively; $P_{Ki}$ is the endogenous price of output energy in sector $K = 1,...,4$ and $i = 1$ (West), $i = 2$ (East).

The model contains typical constraints generally found in such economy-wide energy models relating to material balances, fuel share growth constraints, capacity expansion and retirement of capital stock, oil and gas production decline curves,[3] and so forth; see Fuller (1980: Appendix B) for a detailed description of the model's equations.

The objective function is the discounted sum of consumers plus producers surplus, which equals the sum of the sector and period areas under the demand curve net of energy supply costs. This expression is

$$\sum_{t \in T} [1/(1+d)]^{t-1980} \cdot \{dwd_t \cdot WDFC_t^{(1-1/ed)} + ded_t \cdot EDFC_t^{(1-1/ed)} + dwi_t \cdot$$
$$WIND_t^{(1-1/ei)} + dei_t \cdot EIND_t^{(1-1/ei)} + dwr_t \cdot WRTR_t^{(1-1/er)} + der_t \cdot$$
$$ERTR_t^{(1-1/er)} + dwo_t \cdot WOTR_t^{(1-1/eo)} + deo_t \cdot EOTR_t^{(1-1/eo)} - EC_t\}$$

where $d$ is the social discount rate; $EC_t$ are energy costs in period $t$; $T$ is the set of model time periods; $ed, ei, er,$ and $eo$ are price elasticities of demand for output energy in the sectors ($DFC$), industry ($IND$), road transportation ($RTR$), domestic, farm, and commercial and other transportation, respectively; $dwd, dwi, dwr, dwo, ded, dei, der,$ and $deo$ are parameters derived from demand equation parameters for the sectors $DFC, IND, RTR,$ and $OTR$ in the West and East, respectively; $WDFC_t$ and $EDFC_t$ are output energy levels for the domestic, farm, and commercial sector in the West and East, respectively, in period $t$ and similarly for the variables for the industrial, road transportation, and other transportation.

The model is formally a nonlinear program with linear constraints. It has 1,002 columns, 774 rows, and 3,517 nonzero matrix elements, with 56 variables entering the objective nonlinearly. It takes about five minutes of CPU time to solve (solution plus printed output and plots) the model from a "cold start" with about 2,700 iterations of the generalized reduced gradient algorithm using the code MINOS on the University of Waterloo's IBM 3031. Solutions obtained using good initial feasible solutions require much less CPU time. Some of the key model assumptions and limitations follow.

1.    The data that represents end use conversion processes are the conversion factor (the ratio of output energy to secondary fuel input) and the nonfuel conversion cost (representing the other inputs). In reality, the conversion factors and nonfuel costs are price responsive, but in

---

3. Such decline curves, as well as the total resources, constitute perhaps the greatest data uncertainty in this and most economywide energy models. In this model it is assumed that the total resource is fixed (see below for precise assumptions) at best estimated values given specified current and exogeneous cost level projections. The marginal cost of extraction was then assumed to be constant at $C_1$/unit up to $R_1$, $C_2$/unit from $R_1$ to $R_2$, and so on.

the model they are fixed exogenously. However, this theoretical deficiency is likely minor in the case of space heating, since interfuel substitution (which is represented in the model) will probably dominate the effect of fuel price on the conversion coefficients and costs. For oil use in the two transportation sectors, the conversion coefficients are varied over time exogenously to indicate expected increases in fuel efficiencies. This theoretical deficiency may have a significant effect in the industrial sector.

2.  There is an upper limit on the fraction of Eastern crude oil demand that can be met from Western Canadian sources (see the following section for specific data). This constraint represents the physical extent of the pipeline that carries Western oil to Eastern markets. If the upper limit on the fraction is less than one, as it is in the early periods, then the Eastern region is forced to rely on imported oil or on Eastern offshore supplies as available.

3.  To represent factors involving geography, climate, the introduction dates and rates of new technologies and so on, there are upper limits on some shares—the shares of hydro in electricity generation in each region; the share of electric automobiles in road transportation services; and the shares of solar heat, the heat pump, and district heating by cogeneration in the supply of heating in the domestic, farm, and commercial sector. In other cases of new technologies or new primary supply sources, upper bounds have been used to model the introduction dates and rates, with a zero bound prior to the earliest date of introduction. Specific data is given in the next section.

4.  Coal, oil and gas may be exported from the West, and electricity may be exported from either region. Since the assumed export prices are much higher than domestic prices and export revenues are benefits in the model, upper limits are imposed on all exports, consistent with reasonable projections (see the next section for specific data). One reason for the need for export limits is that the model is deterministic, viewing resources and future conditions as known. If this were true, it would make sense to export cheap supplies quickly to reap the large benefits of export revenues very early. Domestic energy prices would then rise to the export prices and the "backstop" energy supplies would more quickly become the chief domestic energy sources. However, in reality, resources and all future conditions (e.g., the availability of the backstop supplies) are uncertain, which has led Canadian policymakers to place restrictions on exports. Therefore, upper limits on exports in the model are realistic representations of Canadian decisionmakers' risk-averse,

nationalistic, behavior. This formulation has important implications for model behavior: Domestic energy prices will not rise to world prices, but will rise at most to the backstop costs; the introduction of new, more costly technologies may be much later than in an unrestricted export model; and of course, resources will be depleted much less quickly than in an unrestricted export model. In short, the limitation of exports, with the implied two-price system (domestic and international), is a key assumption and designed so that our analysis of energy self-sufficiency would be consistent with the traditional Canadian policy of low-priced domestic energy supplies.

## DATA FOR THE BASE CASE AND OTHER SCENARIOS

The data for the base case consist of our most likely projections for all input variables. Table 4–2 gives the economic and demographic projections. Population and real domestic product per capita are expected to grow more rapidly in the West than the East in the early periods and then equally in the post-2000 era. For a full discussion of this data and its sources, see Fuller (1980). Following Jenkins' (1977) study, we have used 8 percent for the real rate of return on capital and 10 percent for the real social discount rate.

The energy resource costs, availability and limits on rates of development and utilization for coal, oil, gas and electricity are given in Table 4–3. The

**Table 4–2.**    Economic and Demographic Projections, 1980–2030.

| | 1983 | 1988 | 1995 | 2005 | 2015 | 2025 | 2035+ |
|---|---|---|---|---|---|---|---|
| | | | *Percent Change per Year* | | | | |
| Population | | | | | | | |
| West | 1.2 | 1.1 | 0.9 | 0.6 | 0.5 | 0.3 | 0.2 |
| East | 0.9 | 0.8 | 0.7 | 0.6 | 0.5 | 0.3 | 0.2 |
| Real domestic product | | | | | | | |
| West | 4.0 | 3.7 | 3.8 | 2.9 | 2.8 | 2.6 | 2.5 |
| East | 3.7 | 3.4 | 3.6 | 2.9 | 2.8 | 2.6 | 2.5 |
| Income per capita | 1.9 | 2.3 | 2.5 | 2.3 | 2.3 | 2.3 | 2.3 |
| Capital output ratio | 2.1 | 2.8 | 1.0 | 0.5 | 0 | 0 | 0 |

price elasticities of demand are DFC, 0.81; IND, 0.48; RTR, 0.36 and OTR, 0.36.

The assumptions for the alternative scenarios mirror the base case except for

- Double elasticity (DE), the price elasticities of demand are double those of the base case;
- No frontier oil and gas (NF), Northwest Arctic and Eastern offshore oil and gas are assumed to be unavailable;
- No new nuclear (3N), only existing and under construction nuclear capacity is allowed; and
- Low coal (LC), coal production is constrained to be no more than the optimal production level in the base case.

These four cases are combined to form the six scenarios that supplement the base case and provide input concerning various levels of future supply constraints and energy conservation activity. The double elasticity scenarios are used to explore the impact of increased conservation activity, which displays greater sensitivity to price.

The model also contains other limits on fuel shares and market penetration—such as hydro's share in total electricity, solar's share of DFC heating, and so forth—to reflect the inadequacies of the linear process-modeling technique to represent reality adequately. There are also numerous conversion efficiencies for the linear process modeling of primary to secondary to output energy demand and production decline coefficients. See Fuller (1980) for more discussion of these points and specific numerical data.

## SCENARIO RESULTS

To investigate possible Canadian energy futures and, in particular, questions related to self-sufficiency, we developed a most likely base case and six alternative scenarios. The scenarios respond to the possibility of major changes in the supply and demand sides of the Canadian energy economy. The supply restrictions (for economic, environmental, political, or other reasons) are of three types—(1) unavailability of frontier oil and gas; (2) a prohibition against "new" nuclear development; and (3) a low availability of coal. The demand side modification is that there is intensified conservation activity and this phenomenon is modeled by a doubling of the demand elasticities. The seven scenarios are (1) base; (2) double elasticity (DE); (3) no frontier oil and gas (NF); (4) no new nuclear (3N); (5) no new nuclear and

**Table 4-3.** Energy Resource Cost, Availability, and Bounds and Limits Placed on the Rate of Development and Utilization.

| | Resource Cost and Availability Cost 1980$ | Initial Amount | Distribution Within Region Margin Within Region | West to East Transport Cost | Bounds and Limits | | | | |
|---|---|---|---|---|---|---|---|---|---|
| **COAL** | | | | | 1980 capacity in East × (1.15)$^t$ –i.e., double every 5 years 1980–90; then unbounded | | | | |
| W | 0.30/MMbtu | 1584×10$^{15}$ btu | 1.22W | | | 1983 | 1988 | 1995 | 2005 |
| W high cost | 0.61 | 106.0 | | | | | | | |
| E | 1.22 | 21.6 | 0.61 E | 1.57 | W-E transport lower 10$^{15}$ btu/yr | 0 | 0.116 | 0.176 | 0.176 |
| E high cost | 2.43 | 1.4 | | | upper | 0.116 | 0.176 | none | none |
| Imports | 2.08(1.025)$^t$ | | | | | | | | |
| Exports (West) | 2.17(1.025)$^t$ | | | | | | | | |
| **OIL** | | | | | | 1983 | 1988 | 1995 | 2005+ |
| W conventional | 6.08/bbl | 3.6×10$^9$ bbl | DFC | | | | | | |
| W conventional high | 12.16 | 5.5 | | | | | | | |
| W enhanced recovery | 21.28 | 2.5 | | | | | | | |
| NW Arctic | 9.12 | 2.0 | | | | | | | |
| NW Arctic medium | 16.72 | 2.5 | 4.86 W | 0.76 | Tar sands lower 10$^9$ bbl/yr | 0.074 | 0.153 | none | none |
| NW Arctic high | 24.32 | 1.5 | 3.19 E | | E offshore low 10$^9$ bbl/yr | 0.01 | 0.05 | unlimited | unlimited |
| Tar sands | 27.36 | 50.0 | IND | | high | 0 | 0.01 | 0.025 | unlimited |
| | | | 0.61 W | | | | | | |
| | | | 0.15 E | | Percent East demand served by West | | | | |
| E offshore | 18.24 | 1.5 | RTR | | | | | | |
| E offshore high | 22.80 | 2.0 | 29.18 W | | Oil trade price (1980$) (imports and exports) | 65 | 80 | 100 | 100 |
| From coal, West | 34.69 | see coal | 31.16 E | | | 42.70 | 52.00 | 68.40 | 68.40 |
| Backstop | 38.00 | | OTR 11.70 W | | | | | | |
| | | | 19.49 E | | Exports upper 10$^9$ bbl/yr | 0.030 | 0.015 | 0.007 | 0 |

## GAS

| | ($/mcf) | ($23\times10^{12}$ cf) | DFC |
|---|---|---|---|
| W conventional | 0.53/mcf | $23\times10^{12}$cf | |
| W conventional high | 2.28 | 50 | |
| W deep gas | 4.99 | 77 | |
| NW Arctic | 3.28 | 58 | DFC |
| NW Arctic high | 4.04 | 41 | 1.13 W |
| E offshore | 3.72 | 13 | 1.29 E |
| E offshore high | 6.08 | 9 | IND |
| From coal | 5.50 | see coal | 0.24 W |
| From biomass | 3.80 | | 0.08 E |
| | | | 0.67 |
| Exports | 2.92(1.04)[a] | | |

| | 1983 | 1988 | 1995 | 2005 | 2015 | 2025 |
|---|---|---|---|---|---|---|
| E offshore | 0 | 0.48 | unlimited | unlimited | unlimited | unlimited |
| E offshore high | 0 | 0 | 0.48 | unlimited | unlimited | unlimited |
| From biomass, East | 0.012 | 0.024 | 0.025 | 0.027 | 0.029 | 0.031 |
| West | 0.005 | 0.010 | 0.011 | 0.012 | 0.013 | 0.014 |
| W-E transport, upper | 0.972 | 1.40 | unlimited | | | |
| Exports | 1.68 | 0.74 | 0.03 | 0 | 0 | 0 |

## ELECTRICITY

| | (mills/kwh) | DFC |
|---|---|---|
| hydro | 11.7 mills/kwh | DFC |
| nuclear | 15.2 | 23.6 W |
| | | 15.2 F |
| gas | 8.2[a] | IND |
| oil | 10.0[a] | 2.7 W |
| coal | 11.6[a] | −1.5 E |
| biomass | 34.8 | RTR |
| | | 15.7 W |
| | | 15.7 E |

| | 1983 | 1988 | 1995 | 2005 | 2015 | 2025 |
|---|---|---|---|---|---|---|
| Hydro West ($10^3$kwh/yr) | 0.130 | 0.172 | 0.254 | 0.254 | 0.254 | 0.254 |
| Hydro East | 0.262 | 0.322 | 0.442 | 0.442 | 0.442 | 0.442 |
| Exports West | 0.0034 | 0.0036 | 0.0039 | 0.0043 | 0.0048 | 0.0053 |
| Exports East | 0.0070 | 0.0074 | 0.0081 | 0.0088 | 0.0099 | 0.0110 |
| Export price (mills/kwh) | 22.0 | 22.0 | 28.3 | 28.3 | 28.3 | 28.3 |
| Percent new capacity that can be hydro | | | West 75.3 | East 77.9 | | |

[a]Nonfuel capital and operating cost.

low coal (3NLC); (6) no new nuclear, low coal, and no frontier oil and gas (3NLCNF); and (7) no new nuclear, low coal, no frontier oil and gas, and double elasticity (ALL). The least supply-constrained case is thus scenario 2, and scenario 6 is the most supply-constrained case.

## Total Energy

The scenarios indicate that total energy output increases about one and a half times over the fifty-year horizon, growing at an average annual rate of about 2.25 percent. As shown in Figure 4–9, in the base case primary energy production reaches 19.4 quads ($10^{15}$ btu) in 2025, while output energy (accounting for all energy losses in production, distribution, and conversion to end use) is 15 quads, with a relative efficiency of 77 percent.

Table 4–4 summarizes the total primary and output energy usage and the relative efficiency for the various scenarios. The more supply-constrained scenarios are less efficient, since such shortages force utilization of less efficient energy sources. For the double elasticity case, the apparently lower efficiency reflects a higher proportion of transportation energy as well as lower utilization of solar energy (which has no transmission loss, as it is supplied at the point of demand). Energy growth peaks in 1988 and then falls off in most scenarios except those for DE, where the peak occurs in 1995.

## Fuel Shares

Figures 4–10 and 4–11 present the output and primary fuel shares over the horizon for the base case. For the output shares, there is a significant increase in solar energy, with big spurts in 2005 and 2015. Co-generation falls, then increases—as does electricity, with a dramatic increase in 2005. Oil's share falls dramatically in 2005. Gas increases to 37 percent of all output energy in 1988 and then falls, reaching 11 percent in 2015. Coal increases and then stabilizes. The biggest shift is from oil and gas to electric and solar.

Though not shown, secondary fuels change in a similar pattern. The big shift to electricity in primary fuel shares is via increased nuclear power generation with a big spurt in 2005. Coal as a primary fuel also increases throughout the periods, reaching 20 percent by 2025.

**Figure 4–9.** Total Primary, Secondary and Output Energy Use in the Base Case, 1980–2030.

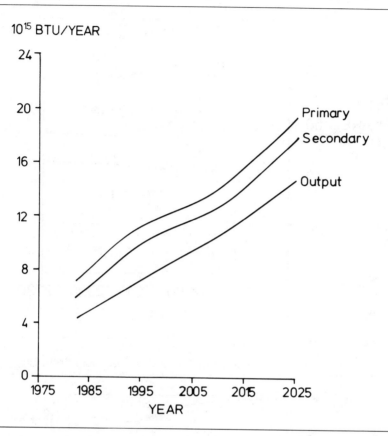

**Table 4–4.** Primary and Output Energy, 2025, and Relative Efficiency in Quads (10^{15} btus).

|  | Base | DE | NF | 3N | 3NLC | NF3NLC | ALL |
|---|---|---|---|---|---|---|---|
| Primary | 19.4 | 15.6 | 19.8 | 19.5 | 17.8 | 17.4 | 12.7 |
| Output | 15 | 11.7 | 14.9 | 14 | 12.9 | 12.7 | 9.4 |
| Efficiency (percent) | 77.2 | 75 | 75.4 | 72 | 72.9 | 72.8 | 73.4 |

**Figure 4–10.**    Primary Fuel Shares, Base Case, 1980–2030.

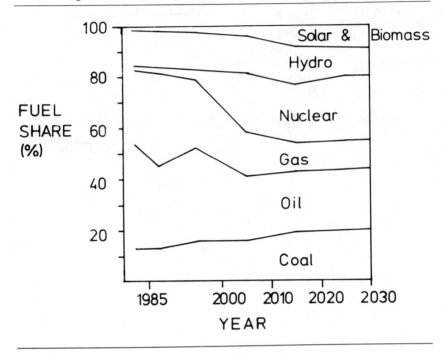

**Figure 4–11.**    Output Energy Fuel Shares, Base Case, 1980–2030.

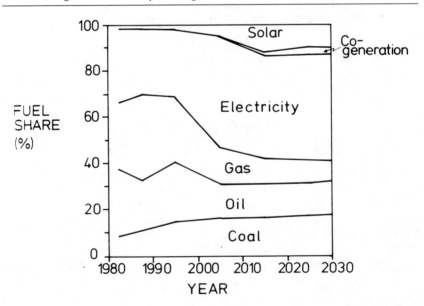

With energy conservation (the DE case), the pattern of output fuel shares holds. However, there is relatively more reliance on oil and gas (6 percent in total) and less on co-generation, electricity, and coal. The primary fuel shares are somewhat more variable, with nuclear and coal falling 4 and 3 percent, respectively, and hydro and oil increasing 2 and 5 percent.

Each supply-constrained scenario reflects a slightly different fuel use pattern (see Table 4–5). The solar share is robust throughout at 13 percent output energy share (3 percent greater than the base case) and for primary at 10 percent (2 percent greater). Coal's output share is roughly equal to the base in all scenarios. This stability in coal's output share does not hold for primary energy where it is clear that coal is a major buffer resource.

Under frontier supply constraints, the output fuel share adjustments are apparently minor—increase solar 3 percent and decrease gas 3 percent. However, this reflects a shift to syngas with no natural gas available. Thus, under primary fuel shares, there is a dramatic 50 percent increase in the share of coal and a total disappearance of natural gas. Under all no nuclear scenarios, the share of electricity falls between 13 and 22 percent. Co-generation varies within output energy depending on the availability of coal— that is, 3N sees a 14 percent increase in co-generation's share. Thus, the shift from nuclear is facilitated by increases in coal for co-generated heat as well as solar. When coal is constrained, there are increases in oil and gas.

**Table 4–5.**  Comparative Primary and Output Energy Fuel Shares, 2025.

| | Base Case | DE | NF | 3N | 3NLC | 3NNFLC | ALL |
|---|---|---|---|---|---|---|---|
| | | Changes from Base Case | | | | | |
| **Primary** | | | | | | | |
| Solar | 8 | | 2 | 2 | 2 | 2 | 2 |
| Biomass | 0.2 | | | | 1 | | |
| Hydro | 12 | 2 | −1 | | 1 | 1 | 5 |
| Nuclear | 25 | −4 | −1 | −25 | −25 | −25 | −25 |
| Gas | 11 | 0 | −11 | −6 | 5 | 4 | −6 |
| Oil | 24 | 5 | −1 | −1 | | 14 | 13 |
| Coal | 20 | −3 | 10 | 30 | 2 | 4 | 11 |
| **Output** | | | | | | | |
| Solar | 10 | | 3 | 3 | 3 | 3 | 3 |
| Co-generation | 3 | −1 | | 14 | 2 | 3 | 7 |
| Electricity | 46 | −2 | | −17 | −22 | −22 | −13 |
| Gas | 9 | 0 | −3 | −1 | 5 | 4 | −5 |
| Oil | 15 | 4 | | 1 | 13 | 13 | 10 |
| Coal | 16 | −1 | | | −1 | −1 | −2 |

For a greater understanding of the specific impacts of the various scenarios, we now investigate output energy demand shares and then the production of various energy resources.

### Demand Use Shares

In terms of output energy, the share of total transportation in the base case is relatively constant at about 9 to 10 percent over the horizon, but there is a decrease of DFC from 46 to 36 percent, while industry increases from 44 to 55 percent. In terms of secondary energy, there are decreases in both transportation and DFC and an increase in industry use reflecting relative efficiency improvements in transportation. The decrease in DFC mirrors the decline in its output share.

Comparing scenarios (see Table 4–6), the changes are small, reflecting the robustness of output energy demand. The NF scenario has no impact on demand shares. The output share for DFC rises slightly for most supply constrained cases, reflecting the availability to DFC of unconstrained alternatives, such as solar and co-generation. Industry's share drops and road transportation increases; this is especially significant in DE and ALL.

*Transportation.*    Transportation demand exhibits relatively constant growth. The most important finding is that there are no electric cars developed under any scenario, electricity is too expensive a fuel to use for trans-

**Table 4–6.**    Comparative Shares by Demand Sector, 2025.

|  | Base Case | Changes from Base Case | | | | | |
|---|---|---|---|---|---|---|---|
|  |  | DE | NF | 3N | 3NLC | NF3NLC | ALL |
| Output |  |  |  |  |  |  |  |
| DFC | 36 |  |  | 1 | 1 | 1 |  |
| IND | 55 | −4 |  | −1 | −2 | −2 | −7 |
| RTR | 7 | 4 |  | 1 | 1 | 1 | 7 |
| OTR | 2 |  |  |  |  |  | 1 |
| Secondary |  |  |  |  |  |  |  |
| DFC | 31 | −1 |  |  | −1 | −2 | −5 |
| IND | 51 | −5 |  | −1 | −1 | −1 | −7 |
| RTR | 12 | 6 |  | 1 | 1 | 1 | 10 |
| OTR | 6 |  |  |  | 1 | 1 | 1 |

portation no matter what the supply constraint unless there is breakthrough in the technology of conversion. Under almost all scenarios, the total transportation output energy is constant at 1.4 quads in 2025; if DE is added, then the demand is higher at 1.6 quads. This reflects the assumed increasing efficiency standards, which are such that the fuel cost per mile decreases over time. Increasing price responsiveness by including the DE assumption thus means that the quantity of transportation service increases even faster in time.

*Industry.*    The total output energy used by industry in the base case increases 374 percent in the East and 279 percent in the West. In the West, over the horizon there is a relative shift from oil and gas to electricity (mostly hydro). However, electricity dips in 1988 before increasing dramatically in 2015. Coal increases throughout. Gas increases and peaks in 2005; then its use falls and grows again. Oil use reaches a minimum in 1995 before increasing. There is also a relative shift to electric from oil and gas in the East. In this region, the electricity is mainly provided by nuclear generation after 1995. Coal maintains approximately the same share throughout. There is a decrease in electricity use in 1995 and then a dramatic 232 percent increase. Gas utilization has a relatively slow growth early and then picks up speed, ending 155 percent higher. Oil use peaks in 1995 then falls dramatically to the previous level and grows again, ending almost twice as high as in 1980.

*DFC Heating.*    In the West, gas heat grows until 2005, when it reaches a 91 percent share; then it falls, as co-generation (with electricity from coal) comes in and grows dramatically to 42 percent (see Figure 4–12). Oil is phased out by 1995, as is electric resistance. No use is made of the heat pump or solar heating. In the East there is dramatic growth in solar until it represents 42 percent (the limit on its share) by the horizon (see Figure 4–13). By that time the rest of the heat is provided by electric resistance (mostly nuclear generated). Gas heat increases in 1988 as the pipeline extensions are completed. However, gas is completely phased out by 2005. Oil is phased out earlier, by 1995. Co-generation (with nuclear electricity) provides a constant 0.025 quads through 2005 and then vanishes, just when it is coming on stream in the West. (Note that this does not make economic sense and may mean that heat by nuclear co-generation is marginally competitive in the East.) In this region as well, no use is made of the heat pump.

Under the DE scenario, total DFC demand falls in both regions. In the East, the same proportions of fuel shares are maintained, and as solar is at

Figure 4-12.    DFC Heating, West, Base Case, 1980–2030.

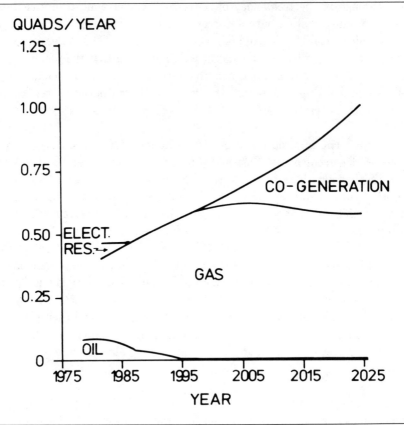

the share limit, this implies that this constraint should be loosened, permitting an even greater reliance on solar. In the West, the same fuels are relied upon as in the base case, but the absolute amount of gas is the same, so the share rises, and that of co-generation falls. In both regions, the supply-constrained scenarios push solar heat to the limits: In the West solar tends to come on stream at the limit, implying that it would be beneficial to begin to encourage solar now in new housing stock.

NF assumptions have impact only in the West, where gas use falls and co-generation comes in to the limit along with solar. With 3N by 2025, co-generation with coal becomes important (57 percent) in the East as well as continuing in the West (45 percent); gas is used in a minor way in the East (1 percent) and significantly in the West (13 percent). Low coal assumptions, further constraining Eastern supplies, make the heat pump

**Figure 4–13.**    DFC Heating, East, Base Case, 1980–2030.

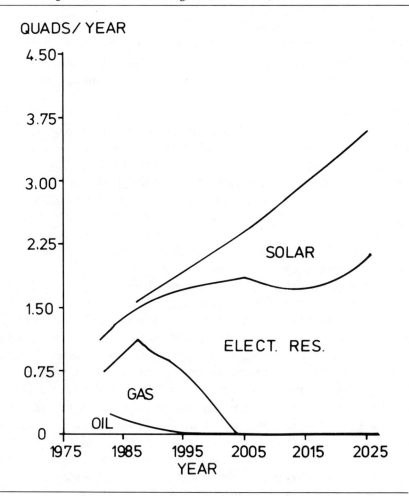

profitable. In the West the heat pump and electric resistance come on stream under the fully constrained case. (This anomaly may be due to changes in industry fuel shares that affect the availability of heat by co-generation.)

In summary, under many of the supply-constrained scenarios, solar and co-generation become profitable. As the model has constrained the shares of these, it is apparent that it would be profitable to encourage alternative sources of heat for co-generation once the district heat capacity is made available (e.g., garbage power, wood waste, and so on).

## Fuel Production and Use

The initial resources levels, as well as the resources remaining under the various scenarios in 2030, appear in Table 4–7. The calculated oil, gas, and coal prices in the West and East are given in Table 4–8. An analysis of production and use of the various fuels over the horizon follows in this section.

*Oil.* There are cycles of oil production (see Figure 4–14). Eastern oil peaks in 1988 and again in 2015, when production of the higher cost Northeast offshore oil is at its greatest. Tar sands production doubles by 1988 as anticipated capacity comes on stream, but then falls a third by 2015 as less expensive Western Arctic oil comes on stream and peaks in 2005. As this source is exhausted, tar sands quickly increases six-fold by 2025. Consequently, there are also swings in production from Western conventional areas. This production declines in 1988, as projected tar sands capacity is completed, but picks up again later as demand increases and as the model is no longer forced to use the tar sands to capacity.

Total oil production by the horizon is remarkably similar under all scenarios that do not include the coal constraints. This is so even though there is no projected oil from coal (see Table 4–9). There are substantial differences in 1995, with NF being lowest (two-thirds of base) and DE approximately 85 percent. However, by 2005 all attain the same level of output, with tar sands and Western conventional making up the differences. Western oil is "conserved" through 1995–2005 until tar sands usage increases. The DE scenario uses less tar sands in the early periods but is similar by 2025 (recall that this is due to increased use of gasoline in this scenario). Under the 3NLC scenario, added pressure is placed on oil; the tar sands are developed more rapidly, and they quickly dominate oil production. Under the most constrained case, NF3NLC, over half of the low cost surface-mined tar sands oil—a huge resource—is used up by 2030 (see Table 4–7).

Throughout the planning period, most of the oil is consumed by transportation (see Figure 4–15). Industry use varies, peaking in 1995 and 2025. DFC use is phased out by 1995, even before exports. Electricity use, which is small in any case, is phased out by 2015. Crude oil prices remain low, never coming near world oil prices (see Table 4–8).

DFC oil use vanishes in all scenarios except 3NLC, where it continues at a low level until 2015. Oil is eliminated for electricity generation by 2015 in all scenarios. Transportation uses are constant given elasticities, so the largest variation comes in industry utilization, which varies from a high of 0.537 quads under 3NLC in 2025 to a low of 0.146 quads in DE as compared with

**Table 4-7.**  Initial Availability, Cost, and Resource Levels Remaining in 2030 of Coal, Oil, and Gas for the Various Scenarios.

| Resource | | Initial Amount | Resources Remaining (2030) | | | | | | |
|---|---|---|---|---|---|---|---|---|---|
| | | | Base Case | DE | NF | 3N | 3NLC | 3NLCNF | ALL |
| COAL | W | $1584 \times 10^{15}$ btu | 1400 | 1431 | 1105 | 959 | 1400 | 1400 | 1400 |
| | W high cost | 106 | 106 | 106 | 106 | 106 | 106 | 106 | 106 |
| | E | 21.6 | b | b | b | b | b | b | b |
| | E high cost | 1.4 | b | b | b | b | b | b | b |
| OIL | W conventional | $3.6 \times 10^{9}$ bbl | b | b | b | b | b | b | b |
| | W conventional high | 5.5 | b | b | b | b | b | b | b |
| | W enhanced recovery | 2.5 | 0.2 | 0.2 | b | 0.2 | 0.2 | b | b |
| | NW Arctic | 2.0 | b | b | a | b | b | a | a |
| | NW Arctic medium | 2.5 | b | b | a | b | b | a | a |
| | NW Arctic high | 1.5 | 0.1 | 0.1 | a | 0.1 | 0.1 | a | a |
| | Tar sands | 50.0 | 39.0 | 40.1 | 32.9 | 39.0 | 35.2 | 23.8 | 32.9 |
| | E offshore | 1.5 | b | 0.1 | a | b | b | a | a |
| | E offshore high | 2.0 | 0.1 | 0.1 | b | 0.1 | 0.1 | b | b |
| GAS | W conventional | $23 \times 10^{12}$ cf | b | b | b | b | b | b | b |
| | W conventional high | 50 | b | b | b | b | b | b | b |
| | W deep gas | 77 | 77 | 77 | 77 | 77 | 77 | 43.4 | 67.6 |
| | NW Artic | 58 | 19.5 | 30.0 | a | 0.6 | b | a | a |
| | NW Arctic high | 41 | 41 | 41 | a | 41 | 12.1 | a | a |
| | E offshore | 13 | b | b | b | b | b | b | b |
| | E offshore high | 9 | 9 | 9 | 9 | 9 | 9 | a | a |

a Frontier oil and gas set equal to zero in these scenarios.
b Indicates that this resource is exhausted.

Table 4–8.    Oil, Gas, and Coal prices, 1980$, Base Case, 1980–2030.

|  |  | 1983 | 1988 | 1995 | 2005 | 2015 | 2025+ |
|---|---|---|---|---|---|---|---|
| COAL $/ton, | W | 6.30 | 6.30 | 6.30 | 6.30 | 6.30 | 6.30 |
|  | E | 55.83 | 63.17 | 39.25 | 39.25 | 39.25 | 39.25 |
| OIL $/bbl. | W | 12.74 | 13.47 | 14.71 | 20.10 | 27.36 | 27.36 |
|  | E | 23.72 | 21.78 | 15.47 | 20.86 | 28.12 | 28.12 |
| Trade |  | 42.70 | 52.00 | 68.40 | 68.40 | 68.40 | 68.40 |
| GAS $/MCF | W | 2.40 | 2.44 | 2.78 | 3.33 | 3.39 | 3.57 |
|  | E | 3.39 | 3.43 | 3.82 | 4.38 | 4.51 | 4.71 |

Figure 4–14.    Oil Production, Base Case, 1980–2030.

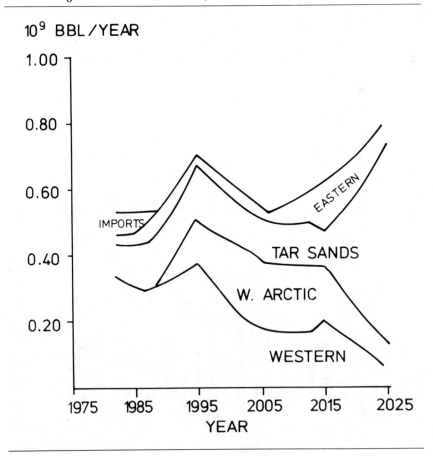

Table 4–9.    Comparative Oil Production, 2025, 10⁶ bbl /yr.

| | Base Case | DE | NF | 3N | 3NLC | NF3NLC | ALL |
|---|---|---|---|---|---|---|---|
| East offshore | 70 | 76 | a | 60 | 60 | a | a |
| Tar sands | 599 | 556 | 781 | 594 | 977 | 1141 | 803 |
| NW Arctic | 61 | 70 | a | 61 | 61 | a | a |
| Western conventional | 77 | 87 | 24 | 75 | 75 | 16 | 19 |
| Total | 807 | 789 | 805 | 790 | 1173 | 1157 | 822 |

ᵃIndicates zero production. Note that imports, backstop technologies and oil from coal are also zero.

Figure 4–15.    Oil Use, Base Case, 1980–2030.

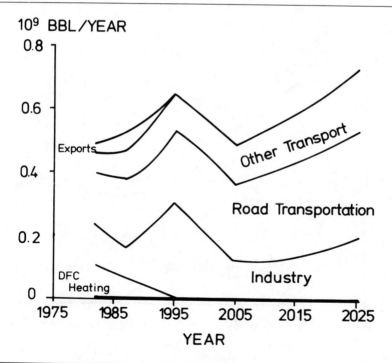

0.2 for the base. Thus, shortfalls in oil production are mostly in industry, as transportation maintains its total allocation. Under DE assumptions, the decisions by industry and DFC to use less frees up more oil for transportation.

*Gas.*    Gas production in the base case peaks in 1988, with Eastern gas providing approximately 10 percent (see Figure 4–16). In the next period, conventional production falls 25 percent, substantially reducing total production; by 2025 it falls to zero. By 2005, when the west-to-east gas pipeline and distribution network are completed, conventional production is so low that total production falls another third. Eastern gas production peaks in 2005 and then decays sharply. Waste is converted to gas at the limits available. There is no production of gas from coal. At the end of the horizon, 57 percent of the gas is still left in frontier areas, which indicates a flexibility to increase incentives to switch from oil to gas.

The DE scenario allows a delay in the development of Eastern gas fields till 2005. Western Arctic penetration is low in 2005, but attains a similar

Figure 4–16.    Gas Production, Base Case, 1980–2030.

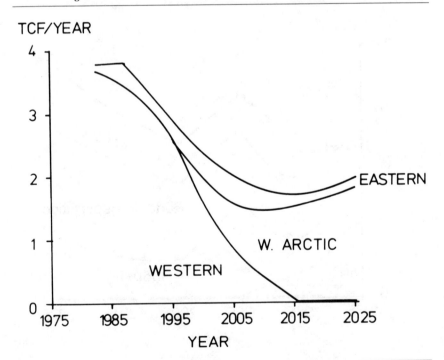

level in 2015 (a ten-year delay). In all, more is left at the horizon. Table 4–10 compares gas production in 2025 across scenarios.

The NF assumptions mean that natural gas production falls off by 2015. Substantial amounts are made up by syngas from coal starting in 2015, and this accounts for all but 3 percent of production in 2025 (this is provided by biomass waste). The 3N scenario leads to an increase in the rate of utilization of gas—faster use of Eastern gas, especially in 1988–95, and of Western Arctic gas in 2005–15, though there is no impact on Western conventional gas. By 2025 there is some production from coal and some from biomass. Adding the "low coal" assumptions puts added pressure on gas, increasing the speed of utilization.

In the base case, gas use changes from mostly exports and DFC to an almost fifty-fifty split between DFC and industry (see Figure 4–17). Industry use grows until 2005, then declines and grows again. DFC use peaks in 1988 and then falls. The small amount allocated to electricity generation ends by 2005. Gas prices rise steadily as low cost resources are used up (see Table 4–8).

The DE scenario shifts the peak industrial use of gas to 2015. NF leads to a sharp reduction (to 57 percent of base) in use of gas by industry in 2005 and in DFC (to 36 percent); industry recovers, while DFC falls further. The 3N scenario generates cycles in industrial use, but the trend is toward increasing use by 2005. Meanwhile, DFC use increases early and falls toward the horizon.

*Coal.* Coal imports are phased out by 1995 in the base case. Eastern production peaks in 1995, and the resource is exhausted by 2025. Western production grows overall. At the end of the period 88 percent of the low cost and all the high cost Western coal remains. Exports continue to

**Table 4–10.**    Comparative Gas Production, 2025, TCF/yr.

| Prod. | Base Case | DE | NF | 3N | 3NLC | 3NNF LC | ALL |
|---|---|---|---|---|---|---|---|
| Biomass | 0.031 | 0.031 | 0.046 | 0.046 | 0.046 | 0.046 | 0.046 |
| Coal | – | | 1.341 | 0.737 | | | |
| East | 0.078 | 0.173 | | 0.042 | 2.627 | | |
| Western Arctic | 1.879 | 1.421 | | 0.888 | | | |
| West | – | | | | | 2.366 | 0.563 |
| Total | 1.988 | 1.625 | 1.387 | 1.713 | 2.673 | 2.412 | 0.609 |

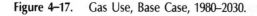

Figure 4–17.    Gas Use, Base Case, 1980–2030.

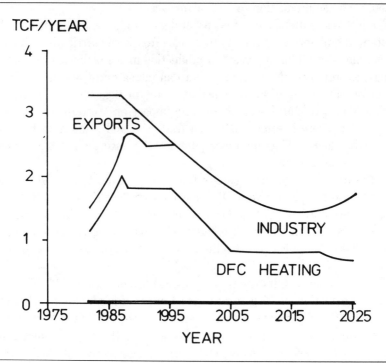

grow at the limits and represent almost 50 percent of production by 2005. Synfuels are not needed. Coal utilization for generating electricity first falls, then dramatically increases (see Figure 4–18). Industry use grows throughout. Coal prices peak in the East in 1988 and then fall as the limits on west-to-east shipment are removed. Prices are constant in the West.

Coal is a resource that provides a cushion in the energy system (see Table 4–11). In the DE scenario, coal production in the horizon period is 85 percent that of the base, while domestic use is only 69 percent. In this case there is relatively little change in coal use from the base proportions.

Under the simple supply constraints, synfuels become important. In NF, domestic coal use is 50 percent higher in 2025 than the base, and almost the entire addition is allocated to synfuels. Under 3N, the production of coal for domestic use in 2025 increases 150 percent over the base case. This time the bulk of the coal (62 percent) goes to electricity production to partially offset nuclear power; industry use falls about 10 percent; synfuels use is still significant.

**Figure 4–18.**     Coal Use, Base Case, 1980–2030.

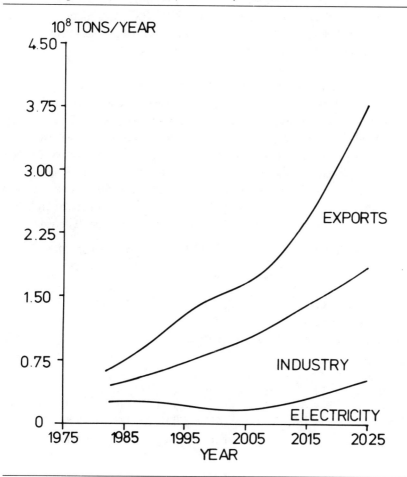

**Table 4–11.**     Comparative Coal Use, 2025, 10⁸ tons/yr.

| | Base Case | DE | NF | 3N | Coal Constrained 3NLC | NF3NLC | ALL |
|---|---|---|---|---|---|---|---|
| Exports | 1.876 | 1.876 | 1.876 | 1.876 | 1.876 | 1.747 | 1.876 |
| Synfuels | – | – | 0.944 | 0.519 | – | – | – |
| Industry | 1.354 | 0.988 | 1.342 | 1.245 | 1.127 | 1.099 | 0.733 |
| Electricity | 0.502 | 0.295 | 0.552 | 2.856 | 0.729 | 0.886 | 1.122 |
| Total | 3.732 | 3.160 | 4.714 | 6.497 | 3.732 | 3.732 | 3.731 |

The multiple constrained scenarios have coal production fixed at the base levels (along with some imports in 2025 in NF3NLC), and there is a variety of allocations between industry and electricity. Of course, as output is constrained, there is not sufficient coal for synfuels production.

*Electricity.*    The electricity generation patterns in the two regions are vastly different, reflecting relative resource base differences (see Table 4–12). In the West there is heavy reliance on hydroelectric generation, whose share peaks at about 75 percent of the capacity generated in the base case. Oil- and gas-fired plants are phased out by 2005. Coal generation grows and represents 32 percent of the electricity generated in 2025. There is a small amount of biomass in the early periods, and there is no need for nuclear power. In the East there is heavy reliance on nuclear (76 percent in 2025); and the rest is hydro, which reaches its capacity by 1995. There is a big

Table 4–12.    Comparative Electricity Production and Use, 2025, $10^{12}$kwh/yr.

| Production | Base Case | DE | NF | 3N | 3NLC | 3NNFLC | ALL |
|---|---|---|---|---|---|---|---|
| EAST[a] | | | | | | | |
| Biomass | – | | | | 0.055 | | |
| Nuclear | 1.416 | 0.95 | 1.409 | | | | |
| Coal | – | | | 0.543 | 0.087 | 0.125 | 0.194 |
| Hydro | 0.442 | 0.442 | 0.442 | 0.442 | 0.442 | 0.442 | 0.442 |
| Total | 1.858 | 1.392 | 1.851 | 0.985 | 0.584 | 0.567 | 0.636 |
| WEST[b] | | | | | | | |
| Coal | 0.117 | 0.069 | 0.129 | 0.124 | 0.083 | 0.082 | 0.068 |
| Hydro | 0.254 | 0.210 | 0.238 | 0.247 | 0.254 | 0.249 | 0.208 |
| Total | 0.371 | 0.279 | 0.367 | 0.371 | 0.337 | 0.331 | 0.276 |
| USE (Total) | | | | | | | |
| Exports | 0.016 | 0.016 | 0.016 | 0.016 | 0.005 | 0.005 | 0.016 |
| IND | 1.208 | 0.882 | 1.198 | 1.023 | 0.556 | 0.543 | 0.572 |
| DFC | 0.821 | 0.634 | 0.822 | 0.199 | 0.275 | 0.268 | 0.242 |
| | 2.045 | 1.532 | 2.036 | 1.238 | 0.836 | 0.816 | 0.830 |

[a]Oil and gas are zero in all scenarios.
[b]Biomass, nuclear, oil, and gas are zero in all scenarios.

spurt in nuclear power in 2005 (increasing more than fourfold from the previous period). Coal generation is phased out by 2015, as Eastern coal is used up. Oil and gas are phased out at the same time.

Industrial use varies throughout the planning period, falling in 1995, only to grow dramatically thereafter. DFC use falls in 1988 and then grows dramatically, reflecting mostly electric resistance heat in the East.

The DE scenario has little impact on hydroelectric production, but does result in a 33 percent decrease in nuclear generation in the East and a 41 percent decline in coal generation in the West. The NF assumptions have relatively little impact on electricity production or use as there was no oil- and gas-fired electric generation in the base. On the other hand, 3N leads to a significant reduction in total electricity generation in the East. It is cut in half by 2025. Coal generation increases to cover 39 percent of the nuclear shortfall. Production in the West is unchanged. (Note that the model does not allow west-east transmission, as the costs due to distances are too great.) The biggest impact on use is on DFC, which declines to less than one-quarter of the base demand, representing the shift from electric resistance heat to co-generation and solar in the East. Industry use is 85 percent of the base demand.

The multiple supply-constrained scenarios have even greater impact. Total electricity generation falls to about 40 percent of the base, with impacts on both industry and DFC. In the West there is only hydro and coal generation under all scenarios, while in the East there is some biomass (approximately 10 percent) with 3NLC.

## SUMMARY OF THE MAJOR FINDINGS AND
## THEIR POLICY IMPLICATIONS

This chapter presents the results of various scenarios run on a long-term deterministic dynamic energy policy model for Canada. The seven scenarios represent a few leading cases out of a myriad of possible energy futures. It is hoped that the scenarios span the range of likely possibilities, so that general conclusions derived have a good measure of credibility, as the approach using scenario analysis instead of attempting to build in stochastic elements is the usual one in large-scale energy modeling (for discussion see Manne, Richels and Weyant 1979; and Ziemba and Schwartz 1980). Thus, with the usual caveats in mind, we are led to the following conclusions.

The notion that Canada can become self-sufficient in all principal energy forms by 1990 and remain so (as hoped by the present government) is robustly supported by all the scenario runs. Table 4–7, where the resources remaining in 2030 are given for the various scenarios, is especially revealing in this regard. Coal and the tar sands are backstop resources that provide a cushion in the system so that the model generates results consistent with current government policy that has the twin premises of energy self-sufficiency and resource prices based on production costs at levels substantially below the world price of oil. As well, coal and tar sands remain in relatively plentiful supply for the post horizon era. Under all scenarios there are substantial remaining reserves of Western coal. Conventional and frontier oil is exhausted and the amount of remaining tar sands varies with the scenario from about 80 percent to about half of the present reserve level in the most supply constrained case. There are likely to be substantial remaining supplies of Western deep gas and high-priced Arctic and Eastern offshore gas, although conventional and much of the low-priced frontier sources are exhausted. Thus there is some possibility of energy resource exports, particularly of electricity and additional coal. However, given historical policy, it is unlikely that there will be synthetic oil exports from the tar sands, as one would expect the government to move plants on stream only as they are needed to fill Canadian demand.

Generally speaking, the results also indicate a substantial growth in solar and co-generation heat, economical use of gas from biomass and coal, non-use of electric cars due to their high cost, and a heavy reliance (if allowed) on nuclear in the East, despite no need for nuclear in the West. Incentives that increase the speed of oil-to-gas conversions are likely to be very worthwhile. The greatest energy conservation and savings benefits are likely to be found in transportation, which is essentially oil based and whose total demand is relatively insensitive to supply option constraints. The internal combustion engine becomes the major user of oil, and research and development resources directed both to improve the technology and develop alternative sources of motive power would be very beneficial. Finally, all scenarios indicate that there is likely to be a transition out of conventional oil and gas—which are exhausted by 2030—into other fuels. Large growth in solar, biomass, nuclear (if allowed), arctic and offshore gas (if allowed), tar sands, synthetic oil, and gradual growth in coal affect the transition (see Figure 4–11 and Table 4–7 for details).

Although conventional oil and gas are exhausted in all scenarios, the future looks quite promising for Canada even under very supply-constrained scenarios. Table 4–13 is concerned with the impact of these supply-constrained scenarios on the objective function values over the horizon. The loss, discounted to 1980, ranges from about $5.5 \times 10^9$ (in 1980$) with the

**Table 4–13.**   Impact of Supply-constrained Scenarios on Objective Function Values Over the Horizon.[a]

| Scenario | Loss of Objective Value from Base Case (in $10^9$ 1980$) | $/Capita Loss | Loss of Objective Value from DE (in $10^9$ 1980$) | $/Capita Loss |
|---|---|---|---|---|
| NF | 11.330 | 472 | 10.565 | 440 |
| 3N | 8.104 | 338 | 5.539 | 231 |
| 3NLC | 11.406 | 475 | 6.155 | 256 |
| NF3NLC | 29.121 | 1213 | 22.825 | 951 |

[a]The base and double elasticity objective values were $1809.625 \times 10^9$ and $2440.593 \times 10^9$, respectively. These values are not directly comparable, as the DE assumption changes the nature of the objective valuation. Only changes from the base and the DE case are intended to have meaning.

estimated elasticities to about $29.1 \times 10^9$ for the double elasticity conservation case. However, the loss per capita is only in the range $231–$1213 (1980$). This is lower than Manne's (1979) similar calculations for the United States and reflects the relatively greater Canadian energy resource base. As expected, in the double elasticity case there is less loss from the supply constraints because of the lower demand levels.

Since the model utilizes a cost-plus method for calculating prices that balance supply and demand, the resulting domestic prices of oil, and gas in particular, remain well below current and projected world prices. The results thus indicate that Canada does not need to move to the world price of oil to become self-sufficient. The problems in attaining a self-sufficient energy future, with prices reflecting Canadian resource development costs rather than world market prices, are likely to be political. "Political" is used here in the broad sense that there is a need for negotiations among the federal and provincial governments and the energy suppliers, as well as a need for the development of socio-economic incentives to replace those that would otherwise be provided by the market.

The infrastructure and resource development problems are likely to be similar whichever energy future evolves. Energy development is never easy or completely clean. The base case requires reliance on nuclear power for heat and industrial energy in the East. Other scenarios project greater reliance on coal, tar sands, and frontier oil and gas. Each energy future confronts us with the need to find ways to protect and maintain the environment. The DE case appears to delay total energy development, so energy conservation measures may provide us with about a decade longer to provide institutions for environmental protection as well as technologies for new, potentially cleaner energy sources and energy saving methods of production.


## REFERENCES

Bank of Montreal. 1980. "Data on World Oil Usage." Montreal. Mimeo.

Dewees, D.N.; R.M. Hyndman; and L. Waverman. 1975. "Gasoline Demand in Canada 1956–1972." *Energy Policy* III:116–23.

Energy, Mines and Resources Canada. 1978. *Energy Futures for Canadians*. Report EP78–1. Ottawa.

———. 1980. *The National Energy Program*. Ottawa.

Fuller, J.D. 1980. "A Long Term Energy Policy Model for Canada." Ph.D. dissertation, University of British Columbia, Vancouver.

Fuller, J.D., and W.T. Ziemba. 1980. "A Survey of Some Energy Policy Models." In W.T. Ziemba and S.L. Schwartz, eds. *Energy Policy Modeling: United States and Canadian Experiences*. Vol. II. Boston: Martinus Nijhoff Publishing.

Fuller, J.D.; S.L. Schwartz; and W.T. Ziemba. 1982. "Long Run Effects of the Canadian National Energy Program." U.B.C. Faculty of Commerce Working Paper.

Grinold, R.C. 1980. "Time Horizons in Energy Planning Models." In W.T. Ziemba and S.L. Schwartz, eds. *Energy Policy Modeling: United States and Canadian Experiences*. Vol. II. Boston: Martinus Nijhoff Publishing.

Helliwell, J.F. 1979. "Canadian Energy Policy." *Annual Review of Energy* 4: 175–229.

Helliwell, J.F., and R.N. McRae. 1981. "The National Energy Conflict." *Canadian Public Policy* 7: 15–23.

Jenkins, G.F. 1977. "Capital in Canada: Its Social and Private Performance 1965–1974." Discussion Paper No. 92. Ottawa: Economic Council of Canada.

Kydes, A.S. 1980. "The Brookhaven Energy System Optimization Model: Its Variants and Uses." In W.T. Ziemba and S.L. Schwartz, eds. *Energy Policy Modeling: United States and Canadian Experiences*. Vol. II. Boston: Martinus Nijhoff Publishing.

Manne, A.S. 1979. "Long-Term Energy Projections for the U.S.A." Stanford, California: Department of Operations Research, Stanford University. Mimeo.

Manne, A.S.; R.G. Richels; and J.P. Weyant. 1979. "Energy Policy Modeling: A Survey." *Operations Research* 27: 1–36.

Sahi, R.K. 1979. "Transportation Sector in the EMR IFSD Model." Ottawa: EMR report, February 15.

———. 1980. Personal communication.

Sahi, R.K., and R.W. Erdmann. 1980. "A Policy Model of Canadian Interfuel Substitution Demands." In W.T. Ziemba, S.L. Schwartz, and E. Koenigsberg, eds., *En-*

*ergy Policy Modeling: United States and Canadian Experiences.* Vol. I. Boston: Martinus Nijhoff Publishing.

Scarfe, B.L. 1981. "The Federal Budget and Energy Program, October 28, 1980: A Review." *Canadian Public Policy* 7: 1–14.

Statistics Canada. (Various Years). "Detailed Energy Supply and Demand in Canada." Catalog No. 57-207. Ottawa.

Ziemba, W. T.; S. L. Schwartz; and E. Koenigsberg, eds. 1980. *Energy Policy Modeling: United States and Canadian Experiences.* Vol. I. Boston: Martinus Nijhoff Publishing.

Ziemba, W. T., and S. L. Schwartz, eds. 1980. *Energy Policy Modeling: United States and Canadian Experiences.* Vol. II. Boston: Martinus Nijhoff Publishing.

# 5 SOME PROBLEMS AND ISSUES IN BUILDING ECONOMETRIC MODELS OF ENERGY DEMAND

*Lester D. Taylor*
*Department of Economics*
*University of Arizona*
*Gail R. Blattenberger*
*Department of Economics*
*University of Utah*
*Robert K. Rennhack*
*Yale University*

## INTRODUCTION

This chapter focuses on the techniques and procedures used in a recent study (Taylor, Blattenberger, and Rennhack 1981) of residential energy demand in the United States to overcome the problems caused by multipart tariffs in the sale of electricity and natural gas. The conventional theory of consumer choice, on which most empirical demand studies are based, assumes that the price of a good is independent of the amount that is purchased. However, this is not the case for goods that are sold on multipart tariffs or that are subject to quantity discounts. Electricity is a prime example, for electricity is sold in most parts of the world on some form of a block tariff in which the price of electricity varies on the margin, usually downward. Because price can no longer be represented by a single parameter, this creates a number of problems for the empirical analysis of demand.

The discussion in the first section of the chapter will concentrate on the theoretical properties of individual demand functions in the face of a decreasing block tariff. Among other things, the demand functions are discon-

We are grateful to the participants in the seminar and to an anonymous referee for comments and critique and to Sonja Eskind for her cheerful and efficient secretarial assistance.

149

tinuous and multivalued, but these are problems that tend to disappear with aggregation. The second section is devoted to a discussion of the various ways that a decreasing block rate schedule can be represented in an econometric equation. Problems of aggregating over the customers on the same rate schedule and then across different schedules are also discussed. Finally, the third section contains some empirical results for residential electricity consumption in the United States. Although the focus in the chapter is on electricity demand and U.S. data are used in illustration, the methods and techniques that are discussed are applicable to any good or service that is sold on a multipart tariff, whether in a developed or developing country.

## CONSUMER EQUILIBRIUM UNDER MULTIPART TARIFFS[1]

The economics of multipart tariffs, of which decreasing block pricing is a special case, is not a simple subject, and there remains much to be learned. However, the implications of multipart tariffs for the theory of consumer choice are now well understood, and while the details are complex, the key ideas and results can be readily grasped in a few simple diagrams. For simplicity, let us assume that a consumer purchases just two goods, electricity $q$ and a composite good $z$. Electricity is supplied on a decreasing block rate schedule with $n$ blocks, while $z$ can be purchased in unlimited quantities at a constant price $p$. Let $r_i$ denote the price of electricity in the $i$th block of the rate schedule, and let $(k_i, k_{i+1})$ denote the kWh demarcations for the $i$th block. Obviously, $k_1 = 0$, and since the last block is open ended, we shall take $k_{n+1}$ to be infinite. Finally, let the consumer's income be denoted by $x$. The budget constraint will accordingly take the form

$$\sum_{i=1}^{j-1} r_i(k_{i+1}-k_i) + r_j(q-k_j) + pz = x, \tag{5.1}$$

where it is assumed that equilibrium occurs in the $j$th block of the rate schedule.

Let

$$h(q) = \sum_{i=1}^{j-1} r_i(k_{i+1}-k_i) + r_j(q-k_j) \tag{5.2}$$

1. The discussion in this section is based primarily on Taylor (1975) and Blattenberger (1977).

denote the expenditure for electricity. By subtracting and adding the quantity $\sum_{i=1}^{j-1} r_j(k_{i+1}-k_i)$, $h(q)$ can be rewritten as

$$
\begin{aligned}
h(q) &= \sum_{i=1}^{j-1} (r_i-r_j)(k_{i+1}-k_i) + r_j \sum_{i=1}^{j-1} (k_{i+1}-k_i) + r_j(q-k_j) \\
&= \sum_{i=1}^{j-1} (r_i-r_j)(k_{i+1}-k_i) + r_j(k_j-k_1) + r_j(q-k_j) \\
&= \sum_{i=1}^{j-1} (r_i-r_j)(k_{i+1}-k_i) + r_j q,
\end{aligned}
\tag{5.3}
$$

since $k_1 = 0$. In the last line of equations (5.3), $r_j q$ represents the amount that would be spent for electricity if the $q$ kWh that are consumed could all be purchased at the price in the marginal block $r_j$. The quantity $\sum_{i=1}^{j-1} (r_i-r_j)(k_{i+1}-k_i)$, on the other hand, represents the "intramarginal premium" that has to be paid as a result of $r_i > r_j$. Let this premium be denoted by $y$. The budget constraint in equation (5.1) can therefore be rewritten as

$$
y + r_j q + pz = x
\tag{5.4}
$$

In order to illustrate graphically what is involved, let us assume that the rate schedule for electricity has the form:

| | |
|---|---|
| first $k_2$ kWh or less | $r_o$ |
| $k_2$ to $k_3$ kWh | $r_2/\text{kWh}$ |
| more than $k_3$ kWh | $r_3/\text{kWh}$ |

where $r_2 > r_3$.[2] It will be assumed that the first part of the tariff $r_o$ must be paid even if no electricity is used. The budget constraint will accordingly be given by

$$
r_o + \delta_1(r_2,q,k_2,k_3) + \delta_2(r_3,q,k_3) + pz = x
\tag{5.5}
$$

where

---

2. This rate schedule differs slightly from the one described by equation (5.1) in that the first block is rolled into a fixed (or customer) charge.

$$\delta_1(r_2, q, k_2, k_3) \quad = \quad \begin{array}{ll} 0 & \text{if } q \leq k_2 \\ r_2(q - k_2) & \text{if } k_2 < q < k_3 \\ r_2(k_3 - k_2) & \text{if } q > k_3 \end{array} \qquad (5.6)$$

$$\delta_1(r_3, q, k_3) \quad = \quad \begin{array}{ll} 0 & \text{if } q \leq k_3 \\ r_3(q - k_3) & \text{if } q > k_3 \end{array} \qquad (5.7)$$

The graph of the budget constraint is given in Figure 5–1. The horizontal segment of the constraint corresponds to the fixed charge of $r_0$ for consumption of the first $k_2$kWh. The linear segment between $k_2$ and $k_3$ has a slope equal to $-r_2/p$ and corresponds to the $r_2$ part of the rate schedule. Finally, the segment from $k_3$ on, with a slope equal to $-r_3/p$, corresponds to the $r_3$ part of the schedule.

The nonlinear, nonconvex budget constraint has a number of implications for the equilibrium of the consumer, his demand functions, and Engel curves. These will be illustrated with the aid of Figures 5–2 through 5–7 (taken from Taylor 1975). Figure 5–2 shows equilibria for two different indifference maps. The indifference map with solid curves yields an equilibrium on the facet of the budget constraint with slope equal to $-r_2/p$, while the indifference map with dashed curves has an equilibrium on the facet with slope equal to $-r_3/p$. Figure 5–3 describes an increase in $r_2$ but not $r_3$,

**Figure 5–1.    Budget Constraint with Decreasing Block Pricing.**

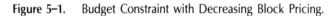

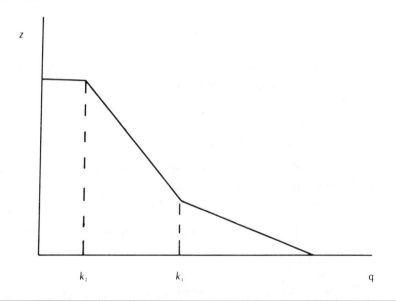

**Figure 5–2.**     Consumer Equilibria with Decreasing Block Pricing.

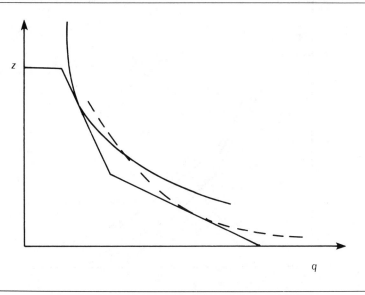

**Figure 5–3.**     Effect of a Change in Intramarginal Price.

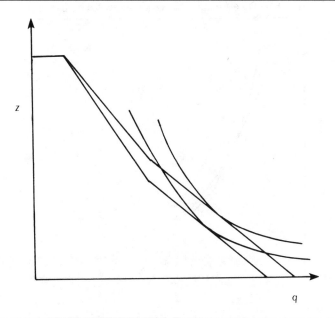

**Figure 5–4.**    Effect of a Change in both Intramarginal and Marginal Price.

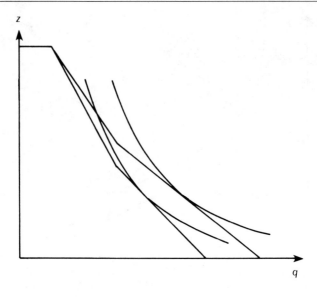

**Figure 5–5.**    Price Change that Leads to Switching Blocks.

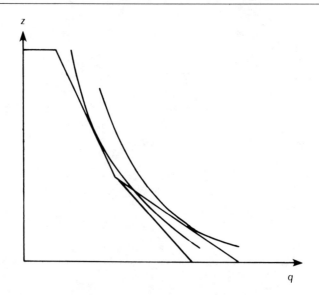

**Figure 5–6.** Effect of an Income Change.

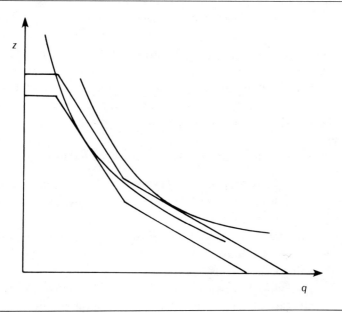

**Figure 5–7.** Multiple Equilibria.

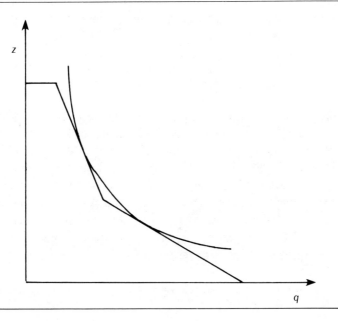

while Figure 5–4 displays an increase in $r_3$ as well as an increase in $r_2$. In these two figures, the equilibrium following the price increases remains on the same facet of the budget constraint. However, it is clear from Figure 5–5 that this need not always be the case, for in this figure we see that the increase in $r_3$ causes the consumer to drop back to a higher marginal rate class. Moreover, as it evident in Figure 5–6, switching into a different rate class can also be brought about by a change in income. Finally, Figure 5–7 depicts a case in which the budget constraint is tangent to the same indifference curve at two different points, thereby resulting in multiple equilibria.

From Figures 5–3 through 5–7, we can draw the following conclusions:

1.  Because of the piecewise linearity of the budget constraint, the equilibrium of the consumer cannot be derived, as is conventionally the case, using differential calculus. While the demand functions and Engel curves still exist, they cannot be derived analytically through solution of the first-order conditions for utility maximization. Moreover, this is true for all goods, not just for electricity.

2.  From Figure 5–5, it is evident that the demand functions are discontinuous, with gaps at the points where the equilibrium switches from one facet of the budget constraint to another.

3.  From Figure 5–6, the same is seen to be true for the Engel curves.

4.  Finally, from Figure 5–7, it is seen that there will be particular configurations of prices for which the demand functions are not single valued. This follows from the nonconvexity of the budget constraint. In particular, the demand functions will be multivalued whenever there is a configuration of prices that yields multiple tangencies of the budget constraint to the same indifference curve.[3]

By far the most detailed examination of the nature of demand functions under decreasing block pricing has been undertaken by Blattenberger (1977). Blattenberger's analysis is for the general case of a rate schedule containing $n$ blocks. She derives and justifies mathematically all of the conclusions just stated and in particular shows that the number of discontinuities in the demand functions when demand is a function of the $j$th block price can never exceed $n - j + 1$. It is also shown that the number of values that a demand function can take at a point of discontinuity is at most $n$. The basic requirement for these results to hold is that the preference rela-

---

3. For a given set of prices, there may also exist a level of income for which the Engel curves are discontinuous and multivalued.

tions of the consumer satisfy a set of axioms that are sufficient for continuity of the ordinary demand function.[4]

The fact that the demand functions with a multipart tariff are discontinuous and multivalued clearly creates a problem for empirical analysis. Econometric analysis requires the use of an analytic function, but the demand functions in this case are correspondences and thus cannot be represented analytically. This is clearly a problem when the data being analyzed refer to the individual households, but it can be shown that the discontinuities tend to disappear when the data refer to a large aggregate of consumers. Specifically, it can be shown that as one aggregates over a group of consumers, the mean demand function for the group is continuous in the limit as the group becomes large.[5] The conditions for this theorem to hold are that tastes or income must vary across consumers in such a way that the probability of a discontinuity at any point in the price set be equal to zero. As far as we know, any reasonable distribution of tastes or income will yield this result as the number of consumers becomes large. Strictly speaking, "large" in this context refers to infinity, but experimental evidence suggests that the mean demand functions may be reasonably continuous for as few as twelve consumers (see Rassenti 1979). Thus, discontinuities appear to present little cause for concern with aggregate data. However, with disaggregate data, the only solution at the moment appears to be to work directly with the first-order conditions (see Wade 1980).

Discontinuities to the side, let us now turn to the way that rate schedules under decreasing block pricing are to be represented in the electricity demand function. To set the stage, consider the following three cases:

1.  An increase in the customer charge $r_0$, $r_2$, and $r_3$ remaining unchanged;
2.  An increase in $r_2$, $r_0$, and $r_3$ remaining unchanged;
3.  An increase in $r_3$, $r_0$, and $r_2$ remaining unchanged.

These cases are illustrated in Figures 5–8, 5–3, and 5–9, respectively.

In Figure 5–8, the increase in $r_0$ shifts the budget constraint downward and accordingly leads to a reduction in the amount of electricity that is consumed. In Figures 5–3 and 5–9, it is seen that increases in $r_2$ and $r_3$ also cause a reduction in $q$. However, it will be noted—and this is the point of the exercise—that the reductions in $q$ in Cases 1 and 2 arise strictly from an income effect. In other words, an increase in the customer charge or an

4. The ordinary demand functions in this context refer to the demand functions that would obtain if electricity were not sold on a multipart tariff.

5. The proof of this theorem is given in Blattenberger (1977).

**Figure 5–8.**    Effect of a Change in the Fixed Charge.

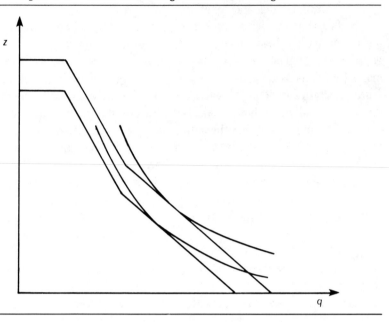

**Figure 5–9.**    Effect of a Change in the Marginal Price.

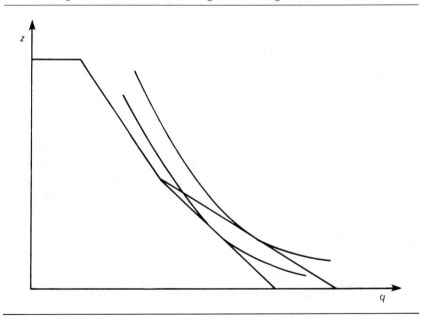

increase in the intramarginal price are equivalent in the sense that they give rise to income effects, but not to substitution effects.[6]  In contrast, a change in $r_3$, the marginal price, yields both an income effect and a substitution effect. Thus, it is clear that it is necessary to treat changes in intramarginal rates separately from a change in the marginal rate.[7]

The budget constraint defined in equation (5.4) provides the appropriate vehicle for doing this. A price change that affects intramarginal rates will show up as a change in the intramarginal premium $y$, while a change that affects the marginal rate will be reflected in a change in $r_j$, since equilibrium is assumed to occur in the $j$th block. In particular, we see that an increase in an intramarginal rate will lead to an increase in $y$, while a decrease in an intramarginal rate will lead to a decrease in $y$. In neither case, however, is the marginal rate $r_j$ affected—unless, of course, the change in an intramarginal price is sufficiently large to cause a switch in blocks.

In Figure 5–10, we have redrawn the budget constraint in Figure 5–1 to correspond to equation (5.4), although we shall now put income, $x$, on the vertical axis, rather than expenditure on all other goods. The customer charge $r_o$ is represented by the distance $ab$ on the vertical axis, while the intramarginal premium $y$ is represented by the distance $ac$. It is clear from the figure that an increase in the intramarginal premium, whether it arises from an increase in $r_o$ or an increase in $r^2$, is indistinguishable from a decrease in income and vice versa for a decrease in the intramarginal premium. In other words, we have

$$\frac{\partial q}{\partial y} = -\frac{\partial q}{\partial x} \tag{5.8}$$

In view of this, one can define the budget constraint as $x - y$, a quantity that Howrey (1979) has referred to as adjusted income.

Changes in the intramarginal premium that arise from a change in the customer charge or a change in an intramarginal rate do not affect the marginal rate, but a change in the marginal rate does affect the intramarginal premium. For, from the definition of $y$,

$$y = \sum_{i=1}^{j-1} (r_i - r_j)(k_{i+1} - k_i) \tag{5.9}$$

6. The only qualification to this statement arises in the situation where the increase in $r_2$ is sufficiently large that equilibrium shifts from the $r_3$ block to the $r_2$ block. In this case, it can be argued that there will be a substitution effect as well as an income effect.

7. Marginal and intramarginal in this context are defined with respect to the block in which the consumer is initially in equilibrium.

Figure 5–10.    Two-Part Tariff Representation of the Budget Constraint.

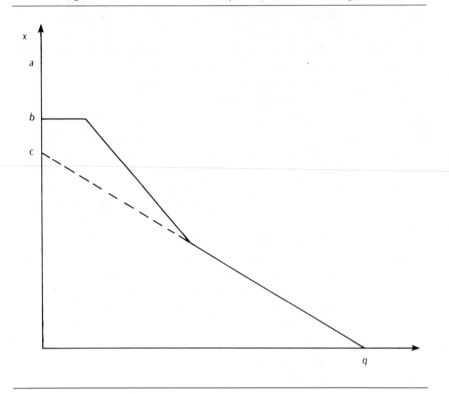

so that

$$\frac{\partial y}{\partial r_j} = - \sum_{i=1}^{j-1} (k_{i+1} - k_i)$$

$$= - k_j \qquad (5.10)$$

since $k_1 = 0$.

A fairly standard practice is to use the ex post average price, calculated by dividing the total expenditure for electricity by the number of kWh sold, for the price variable in the electricity demand function. As has been recognized by Houthakker (1951), Halvorsen (1975, 1976), and others, this leads to problems of simultaneity. For a price schedule with decreasing block tariffs means, in effect, that the consumer faces a downward sloping supply schedule, defined with respect to average price, and this has led to the conclusion that equilibrium is at the price and quantity where demand and "supply" are equal. The apparent details are presented in Figure 5–11. We say "apparent" for, unless interpreted with a great deal of care, this is an erroneous conclusion.

The problem is that while the "supply" function for a given rate schedule is well defined, the demand function (multivaluedness and discontinuities aside) as a function of average price does not exist as a function, but only as a point—in particular, as the point in Figure 5–11 where $D$ crosses $S$. The curve $S$ is defined as the locus of points $(q, \bar{r})$, where

$$\bar{r} = \frac{R(q)}{q} \tag{5.11}$$

and $R(q)$ denotes the expenditure for $q$ kWh of electricity as determined by the rate schedule. The point $S$ finally selected by the consumer will be the $q$, and hence the corresponding $r$, where utility is maximized. However, for a

**Figure 5–11.**    "Supply" and "Demand" with Decreasing Block Pricing.

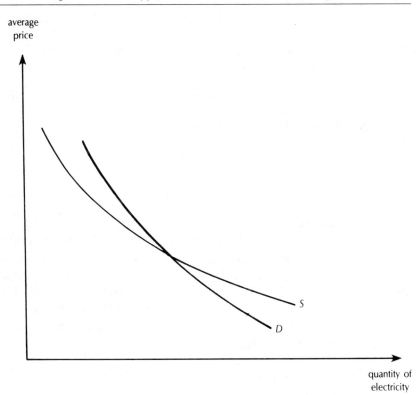

given rate schedule, there is only one equilibrium pair of $q$ and $\bar{r}$. Consequently, to define $q$ as a function of $\bar{r}$ as in the curve $D$ in Figure 5–11 requires a family of rate schedules. In other words, quantity demanded as a function of average price has to be defined as a locus of equilibrium pairs $[q(\alpha), \bar{r}(\alpha)]$, where $\alpha$ is an index representing a family of rate schedules.

We are thus brought to the problem (first pointed out by Houthakker 1951) that arises when electricity consumption is regressed on the ex post average price. Because the amount of electricity consumed and average price are related arithmetically through the rate schedule, one cannot distinguish between the price slope of the demand function and the slope of the "supply" function. The solution proposed by Halvorsen (1975, 1976) is to specify a second equation that explains average price as a function of supply side cost variables and then to treat the demand function and the average price function as a two-equation system of simultaneous equations. For illustrations, let us assume that the demand for electricity as a function of income $x$ and average price $\bar{r}$ is given by

$$q = \alpha \, x^\beta \, \bar{r}^\gamma \qquad (5.12)$$

Further, let us assume that the relationship between $\bar{r}$ and $q$ from the rate schedule can be approximated by

$$\bar{r} = a \, q^\lambda \qquad (5.13)$$

Taking logarithms of both equations, we have

$$\ln q = \alpha^* + \beta \ln x + \gamma \ln \bar{r} \qquad (5.14)$$

$$\ln \bar{r} = a^* + \lambda \ln q \qquad (5.15)$$

where $\alpha^* = \ln \alpha$ and $a^* = a$.

As these equations stand, the average price function [equation (5.15)] is identified, but not the demand function [equation (5.14)]. In order for the demand function to be identified, information that is independent of demand has to be introduced into the average price function. One way of doing this is by postulating the parameters $a^*$ and $\lambda$ to be functions of supply side cost variables.[8] Let $c_1, \ldots c_m$ denote such a set of variables, so that $a^* = a^*(c_1, \ldots c_m)$, $\lambda = \lambda(c_1, \ldots c_m)$, and

$$\ln \bar{r} = a^*(c_1, \ldots c_m) + \lambda(c_1, \ldots c_m) \ln q \qquad (5.16)$$

---

8. Variables representing the regulatory authority may also be relevent.

Halvorsen's procedure is to linearize the right-hand side of this equation, so that

$$\ln \bar{r} = \delta_0 + \delta_1 c_1 + \ldots + \delta_m c_m + \xi \ln q \qquad (5.17)$$

The demand function in equation (5.15) is now identified and can accordingly be estimated by two-stage least squares (or some other appropriate method). An alternatuve procedure is to obtain estimates of $a^*$ and $\lambda$ directly from actual rate schedules and then to use these estimates as predictors in the reduced form equation for $\ln q$. Accordingly, let us return to equations (5.14) and (5.15) and solve them for $\ln q$. We have

$$\ln q = \frac{a^* + \gamma a^*}{1 - \gamma \lambda} + \frac{\beta}{1 - \gamma \lambda} \ln x \qquad (5.18)$$

Given estimates $a^*$ and $\lambda$, $a^*$, $\beta$, and $\gamma$ can be estimated by nonlinear least squares.

To this point, we have discussed three different approaches that can be used in circumventing the problems caused by decreasing block pricing. The first of these represents the rate schedule in the demand function by the marginal price and the intramarginal premium. This method will be referred to as the fixed charge/marginal price (FC/MP) approach. The second and third approaches involve a two-equation simultaneous equations model in which the focus in on demand as a function of average price. Besides the demand function, a "supply" function is specified that describes the relationship (via the rate schedule) between quantity and average price. In Halvorsen's approach, the demand function is identified by assuming average price to be a function of supply side cost variables that are exogenous to demand and then estimating the demand function by two-stage least squares. The alternative is to estimate the parameters of the demand function through the reduced form equation for quantity. The demand function is then identified by estimating the parameters of the average price function with data from actual rate schedules. This last procedure will be referred to as the average price (AP) approach.

Before leaving this section, it is useful to observe as a historical note that Buchanan (1952–53) and Gabor (1955–56) clearly understood the theoretical implications of block tariffs and quantity discounts. However, the contributions of Buchanan and Gabor went unnoticed in the econometric literature, which is unfortunate because, had the insights in Houthakker's 1951 paper been integrated into their theoretical structures, much of the sterile debate of the last twenty-five years concerning which price—marginal or average—

to include in the demand function could have been avoided. Buchanan, among other things, pointed out the ambiguities surrounding the demand function in the presence of quantity discounts, while Gabor's contribution was to show that any multipart tariff can be replaced by an equivalent two-part tariff. Indeed, Gabor's theorem provides the theoretical basis for the fixed charge/marginal price method of parameterizing a rate schedule.[9] Finally, it should also be mentioned that the problems associated with decreasing block pricing for electricity and natural gas are similar to the problems associated with overtime and a progressive income tax in the context of labor-supply models (see Burtless and Hausman [1978] for a discussion).

## CONSTRUCTION OF THE PRICE VARIABLES FOR ELECTRICITY AND NATURAL GAS

We have seen that overcoming the problems caused by decreasing block pricing requires either the use of a simultaneous equations model in which the average price is assumed endogenous or the use of price variables that are constructed from actual rate schedules. The latter has been adopted in the present effort, and in this section we shall describe the ways in which the price variables for electricity and natural gas have been constructed in analyzing the residential demand for electricity in the United States.

The raw input in both cases is the actual rate schedules that residential customers faced during the period of the sample. The rate schedules for electricity have been obtained from the *National Electric Rate Book,* which is published annually by the U.S. Federal Energy Regulatory Commission, while the rate schedules for natural gas have been obtained from publications of the American Gas Association.

We have discussed two methods by which a rate schedule can be incorporated into a demand function. With the fixed charge/marginal price method, the rate schedule is represented by two quantities, the rate in the marginal block and the difference between what the consumer actually pays

---

9. Taylor notes that in his 1975 survey article, he had not grasped the full implications of Gabor's theorem and suggested that a rate schedule be represented by the marginal price and the intramarginal expenditure, as opposed to the intramarginal premium. Nordin (1976) set the record straight, as did also Blattenberger (1977). Finally, we should also note that in early 1976, Professor Aly Ercelawn of Quaid-e-Azam University in Islamabad, Pakistan, brought to Taylor's attention that many of the problems associated with decreasing block pricing were discussed in his Ph.D. dissertation (Ercelawn 1974).

for the electricity purchased and the amount that would be paid if the marginal rate applied throughout the schedule. With the average price method, the average price function (i.e., average price as a function of quantity is calculated from the rate schedule) is approximated by a double logarithmic function, and the least squares coefficients of this function are then included as independent variables in the demand function. In both cases, the parameterization is straightforward and unambiguous.

However, problems arise when, as in the present effort, the unit of observation is a state and one has to aggregate over both customers and rate schedules. Aggregating over customers creates the most problems, for once the customers on a given rate schedule have been dealt with, one can aggregate across schedules using customers as weights. The problems in aggregating across customers arise from the fact that since rate schedules are common to large numbers of customers, one cannot unambiguously identify a block in a rate schedule as being the marginal block. Any given block can be marginal to one group of customers, intramarginal to a second group of customers, and extramarginal to still a third group.

Two methods have been used in aggregating over customers on the same schedule. The first method involves parameterizing the rate schedule in terms of total revenue as a function of quantity and then defining the marginal price as the slope of this function and the fixed charge as its intercept. The second method involves identifying a "typical" customer on the schedule and then defining the marginal price and the fixed charge in terms of the block that contains this customer. The preferred way of defining the marginal price with this latter method would be to take a weighted average of rates across blocks using numbers of customers as weights. However, U.S. utilities as a rule report only the total number of customers on a schedule, so that a true weighted average marginal price cannot be calculated. Our procedure, instead, has been to associate the marginal block with the block that contains the observed mean number of kWhs purchased by the customers on the schedule. The marginal price and the fixed charge are then calculated with respect to this block. The marginal price and the fixed charge for a state as a whole are then obtained as weighted averages of the marginal prices and fixed charges across the schedules in the state using the number of customers on each schedule as weights.

Provided that a linear function gives a good approximation to the total revenue function, the first method is in principle superior to the one that has just been described because it is free of simultaneity bias. With the second method, the marginal block is determined ex post by the observed mean consumption, and this could lead to a simultaneous equations bias if the rate schedules are steeply stepped. Fortunately, with the U.S. data, a linear function turns out to provide a very good approximation to the total revenue function for electricity, and the first method has accordingly been used in parameterizing all of the electricity schedules. However, for reasons that need not be gone into here, the second method has been used in parameterizing the rate schedules for natural gas.

We shall now turn to the complications that arise in aggregating over customers and rate schedules and the ways we have dealt with these complications.

## The Fixed Charge/Marginal Price Approach: Method 1

Let $R(q)$ denote the revenue, as determined by the rate schedule, that is generated by the sale of $q$ kWh of electricity—that is,

$$R(q) = \sum_{i=1}^{j-1} r_i(k_{i+1} - k_i) + r_j(q - k_j) \tag{5.19}$$

where, as in the preceding section, $(k_i, k_{i+1})$ denotes the kWh demarcations for the $i$th block, $r_i$ denotes the rate in this block, and $q > k_j$. This function is defined for an individual rate schedule, and its position and shape obviously depend upon the rates and block demarcations of the schedule. $R(q)$ will be referred to as the total revenue function.

The next step is to define a mean total revenue function for a state as a whole. Let this be denoted by $\bar{R}(q)$. Formally, $\bar{R}(q)$ is defined as

$$\bar{R}(q) = \sum_{i=1}^{m} w_i R_i(q) \tag{5.20}$$

where $R_i(q)$ is the total revenue function for the $i$th rate schedule in the state, $m$ denotes the total number of schedules, and

$$w_i = \frac{\text{number of customers on schedule } i}{\text{total number of customers in the state}} \tag{5.21}$$

The next (and critical) step is to approximate the function $R(q)$ by a function that is linear in $q$,

$$\bar{R}(q) = a + bq + u \tag{5.22}$$

where $a$ and $b$ are parameters and $u$ is the approximation error. The parameters $a$ and $b$ are estimated by a least squares regression of $\bar{R}(q)$ on $q$, using values of $\bar{R}(q)$, as calculated from equation (5.20). With the U.S. data, this has been done for 290 values of $q$ between 50 and 1,500 kWh in increments of 5 kWh. The marginal price is obtained from the total revenue function by differentiation with respect to $q$. With a linear approximation, this derivative is a constant, so that the marginal price is independent of the amount of electricity that is consumed. This is an extremely important result, for it rules out any possibility of simultaneity bias. The marginal price is thus represented by the parameter $b$, while the intramarginal premium is represented by the intercept $a$ and is readily interpreted as a fixed charge.

The time unit of observation in the U.S. analysis is a year, so that the total revenue function defined in equation (5.19) also involves an aggregation over time. For illustration, let us assume that the customers in a particular service area in a particular year faced two rate schedules, the first in effect from January 1 to August 15 and the second from August 15 to December 31. Let $R^1(q)$ denote the total revenue function for the first schedule and $R^2(q)$ that for the second schedule. The total revenue function for the year, $R(q)$, will therefore be defined (ignoring leap years) as

$$R(q) = \frac{1}{365} \left[ 227 \ R^1(q) + 138 \ R^2 \ (q) \right]$$

$$(5.23)$$

where 227 represents the number of days that the first schedule was in effect, while 138 represents the number of days for the second schedule. In general, for a service area that has $m$ rate schedules in a year, the total revenue function for the year will be defined as

$$R(q) = \sum_{\iota=1}^{m} t_i R^i(q)$$

$$(5.24)$$

where $t_i$ denotes the proportion of the year that the $i$th rate schedule is in effect and $R^i(q)$ denotes the total revenue function for this schedule.

Equation (5.22) was estimated for each state for each of the years in our sample. This yielded a set of 768 estimates of $a$ and $b$ (forty-eight states and sixteen years) that was subsequently used as "observations" for the fixed charge and the marginal price. These mean $R^2$s for these regressions are greater than 0.99 for forty-six of the forty-eight contiguous states, so that fits are tight. In addition, spot checks of the residuals from a number of individual equations fail to reveal any systematic departures from linearity.

Consequently, a linear approximation to the total revenue function appears to be a very good assumption for the rate schedules in the U.S. data set.

## The Fixed Charge/Marginal Price Approach: Method 2

Let us now turn to the procedure for constructing the fixed charge and the marginal price that was used extensively in the preliminary stages of the U.S. study, which involved identifying a particular block in a schedule as the marginal block and then calculating the marginal price and the intramarginal premium with respect to this block. As noted, our preference was to define the marginal price as a weighted average of the rates in the schedule or, alternatively as the rate in the block containing the plurality of customers. However, both of these procedures require the distribution of customers across blocks—information that utilities as a rule do not publish. In general, the information that is available consists of the observed mean level of consumption, the observed mean level of expenditure, and the observed mean expenditure per kWh. The problem, therefore, is how best to approximate the modal level of consumption using this information.

Figure 5–12 depicts an individual's expenditure for electricity, $R(q)$, as a function of quantity, $q$, for a hypothetical decreasing block rate schedule. The observed mean level of consumption, $q$, and the observed mean level of expenditure, $E$, are also shown on the graph.[10] The concavity of $R(q)$, which reflects the decreasing block rate schedule, implies that $R(q) > E$. The point $q^o$ on the horizontal axis indicates the level of consumption at which the cost of electricity, as calculated from the rate schedule, is equal to the observed mean level of expenditure—namely, $R(q^o) = \bar{E}$. Finally, the point $q'$ on the horizontal axis indicates the level of consumption at which the average price of electricity per kWh is equal to the observed average price— namely, $R(q')/q' = \bar{E}/\bar{q}$. Since $\bar{E} < R(\bar{q})$ and $R(q)$ is monotonic and concave, it follows that $q^o < \bar{q} < q'$. Since the distribution of customers across rate classes is observed to be skewed to the right, the modal level of consumption is necessarily less than $\bar{q}$. Consequently, modal consuption is better approximated by $q^o$ or $\bar{q}$ than by $q'$. In most of our empirical work, the marginal price has been identified with the block that contains $\bar{q}$. The foregoing can

10. We should emphasize that $R(q)$ is the total revenue function for the hypothetical rate schedule as defined by equation (5.19), whereas $.q$ and $\bar{E}$ are calculated with reference to the customers who consume on the rate schedule.

**Figure 5–12.**   Total Revenue Function for a Decreasing Block Rate Schedule.

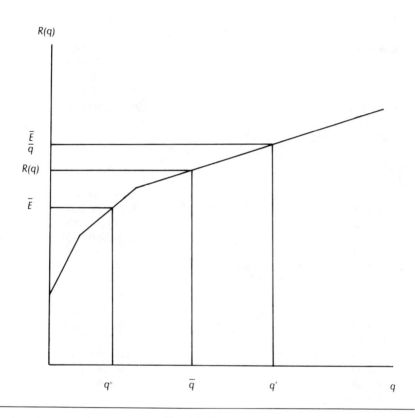

be usefully illustreated with an example involving three rate districts, as shown in Table 5–1.

With the method of this subsection, the total revenue function is accordingly approximated by

$$\hat{R}(q) = r_o + r_1 q \qquad (5.25)$$

where $\hat{R}(q)$ denotes the approximation to $R(q)$, $r_o$ denotes the intramarginal premium, and $r_1$ denotes the marginal price. Table 5–2 tabulates the values of $r_o$ and $r_1$ corresponding to the three alternative ways of selecting the marginal block for the rate schedules given above. Note that the three methods yield the same marginal blocks, except for *rate schedule 2*, for which $\bar{q}'$ lies in a higher block than $\bar{q}$ and $q^o$.

**Table 5–1.**  Modal Consumption Estimates for Alternative Rate
Schedules.

Rate Schedule 1

| | |
|---|---|
| $1.50 | <       15 kWh |
| 4.40¢/kWh | 15 to    70 kWh |
| 3.00¢/kWh | 70 to   150 kWh |
| 2.50¢/kWh | 150 to   300 kWh |
| 2.00¢/kWh | 300 to   500 kWh |
| 1.60¢/kWh | 500 to 2,000 kWh |
| 1.45¢/kWh | ≥     2,000 kWh |

$q = 350$ kWh $N = 50,000$ customers $E = \$10.40$

Rate Schedule 2

| | |
|---|---|
| $1.60 | <       20 kWh |
| 5.40¢/kWh | 20 to    50 kWh |
| 3.50¢/kWh | 50 to   200 kWh |
| 2.70¢/kWh | 200 to   600 kWh |
| 2.20¢/kWh | 600 to 2,000 kWh |
| 1.80¢/kWh | ≥     2,000 kWh |

$q = 450$ kWh $N = 50,000$ customers $E = \$12.15$

Rate Schedule 3

| | |
|---|---|
| $0.75 | <       10 kWh |
| 5.50¢/kWh | 10 to    55 kWh |
| 3.00¢/kWh | 55 to   110 kWh |
| 2.50¢/kWh | 110 to   500 kWh |
| 2.00¢/kWh | 500 to 1,000 kWh |
| 1.70¢/kWh | ≥     1,000 kWh |

$q = 558$ kWh $N = 50,000$ customers $E = \$15.36$

Note: Data in table correspond roughly to data for Rhode Island for 1972.

Written out in full, equation (5.25) for the three rate schedules with the
marginal block defined by $\bar{q}$ are:

$$\hat{R}(q) = 4.07 + 0.020q \text{ (rate schedule 1)} \qquad (5.26)$$

$$\hat{R}(q) = 3.07 + 0.027q \text{ (rate schedule 2)} \qquad (5.27)$$

$$\hat{R}(q) = 4.63 + 0.020q \text{ (rate schedule 3)} \qquad (5.28)$$

In aggregating to the level of the state, each of these total revenue functions
is given equal weight, since it is assumed that there are the same number of

Table 5–2.  Fixed Charges and Marginal Prices for Hypothetical Rate Schedules

| Rate Schedule | Method of Selecting Marginal Block | | |
| --- | --- | --- | --- |
| | $q$ | $q^o$ | $q'$ |
| Rate Schedule 1 | | | |
| $r_0$ | $4.07 | $4.07 | $4.07 |
| $r_1$ | 0.020 | 0.020 | 0.020 |
| Rate Schedule 2 | | | |
| $r_0$ | 3.07 | 3.07 | 6.07 |
| $r_1$ | 0.027 | 0.027 | 0.022 |
| Rate Schedule 3 | | | |
| $r_0$ | 4.63 | 4.63 | 4.63 |
| $r_1$ | 0.02 | 0.02 | 0.02 |

customers in each district—namely, 50,000. The aggregate total revenue for the state will then be given by

$$\hat{R}(q) = 3.92 + 0.0223q \tag{5.29}$$

Thus in this case, the marginal price and the intramarginal premium for the state are 2.23¢/kWh and $3.92, respectively.

## The Average Price Approach

In section two we described an alternative approach to parameterizing a decreasing block rate schedule that focuses on the average revenue function rather than on the calculation of a fixed charge and marginal price. The mechanics of this approach are very similar to those employed with Method 1 of the fixed charge/marginal price framework, the only essential difference being that the average revenue function is parameterized, rather than the total revenue function.

As in section two, let

$$\bar{r}(q) = \frac{R(q)}{q} \tag{5.30}$$

denote the average revenue function for an individual rate schedule, and let us assume that the function $r(q)$ can be approximated by a double logarithmic function

$$\ln \bar{r}(q) = \lambda_0 + \lambda_1 \ln q + u \qquad (5.31)$$

where $u$ denotes the approximation error. As with Method 1 of the FC/MP framework, the parameters $\lambda_0$ and $\lambda_1$ are estimated in a least squares regression of $\bar{r}(q)$ on $q$ using 290 points on the function $\bar{r}(q)$ in equation (5.30), calculated at values of $q$ between 50 and 1,500 kWh in increments of 5 kWh. Once again, a separate equation is estimated for each state for each year in the sample, so that estimates of the parameters $\lambda_0$ and $\lambda_1$ vary both across states and time.

The average revenue function for a state has been arrived at in the same manner as the total revenue function in the preceding section—that is, the average revenue function in a service area is obtained as a weighted average over the rate schedules in the area using as weights the proportion of the year that each schedule was in effect. The average revenue function for the state is then obtained as a weighted average across service areas using the mean numbers of customers as weights.

## AN ILLUSTRATION WITH U.S. DATA

It will be useful to illustrate the foregoing with two equations for residential electricity demand from our U.S. study. The first equation uses Method 1 of the FC/MP framework to parameterize the electricity rate schedules, while the second equation uses Method 2 of the FC/MP framework.[11] The equations are otherwise identical and are based on a double logarithmic Houthakker-Taylor flow adjustment model (see Houthakker and Taylor 1970; and Houthakker, Verleger, and Sheehan 1974) as follows:

$$
\begin{aligned}
\ln q_t = {} & \alpha_0 + \alpha_1 \ln q_{t1} + \alpha_2 \ln x_t + \alpha_3 ga_t \ln x_t + \alpha_4 \Delta ga_t \ln x_t \\
& + \alpha_5 \ln fce_t + \alpha_6 ga_t \ln fce_t + \alpha_7 \Delta ga_t \ln fce_t + \alpha_8 \ln mpe_t \\
& + \alpha_9 ga_t \ln mpe_t + \alpha_{10} \Delta ga_t \ln mpe_t + \alpha_{11} ga_t dg_t \ln fcg_t \\
& + \alpha_{12} \Delta ga_t dg_t \ln fcg_t + \alpha_{13} ga_t dg_t \ln mpg_t \\
& + \alpha_{14} \Delta ga_t dg_t \ln mpg_t + \alpha_{15} \ln po_t + \alpha_{16} ga_t \ln po_t \\
& + \alpha_{17} \Delta ga_t \ln po_t + \alpha_{18} wh_t \ln ddhd_t + \alpha_{19} ga_t wh_t \ln ddhd_t \\
& + \alpha_{20} \Delta ga_t wh_t \ln ddhd_t + \alpha_{21} wc_t \ln ddcd_t + \alpha_{22} ga_t wc_t \ln ddcd_t \\
& + \alpha_{23} \Delta ga_t wc_t \ln ddcd_t + \alpha_{24} ga_t + \alpha_{25} \Delta ga_t + u_t \qquad (5.32)
\end{aligned}
$$

where

---

11. Equations estimated using the AP framework are not reported here, but may be found in Blattenberger (1977) and Taylor, Blattenberger and Rennhack (1981).

$q$ = electricity sales per customer (kWh/month);

$x$ = personal income per customer (in 1972 dollars);

$ga$ = availability of natural gas, defined as the proportion of a state's population that has access to pipeline-delivered natural gas;

$\Delta ga$ = first difference in $ga$;

$fce$ = fixed charge for electricity, calculated according to Method 1 (or Method 2) as described in section two (in 1972 dollars);

$mpe$ = marginal price for electricity, calculated according to Method 1 (or Method 2) as described in section two (cents/kWh in 1972 dollars);

$dg$ = a dummy variable denoting high gas availability combined with significant penetration of all electric homes (1 for Florida, Oregon, Tennessee, Washington, and West Virginia);

$fcg$ = fixed charge for natural gas, calculated according to Method 2 as described in section two (in 1972 dollars);

$mpg$ = marginal price for natural gas, calculated according to Method 2 as described in section two (cents/therm in 1972 dollars);

$po$ = price of fuel oil (1972 = 100, in 1972 dollars);

$w_h$ = proportion of homes in a state that are all electric;

$ddhd$ = ratio of heating degree days to normal heating degree days, where normal heating degree days for a state are defined as the mean heating degree days for the sample period;

$w_c$ = proportion of homes in a state that have central air conditioning; and

$ddcd$ = ratio of cooling degree days to normal cooling degree days, where normal heating degree days for a state are defined as the mean cooling degree days for the sample period.

The only definitions that require further elaboration are the fixed charges for electricity and natural gas, as these are defined as one minus the ratio of the intramarginal premium to personal income. This way of defining the fixed charge allows one to test the hypothesis (implied by the conventional theory of consumer choice) that the impacts on demand of equal changes in the intramarginal premium and income are the same except for sign. To see this, let $x$ and $\pi^o$ denote income and the intramarginal premium. Then

$$
\begin{aligned}
\ln(x - \pi_o) &= \ln[x(1 - \pi_o/x)] \\
&= \ln x + \ln(1 - \pi_o/x) \\
&= \ln x + \ln fce
\end{aligned}
\tag{5.33}
$$

where $fce = 1 - \pi^o/x$. Consequently, if consumers view the intramarginal premium as a subtraction from income, the coefficient for $\ln fce$ should be minus the coefficient for $\ln x$. This can be tested as a hypothesis.[12]

The data set used in estimation consists of annual observations on the forty-eight contiguous U.S. states for the years 1960 through 1975. There are thus 768 pooled time series, cross-section observations (sixteen years, forth-eight states). The equations have been estimated by the variance components technique of Balestra and Nerlove (1966). The equations are tabulated in Table 5–3. The numbers in parentheses are the $t$-ratios of the coefficients. Method 1 obtains the fixed charge and the marginal price for electricity as the intercept and slope, respectively, in a least squares linear approximation to the mean total revenue function, while Method 2 identifies the marginal block on a rate schedule with the block that contains the mean level of electricity consumption for the customers on the schedule and then defines the marginal price and the fixed charge with respect to this block. It was noted earlier that, provided the total revenue function can be well approximated by a linear equation, Method 1 is to be preferred because it is a totally ex ante procedure and hence is free of simultaneous equations bias. As it turns out, a linear equation does provide an excellent approximation to the total revenue function, but a comparison between the two methods is nevertheless of interest, since there may be situations where because the total revenue function is not linear, Method 2 has to be used instead.

The results for the two methods are clearly very similar. The fixed charge for electricity is a bit more significant and the coefficient for income is a bit smaller with Method 2, but these are the only differences of note. Of particular interest in both equations is the highly significant coefficient for the marginal price of electricity. Note, too, the very substantial difference (in absolute value) in the coefficients for the logarithms of income and the fixed charge for electricity, which belies the hypothesis that consumers react to a change in the fixed charge in the same way as an equal change in regular income. The price and income elasticities from the two equations are presented in Table 5–4. The income elasticity is estimated to be about 0.08 in the short run and about

---

12. This formulation of the fixed charge was suggested by E.P. Howrey of the University of Michigan (see Howrey 1979).

**Table 5–3.**   Demand Equations for U.S. Residential Electricity Consumption, Comparison of Methods 1 and 2 of the FC/MP Framework (t-ratios in parentheses).

| Independent Variable | Method 1 | Method 2 |
|---|---|---|
| $\ln q_{t1}$ | 0.904 | 0.904 |
| | (99.59) | (97.69) |
| $\ln x_t$ | 0.077 | 0.073 |
| | (3.11) | (3.02) |
| $\Delta ga_t \ln x_t$ | −0.714 | −0.813 |
| | (−1.37) | (−1.56) |
| $\ln fce_t$ | 3.49 | 4.85 |
| | (1.70) | (3.04) |
| $\ln mpe_t$ | −0.101 | −0.096 |
| | (−8.58) | (−8.16) |
| $ga_t dg_t \ln fcg_t$ | 16.04 | 14.81 |
| | (1.39) | (1.29) |
| $ga_t dg_t \ln mpg_t$ | 0.026 | 0.022 |
| | (1.48) | (1.31) |
| $wh_t \ln ddhd_t$ | 1.07 | 1.10 |
| | (4.94) | (5.10) |
| $\Delta ga_t wh_t \ln ddhd_t$ | −23.64 | −24.98 |
| | (−1.46) | (−1.54) |
| $wc_t \ln ddcd_t$ | 0.735 | 0.734 |
| | (7.34) | (7.27) |
| $ga_t$ | −0.057 | −0.061 |
| | (−2.18) | (−2.34) |
| $\Delta ga_t$ | 4.84 | 5.51 |
| | (1.36) | (1.54) |
| $R^2$ | 0.985 | 0.985 |
| $S_e$ | 0.052 | 0.051 |

0.8 in the long run, while the elasticity with respect to the marginal price is estimated to be about −0.1 in the short run and about −1 in the long run.

The comparison in this section between Methods 1 and 2 is of more than just passing interest, because it suggests that simultaneous equations bias is not de facto a problem with Method 2. If this were the case, we should expect the marginal price elasticity with Method 2 to differ from that of Method 1, but this is clearly not the case. This is an important result, because it suggests that Method 2, which is straightforward to apply, can be

**Table 5–4.**   Income and Price Elasticities for Equations in Table 5–3.

| Elasticity | Method 1 | Method 2 |
|---|---|---|
| Income | | |
| Short run | 0.077 | 0.073 |
| Long run | 0.802 | 0.760 |
| Fixed Charge for Electricity | | |
| Short run | −0.041 | −0.058 |
| Long run | −0.430 | −0.600 |
| Marginal Price of Electricity | | |
| Short run | −0.101 | −0.096 |
| Long run | −1.052 | −1.000 |
| Fixed Charge for Natural Gas | | |
| Short run | 0.030 | 0.028 |
| Long run | 0.311 | 0.291 |
| Marginal Price of Natural Gas | | |
| Short run | 0.002 | 0.002 |
| Long run | 0.018 | 0.016 |

used with confidence in situations where, because of nonlinearity in the total revenue function, Method 1 cannot be used.


## CONCLUSION

In closing, we would like to return to the point made in the introduction that while the focus in this chapter has been on electricity demand in the United States, the problems discussed are generic, and the techniques described are applicable to any good or service that is sold on a multipart tariff. We should also mention that although the analysis has been with regard to decreasing block pricing, the Gabor theorem also applies to increasing block pricing. The intramarginal "premium" in this case would be negative and would represent a subsidy as opposed to a lump sum tax. This is an important implication of the analysis, for it means that the demand functions that are estimated using historical data that embody decreasing block pricing can be used in evaluating the impact of so-called lifeline and other forms of inverted rate structures.

## REFERENCES

Balestra, P. and M. Nerlove. 1966. "Pooling Cross-Section and Time-Series Data in the Estimation of a Dynamic Model: The Demand for Natural Gas." *Econometrica* 34, no. 3 (July): 585–612.

Blattenberger, G.R. 1977. "The Residential Demand for Electricity." Ph.D. dissertation, Department of Economics, University of Michigan, Ann Arbor, Michigan.

Buchanan, J.M. 1952–53. "The Theory of Monopolistic Discount Pricing." *Review of Economic Studies* 20: 463–471.

Burtless, G., and J.A. Hausman. 1978. "The Effect of Taxation on Labor Supply: Evaluating the Gary Negative Income Tax Experiment." *Journal of Political Economy* 86, no. 6 (December): 1103–30.

Ercelawn, A.A. 1974. "An Econometric Analysis of the Residential Demand for Electricity in the United States." Ph.D. dissertation, Vanderbilt University, Nashville, Tennessee, December.

Gabor, A. 1955–56. "A Note on Block Tariffs." *Review of Economic Studies* 23: 32–41.

Halvorsen, R. 1975. "Residential Demand for Electric Energy." *Review of Economics and Statistics* 57 (February): 12–18.

Halvorsen, R. 1976. "Demand for Electric Energy in the United States." *Southern Economic Journal* 42, no. 4 (April): 610–625.

Houthakker, H.S. 1951. "Some Calculations on Electricity Consumption in Great Britain." *Journal of the Royal Statistical Society (A)* CXIV, pt. III: 351–71.

Houthakker, H.S., and L.D. Taylor. 1970. *Consumer Demand in the United States.* 2d ed. Cambridge, Massachusetts: Harvard University Press.

Houthakker, H.S.; P.K. Verleger, Jr.; and D.P. Sheehan. 1974. "Dynamic Demand Analysis for Gasoline and Residential Electricity." *American Journal of Agricultural Economics* 56, no. 2 (May): 412–418.

Howrey, E.P. 1979. "The Demand for Electricity with Declining Block Rates." Department of Economics, University of Michigan. Unpublished.

Nordin, J.A. 1976. "A Proposed Modification of Taylor's Demand Analysis: Comment." *The Bell Journal of Economics* 7, no. 2 (Autumn): 719–721.

Rassenti, S. 1979. "The Effect of Decreasing-Block Tariffs on Demand: An Experimental Study." Department of Systems Engineering, University of Arizona, Tucson.

Taylor, L.D. 1975. "The Demand for Electricity: A Survey." *The Bell Journal of Economics* 6, no. 1 (Spring): 74–110.

Taylor, L.D.; G.R. Blattenberger; and R.K. Rennhack. 1981. "The Residential Demand for Energy in the United States." Report to the Electric Power Research Institute on RP 1098. Lexington, Massachusetts: Data Resources, Inc., August.

Wade, S.H. 1980. "The Implications of Decreasing Block Pricing for Individual Demand Functions: An Empirical Approach." Ph.D. dissertation, University of Arizona, Tucson, Arizona, April.

7230
6130
2120

# 6 OPTIMAL INVESTMENT PLANNING AND PRICING POLICY MODELLING IN THE ENERGY SECTOR
## Electric Power

Mohan Munasinghe
Senior Economist-Engineer, Energy Department
The World Bank, Washington, D.C.

## INTRODUCTION

Modern societies have become increasingly dependent on various types of energy sources, among which electricity occupies a dominant position. Therefore, it is not surprising that investments in the electric power sector are estimated to be about US$450 billion in the developing countries during the next decade.

There is already a general worldwide rising trend in the real unit costs of supplying electric power, and this is likely to continue owing to several factors. These include the shift toward more costly coal and nuclear generating plants following the oil crisis; the increasing scarcity of cheaply exploitable hydroelectric sources; and the limited possibilities for realizing further significant economies of scale, especially as systems continue to expand into regions of lower population density such as rural areas. The massive investment needs for power imply that even small efficiency improvements in the sector will lead to significant savings, which are especially important in the case of developing countries experiencing shortages of both local and foreign exchange resources.

The views and opinions expressed in this chapter are the author's and do not necessarily represent those of the World Bank or affiliated organizations.

179

In recent years, decisionmakers in an increasing number of countries have also realized that energy sector planning should be carried out on an integrated basis across all sources and uses of energy—for example, within the framework of a national energy master plan that determines energy policy ranging from short-run supply-demand management decisions to long-run planning. However, in practice, investment planning and pricing are still carried out on an ad hoc and at best partial or subsector basis. Thus typically, electricity planning has traditionally been carried out essentially independently of other energy subsectors such as oil or wood fuel. As long as energy was cheap, such partial approaches were acceptable, but lately, with the significant fluctuations in relative fuel prices and sudden energy shortages, the advantages of integrating energy policy planning have become evident.

In this chapter, we will discuss in detail investment planning and pricing policy modeling in the electric power sector, with due regard for interactions with other energy sources and the rest of the economy. We will also focus on the less-developed country context where, generally, higher levels of market distortion, shortages of foreign exchange and resources for development, larger numbers of poor households whose basic needs must be met, greater reliance on traditional fuels, and relative paucity of energy data, add to the already complicated problems faced by energy planners in the developed countries.

In the next section, the scope and framework of electricity policy modeling are defined. Section three outlines the basic principles and concepts underlying the pricing and investment decisions. Finally, a more detailed state of the art discussion of the methodology and practical application of electricity pricing and investment policy modeling is provided in sections four and five, respectively.

## SCOPE AND FRAMEWORK OF POLICY MODELING IN ELECTRIC POWER

The relationship of the electric power sector to the whole energy sector and the rest of the economy is shown in the hierarchical framework of Figure 6–1. At the highest and most aggregate level, it should be clearly recognized that the energy sector is a part of the whole economy. Therefore, energy planning requires analysis of the links between the energy sector and the rest of the economy. Such links include the input requirements of the energy sector such as capital, labor, and raw materials, as well as energy outputs

**Figure 6–1.**    Hierarchy of Interactions in Integrated National Energy Planning (INEP).

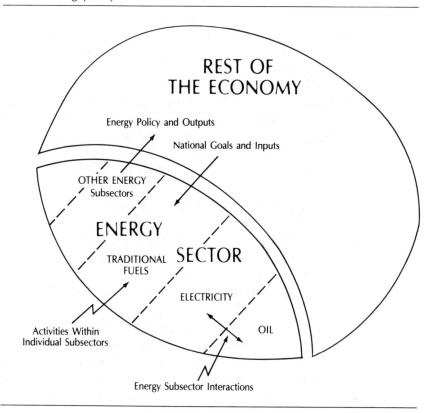

such as electricity, petroleum products, wood fuel and so on and the impact on the economy of policies concerning availability of supply, pricing, and so forth in relation to national objectives.

The second level treats the energy sector as a separate entity composed of subsectors such as electricity, petroleum products, and so on. This permits detailed analysis of the sector, with special emphasis on interactions among the different energy subsectors, and the resolution of any resulting policy conflicts—for example, competition between kerosene and electricity for lighting or wood fuel and kerosene for cooking (Schramm and Munasinghe 1981). The third and most disaggregate level pertains to planning within each of the energy subsectors. Thus, for example, the electricity subsector must determine its own long-run investment program; the wood fuel subsector must develop detailed plans for reforestation, harvesting of timber, and so on.

Energy planning is an essential part of overall national economic planning and should be carried out and implemented in close coordination with the latter. It is important to realize that lack of data, time, and manpower resources, particularly in the developing country context, will generally preclude the analysis of a full, economywide model when energy-related decisions are made.[1] Instead, the partial approach shown in Figure 6–1 may be used, where key linkages and resource flows between the energy sector and the rest of the economy, as well as interactions among different energy subsectors, are selectively identified and analyzed, using appropriate shadow prices such as the opportunity cost of capital, shadow wage rate, and marginal opportunity cost for different fuels (Munasinghe 1980d). In practice, surprisingly valuable results may be obtained from relatively simple models and assumptions.

Two principal policy decisions to be taken by developing country governments relate to investments in and the pricing of electric power; since the government is invariably the main supplier of electricity services, it can intervene directly in the sector. Successful policy modeling in relation to the framework discussed above requires the following items:

First, the national policy objectives must be clearly defined. Second, the policy models must explicitly define and quantify the most important technical-economic relationships within the electricity sector and interactions with the outside world. Third, other social and political constraints that are difficult to quantify must be systematically accounted for. Finally, the results should be readily translatable into straightforward policy options, and the methodology should be practical and applicable even when data are poor.

## BASIC ECONOMIC PRINCIPLES FOR OPTIMIZING PRICING AND INVESTMENT POLICY

From the economic viewpoint, the basic objective of modeling is to determine a set of policies that will maximize the net benefits of electricity consumption. This also corresponds to the most efficient use of scarce economic resources and maximization of output-GNP. In this section, we will focus on

---

1. This holistic approach or general equilibrium analysis is conceptually important. For example, the efficient shadow price of a given resource may be represented by the change in value of aggregate national consumption or output due to a small change in the availability of that resource.

the economic viewpoint. As discussed later, there are several other important objectives, such as meeting the basic energy needs of poor consumers, independence from foreign sources, raising financial resources for future investments, and the like, that will also influence both pricing and investment policy.

The investment decision has traditionally been treated within the framework of the least cost system expansion plan. In recent times sophisticated system planning models and techniques have been developed, based on the criterion of minimizing the cost of supplying a given long-range demand forecast at some acceptable reliability level (or quality of supply) (Anderson 1972; Sullivan 1977). The optimal size, mix, and timing of new capacity additions are treated in this way, and related models also provide for optimal (least cost) operation of the system.

The theoretical foundations of optimal electricity pricing date back as far as the pathbreaking efforts of Dupuit (1932) and subsequently of Hotelling (1938); Ruggles (1949a,b) provides a comprehensive review of work in this area up to the 1940s. The development of the theory, especially for application in the electric power sector, received a strong impetus from the work of Boiteaux, Steiner, and others (see Boiteaux, 1949; Boiteaux and Stasi 1964; Steiner 1957; Turvey 1968; Williamson 1966) from the 1950s onwards. Recent work has led to more sophisticated investment models that permit determination of marginal costs, developments in peak load pricing, consideration of the effects of uncertainty and the costs of power shortages, and so on (see Symposium 1976; Turvey and Anderson 1977; Crew and Kleindorfer 1978; Sherman and Visscher 1978; Canadian Electrical Association 1978; Munasinghe and Gellerson 1979).

While the close relationship between optimal investment and pricing policies has been recognized for some time, these links were systematically analyzed only in some of the more recent studies. By explicitly incorporating effects due to the stochasticity of supply and demand and introducing the notion of shortage costs in welfare-maxmizing models of electricity consumption, it has been shown that the optimal conditions for price and capacity levels must be simultaneously satisfied (Crew and Kleindorfer 1979; Turvey and Anderson 1977; Ch. 14). In this context, determining the optimal capacity level is equivalent to establishing the optimal level of reliability, since in general, greater excess capacity implies better reliability and vice versa. Problems relating to the dichotomy of having to choose between short- and long-run marginal costs and the correct allocation of capacity costs among peak, shoulder, and off-peak consumers have been illuminated in recent work.

We may summarize this complex analysis in simple terms, as follows: The optimal price is the marginal cost of supply. Simultaneously, the optimal reliability (capacity) level is defined by the point at which the marginal cost of increasing reliability is exactly equal to the corresponding reduction in marginal outage costs. Furthermore, let us define the short-run marginal cost (SRMC) as the cost of meeting additional electricity consumption with capacity fixed, while the long-run marginal cost (LRMC) is the cost of providing an increase in consumption (sustained indefinitely into the future) in a situation where optimal capacity adjustments are possible. When the system is optimally planned and operated (i.e., capacity and reliability are optimal), SRMC and LRMC coincide. However, if the system plan is suboptimal, significant deviations between SRMC and LRMC will have to be resolved within the pricing policy framework. Finally, if there are substantial outage costs outside the peak period, then the optimal marginal capacity costs may be allocated among the different rating periods (i.e., peak, intermediate, and off-peak) in proportion to the corresponding marginal outage costs.

For practical purposes, the joint optimal price and reliability conditions are used in an essentailly uncoupled form. Thus, the optimal price is determined at some target reliability level and optimal reliability is set assuming fixed price. By iteration, the solutions may be made mutually consistent. Application of marginal cost pricing rule has been attempted in several countries (most notably France), and while interpretations vary among practitioners, the approach is gaining wide acceptability (Munasinghe and Warford 1982). The optimal reliability rule is more difficult to apply, especially because outage costs are difficult to estimate (Munasinghe 1979).

## Optimal Pricing Decision

The basic rule for maximizing net benefits of consumption is that price should be set equal to marginal cost. This may be clarified using the simple static model summarized in Figure 6–2. Let EFGD$_0$ be the demand curve (which determines the kWh of electricity demanded per year, at any given average price level), while AGS is the supply curve (represented by the marginal cost MC of supplying additional units of output).

At the price $p$ and demand $Q$, the total benefit of consumption is represented by the consumers willingness to pay—namely, the area under the demand curve OEFJ—while the corresponding cost of supply is the area under the supply curve OAHJ. Therefore, the net benefit, or total benefit minus

**Figure 6–2.**   Supply and Demand Diagram for Electricity Consumption.

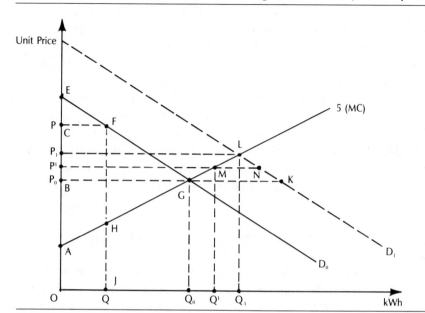

supply costs, is given by the area AEFH. Clearly, the maximum net benefit AEG is achieved when price is set equal to marginal cost at the optimum market clearing point G—that is, $(p_0, Q_0)$. In mathematical terms, the net benefit is given by:

$$NB = TB - SC = \int p\,(Q) \cdot dQ - \int MC(Q) \cdot dQ$$

where $TB$ is the total benefit of electricity consumption and $SC$ is the supply cost at some fixed reliability level. $TB$ and $SC$ are represented by the areas under the demand and supply curves $p(Q)$ and $MC(Q)$, respectively. Maximizing $NB$ yields $d(NB)/dQ = p(Q) - MC(Q) = 0$, or $p = MC$ at the market clearing point of intersection $(p_0, Q_0)$ of the demand and marginal cost curves.

Next, we add to this static analysis the dynamic effect of growth of demand from year 0 to year 1, which leads to an outward shift in the demand curve from $D_0 D_1$. Assuming that the correct market clearing price $p_0$ existed in year 0, excess demand GK will occur in year 1. Ideally, the supply should be increased to $Q_1$ and the new optimal market clearing price established at $p_1$. But data concerning the demand curve $D_1$ may be incomplete, making it difficult to locate the point $L$.

Fortunately, system data permit the marginal cost curve to be determined more accurately. Therefore, as a first step, the supply may be increased to an intermediate level $Q'$, at the price $p'$. Observation of the excess demand $MN$ indicates that both the supply and the marginal cost price should be further increased. Conversely, if we overshoot $L$ and end up in a situation of excess supply, then it may be necessary to wait until the growth of demand catches up with the overcapacity. In this iterative manner, it is possible to move along the marginal cost curve toward the optimal market clearing point. Note that, as we approach the optimum, it is also shifting with demand growth, and therefore we may never hit this moving target. However, the basic rule of setting price equal to the marginal cost and expanding supply until the market clears is still valid.

## Capital Indivisibilities and Peak Load Pricing

Owing to economies of scale, capacity additions to power systems (especially generation) tend to be large and long lived, resulting in lumpy investments. Suppose that in year 0, the maximum supply capacity is $Q$, as shown in Figure 6–3, while the optimal price and output combination $(p_0, O_0)$ prevails, corresponding to the demand curve $D_0$ and the short-run marginal system cost curve SRMC (e.g., fuel, operating, and maintenance costs). As demand grows from $D_0$ to $D_1$ over time, with capacity fixed, the price must be increased to $p_1$ to clear the market. When the demand curve has shifted to $D_2$ and the price is $p_2$, new plant is added. Once the capacity increases to $Q$, $P_3$ becomes the optimal price corresponding to demand $D_3$ and the SRMC line. Generally, the resulting large price fluctuations over time will be unacceptable to consumers. This practical problem may be avoided by adopting a long-run marginal cost (LRMC) approach and peak load pricing.

The basic static peak load pricing model shown in Figure 6–4 has two demand curves: For example, $D_{pk}$ could represent the peak demand during the $x$ daylight and evening hours of the day when electric loads are light. For simplicity, a single type of plant is assumed, with the SRMC of fuel, operating, and maintenance costs given by the constant $a$ and the LRMC of adding to capacity (e.g., investment costs suitably annuitized and distributed over the lifetime output of the plant) given by the constant $b$. The diagram indicates that the pressure on capacity arises due to peak demand $D_{pk}$, while the off-peak demand $D_{op}$ does not infringe on the capacity $Q$. The optimal pricing rule now has two parts corresponding to two distinct rating periods (i.e., differentiated by the time of day)—(1) peak period price of

**Figure 6–3.**    The Effect of Capital Indivisibilities on Price.

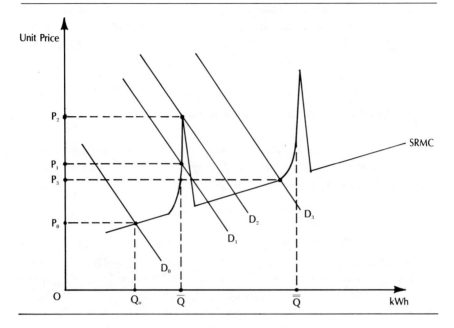

**Figure 6–4.**    Basic Peak Load Pricing Model.

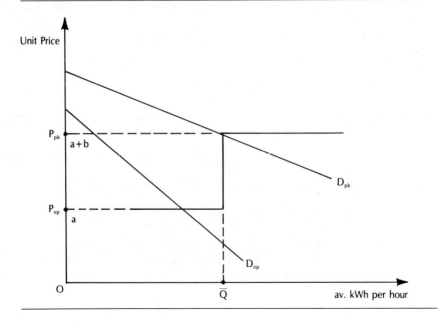

$p_{pk} = a + b$; and (2) off-peak period price of $p_{op} = a$. The logic of this simple result is that peak period users, who are the cause of capacity additions, should bear full responsibility for the capacity costs as well as fuel, operating, and maintenance costs, while off-peak consumers only pay the latter costs (Munasinghe 1981).

## Optimal Investment and Reliability Decisions

Consider a power system in which the evolution of electricity demand over a long period of $(T)$ years in given by $D_t$ where $t$ varies from $0$ to $Y$. $D$ is a function of other variables and may be written:

$$D_t = D_t (P_t, Y_t, R^*_t, \underline{Z}_t) \tag{6.1}$$

where $P$ is the electricity price, $Y$ is the income variable that represents the level of economic activity, $R^*$ is the value of reliability expected by consumers, and $Z$ is a vector of other independent variables affecting demand. Initially, it is assumed that the values of arguments $P_t$, $Y_t$, and $Z_t$ on the right-hand side of equation (6.1) are exogeneously fixed. Prespecifying $P_t$ allows us to uncouple the joint optimal pricing and reliability conditions at this stage. This constraint may be subsequently relaxed, as described later.

The economic costs suffered by electricity consumers due to electric power shortages associated with each system plan may be represented as a function of the generalized reliability level $R_t$, forecast demand, and reliability expectation:

$$OC_t = OC_t (R_t, D_t, R^*_t) \tag{6.2}$$

Corresponding power system supply costs, incurred as a consequence of providing electricity services may be written:

$$SC_t = SC_t (R_1, \ldots, R; D_1, \ldots, D) \tag{6.3}$$

The supply costs described in equation (6.3) correspond to least cost system designs. We note that $SC$ should include the capital and operating expenses as well as the kW and the kWh losses in the system, appropriately valued (at the marginal cost of supply), but net of the marginal supply costs of kWh not delivered due to outages. Finally, since reliability expectation depends on past reliability, we may write:

$$R^*_t = R^*_t (R_{t-1}, \ldots, R_{t-s}) \tag{6.4}$$

A simple expression for the net benefit of electricity consumption to society (in present discounted value terms) is:

$$NB = \sum_{t=0}^{T} (TB_t - OC_t - SC_t)/(1 + r)^t$$

(6.5)

where $TB_t = TB_t (D_t)$ is the total benefit of electricity consumption in the absence of outages and $r$ is the appropriate discount rate. Because of the long lifetime of some investments, the discounting time horizon $T$ may be chosen to be greater than the planning time horizon $\theta$ to eliminate end effects.

In order to identify the marginal conditions that maximize $NB$, we formulate the Lagrangian:

$$L = \sum_{t=0}^{T} \{(TB_t - OC_t - SC_t)/(1+r)^t - \lambda_t[R^*_t - R^*_t (R_{t1}, \ldots, R_{ts})] - \mu_t[D_t - D_t(R^*_t)]\}$$

The three first order conditions of relevance are:

$$(\partial L/\partial R_j) = -[(\partial OC_j/\partial R_j)/(1+r)^j + \sum_{t=0}^{T} (\partial SC_t/\partial R_j)/(1+r)^t] + \sum_{t=0}^{T} \lambda_t(\partial R^*_t/\partial R_j) = 0$$

$$(\partial L/\partial R^*_j) = - (\partial OC_j/\partial R^*_j)/(1 + r)^j + \mu_j(\partial D_j/\partial R^*_j) - \lambda_j = 0$$

$$(\partial L/\partial D_j) = [(\partial TB_j/\partial D_j) - (\partial OC_j/\partial D_j)]/(1+r)^j - \sum_{t=0}^{T} (\partial SC_t/\partial D_j)/(1+r)^t - \mu_j = 0$$

for $j = 0, 1, \ldots, T$.

Combining these three equations yields:

$$\{-(\partial OC_j/\partial R_j)/(1+r)^j - \sum_{t=0}^{T} (\partial SC_t/\partial R_j)/(1+r)^t\} + \sum_{t=0}^{T} (\partial R^*_t/\partial R_j) \{[-(\partial OC_t/\partial R^*_t)$$

$$+ (\partial D_t/\partial R^*_t)\{(\partial TB_t/\partial D_t) - (\partial OC_t/\partial D_t)\}]/(1+r)^t - \sum_{t=0}^{T} (\partial SC_u/\partial D_t)/(1+r)^u\} = 0$$

The first term $\{\ldots\}$ captures the direct impact of reliability changes on $OC$ and $SC$, while the rest of the equation represents the corresponding indirect effects via the reliability expectation. To simplify interpretation of the above condition, we might assume to first order that $(\partial R^*_t/\partial R_j) \cdot (\partial OC_t/$

$\partial R^*_t$) and $(\partial R^*_t/\partial R_j) \cdot (\partial D_t/\partial R^*_t)$ are negligible. In other words, the effect of changes in reliability level $R$ on both $OC$ and $D$, via the reliability expectation $R^*$, are small. This assumption would be especially valid if the range of variation of $R$ is not very wide.

Therefore,

$$-(\partial OC_j/\partial R_j)/(1 + r)^j - \sum_{t=0}^{T} (\partial SC_t/\partial R_j)/(1 + r)^t = 0 \qquad (6.6)$$

Equation (6.6) indicates that the net benefits to society will be maximized at the point where the marginal outage costs associated with a change in reliability are exactly offset by the corresponding change in supply costs. Although this equation relates to reliability in time period $j$, in practice, changes in reliability are likely to be implemented over several time periods. Therefore, a more useful form of equation (6.6) would be:

$$\sum_{j=0}^{T} [-(\partial OC_j/\partial R_j) \cdot \Delta R_j/(1+r)^j - \sum_{t=0}^{T} (\partial SC_t/\partial R_j) \cdot \Delta R_j/(1+r)^t] = 0 \qquad (6.7)$$

where $\Delta R_j$ is a small change in reliability during period $j$.

For practical application of this rule, let us consider $n$ alternative long-range system expansion programs, where the reliability level of the $i$th program in year $t$ is $R^i_t$. Suppose that expansion plan $(i+1)$ is derived from plan $i$, by a small change in reliability given by:

$$\Delta R^i_t = R^{i+1}_t - R^i_t \text{ for } i = 0, 1, \ldots, n.$$

Examining equations (6.4) and (6.7), the corresponding change in net benefits may be written:

$$\Delta NB^i = NB^{i+1} - NB^i = -\Delta OC^i - \Delta SC^i \qquad (6.8)$$

where

$$\Delta OC^i = \sum_{j=0}^{T} (\partial OC^i_j/\partial R^i_j) \cdot \Delta R^i_j/(1 + r)^j$$

and

$$\Delta SC^i = \sum_{j=0}^{T} \sum_{t=0}^{T} (\partial SC^i_t/\partial R^i_j) \cdot \Delta R^i_j/(1 + r)^t$$

In order to interpret equation (6.8), it is assumed that the change from system expansion plan $i$ to plan $(i+1)$ involves an overall unambigous improvement in reliability—that is, that each component $\Delta R^i{}_t$ is nonnegative. In general, this implies correspondingly that $\Delta OC^i \leq 0$ and $\Delta SC^i \geq 0$. In this case, equation (6.8) yields:

$$| \Delta NB^i | = | \Delta OC^i | - | \Delta SC^i |$$

Therefore, in order to maximize the net economic benefits of supplying electricity to society, the reliability level should be increased in successive system plans as long as the corresponding decrease in incremental outage costs exceeds the increase in incremental supply costs, and vice versa. Equivalently, since the total benefit $TB$ is assumed to be independent of reliability $R$, the net benefit $NB$ is maximized when the present discounted value of the sum of outage costs and supply costs is minimized.

Figure 6–5 shows a typical graph of outage costs ($OC$) and supply costs ($SC$) associated with different system expansion programs and reliability levels. The total costs $TC = SC + OC$ are also plotted. As $R$ increases, $SC$ rises more and more rapidly; clearly a perfectly reliable system ($R=1$) is not attainable. Correspondingly, $OC$ falls toward zero as $R$ increases toward uni-

**Figure 6–5.**    Outage Costs, Supply Costs, and Total Costs as Functions of the Reliability Level.

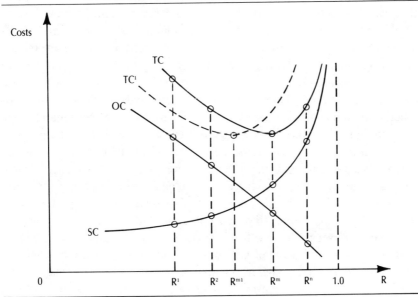

ty. The optimal reliability level $R^m$ is at the minimum point of the $TC$ curve, when the slope of $SC$ is equal to minus the slope of $OC$, corresponding to equation (6.2).

In this formulation, the reliability measure is defined in a very generalized way. Therefore, the selection of the optimum system plan and the associated reliability level is made on the basis of economic cost-benefit analysis and is quite independent of the actual index of reliability. However, from a practical point of view, it is important to develop reliability indexes that not only characterize future system performance in a satisfactory manner, but are also meaningful at the consumer level and could be easily used to determine the costs of shortages incurred by users. From this viewpoint, load point indexes of the frequency and duration type, referred to individual consumers on a disaggregate basis, would be the most convenient measures to use. It would also be very important to know the times of occurrence of outages. Since outage costs are generally a nonlinear function of outage duration, ideally, the probability distribution of outage duration should be computed. However, in practice, a knowledge of the mean duration at specific times, may be sufficient—for example, during the periods of peak, shoulder, and off-peak demand.

Next, let us relax the assumption regarding the original fixed price $p_t$. Consider the situation where the stream of system supply costs $SC^m{}_t$ associated with the optimum expansion plan $i = m$ on the first round, necessitate significant changes in the assumptions regarding the evolution of prices $p_t$ that were themselves used to determine the initial demand forecast. For example, the use of a marginal cost pricing rule or some simple financial requirement such as an adequate rate of return on fixed assets may require previously unforeseen changes in future electricity tariffs to compensate for the new supply costs. Such a shift in prices would directly affect load growth. Furthermore, the new target reliability levels implied by the first-round optimum expansion path $i = m$, may themselves affect reliability expectation and thus have a secondary impact on demand and outage costs.

In such a situation, the impact of the new sets of price and expected reliability levels on the demand forecast and outage cost estimates should be considered when iterating through the model again. In general, this procedure would shift the whole total cost ($TC'$) curve as shown by the broken line in Figure 6–5, leading to a new optimum plan $m'$. In this fashion, the direct and indirect feedback effects of reliability on demand may be considered iteratively until a set of self-consistent price, demand, and reliability levels was determined. Thus, in the approach described in this chapter, the reliability level is also a variable to be optimized. Therefore, the system planner must design a number of alternative systems to meet the future demand (which is initially assumed to be fixed) at each of several target reliability levels and select as the optimal one the system that minimizes the total costs, defined as the sum of the outage costs and the system costs. In other words, the conventional system-planning criterion of minimizing only the system costs is subsumed within the new procedure, where the total social costs are minimized (Munasinghe 1980).

The framework for evaluating outage costs as well as system costs in this new approach is basically economic and more appropriate in the context of the national economy or society as a whole. The goods and services used as inputs to the electric power system—for example, labor, land, physical assets, materials, and the like—are considered as scarce economic resources that could be used in alternative production, and they are valued at opportunity cost. In particular, if markets are highly distorted, shadow prices may be used. Such an approach is particularly appropriate in the case of a publicly owned power utility, a situation that occurs very often in the developing countries. In contrast, the traditional system-planning approach is more compatible with the financial or accounting viewpoint of a private utility. Finally, the model may be suitably disaggregated to permit optimization of an interconnected system at various levels of aggregation ranging from the global (e.g., in terms of systemwide generation reliability) to the specific (e.g., in terms of distribution reliability for small geographic areas).

Figure 6–6 illustrates the new procedure in a different way. Suppose that in the starting year the optimal price $p_0$ has been set equal to the long-run marginal cost $LRMC(R^0)$ at the market clearing point $A$. The $LRMC(R^0)$ curve is derived from the system plan with the optimal reliability level $R^0$, keeping $R^0$ fixed. Thus initially both price and reliability are jointly optimized.

Now if the demand curve shifts from $D_0$ to $D_1$ after some time, the optimal price is not necessarily $p'_1$ on the same $LRMC(R^0)$ curve; using this static, LRMC corresponds to the traditional method of system planning with a fixed target reliability level $R^0$. The optimal reliability may have changed to $R^1$ and the appropriate curve is $LRMC(R^1)$ with optimal price $p_1$. Thus, as demand increases, the dynamic optimal long-run marginal cost curve $LRMC_{dyn}$ lies along AB.

In practice, B is unlikely to be a well-defined point because although the LRMC curve is generally known from known supply side (technological-economic) considerations, the slope and position of the demand curve are not. Therefore, since B is a poorly defined and shifting target, a trial and error

**Figure 6–6.**    Evolution of Demand and Reliability.

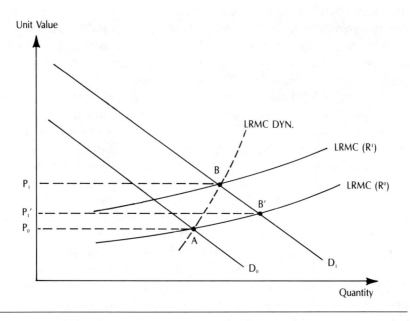

approach is required. As demand grows, capacity is added to expand output, while price and reliability are optimized iteratively, as described earlier. Thus, when reliability is optimized, price and demand growth are assumed to be fixed; and when price is optimized, reliability and demand are assumed to be unaffected. Through successive iterations, the mutually self-consistent set of optimal price, reliability, and demand levels would be reached at point B.

## PRACTICAL APPLICATION OF OPTIMAL PRICING METHODOLOGY[2]

### Objectives of Power Pricing Policy

The modern approach to power pricing recognizes the existence of several objectives or criteria, not all of which are mutually consistent. First, national economic resources must be allocated efficiently, not only among different

---

2. For more details, see Munasinghe (1981) or Munasinghe and Warford (1982).

sectors of the economy, but within the electric power sector. This implies that cost-reflecting prices must be used to indicate to the electricity consumers the true economic costs of supplying their specific needs, so that supply and demand can be matched efficiently.

Second, certain principles relating to fairness and equity must be satisfied, including (a) the fair allocation of costs among consumers according to the burdens they impose on the system; (b) the assurance of a reasonable degree of price stability and avoidance of large price fluctuations from year to year; and (c) the provision of a minimum level of service to persons who may not be able to afford the full cost.

Third, the power prices should raise sufficient revenues to meet the financial requirements of the utility, as described earlier. Fourth, the power tariff structure must be simple enough to facilitate the metering and billing of customers. Fifth and finally, other economic and political requirements must also be considered. These might include, for example, subsidized electricity supply to certain sectors in order to enhance growth or to certain geographic areas for regional development.

Since the above criteria are often in conflict with one another, it is necessary to accept certain trade-offs between them. The LRMC approach to price setting described below has both the analytical rigor and inherent flexibility to provide a tariff structure that is responsive to these basic objectives.

## LRMC-Based Tariffs

A tariff based on LRMC is consistent with the first objective—that is, the efficient allocation of resources. The traditional accounting approach is concerned with the recovery of historical or sunk costs, while in the LRMC calculation, the important consideration is the amount of future resources used or saved by consumer decisions. Since electricity prices are the amounts paid for increments of consumption, in general they should reflect the incremental cost incurred. Supply costs increase if existing consumers increase their demand or if new consumers are connected to the system. Therefore, prices that act as a signal to consumers should be related to the economic value of future resources required to meet consumption changes. The accounting approach that uses historical assets and embedded costs implies that future economic resources will be as cheap or as expensive as in the past. This could lead to overinvestment and waste or to underinvestment and the additional costs of unnecessary scarcity.

To promote better utilization of capacity, and to avoid unnecessary investments to meet peak demands, which tend to grow very rapidly, the LRMC approach permits the structuring of prices so that they vary according to the marginal costs of serving demands—(1) by different consumer categories, (2) in different seasons, (3) at different hours of the day; (4) by different voltage levels, (5) in different geographical areas, and so on.

In particular, with an appropriate choice of the peak period, structuring the LRMC-based tariffs by time of day generally leads to the conclusion that peak consumers should pay both capacity and energy costs, whereas off-peak consumers should pay only the energy costs. Similarly, analysis of LRMC by voltage level usually indicates that the lower the service voltage, the greater the costs consumers impose on the system.

The structuring of LRMC-based tariffs also meets subcategories (a) and (b) of the second, or fairness, objective mentioned earlier. The economic resource costs of future consumption are allocated as far as possible among the customers according to the incremental costs they impose on the power system. In the traditional approach, fairness was often defined rather narrowly and led to the allocation of arbitrary accounting costs to various rating periods and consumers, thus violating the economic efficiency criterion. Because the LRMC method deals with future costs over a long period—for example at least five to ten years—the resulting prices in constant terms tend to be quite stable over time. This smoothing out of costs over a long period is especially important given capital indivisibilities or "lumpiness" of power system investments.

Using economic opportunity costs (or shadow prices—especially for capital, labor, and fuel) instead of purely financial costs and taking externalities into consideration whenever possible also link the LRMC method and efficient resource allocation. The development of LRMC-based tariff structures that also meet the other objectives of pricing policy mentioned earlier are discussed next.

## Practical Tariff Setting

The first stage of the LRMC approach is the calculation of pure or strict LRMC that reflect the economic efficiency criterion. If price was set strictly equal to LRMC, consumers could indicate their willingness to pay for more consumption, thus signaling the justification of further investment to expand capacity.

In the second stage of tariff setting, ways are sought in which the strict LRMC may be adjusted to meet the other objectives, among which the financial requirement is most important. If prices were set equal to strict LRMC, it is likely that there will be a financial surplus. This is because marginal costs tend to be higher than average costs when the unit costs of supply are increasing. In principle, financial surpluses of the utility may be taxed away by the state, but in practice the use of power pricing as a tool for raising central government revenues is usually politically unpopular and rarely applied. Such surplus revenues can also be utilized in a way that is consistent with the other objectives. For example, the connection charges can be subsidized without violating the LRMC price, or low income consumers could be provided with a subsidized block of electricity to meet their basic requirement, thus satisfying sociopolitical objectives. Conversely, if marginal costs are below average costs—typically as a result of economies of scale—then pricing at the strict LRMC will lead to a financial deficit. This will have to be made up, for example, by higher lump sum connection charges, flat rate charges, or even government subsidies.

Another reason for deviating from the strict LRMC arises because of second-best considerations. When prices elsewhere in the economy do not reflect marginal costs, especially for electric power substitutes and complements, then departures from the strict marginal cost pricing rule for electricity services would be justified. For example, in rural areas inexpensive alternative energy may be available in the form of subsidized kerosene and/or gas. In this case, pricing electricity below the LRMC may be justified to prevent excessive use of the alternative forms of energy. Similarly, if incentives are provided to import private generators and their fuel is also subsidized, then charging the full marginal cost to industrial consumers may encourage them to purchase their own or captive power plant. This is economically less efficient from a national perspective. Since the computation of strict LRMC is based on the power utilities' least cost expansion program, LRMC may also need to be modified by short-term considerations if previously unforeseen events make the long-run system plan suboptimal in the short run. Typical examples include a sudden reduction in demand growth and a large excess of installed capacity that may justify somewhat reduced capacity charges, or a rapid increase in fuel prices, which could warrant a short-term fuel surcharge.

As discussed earlier, the LRMC approach permits a high degree of tariff structuring. However, data constraints and the objective of simplifying metering and billing procedures usually require that there should be a practical limit to differentiation of tariffs by (1) major customer categories (residential, industrial, commercial, special, rural, and so on); (2) voltage levels (high, medium, and low); (3) time of day (peak, off-peak); and (4) geographic region. Finally, various other constraints also may be incorporated into LRMC-based tariffs such as the political requirement of having a uniform national tariff, subsidizing rural electrification, and so on. In each case, however, such deviations from LRMC will impose an efficiency cost on the economy.

## Summary

In the first stage of calculating LRMC, the economic (first-best) efficiency objectives of tariff setting are satisfied, because the method of calculation is based on future economic resource costs rather than sunk costs and also incorporates economic considerations such as shadow prices and externalities. The structuring of marginal costs permits an efficient and fair allocation of the tariff burden on consumers. In the second stage of developing a LRMC-based tariff, deviations from strict LRMC are considered to meet important financial, social, economic (second-best), and political criteria. This second step of adjusting strict LRMC is generally as important as the first-stage calculation.

The LRMC approach provides an explicit framework for analyzing system costs and setting tariffs. If departures from the strict LRMC are required for noneconomic reasons, then the economic efficiency cost of these deviations may be estimated roughly by comparing the impact of the modified tariff relative to strict LRMC. Thus strict LRMC is used as the benchmark. Since the cost structure may be studied in considerable detail during the LRMC calculations, this analysis also helps to pinpoint weaknesses and inefficiencies in the various parts of the power system—for example, overinvestment, unbalanced investment, or excessive losses at the generation, transmission, and distribution levels, in different geographic areas; and so on. This aspect is particularly useful in improving system expansion planning.

Finally, any LRMC-based tariff is a compromise between many different objectives. Therefore, there is no "ideal" tariff. By using the LRMC approach, it is possible to revise and improve the tariff on a consistent and ongoing basis and thereby to approach the optimum price over a period of several years, without subjecting long-standing consumers to "unfair" shocks in the form of large abrupt price changes.

## Extensions of Simple Models

The simplified models presented so far must be extended to analyze the economics of real world power systems. First, the usual procedure adopted in marginal cost pricing studies may require some iteration, as shown in Figure 6–7. Typically, a deterministic long-range demand forecast is made assuming some given future evolution of prices. Then, using power system models and data, several plans are proposed to meet this demand at some fixed target reliability level (see below). The cheapest or least cost system expansion plan is chosen from these alternatives. Finally, strict LRMC is computed on the basis of this least cost plan, and an adjusted LRMC tariff structure is prepared. If the new tariff that is to be imposed on consumers is significantly different from the original assumption regarding the evolution of prices, however, then this first-round tariff structure must be fed back into the model to revise the demand forecast and repeat the LRMC calculation.

In theory, this iterative procedure could be repeated until future demand, prices, and LRMC-based tariff estimates become mutually self-consistent. In practice, uncertainties in price elasticities of demand and other data may dictate a more pragmatic approach in which the LRMC results would be used after only one iteration to devise new power tariffs and to implement them. The demand behavior is then observed over some time period; the LRMC is reestimated, and tariffs are revised to move closer to the optimum, which may itself have shifted, as described previously. An extreme form of price feedback could result in a shift of the peak outside the original peak period, especially if the latter was too narrowly defined. That is, peak load pricing may shift the demand peak from one pricing period to another. If sufficient data on the price elasticity of demand were available, theory indicates that each potential or secondary peak should be priced to keep its magnitude just below the available capacity level. Since the necessary information would rarely be available in practice, a combination of techniques—including use of a sufficiently wide peak period, redefining the peak period to include both the actual and potential peaks, direct switching of certain consumer loads, and on—may be used to avoid the shifting peak problem.

Second, the interrelated issues of supply and demand uncertainty, reserve margins, and cost of shortages suggest that reliability should also be treated as a variable to be optimized, and both price and capacity (or equivalantly, reliability) levels should be optimized simultaneously. These considerations

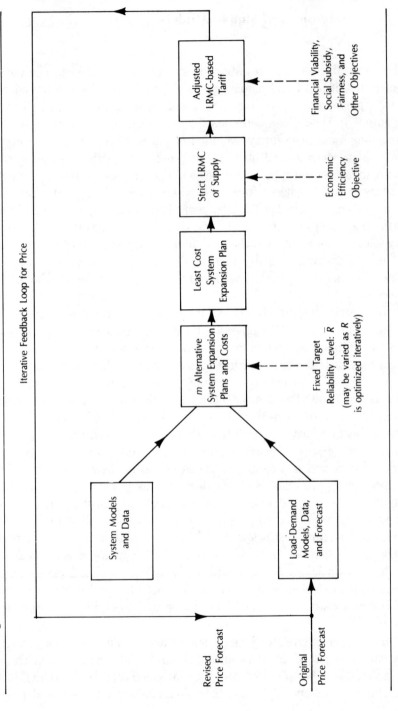

**Figure 6–7.** Use of Price Feedback in Estimating LRMC–Based Tariffs.

lead to a more generalized approach to system expansion planning as described earlier, which will affect the estimates of LRMC.

Third, consider again the choice between short-and long-run marginal costs for pricing. The short-run marginal cost (SRMC) may be defined as the cost of meeting additional electricity consumption (including the costs of shortages) with capacity fixed. The long-run marginal cost (LRMC) is the cost of providing an increase in consumption (sustained indefinitely into the future) in a situation where optimal capacity adjustments are possible. When the system is optimally planned and operated (i.e., capacity and reliability are optimal), SRMC and LRMC coincide. However, if the system plan is temporarily suboptimal, significant deviations between SRMC and LRMC will have to be carefully resolved. For example, in the post-1973 period, many utilities are replacing oil-fired plant with coal-fired units to realize fuel cost savings. This may result in significant excess capacity and low marginal capacity costs in the short run, thus justifying a reduction in demand charges below the LRMC level. However, as peak demand grows and the system approaches optimality again, the capacity charges should rise smoothly toward LRMC. This transition could become undesirably abrupt if the initial reduction in demand charges was too large and demand growth was overstimulated.

Finally, if there are substantial outage costs outside the peak period, then the optimal marginal capacity costs may be allocated among the different rating periods in proportion to the corresponding marginal outage costs. It has been suggested that capacity costs should be allocated to different rating periods in inverse proportion to loss–of–load–probability (LOLP), but this would be only an approximation because aggregate reliability indexes such as LOLP are poor proxies for prorating outage costs.

### Shadow Pricing[3]

In the idealized world of perfect competition, the interaction of many small profit-maximizing producers and welfare-maximizing consumers gives rise to market prices that reflect the true economic costs, and scarce resources are efficiently allocated. However, conditions are likely to be far from ideal in the real world. Distortions due to monopoly practices, external economies and diseconomies (which are not internalized in the private market), interventions in the market process through taxes, import duties and subsidies,

3. For details, see Munasinghe (1979).

and so forth all result in market (or financial) prices for goods and services, which may diverge substantially from their shadow prices or true economic opportunity costs. For example, in a country where subsidized diesel fuel is available for electricity generation, the appropriate shadow price would be the import price rather than the artificially low market price. Moreover, if there are large numbers of poor consumers, pricing based only on strict efficiency criteria may be socially and politically unacceptable. Such considerations necessitate the use of appropriate shadow prices (instead of market prices) of inputs to the electricity sector to determine the optimal investment program as well as LRMC.

## PRACTICAL APPLICATION OF OPTIMAL INVESTMENT AND RELIABILITY METHODOLOGY

Next we discuss a practical methodology to implement the investment-optimizing model. Figure 6–8 is a flow chart of the reliability-optimizing methodology presented in this chapter. To begin with, a framework and set of models are developed to analyze the economic costs incurred by different categories of consumers (e.g., residential, industrial, etc.) due to electric power shortages of varying intensity. Concurrently, a disaggregate long-range (e.g., twenty years) load-demand forecast is estimated, based on a predetermined evolution of electricity prices within the area to be served by the electric power utility. Next, several alternative (least cost) power system plans are prepared to meet this future load at several different levels of reliability. The expected annual frequency (i.e., the number) and duration of power failures associated with each alternative system design or plan, as well as the time of occurrence of these shortages and the average numbers and types of consumers affected by them, are estimated for the entire forecast period.

By substituting the estimated outage frequency and duration results in the consumer outage cost models, it is possible to determine the total future outage costs for each system plan. On the supply side, the investment and operating costs of each alternative design may also be estimated. Then a cost-benefit model is used to compare the outage costs with the corresponding power system costs attributable to each alternative plan. At this stage, some preliminary feedback of forecast frequency and duration data, as well as disaggregate outage costs and system costs from the cost-benefit module, may be used to further improve system design. Finally the optimum long-

**Figure 6-8.**  Flow Chart for the Implementation of the Optimal Investment and Reliability Methodology.

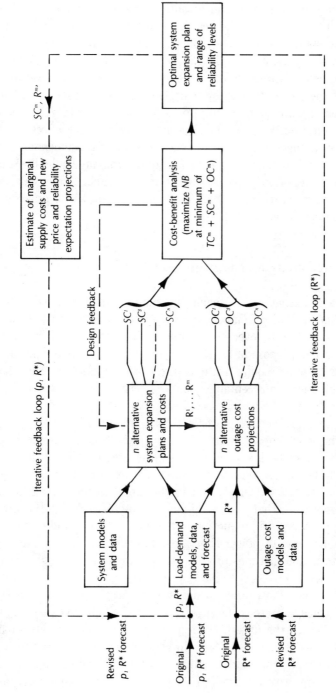

*Note: $p$ = price; $R^*$ = consumer's reliability expectation; $R$ = reliability level; $SC$ = supply costs; $Oc$ = outage costs; $TC$ = total costs; and $NB$ = net benefits. Maximizing $NB$ yields the optimal system plan $m$ and the corresponding reliability $R^m$ at the minimum value of $TC^m = SC^m + OC^m$.*

run system expansion plan and a range of associated reliability levels are established that maximize the net social benefits or, equivalently, minimize the total costs (i.e., system costs plus outage costs) to society.

Two further possibilities exist for including feedback effects. The principal return path is via the impact of electricity prices on the load forecast— that is, if the new optimized system plan requires changes in the original assumptions regarding the future prices that were used to make the initial demand projection. A similar but less important feedback effect due to the influence of changes in the reliability expectation of consumers on both the demand and the outage costs may also be incorporated into the analysis. Therefore, if necessary, it is possible to iterate through the model several times, in order to arrive at a mutually self-consistent set of price, demand, and optimum reliability levels.

## Reliability and Outage Costs

The concept of reliability in engineering may be simply defined in terms of the probability that a component or a system will perform its intended functions satisfactorily over some period of time subject to actual operating conditions. The purpose of an electric power system is to supply power to consumers at some required rate, at the time and place of their choosing, while maintaining an acceptable quality of service—that is, voltage and frequency levels must lie within specified limits.

Thus, an ideal electric power system that unfailingly supplies power to consumers, whenever required, is by definition a perfectly reliable one; and conversely, a system that is never able to deliver electricity to users could be termed totally unreliable. All real world power systems lie between these two extremes, and furthermore, as the system reliability level is improved, there is an inherent trade-off between the increased costs of supply and the reduction in the inconvenience and costs imposed on consumers due to power shortages. Therefore, it is important to develop criteria and methods of assessing and ranking systems according to reliability level.

As in the case of any other good or service, electric power shortages occur when the demand exceeds the supply, due to the failure of planners to correctly predict all the uncertainties in supply and demand. The stochastic nature of demand manifests itself through unforeseen increases in the load level—for example, the sudden build-up in the air-conditioning load due to unusually warm weather. Similarly, the randomness of supply is characterized by the unexpected failure or outage of the various components that make up a power system, the unavailability of water for hydroelectric generation, and so on.

From the consumers' viewpoint, power shortages manifest themselves in a number of ways, including complete interruptions of supply (blackouts), frequency and voltage reductions (brownouts), and instability effects such as erratic frequency fluctuations and power surges. While all these phenomena are likely to inconvenience and impose costs on electricity users, the consequences of supply interruptions are the most severe and probably also the easiest to define. For example, a blackout will disrupt productive activity and prevent the enjoyment of leisure, whereas a voltage reduction may have lesser effects such as the inconvenience caused by the dimming of lights and so on. Frequency variations would effect a power system's own automatic control equipment, as well as other synchronous devices such as electric clocks, while power surges could also cause some damage to equipment, but these consequences are difficult to isolate. Therefore, although the term outage cost (which is used throughout) is meant to encompass the expenses incurred by consumers due to all types of shortages, in practice, the principle emphasis will be on the impact of supply interruptions. Moreover, the effects of random or unexpected interruptions will be stressed, since they are likely to impose much greater hardships on users than known or planned power cuts.

Outage costs may be defined as direct or indirect according to whether they are incurred because an outage actually takes place or simply because an outage is expected to occur. For example, during an outage, direct outage costs are likely to be incurred since normal productive activity is disrupted. In contrast, indirect outage costs are incurred in the absence of an outage itself, because consumers may adapt their behavior patterns in ways that are less efficient or more costly but less susceptible to outage disruptions, or they may purchase alternative (standby) sources of energy. Although indirect outage costs cannot be attributed to any particular outage, they depend on the general level of reliability and represent real resource costs that should be considered when attempting to estimate the economic costs associated with alternative reliability levels. Generally, direct outage costs are related more to the short-term impact of unexpected outages, whereas indirect outage costs arise from longer term considerations of outage expectation, including the effects of planned power cuts. In practice, it would often be difficult to estimate outage costs associated with a particular level of reliability because such costs may consist of a combination of direct and indirect components.

Within the economics literature there are two schools of thought concerning how outage costs should be estimated. One approach is to estimate these costs on the basis of observed (or estimated) willingness to pay for planned electricity consumption (Brown and Johnson 1969; Sherman and Visscher 1978; Crew and Kleindorfer 1978). The other approach, which is the one used in this chapter, estimates such costs in terms of the effect of outages on the production of various goods and services (Telson 1975; Turvey and Anderson 1977: ch. 14; Munasinghe 1980a; Munasinghe and Gellerson 1979).

As described earlier, attempts to estimate outage costs according to willingness to pay are actually part of a more general literature on optimal pricing for public utilities under conditions of uncertainty—namely, stochastic demand and supply. In this approach, the variable to be maximized is net welfare, which is generally set equal to the expected area under the demand curve corresponding to planned electricity consumption, minus the sum of the expected costs of supplying electricity, plus the expected costs (if any) of rationing available electricity among consumers if an outage occurs. Thus, outage costs are measured by the expected reduction in net welfare or the amount that those who are deprived of electricity would be willing to pay for it, minus the costs saved by not supplying it.

Studies that estimate outage costs on the basis of willingness to pay assume that electricity provides direct satisfaction to its consumers. Outage costs are therefore estimated in terms of lost consumers' surplus. Other studies that estimate outage costs in terms of the effect of outages on various types of production do not make this assumption. Instead, they treat electricity as an intermediate input used to produce various goods and services that provide consumers with satisfaction, rather than as a final good that itself provides satisfaction to consumers. Outage costs are therefore measured primarily by the costs to society of outputs not produced because of outages.

The studies that estimate outage costs on the basis of willingness to pay have several important shortcomings: (1) It seems clear that observed willingness to pay for planned electricity consumption is not an accurate indicator of what one would be willing to pay to avoid an unplanned outage. Such an unplanned outage is apt to disrupt activities that are complementary with electricity consumption, and therefore, actual outage costs may be greatly in excess of observed (long-run) willingness to pay. (2) These studies measure losses of consumers' surplus on the basis of the assumption that load shedding takes place according to willingness to pay—that is, those with the lowest willingness to pay are the first to have their electricity cut off. Thus, lost consumers' surplus is the triangle-shaped area defined by the downward sloping demand curve, the horizontal price line, and the vertical line representing the quantity of electricity supplied in spite of the outage. However, in many instances it is not reasonable to assume that load shedding takes place according to willingness to pay. For example, if the outage is caused by a distribution system failure (rather than a generation system failure), the ability to carry out load shedding according to some predetermined order may be severely limited. If such is the case, the resulting loss in consumers' surplus is a trapezoid-shaped area defined by the demand curve, the price line, and the inframarginal units of electricity not supplied. The implication of both the above arguments is that actual outage costs will exceed outage costs estimated on the basis of the marginal consumers' surplus lost. Finally, with this approach, the empirical estimation of outage costs requires exact knowledge of various consumers' demand functions for electricity. Given the problems associated with empirically estimating such demand functions (Taylor 1975), it is likely that any estimates of outage costs obtained in this fashion will be subject to considerable error. Given these criticisms, outage costs would be more appropriately measured in terms of the effects of outages on various kinds of productive activity.

Production is a process in which capital and labor are combined with other inputs such as raw materials and intermediate products to produce a time stream of outputs. Under conditions approximating those of perfect competition, the net social benefit of a marginal unit of output in a given time period equals the value of the output minus the value of inputs. For inframarginal units of output, producers' and consumers' surplus must be included when measuring the net benefits of production. When market distortions are present in the economy, appropriate shadow prices have to be used to value inputs and outputs. The net social benefit resulting from a time stream of marginal outputs equals the present value of the resulting stream of net social benefits. Thus, the opportunity cost of supplying electricity with less than perfect reliability can be measured in terms of the resulting reduction in the present value of this stream of net social benefits.

When an outage disrupts production, the net benefits derived from such activities are reduced—that is, direct outage costs are incurred, since the costs of inputs are increased, and/or the value of outputs is reduced. Specifically, an outage can cause raw materials, intermediate products, or final outputs to spoil; and it can also result in productive factors being made idle. The spoilage effect leads to an opportunity cost equal to the value of the final product not being made available as a result of the outage, minus the value of additional inputs not used because the final product was not produced. However, if the value of the output is not easily determined, as in the case of household and public sector outputs that are not directly sold on the market, then it is necessary to use the cost of producing the spoiled product or output as a minimum estimate of the value of the output.

## Case Study

A case study was carried out to empirically test the new methodology described above. The long-range distribution plan of the city of Cascavel in Brazil was optimized according to the procedure summarized in Figure 6–8. For simplicity, only the distribution system reliability was varied, while the reliability of the generation and transmission system was held constant; although it does not affect the results of the case study, we note that varying the latter would have yielded a better optimum. The details relating to the demand forecast and design of alternative distribution system plans have been described elsewhere (Munasinghe and Scott 1978). The more novel aspects of the analysis relating to the measurement of outage costs are summarized below.

For residential consumers, during an outage, electricity-dependent housekeeping chores could be effectively rescheduled without much inconvenience, and cooking activity was not disrupted, since it is done almost entirely by gas in Cascavel. However, leisure activities were significantly affected by outages, since the enjoyment of leisure in most households was constrained to occur over a relatively fixed period of time in the evening, especially for wage earners, and the use of electricity could be considered essential to the enjoyment of certain leisure activities (e.g., watching TV, reading, dining, etc.) during these nighttime hours.

The results of a survey of residential consumers and an analysis of their outage costs confirmed the result of a detailed theoretical model presented elsewhere (Munasinghe 1980a), and showed that (1) the chief impact of unexpected outages on electricity-using households was the loss of a critical ninety-minute period of leisure during the evening hours, when electricity was considered essential, whereas domestic activities interrupted during the daytime could be rescheduled with relatively little inconvenience; and (2) over this one-and-a-half-hour period, the monetary value of lost leisure could be measured in terms of the net wage or income-earning rate of affected households, as confirmed by their short-term willingness to pay to avoid outages. Estimated residential outage costs were in the range of US$1.30 to $2 per kilowatt hour lost or not consumed due to outages. The principal advantage of this method for estimating the leisure costs of outages to residential consumers was its reliance on relatively easy to obtain income data.

In general, industrial consumers suffer outage costs because materials and products are spoiled and normal production cannot take place; the disrupted production results in an opportunity cost in the form of idle capital and labor, both during the outage and during any restart period following the outage. If there is slack capacity, some of the lost value added may be recovered by using this productive capacity more intensively during normal working hours. In addition, the firm may operate overtime to make up lost production. Based on these considerations, the twenty principal industrial users of electricity in Cascavel were surveyed to determine outage costs for outages of various durations (i.e., one minute to five hours). The results of the analysis indicated that there were wide variations in the effects of outages on industrial consumers—for example, US$1 to $7 per kWh lost, depending on the type of industry, the duration of the outage, and the time of day during which it occurred. This approach was helpful for ranking industries in terms of sensitivity to outages—for example, for emergency load-shedding purposes.

An outage that affects public illumination imposes a cost in the form of foregone community benefits such as security, improved motoring safety, and so forth. One can argue that these foregone benefits are worth at least as much as the net supply cost that the community would have incurred for public illumination during the outage periods—for example, the annuitized value of capital equipment and routine maintenance expenditures; electricity costs are not included since they are not incurred during outages. Two hospitals (eighty beds and 200 beds) were surveyed to estimate the opportunity costs both of productive factors that are made idle (e.g. electricity using equipment, labor, etc.) and of intermediate products such as blood and medicines that might spoil because of outages. The principal outage costs of US¢5.5 per hospital bed per hour of outage were found to occur during the night period (i.e., 7:00 p.m. to 6:00 a.m.), due to idle labor and capital. Estimating the outage costs resulting from possible loss of life is a task exceeding the scope of this sutdy, and therefore, such costs are not considered here. The existence of standby batteries for the intensive care and surgical equipment suggests that death will be avoided in most cases; the cost of these batteries is very small.

Outage costs for government offices and commercial customers were found to be minimal, because in most cases, reliance on electricity-using equipment such as calculators and Xerox machines was small, thus permitting work to continue by daylight. Furthermore, there was sufficient slack during the normal hours of work for jobs delayed by any outage to be made up. Supermarkets and hotels reported minor amounts of spoilage for long outages (i.e., over five hours); however, such outages are extremely rare. Rural consumers in the vicinity of Cascavel could be neglected, since their energy consumption was less than 2 percent of the total throughout the plan period.

The residential and industrial categories incurred the highest losses. The cost-benefit comparison of the outage costs and system costs for Cascavel indicated that as global reliability improved, outage costs decreased fairly steadily, whereas supply costs were practically constant until a critical level of reliability was reached, after which these costs increased sharply. The outage cost results disaggregated by cell and by consumer category indicated that the high population density areas in the city center and in the industrial area suffered the highest outage costs. Therefore, several additional mixed or hybrid network expansion plans were designed, based on the principle of providing the highest reliability service to areas with the highest outage costs, and so on. This feedback procedure yielded the best system expansion plan, which provided high reliability service in the city center area, with a high population density, and in the main industrial zone, while other areas of the city were served at a lower reliability level. The range of global optimal reliability levels was $0.9987 \geq R \geq 0.9983$, where $R$ is defined as the ratio of energy consumed to the energy consumed plus energy not consumed due to outages.

The effects of the new optimum reliability levels on the demand forecast and outage costs via the price and reliability expectation feedback loops shown in Figure 6–5 were not investigated because of lack of information on how the original prices and expected reliability levels should be revised. However, the results were found to be relatively insensitive to an arbitrary 10 percent change in the demand forecast.

Finally, the residential outage costs of US$1.3 to $2 per kWh lost (depending on the duration) in Cascavel may be compared with corresponding results of other studies: US$0.4 to $0.7 (Sweden, 1948), $0.7 to $1.5 (Sweden, 1969), and $0.5 to $1.5 (England, 1975). Similarly, Cascavel industrial outage costs of US$1 to $7 per kWh lost correspond to values of US$1 to $2 (Sweden, 1948); $0.1 to $3 (Sweden, 1969); $0.2 to $8 (Chile, 1973); and $1 to $9 (Canada, 1976). (All values are given in 1977 dollars.)

## SUMMARY

The rapid increases in the costs of energy supply in recent times have highlighted the need for improving the efficiency of producing and using energy, especially in the capital- and foreign-exchange-scare developing countries. Integrated national energy planning must begin with a clearcut definition of national objectives, in relation to which the links between the energy sector and the rest of the economy, as well as the interactions between and within the different energy subsectors, must be analysed.

The two critical decisions facing the policymaker in the electric power subsector relate to the optimal levels of output price and investment, which are closely interrelated. Economic theory indicates that the net social benefits of electricity consumption would be maximized if the price was set equal to marginal cost, while investments should continue until the marginal system costs of improving reliability were equal to the averted marginal outage costs. Although these optimality conditions should be satisfied simultaneously, in practice each rule is implemented separately, with the option of iterating between solutions to ensure mutual consistency.

Practical electricity pricing requires a two-stage procedure. In the first stage, the strict long-run marginal costs (LRMC) of electricity supply are estimated. Setting price equal to strict LRMC satisfies the economic efficiency objective. The second stage involves adjusting strict LRMC to meet other national goals and constraints such as the financial viability of the electricity producer, meeting the basic energy needs of poor consumers, economic second-best considerations, limitations of metering and billing, and various special considerations.

The practical implementation of the investment rule involves the use of a reliability-optimizing model in which the sum of system costs and outage costs is minimized. This operational criterion subsumes the traditional system-planning approach in which only system costs are usually minimized subject to an arbitrary target-reliability level. The results of a case study demonstrate that the new methodology may be applied empirically. The importance of measuring the outage costs of electricity consumers, and models for doing this, are discussed.

## REFERENCES

Anderson, D. 1972. "Models for Determining Least-Cost Investments in Electricity Supply." *The Bell Journal of Economics* 3 (Spring): 267–301.

Boiteaux, M. 1949. "La Tarification des Demandes en Pointe." *Revue Generale de l'Electricité* 58.

Boiteaux, M., and P. Stasi. 1964. "The Determination of Costs of Expansion of Inter-connected System of Production and Distribution of Electricity." In James Nelson, ed., *Marginal Cost Pricing in Practice.* Englewood-Cliffs, New Jersey: Prentice-Hall.

Brown, G., Jr., and M.B. Johnson. 1969. "Public Utility Pricing and Output Under Risk." *American Economic Review* (March): 119–28.

Canadian Electrical Association. 1978. *Marginal Costing and Pricing of Electrical Energy.* Montreal.

Crew, M.A., and P.R. Kleindorfer. 1978. "Reliability and Public Utility Pricing." *American Economic Review* (March): 31–40.

1979. *Public Utility Economics.* New York: St. Martin's Press.

Dupuit, P. 1932. "De l'Utilité et de sa Mesure." *La Reforma Soziale* (Turin).

Hotelling, H. 1938. "The General Welfare in Relation to Problems of Taxation and of Railway and Utility Rates." *Economethica* 6 (July): 242–69.

Munasinghe, M. 1979. *Economics of Power System Reliability and Planning.* Baltimore: Johns Hopkins University Press.

_____. 1980a. "The Costs of Electric Power Shortages to Residential Consumers." *Journal of Consumer Research* 6 (March): 361–69.

_____. 1980b. "A New Apporach to System Planning." *IEEE Transactions on Power Apparatus and Systems,* PAS-99 (May-June).

_____. 1980c. "An Integrated Framework for Energy Pricing in Developing Countries." *The Energy Journal* 1 (July): 1–31.

_____. 1980d. "Integrated National Energy Planning in Developing Countries." *Natural Resources Forum* (October): 359–74.

_____. 1981. "Principles of Modern Electricity Pricing." *Proceedings of the IEEE* 69 (March): 332–48.

Munasinghe, M., and M. Gellerson. 1979. "Economic Criteria for Optimizing Power System Reliability Levels." *The Bell Journal of Economics* 10 (Spring): 352–65.

Munasinghe, M., and W. Scott. 1978. "Long Range Distribution System Planning Based on Optimum Economic Reliability Levels." *Proceedings, IEEE PES Summer Meeting,* Los Angeles, July, Paper No. A78576-1.

Munasinghe, M., and J.J. Warford. 1982. *Electricity Pricing.* Baltimore: Johns Hopkins University Press.

Ruggles, N. 1949a. "The Welfare Basis of the Marginal Cost Pricing Principle." *Review of Economic Studies* 17:28–46.

_____. 1949b. "Recent Developments in the Theory of Marginal Cost Pricing." *Review of Economic Studies* 17: 107–26.

Schramm, G., and M. Munasinghe. 1981. "Interrelationships in Energy Planning: The Case of Tobacco Curing Industry in Thailand." *Energy Systems and Policy* 5:no. 2.

Sherman, R., and M. Visscher. 1978. "Second Best Pricing with Stochastic Demand." *American Economic Review* 68 (March): 42–53.

Steiner, P. 1957. "Peak Loads and Efficient Pricing." *Quarterly Journal of Economics* (November).

Sullivan, R.L. 1977. *Power System Planning.* New York: McGraw-Hill.

Symposium on Peak Load Pricing. 1976. *The Bell Journal of Economics* 7 (Spring): 197–250.

Taylor, L.D. 1975. "The Demand for Electricity: A Survey." *The Bell Journal of Economics* 6 (Spring): 74–110.

Telson, M.L. 1975. "The Economics of Alternative Levels of Reliability for Electric Generating Systems." *The Bell Journal of Economics* 6 (Fall): 679–94.

Turvey, R. 1968. *Optimal Pricing and Investment in Electricity Supply.* Cambridge, Massachusetts: MIT Press.

Turvey, R., and D. Anderson. 1977. *Electricity Economics.* Baltimore: Johns Hopkins University Press.

Williamson, O.E. 1966. "Peak Load Pricing and Optimal Capacity Under Indivisibility Constraints." *American Economic Review* 56 (September): 810–27.

1323
6352
7230
Israel

# 7 A TIME STEP EQUILIBRIUM MODEL FOR THE ELECTRICITY SECTOR

*Nissan Levin*
*Faculty of Management, Tel-Aviv University*
*Asher Tishler*
*Faculty of Management and Department of Economics, Tel-Aviv University*
*Jacob Zahavi*
*Faculty of Management, Tel-Aviv University*

## INTRODUCTION

The 1973 energy crisis, with the resulting increase in and instability of oil prices, has stimulated considerable interest in developing large-scale energy models as a means to set up national priorities and evaluate alternative energy policies. A variety of large-scale energy models has been developed in recent years to help national energy planning and support the decisionmaking process in this field. The various models can be classified into macroeconomic models, interindustry models, energy sector models, and models of individual energy industries. Macroeconomic models were developed, among the rest, by Preston (1972), Jorgenson and Hudson (1974), Manne (1977) and Connolly, Dantzig, and Parikh (1977). Interindustry models, in addition to Preston (1972) and Hudson and Jorgenson (1974), include the models by Bullard and Sebald (1975) and Hnyilicza (1975). The energy sector models include the Brookhaven models (see Cherniavsky 1974; Kydes and Rabinowitz 1979; and Marcuse et al. 1976), the ETA model (see

The present research was sponsored by the Israeli Ministry of Energy and Infrastructure and performed within the framework of the Israel Institute of Business Research, Faculty of Management, Tel-Aviv University, as part of the institute's masters program on Economics and Management of Energy.

215

Manne 1977), and the SRI-Gulf model (described by Cazalet 1977). Finally, the individual industry models include the natural gas model of MacAvoy and Pindyck (1975), the coal model of Zimmerman (1977), the electricity model by Joskow and Baughman (1976), and the models of Anderson (1972) and Munasinghe (1979). This list of models is not intended to be exhaustive, but only to indicate a few representative models in each category. A survey of existing large-scale energy models and additional references has recently been compiled in an EPRI (1979) report. The methodological basis of those models appears in Brock and Nesbitt (1977).

In this chapter we develop an equilibrium model for the electricity sector. The equilibrium issue has been dealt with by several of the above-mentioned models, including the Brookhaven Illinois model, the PIES model, the SRI-Gulf model, the Hudson-Jorgenson energy model, and others. All these models attempt to find the optimal equilibrium prices and quantities for the energy market, sometimes even for the whole economy, using complex mathematical programming models that require large amounts of input data and long processing times. The purpose of this chapter is to offer a simpler approach to finding the equilibrium solution for the electricity sector over time, by solving the problem year by year, rather than simultaneously across time, with the output of each year being the input to the following year. This process of solving a dynamic problem period after period rather than by making a complete lifetime planning is known in the literature as a myopic optimization (see, for example, Day, Morley, and Smith 1974). The planning horizon problems also belong to this type of model (see Modigliani and Hohn 1955). Several of the above-mentioned energy models also solve for the equilibrium prices and quantities in a serial fashion, including the FEA PIES model, the Hnyilicza model, the Hudson-Jorgenson model, and the Brookhaven TESOM model. We refer to this model, after the TESOM model (see Marcuse et al. 1976), as the time step model, to distinguish it from dynamic equilibrium models that view the problem simultaneously over time.

With the time step approach, the core of the model is the one-step (also myopic or static) problem, whose objective is to solve for the equilibrium prices and quantities of electricity at any given year in the future. In our model, we use a variation of the Joskow-Baughman model with one region to find the one-step equilibrium solution. Basically, the model consists of a demand side and a supply side, integrated through a price mechanism to balance the supply and the demand. A breakeven point analysis approach, extended to deal with both new and existing units, is used to find the optimal mix of units to meet electrical energy demand at any given year in the future.

Obviously, the time step approach offers significant computational savings over dynamic models that view the problem simultaneously over time, since each year is dealt with separately. The main obstacle with the time approach is that it cannot account for future developments in determining present investment decisions, thus yielding solutions that might not be optimal in the dynamic sense. Levin, Tishler, and Zahavi (1980b) have recently derived several conditions under which the time step model solution coincides with the overall dynamic model solution. Fortunately, these conditions prove to be most common in power systems that exhibit growing demand for electrical energy over time, thus rendering the time step approach very useful for policy analysis in the power field under quite general conditions.

Because of the simplicity of the model, we were able to find conditions under which the equilibrium solution exists and is unique and to investigate the sensitivity of the equilibrium solution to changes in the demand parameters. In the following sections, we proceed to describe the various components of the electricity model and the properties of the equilibrium solutions. For detailed proofs of the algorithms and properties, see Levin, Tishler, and Zahavi (1980a, b). The model has been programmed and applied to a realistic system, and some of the results will also be discussed. Further extensions of the model to encompass the entire energy sector for an economy that is a price taker in the world energy market and to consider uncertainties in the prices of primary energy resources are found in Levin, Tishler, and Zahavi (1980c, d, e).

## THE ONE-STEP SUPPLY MODEL

### The Load Duration Curve (LDC)

Investment decisions in electrical systems are governed by the projected load duration curve (LDC). The LDC is a conventional means to describe the demand for electrical energy over a given period of time, usually a year. We denote the LDC by $L(\tau)$, with $L_{min}$ denoting the load required by customers throughout the entire period (the base load) and $L_{max}$ the maximum demand in the period (the peak load). The area under the LDC represents the total amount of electrical energy required by customers, for all uses, in the period involved. By definition, the LDC is a monotonically decreasing and continuous function over the range between zero and the number of time units in the period concerned. By experience, the LDC is neither convex nor concave. For convenience, we consider normalized LDCs with time periods of one year, thus expressing the energy required in units of megawatt year (MWY).[1] Since the curve is monotonically decreasing, it possesses an inverse, denoted by $g(x)$. The inverse function $g(x)$ has the same properties as $L(\tau)$, except that for loads satisfying $x \leq L_{min}$, $g(x)$ has a constant value of one.

## The Optimization Problem: New Units Only

Given the LDC for the target year, the one-step problem is to find the mix of generating means to meet the load at minimum cost. The generating means could be of several types—for example, nuclear, oil-fired, coal-fired, hydroelectric, gas turbine, and so forth—and different sizes, as measured in MW. We refer to any generating means of a given type and size as a generating unit or simply, a unit, and denote it with an index $i$. To formulate the optimization problem, we introduce the following notation:

$n$ = number of units in the target year,
$t$ = the target year,
$x_i$ = capacity of unit $i$ (MW),
$c_i$ = total fixed costs for unit $i$ per year ($/MW), and
$b_i$ = total variable costs for unit $i$ ($/MWY)

Unless stated otherwise, all the variables will correspond to the given target year $t$. The index $t$ will be omitted for brevity.

Following Joskow and Baughman (1976), we assume that $c_i$ is constant, regardless of the unit's capacity (no economies of scale) and that $b_i$ is constant regardless of the unit's output. It can be shown that if there are no set-up costs to bring the generating unit to a working condition, these assumptions imply that the least cost procedure to operate the power plants is to load the generating units to production, at their rated capacity, in increasing order of their total variable costs (the merit order loading). To take forced outages and maintenance requirements of the generating units into account, one can multiply the rated capacity by an availability factor $\Theta_i$[2]

---

1. MWY of energy is defined as the energy output of a generating unit with capacity 1 MW over a period of one year.

2. The availability of a generating unit, $\Theta, o \leq \Theta \leq 1$, denotes the fraction of time the unit is available to meet customer demand when required, accounting for both forced outages and maintenance requirements.

and divide up the corresponding fixed cost $c_i$ by $\Theta_i$. However, without loss of generality, we assume $\Theta_i = 1$ for all $i$. In compliance with the merit order loading, we therefore arrange the generating units so that

$$b_1 < b_2 < \ldots b_i < \ldots b_n$$

It is further assumed that $c_1 > c_2 > \ldots > c_i > \ldots > c_n$, because otherwise, if $b_i < b_j$ and $c_i < c_j$, unit $j$ is inefficient and could be discarded from the mix of units to supply the demand.

Assuming that the power system starts out from scratch at the target year, the optimization problem is to find the capacity vector $\underline{x} = (x_1, \ldots, x_n)$ that solves

$$\operatorname*{Min}_{\underline{x}} \; TC\,(\underline{x}) = \sum_{i=1}^{n} c_i\, x_i + \sum_{i=1}^{n} b_i \int_{D_i}^{D_{i+1}} g(x)\, dx \tag{7.1}$$

s.t.

$$x_i \geq 0 \qquad i = 1, \ldots, n \tag{7.2}$$

$$\sum_{i=1}^{n} x_i \geq L_{max} \tag{7.3}$$

where $D_i$ is the loading point of unit $i$, defined as

$$D_1 \overset{\Delta}{=} 0$$

$$D_i \overset{\Delta}{=} \sum_{j=1}^{i-1} x_i \qquad i = 2, \ldots, n+1 \tag{7.4}$$

We note that the first expression in equation (7.1) is the total fixed costs incurred; the second expression is the total operating expenses.

The optimization problem [equations (7.1) through (7.3)] is a convex non-linear programming problem whose solution is obtained using a simple breakeven point analysis (see for example Levin, Tishler, and Zahavi 1980a: Section 3.3. and Appendix B).

The solution procedure can also be demonstrated graphically, as shown in Figure 7–1, for a three-unit system containing a coal-fired, an oil-fired, and a gas turbine unit. Since the costs $b_i$ and $c_i$ are constant for any unit $i$ regardless of its capacity and time of operation, the cost function representing the total cost for unit $i$ as a function of operating time is linear, with the

**Figure 7-1.**    Optimal Mix Algorithm, New Units Only.

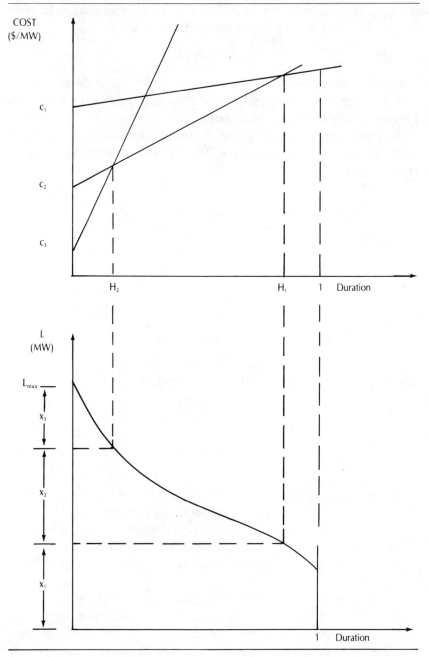

intercept representing the total investment cost per MW per year ($c_i$) and the slope denoting the total variable cost for a unit of energy (1 MWY) produced by unit $i$ ($b_i$). These curves are plotted in the upper portion of Figure 7–1. Since the operating and investment costs for the various units are inversely related, the curve describing the minimum total expenses for the system as a function of time is a piecewise concave function, as shown in the upper portion of Figure 7–1. We refer to this function as the minimum cost polygon. Thus, the gas turbine unit is not economical if operated more than $H_2$ percent of the time, and the oil-fired unit is economical only if operated more than $H_2$ but less than $H_1$ percent of the time, whereas the coal-fired unit is economical only if operated continuously throughout the time period. The breakeven points are obtained at the intersection point of consecutive costs curve. The optimal capacity to install of each unit is then obtained by projecting the breakeven points onto the LDC, as demonstrated in the lower portion of Figure 7–1.

Because of its simplicity, the optimal mix algorithm used here has been used for many years to find the least cost mix of units to meet electrical energy demand and is widely reported in the literature. Joskow and Baughman (1976) have also used this model to find the optimal mix of units in their model.

## Optimization with Existing Units: 1 EMU

Clearly, the assumption that the power system in the target year consists of new units only is not realistic, especially when dealing with short- and medium-range planning. Phillips et al. (1969) and, more recently, Stoughton, Chen, and Lee (1980) have extended the above optimal mix algorithm to also account for existing units. In this study we devise a more efficient approach, to allow existing units to enter the optimal mix solution in the target year, distinguishing between two cases—(1) only efficient[3] existing units are allowed in the optimal mix of units; (2) all existing units, even if inefficient, are required to participate in the mix of units in the target year.

To develop the algorithm, we arrange the new and existing units in the merit order. We refer to any consecutive series of existing units in the merit order as an existing multiunit (EMU). To start with, we assume only 1 EMU, consisting of $s-r+1$ units occupying positions $r, r+1, \ldots, s$ in the merit order. The optimization problem is the same as in equations (7.1)

---

3. The terms "efficient" and "inefficient" existing units will be made clear later.

through (7.3). To allow for efficient existing units to enter the optimal mix of units in the target year, we add the additional set of constraints:

$$x_i \leq y_{i+1-r} \qquad\qquad i = r, \ldots, s \qquad\qquad (7.5)$$

where $y_1, \ldots, y_l$, $l = s - r + 1$, are given constants, expressing the capacities, in MW, of the existing units.

While not required mathematically, it is plausible to assume that the peak demand at the target year, $L_{max}$, is higher than the peak demand at the base year—that is,

$$\sum_{i=1}^{l} y_i \leq L_{max} \qquad\qquad (7.6)$$

Letting

$u_i$, $i = 1, \ldots, n$ be the dual variables (Lagrange multipliers) of the nonnegativity constraints [equation (7.2)], expressing the marginal cost to the system of installing an increment of unit $i$;

$u =$ the dual variable of the peak demand constraint (7.3), expressing the marginal cost to the system of increasing the peak demand ($L_{max}$) by one unit (1 MW),

$\lambda_{i+1-r}$, $i = r, \ldots, s$ be the dual variables of the existing units constraints [equation (7.5)]

the Kuhn-Tucker conditions are

$$c_i + R_i - u_i - u = 0 \qquad\qquad i < r \text{ or } s < i \leq n \qquad\qquad (7.7)$$

$$c_i + R_i + \lambda_{i+1-r} - u_i - u = 0 \qquad\qquad i = r, \ldots, s \qquad\qquad (7.8)$$

where

$$R_i \overset{\Delta}{=} \sum_{j=i}^{n} (b_j - b_{j+1}) g(D_{j+1}) \qquad\qquad (7.9)$$

$$x_i \geq 0 \qquad\qquad i = 1, \ldots, n \qquad\qquad (7.10)$$

$$\sum_{i=1}^{n} x_i - L_{max} \geq 0 \qquad\qquad (7.11)$$

$$y_{i+1-r} - x_i \geq 0 \qquad\qquad i = r, \ldots, s \qquad\qquad (7.12)$$

$$u_i \cdot x_i = 0 \qquad\qquad i = 1, \ldots, n \qquad\qquad (7.13)$$

$$u \cdot \left( \sum_{i=1}^{n} x_i - L_{\max} \right) = 0 \qquad\qquad (7.14)$$

$$\lambda_{i+1-r}(y_{i+1-r} - x_i) = 0 \qquad\qquad i = r, \ldots, s \qquad\qquad (7.15)$$

$$u_i \geq 0 \qquad\qquad i = 1, \ldots, n \qquad\qquad (7.16)$$

$$u \geq 0 \qquad\qquad (7.17)$$

$$\lambda_{i+1-r} \geq 0 \qquad\qquad i = r, \ldots, s \qquad\qquad (7.18)$$

By definition, the dual variable $\lambda_{i+1-r}$ denotes the shadow price of increasing the capacity of the existing unit $i$, $r \leq i \leq s$, by 1 MW. Hence, if the dual variable is positive, we define the existing unit as an "efficient" unit and include it in the optimal mix solution at its rated capacity. If the dual variable is zero, we define the corresponding unit as "inefficient." By the Kuhn-Tucker condition [equation (7.15)], this unit should either be discarded from the optimal mix of units or else utilized at a capacity that is less than its rated capacity.

Another interpretation of the dual variables $\lambda_{i+1-r}$ can be obtained by comparing the Kuhn-Tucker conditions (7.7) and (7.8). We recall that the fixed cost for a given unit is composed of a capital cost component and a fixed operating and maintenance cost component. Since the capital costs for the existing units are actually sunk costs, we can set them equal to zero in the optimization problem. Furthermore, assuming that the fixed operating and maintenance cost component for a generating unit is negligible as compared to its capital cost component, we can assume $c_i = 0$ for all existing units. Substituting in equation (7.8), we obtain

$$R_i + \lambda_{i+1-r} - u_i - u = 0 \qquad\qquad r \leq i \leq s \qquad\qquad (7.19)$$

By comparing equation (7.7) to equation (7.19), the dual variables $\lambda_1, \ldots, \lambda_l$, $l = s - r + 1$, can be interpreted as the "effective" fixed cost for the existing units—that is, if we were to install a generating unit in an all new power system whose total variable expenses are given by $b_i$ \$/MWY and total fixed costs by $\lambda_{i+1-r}$ \$/MW, we would obtain this unit in the optimal mix solution with capacity identical to that of existing unit $i$. Since unit $i$ is already installed, we actually "earn" the capital cost by keeping it in the optimal solution. Hence, the unit is efficient. If the dual variable is zero, we actually gain nothing by keeping the unit in the optimal mix solution at its rated capacity. Thus, the unit is inefficient.

It can be shown that the existing units in the optimal mix solution satisfy the following rules (see Levin, Tishler, and Zahavi 1980a: Appendixes C, D, E): First, at least one existing unit appears in the optimal mix of units in the target year at capacity greater than zero. There exist exactly two cases:

1.  Either $x^*_i = y_{i+1-r}$ for all $i = r, \ldots, s$, or
2.  There exists $\hat{s}$ such that

$$\hat{s} < i \leq s \Rightarrow x^*_i = 0$$
$$r \leq i < \hat{s} \Rightarrow x^*_i = y_{i+1-r}$$

and also, $0 \leq x^*_{\hat{s}} \leq y_{\hat{s}}$. Case (1) corresponds to the case where all existing units are efficient; case (2) to that where some or all of the existing units are inefficient.

We demonstrate the algorithm graphically for a system containing two new units, say one coal-fired unit and one gas turbine unit, and an EMU consisting of two oil-fired units, denoted as units 1 and 2, respectively. In Figure 7–2 we describe the algorithm for the case where all existing units are efficient. Without loss of generality, we assume that the merit order locations of the existing units fall in between the coal-fired and the gas turbine units, so that the minimum cost polygon for the EMU lies below the minimum cost polygon for the new units, as shown in the upper portion of Figure 7–2. We start the solution procedure by solving for the optimal mix of the new existing units only. We then shift the minimum cost polygon for the EMU up and down, right or left, until the projections of the breakeven points onto the LDC yield the capacities of the existing units, as demonstrated in the lower portion of Figure 7–2. As can be seen from the figure, the two dual variables $\lambda_1$ and $\lambda_2$ are positive. Thus, by definition, both existing units are efficient and appear in the optimal mix of units at their rated capacities. Given the loading points of the existing units, the capacities of the new coal-fired and gas turbine units are then read directly off the LDC. Clearly, these capacities are smaller than those obtained when no existing units are allowed in the optimal mix of units (denoted with a "hat" in Figure 7–2).

The case of inefficient existing units is illustrated in Figure 7–3. Repeating the procedure described above, we obtain that in this case $\lambda_2$, the dual variable for the second existing unit, is negative. Since by the Kuhn-Tucker condition [equation (7.18)] $\lambda_2$ cannot be negative, we slide the minimum cost polygon of the EMU upwards, until $\lambda_2$ becomes zero, as demonstrated in Figure 7–4, thus obtaining the new breakeven points. The optimal capacities

**Figure 7-2.** Optimal Mix Algorithm, 1 EMU.

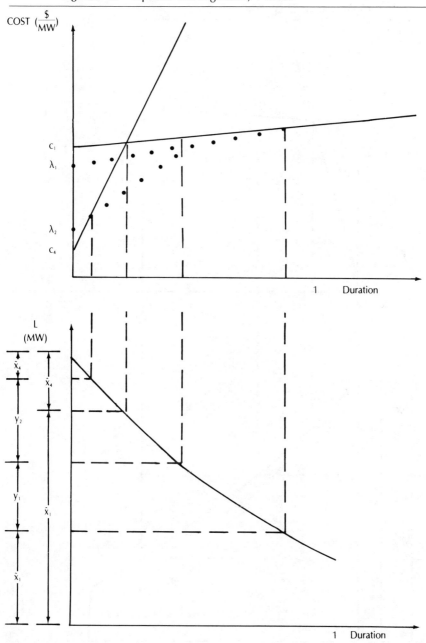

**Figure 7-3.**     Optimal Mix Algorithmal, 1 EMU, All Existing Units Required to Operate at Target Year.

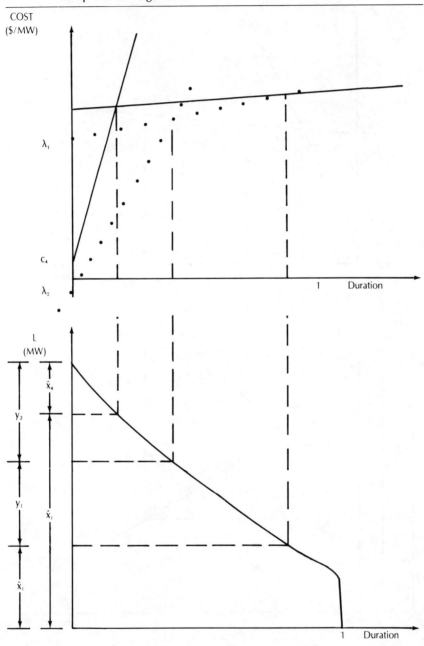

**Figure 7–4.**     Optimal Mix Algorithm, 1 EMU, Only Efficient Existing Units Are Allowed in Optimal Mix.

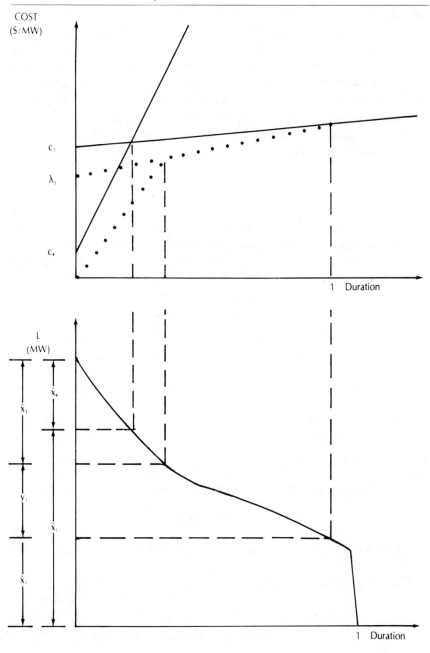

to install of each unit are then obtained by projecting the breakeven points onto the LDC. We note that the second existing unit is utilized, in the optimal mix of units, at a capacity that is less than its rated capacity.

While economically inefficient units should be discarded from the optimal mix of units in the target year or utilized at reduced capacities, we might conceive of cases where because of short-run budget constraints that limit the amount of money that can be invested in power system expansion, all the existing units, including inefficient ones, will be called upon to meet the energy demand at the target year. The optimization problem in this case is given again by equations (7.1) through (7.3). Constraint (7.5), however, takes the form of an equality—that is,

$$x_i = y_{i+1-r} \qquad\qquad i = r, \ldots, s \qquad\qquad (7.20)$$

The solution procedure for this case was demonstrated in Figure 7–3. As can be seen from the figure, existing unit 2 appears in the optimal mix of units at its rated capacity, in compliance with constraint (7.20). We note that since (7.20) is an equality constraint, the dual variables of the existing units could be negative, as is the case with $\lambda_2$. The negative dual variables yield, in this case, the losses incurred to the system by the requirement to include the inefficient existing units in the optimal mix of units in the target year.

## Optimization with Multiple EMUs

We now extend the previous algorithm to the more general case where there are multiple EMUs. We again arrange the new and existing units in a merit order, assuming $J$ EMUs, with the $j$th EMU containing $l_j = s_j - r_j + 1$ units, occupying merit order locations $r_j, \ldots, s_j$. Let $y^j_{i+1-r_j}$ denote the capacity of the existing unit $i$ in the $j$th EMU. Constraint (7.5) takes the form

$$x_i \leq y^j_{i+1-r_j} \qquad\qquad i = r_j, \ldots, s_j \qquad\qquad (7.21)$$

The objective function (7.1) and the constraints (7.2) and (7.3) do not change.

To demonstrate the algorithm, we assume that there are two EMUs, with the first EMU loaded to generation before the second EMU. The algorithm proceeds as follows: Solve the optimal mix problem for each EMU separately, using the algorithm described in the previous section and in Figures 7–1 and 7–3. Let

$m_1$ be the loading point (in the optimal mix solution) of the first EMU;

$M_1$ be the loading point (in the optimal mix solution) of the unit loaded to
generation following the first EMU; and

$m_2$, $M_2$ be the corresponding loading points for the second EMU.

If there is no overlapping between the two separate solutions—that is, if
$m_2 \geq M1$—then the loads in the interval $[0 - m_1]$, $[M_1 - m_2]$, $[M_2 - L_{max}]$ will
be met by the new units, whereas the loads in the interval $[m_1 - M_1]$,
$[m_2 - M_2]$ will be covered by the two EMUs, respectively. Otherwise—namely, if $M_1 > m_2$—we discard all new units occupying the merit order locations
between the two EMUs, combine the two EMUs into one, and solve the
optimal mix problem for the combined EMU using the previous model.

Using similar arguments to the above, the algorithm can be easily extended to any number of EMUs. We have used this extended algorithm to
solve the optimal mix problem for the application described later in the
chapter. Further discussion and the optimality proofs of the algorithms for
all cases described above are found in Levin, Tishler, and Zahavi (1980a:
Appendixes B through G).

## THE EQUILIBRIUM MECHANISM

### The Demand Function

Under equilibrium, the quantity demanded of electricity should be equal to
the quantity supplied of electricity for the given price. In the present work,
the demand for electricity is represented by a single demand function $f(p)$.
Most of the theoretical analysis to follow does not require an explicit specification of the demand function, except that it be a continuous, decreasing
function. For some uniqueness theorems and sensitivity analyses and, in
particular, in the application of section five, we assume that the demand for
electricity is given by the following aggregate function:

$$f(p) = aY^\alpha (p/p_c)^\beta \qquad (7.22)$$

where $Y$ is the GNP in the target year, $p$ is the electricity price, $p_c$ is the
price index of all other commodities in the market, $\alpha$ and $\beta$ are the output
(income) and price elasticities, respectively, and $a$ is a constant coefficient
representing all other explanatory variables that are not specifically expressed in the aggregate demand function. Methods to estimate demand
functions for electricity have been discussed widely in literature (see, for

example, Berndt and Wood 1975; Fuss 1977; Halvorsen 1978; Maddala, Chern, and Gill 1978 and Pindyck 1979) and will therefore not be discussed here.

## Pricing Mechanism

The electricity price is the driving force leading to the equilibrium solution. A variety of methods have been devised to determine the end use price of electricity. Joskow and Baughman (1976), for example, have used the common rate of return criterion to set up electricity prices in their model. In the present work, we use a simplified mechanism to determine end use electricity price, based on the average total cost—namely,

$$p = U\left(\frac{TC}{E}\right)$$
(7.23)

where $p$ is end-use price of electricity, $TC$ is total fixed and variable costs, and $E$ is total energy produced (MWH).

In most cases discussed below, it suffices to assume that $U(\cdot)$ is any scalar, positive, and monotonically increasing function. In the sensitivity analysis of section four, we chose the mark-up approach in order to translate the average total cost into end use electricity price—that is,

$$p = \mu \cdot \frac{TC}{E}$$
(7.24)

where $\mu$ is a given constant satisfying $\mu > 0$.

## Changing the LDC

Clearly, any change in the relative price of electricity will cause the LDC for the system to change. The precise effect of a relative price change on the shape of the LDC should be determined by estimating the demand functions for electricity for several intervals of the day. This information is generally unavailable when only one price for electricity is used and only partially available when peak load prices are used (see Acton and Mitchell 1980). Thus, in this chapter we consider three possibilities of changing the LDC as a result of a change in the relative price of electricity—scaling, shifting, and combined shifting and scaling, as demonstrated graphically in Figure 7–5.

**Figure 7-5.**   Scaling and Shifting of the LDC.

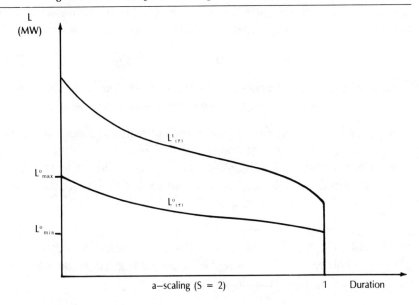

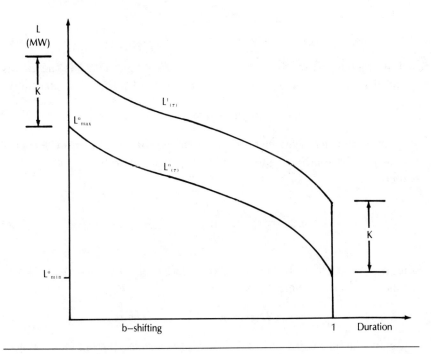

*Scaling the LDC.* In this case, the LDC is scaled upwards or downwards by a constant amount $S$. Denoting the LDC in the base year by $L^o(\tau)$ and the LDC in the target year $t$ by $L^t(\tau)$, we have, under scaling,

$$L^t(\tau) \; = \; S \; L^o(\tau) \qquad\qquad S\varepsilon \; [\tilde{S}, \infty] \qquad\qquad (7.25)$$

Clearly, the maximal value of $S$ is infinity. To determine the minimal value of $S$, denoted by $\tilde{S}$, we distinguish between the following cases:

- If only new units are allowed in the optimal mix of units in the target year, then, at least theoretically, $\tilde{S} \; = \; 0$.
- Otherwise—that is, if existing units are also allowed in the mix of units in the target year, producing altogether $\tilde{E}$ MWY of electricity— $\tilde{S}$ is that value of $S$ that satisfies $\tilde{S}E^o{}_s \; = \; \tilde{E}$—namely, $\tilde{S} \; = \; \tilde{E}/E^o{}_s$

The equilibrium price is also a function of the scaling factor and will be denoted by $p(S)$. Let $E_s(p(S))$ denote the energy supplied with the price $p(S)$. By definition, the energy supplied in a year is given as the area under the corresponding LDC—that is,

$$E_s(p(S)) \; = \; \int_0^1 L^t(\tau) \; d\tau \; = \; S \; \int_0^1 L^o(\tau) \; d\tau \qquad\qquad (7.26)$$

But the integral on the right hand side of equation (7.26) is the energy supplied with the original LDC, which we denote by $E^o{}_s$. Thus, in scaling,

$$E_s(p(S)) \; = \; S \; \cdot \; E^o{}_s \qquad\qquad (7.27)$$

Equating the energy demanded at the price $p(S)$, $f(p(S))$, with the energy supplied at price $p(S)$, $E_s(p(S))$, and using equation (7.27), we have, under equilibrium,

$$S \; = \frac{f(p(S))}{E^o{}_s} \qquad\qquad (7.28)$$

*Shifting the LDC.* In this case, the LDC is shifted upwards or downwards by a constant amount $K$—that is,

$$L^t(\tau) \; = \; L^o(\tau) \; + \; K \qquad\qquad K\varepsilon \; [\tilde{K}, \infty] \qquad\qquad (7.29)$$

Again, the maximal value of $K$ is $\infty$. To determine the minimal value of $K$, denoted $\tilde{K}$, we also have to distinguish between two cases:

- If the power system in the target year consists of new units only, or new units plus the efficient existing units only, then $\check{K}$ is that value of $K$ for which min $L^t(\tau) = 0$. Since the LDC is a monotonically decreasing function, we have by equation (7.29)

$$\check{K} = \min(K) = -L^o_{\min} \tag{7.30}$$

- If all the existing units are required to participate in the mix of units in the target year, $K$ is determined by

$$\check{K} = -\min\left\{ L^o_{\min}, L^o_{\max} - \sum_{i=1}^{N_o} y_i \right\} \tag{7.31}$$

where $N_o$ is the number of existing units and $y_i$ the capacity (in MW) of existing unit $i$.

As in the previous case, the equilibrium price under shifting is a function of the shifting factor and is denoted by $p(K)$.

The energy produced to meet the demand at the target year, denoted by $E_s(p(K))$, is given by

$$E_s(p(K)) = \int_0^1 L^t(\tau)d\tau = \int_0^1 (L^o(\tau) + K)d\tau = \int_0^1 L^o(\tau)\,d\tau + K = E^o_s + K \tag{7.32}$$

Equating the energy supplied to the energy demanded, we have under equilibrium

$$K = f(p(K)) - E^o_s \tag{7.33}$$

We note that in equation (7.29), $K$ is expressed in units of capacity (MW), whereas in equation (7.32), it is expressed in units of energy (MWY). This is permissible, because we use yearly LDC with normalized time axes.

*Combined shifting and scaling.*    Finally, we consider the more general case in which the new LDC resulting from the change in the relative price of electricity is obtained by combined shifting and scaling of the original LDC—that is,

$$L^t(\tau) = S \cdot L^o(\tau) + K \tag{7.34}$$

Using similar development as above, the energy produced to meet the demand in the target year is given by

$$E_s \left( p(K) \right) = S \cdot E^o{}_s + K \tag{7.35}$$

However, unlike the previous cases, it is impossible to solve for $S$ and $K$ that equate the energy demanded to the energy supplied, unless the function $S = q(K)$ is given. Clearly, for shifting $q(K) = 1$; for scaling $K=0$.

The minimal value of $K$, $\tilde{K}$, in this case depends on the function $q(\cdot)$ and is obtained by solving

$$\underset{K}{\text{Min}} \; (K + q(K) \, E^o{}_s) = \tilde{K} + q(\tilde{K}) \, E^o{}_s \tag{7.36}$$

s.t.

$$K + q(K) \, L^o{}_{min} \geq 0 \tag{7.37}$$

$$K + q(K) \, L^o{}_{max} > \sum_{i=1}^{N_0} y_i \tag{7.38}$$

where $y_i$ and $N_0$ are as defined in equation (7.31). In case the optimal mix solution contains new units only, or new and efficient existing units, the second constraint should be ignored.

*Example*    As an example, we evaluate the function $S=q(K)$ for a given change in the expected system load factor.[4] Assuming the system load factor in the target year, denoted by $r^t$, is given as

$$r^t = ar^o$$

where $r^o$ is the load factor in the base year and $a > o$ is a given constant, then by definition of the load factor

$$r^t = \frac{E_s(p(K))}{L^t{}_{max}} = \frac{S \cdot E^o{}_s + K}{S \cdot L^o{}_{max} + K} = a \, \frac{E^o{}_s}{L^o{}_{max}}$$

Solving, we obtain

$$S = \frac{r^t - 1}{E^o{}_s - r^t \, L^o{}_{max}} \cdot K$$

which is the resulting $S = q(K)$ function.

4. The load factor is the ratio of the energy produced (the area under the LDC) to the maximum possible energy output (the area of the rectangle whose base is the time duration involved and whose height is the peak demand).

## Finding the Equilibrium Solution

In the case where no existing unit is allowed in the optimal mix solution for the target year, the equilibrium solution can be obtained analytically. Properties of the above solution, as well as theorems stating the condition for existence and uniqueness of the equilibrium solution for scaling, shifting, and combined scaling and shifting, are found in Levin, Tishler, and Zahavi (1980a).

In the case where some or all of the existing units are required to be operating in the target year, the equilibrium solution is obtained in an iterative manner, as described in the internal loop of Figure 7–6. For given predictions of the prices of primary energy resources and the LDC in the target year, the supply model of section two is first used to find the optimal mix of units to meet the demand for electrical energy as given by the area under the LDC. The resulting investment program is then translated into price of electricity $p$ and matched with the demand curve $f(p)$ to yield the quantity demanded of electrical energy at that price. Under equilibrium, the quantity demanded of electricity, as determined by the demand curve, should be equal to the quantity supplied of energy as given by the area under the LDC. Otherwise, the LDC is updated by scaling, shifting, or combined shifting and scaling, until the area under the LDC is equal to the energy demanded. The updated LDC is then used to find the new optimal mix of units, the new electricity price, and the new energy demanded, and so on, until convergence occurs.

## The Time Step Solution

Figure 7–6 also describes the time step approach. As mentioned above, the internal loop constitutes the one-step equilibrium model. The output of the one-step model—namely, the investment program under equilibrium—is used to update the inventory of units facing the system at the start of the following year. The algorithm then proceeds to find the equilibrium solution for the successive year (year $t+1$), starting with the LDC for year $t$, which is updated to reflect the expected increase in peak demand, to express the demand distribution at year $t+1$. The algorithm continues in this manner until all years in the planning horizon are considered.

As mentioned above, Levin, Tishler, and Zahavi have recently derived several conditions under which the time step model solution coincides with an overall dynamic model solution. The conditions pertain to two basic

**Figure 7–6.** Flow Chart of Time Step Equilibrium Model.

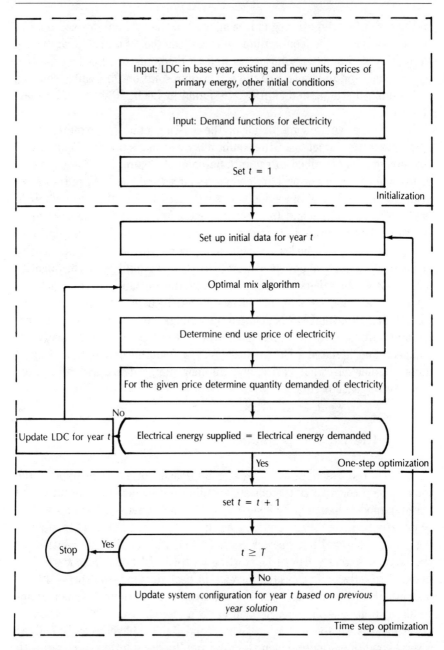

cases: In the first case, it is assumed that all present power generation technologies are available for erection at the first year of the planning horizon, allowing for new technologies only to become available at a later date. In the second case, it is assumed that some of the more advanced technologies, occupying low merit order locations (such as nuclear technology), will not be available at the beginning of the planning horizon because of lead time constraints. Then, under certain conditions (see Levin, Tishler, and Zahavi 1980b), the time step model solution and the dynamic model solution are identical. Fortunately, the conditions derived are found to be most common in power systems that exhibit growing demand for electrical energy over time. Even if some of these conditions do not hold in reality, the time step approach has a value of its own, because it reflects the manner in which decisions are actually being made in practice. The uncertainty involved in estimating parameters over time also makes it difficult, if not impossible, to attain the necessary data to solve the dynamic model simultaneously over time. Instead, decisions are made one by one as more information becomes available.

## PROPERTIES OF THE EQUILIBRIUM SOLUTION

In the following section, we state several existence and uniqueness theorems of the equilibrium solution described above that apply to each of the one-step solutions obtained using the time step approach. These theorems, as well as some additional sensitivity analysis results, are proved and discussed in Levin, Tishler, and Zahavi (1980a).

We start by stating the conditions for existence and uniqueness of the equilibrium solution for various procedures of updating the LDC. Note that for all theorems, the pricing mechanism is given by equation (7.23). Theorems 1, 3, and 5 are proved for any demand function $f(p)$ that is positive, monotonically decreasing, and differentiable. Theorems 2 and 4 are proved only for the demand function (7.22), which is later used in the application of section five.

### Theorem 1 (Existence and Uniqueness)

In the case where only efficient existing units, as well as new units, are allowed in the optimal mix solution and the LDC is updated using scaling, the equilibrium solution exists and is unique.

## Theorem 2 (Existence and Uniqueness)

In the case where all existing units are required to participate in the optimal mix solution at their present capacities and the LDC is updated using scaling, a sufficient condition that there exists a unique equilibrium solution is that

$$f(p\left(\frac{\hat{E}}{E^o{}_s}\right)) > \hat{E}$$

where $\hat{E}$ is the energy produced in the target year by a system containing existing units only and $f(\cdot)$ is the demand function.

## Theorem 3 (Existence)

In the case where the mix of units in the target year contains new and existing units and the LDC is updated using shifting, then a sufficient condition that there exists at least one equilibrium solution is that $f(p(\tilde{K})) > E^o{}_s + \tilde{K}$, where $\tilde{K}$, the minimal value of $K$, is defined by equation (7.31).

## Theorem 4 (Uniqueness)

If, under the conditions of Theorem 3, the base load is provided by a new base unit, then a sufficient condition that the equilibrium solution is unique is given by

$$\frac{E^o{}_s + \tilde{K}}{f(p(\tilde{K}))} > \left(\frac{b_1 + c_1}{p(\tilde{K})} - 1\right)\beta$$

where $\beta$ denotes the price elasticity of demand and $b_1$, $c_1$ are, respectively, the total variable and fixed costs of the first (base) unit.

## Theorem 5 (Existence)

In the case where the mix of units in the target year consists of new and existing units and the LDC is updated using combined shifting and scaling, a sufficient condition that there is at least one equilibrium solution is that

$$f(p(\tilde{K})) > \tilde{K} + q(\tilde{K})E^o{}_s$$

where $\tilde{K}$ is determined by equations (7.36) through (7.38).

The uniqueness conditions for the case of combined scaling and shifting are much more complex to obtain and depend, among the rest, on the functional relationship between the scaling and the shifting factors, $S = q(K)$.


## AN APPLICATION

### Basic Assumptions

The time step model has been programmed and applied to yield the equilibrium solution for the Israeli power system under the following assumptions:

1. The planning horizon extends from 1985 through 2000.
2. Twenty-nine units will be in operation at the beginning of the year 1985; all are required to participate in the optimal mix of units in the future years.
3. New units to satisfy increasing demand in the planning horizon consist of four types—nuclear, coal-fired, oil-fired, and gas turbine units.
4. An earliest commencing time is introduced for new coal-fired and nuclear units (1990 for coal fired units and 1995 for nuclear units).
5. No constraints are imposed on either the minimum or the maximum capacity of the new units.
6. The generating units' availability changes with the age of the machine. Typically, the older the unit, the smaller the availability.
7. The aggregate demand function for electricity is given by equation (7.22), with the GNP at any target year, $Y_t$, obtained from the GNP at the base year, $Y_o$, using the formula

$$Y_t = Y_o (1+\delta)^{t-t_o}$$

   where $\delta$ is the annual rate of increase in the GNP (percent) and $t_o$ is the base year ($t_o = 1977$). The GNP for year $t$ is derived parametrically for various values of $\alpha, \beta$, and $\delta$ as described below.
8. The electricity price is determined by marking up the average total cost. Without loss of generality, we assume $\mu = 1$.
9. The LDC is updated using scaling.
10. Initial conditions for the calculations are

$$Y_o = \$12.6 \cdot 10^9 \qquad p_c = 25 \ \$/MWH \qquad E^o_s = 9.3 \cdot 10^6 \ MWH$$

11.  To examine the sensitivity of the equilibrium solution, we ran the model under the following values of the parameters:

- Time steps: 1, 2, 3, and 4 years;
- Yearly increase in the GNP ($\delta$): 3, 5, and 7 percent;
- Price elasticity ($\beta$): $-$ 0.3;
- Income elasticity ($\alpha$): 1.1, 1.3, 1.5, 1.7;
- Yearly change in primary energy prices as described in Table 7–1.

The old and new units characteristics, as well as fuel characteristics, are given in detail in Levin, Tishler, and Zahavi (1980b: Tables 5.1, 5.2, 5.3). We summarize the main conclusions in the following sections.


## Time Step Impact

Table 7–2 summarizes the equilibrium solution for several time steps for moderate and accelerated change in the prices of primary energy resources. The main conclusion drawn from the table is that the equilibrium solution is well behaved—that is, new units are added to the system at each time period, and the differences in the cumulative new capacity for various time steps is minimal. Differences in the cumulative new capacities are due mainly to the earlier time constraints imposed on coal-fired and nuclear units. For example, since the earliest introduction time for nuclear units is 1995, no nuclear unit will be allowed in the period 1994–97 (a time step of four years), whereas if a time step of three years is used, the corresponding period is 1995–97, for which a nuclear unit can be erected. And indeed, we notice a substantial difference in the total cost for time steps of four years in 1997 versus the corresponding cost for time steps of three years. By and large, the smaller the time steps, the less the total costs, since cheaper and

Table 7–1.  Yearly Change (percent) in the Real Prices of Primary Energy Resources.

|  | Nuclear | Coal | Fuel Oil | Diesel Oil |
|---|---|---|---|---|
| Slow | 1 | 2 | 3 | 3 |
| Moderate | 1 | 2.5 | 5 | 5 |
| Accelerated | 2 | 5 | 8 | 8 |

more efficient units can be introduced at a faster rate to meet the increasing demand for power.

## Capacity Increase by Type of Unit

Table 7–3 summarizes the new capacity by type of unit for $\alpha = 1.3$, $\beta = -0.3$, $\delta = 5$ percent, and moderate increase in the prices of primary energy resources. As can be seen, capacity is added in bulk, approximately one unit per period. Also, the solution obtained corresponds to the conditions of Theorem 4.4 in Levin, Tishler, and Zahavi (1980b). Hence, the time step solution, in this particular case, is identical to the dynamic model solution, at least for the time period considered.

## Rate of Increase in the GNP

Table 7–4 summarizes the equilibrium solution for various rates of increase in the GNP, assuming moderate changes in the prices of primary energy, price elasticity of $-0.3$, income elasticity 1.3, and time steps of one year. The results indicate that the larger the rate of increase in the GNP, the larger the energy produced and the resulting total cost. It is interesting to note that the impact of the GNP increase on the required energy and total cost is more or less linear. Clearly, the more distant the target year, the greater the GNP impact on the equilibrium solution, due to the cumulative effects of the GNP increase on the demand for energy. The sensitivity of the system performance measures to changes in the rate of increase in the GNP emphasizes how important it is to accurately predict this parameter over time.

## Changes in Prices of Primary Energy

While the total cost and the equilibrium price react very strongly to changes in prices of primary energy, energy produced changes very little (for price elasticities smaller than $-0.3$). Table 7–5 summarizes the results for $\delta = 5$ percent, $\alpha = 1.3$, $\beta -0.3$, and time steps of one year. Clearly, the larger the absolute value of the price of elasticity of demand, the more pronounced is the impact of changes in the primary energy prices on the equilibrium solution.

**Table 7-2.** Time Step Impact ($\alpha = 1.3$, $\beta = -0.3$, $\delta = 5\%$)

| Increase in Primary Energy Price / Time Step | Max Load (MW) | | | | | Annual Total Cost $10^9$ $ | | | | | Equilibrium Price $/MWH | | | | |
|---|---|---|---|---|---|---|---|---|---|---|---|---|---|---|---|
| | 1 | 2 | 3 | 4 | static | 1 | 2 | 3 | 4 | static | 1 | 2 | 3 | 4 | static |
| Moderate | | | | | | | | | | | | | | | |
| 1986 | 2,988 | | | | | 0.431 | | | | | 24.8 | | | | |
| 1987 | 2,986 | 2,986 | | | | 0.447 | 0.447 | | | | 25.7 | 25.7 | | | |
| 1988 | 3,126 | | 3,123 | | | 0.495 | | 0.499 | | | 27.2 | | 27.5 | | |
| 1989 | 3,275 | 3,279 | | 3,259 | | 0.599 | 0.550 | | 0.561 | | 28.8 | 28.8 | | 29.6 | |
| 1990 | 3,483 | | | | | 0.589 | | | | | 29.1 | | | | |
| 1991 | 3,699 | 3,695 | 3,598 | | | 0.633 | 0.634 | 0.676 | | | 29.4 | 29.5 | 32.3 | | |
| 1992 | 3,924 | | | | | 0.681 | | | | | 29.8 | | | | |
| 1993 | 4,164 | 4,163 | | 4,158 | | 0.733 | 0.733 | | 0.733 | | 30.2 | 30.3 | | 30.3 | |
| 1994 | 4,427 | | 4,336 | | | 0.785 | | 0.820 | | | 30.5 | | 32.5 | | |
| 1995 | 4,745 | 4,701 | | | | 0.822 | 0.843 | | | | 29.8 | 30.8 | | | |
| 1996 | 5,077 | | | | | 0.868 | | | | | 29.4 | | | | |
| 1997 | 5,450 | 5,387 | 5,407 | 5,286 | 5,706 | 0.909 | 0.931 | 0.927 | 0.972 | 0.820 | 28.7 | 29.7 | 29.4 | 31.6 | 24.7 |

Accelerated

| Year | | | | | | | | | | | | | | | |
|------|------|------|------|------|------|-------|-------|-------|-------|-------|------|------|------|------|------|
| 1986 | 2,988 |       |       |       |       | 0.548 |       |       |       |       | 31.5 |      |      |      |      |
| 1987 | 2,940 | 2,940 |       |       |       | 0.569 | 0.569 |       |       |       | 33.3 | 33.3 |      |      |      |
| 1988 | 2,899 |       | 2,899 |       |       | 0.594 |       | 0.594 |       |       | 35.2 |      | 35.2 |      |      |
| 1989 | 3,013 | 3,013 |       | 3,010 |       | 0.667 | 0.667 |       | 0.672 |       | 38.0 | 38.0 |      | 38.3 |      |
| 1990 | 3,193 |       |       |       |       | 0.721 |       |       |       |       | 38.8 |      |      |      |      |
| 1991 | 3,374 | 3,371 | 3,265 |       |       | 0.784 | 0.783 | 0.848 |       |       | 39.9 | 39.9 | 44.6 |      |      |
| 1992 | 3,564 |       |       |       |       | 0.852 |       |       |       |       | 41.1 |      |      |      |      |
| 1993 | 3,764 | 3,763 |       | 3,758 |       | 0.927 | 0.927 |       | 0.925 |       | 42.3 | 42.3 |      | 42.3 |      |
| 1994 | 3,992 |       | 3,869 |       |       | 0.999 |       | 1.057 |       |       | 43.0 |      | 46.6 |      |      |
| 1995 | 4,311 | 4,223 |       |       |       | 1.029 | 1.082 |       |       |       | 41.0 | 44.0 |      |      |      |
| 1996 | 4,629 |       |       |       |       | 1.078 |       |       |       |       | 40.0 |      |      |      |      |
| 1997 | 5,017 | 4,901 | 4,971 | 4,707 | 5,480 | 1.103 | 1.163 | 1.127 | 1.283 | 0.899 | 37.8 | 40.8 | 39.0 | 46.8 | 28.2 |

Table 7–3.    Required Capacity Increase (in MW) by Type of Unit.

| Type Year | Nuclear | Coal-fired | Oil-fired | Gas Turbine |
|---|---|---|---|---|
| 1986 | 0 | 0 | 0 | 0 |
| 1987 |  |  |  | 54 |
| 1988 |  |  | 238 |  |
| 1989 |  |  | 250 |  |
| 1990 |  | 390 |  |  |
| 1991 |  | 344 |  |  |
| 1992 |  | 360 |  |  |
| 1993 |  | 383 |  |  |
| 1994 |  | 544 |  |  |
| 1995 | 662 |  |  |  |
| 1996 | 581 |  |  |  |
| 1997 | 321 |  |  |  |
| 1998 | 626 |  |  |  |
| 1999 | 667 |  |  |  |
| 2000 | 1,587 |  |  |  |

## Other Experiments

The effect of a change in the price or income elasticity of demand is reported in Levin, Tishler, and Zahavi (1980b). In addition, we investigated the
steady state characteristics of the equilibrium solution over a long period of
time (one hundred years). It is found that using the initial conditions stated
above, the solution stabilizes in about thirty years and reaches a steady
state in about seventy-five years (see details in Levin, Tishler, and Zahavi
1980b).

## CONCLUSIONS

In this chapter we have presented an engineering-economic model of electricity supply, to determine the equilibrium end use prices and quantity
demanded of electrical energy over time, using a time step approach. As
shown by Levin, Tishler, and Zahavi (1980b), the time step approach
yields solutions that are also optimal in the dynamic sense, under quite
general conditions. In addition, we have derived conditions under which

**Table 7-4.** Equilibrium Solution as a Function of Rate of Increase in GNP.

| Year | GNP Increase per Year (percent) | Energy Produced (GWH) | Total Cost ($10⁹) | Equilibrium Price ($/MWH) | Max Load (MW) |
|---|---|---|---|---|---|
| | 3 | 15,911 | 0.440 | 27.65 | 2,734 |
| 1990 | 5 | 20,270 | 0.589 | 29.06 | 3,483 |
| | 7 | 27,047 | 0.867 | 32.07 | 4,648 |
| Percentage change | | | | | |
| GNP increase 5 versus 3 percent | | +27.4 | +33.9 | +5.1 | +27.4 |
| GNP increase 7 versus 5 percent | | +33.4 | +47.2 | +10.4 | +33.4 |
| GNP increase 7 versus 3 percent | | +70.0 | +97.0 | +16.0 | +70.0 |
| | 3 | 17,842 | 0.508 | 28.48 | 3,066 |
| 1995 | 5 | 27,614 | 0.322 | 29.76 | 4,745 |
| | 7 | 42,441 | 1.311 | 30.89 | 7,293 |
| Percentage change | | | | | |
| GNP increase 5 versus 3 percent | | +54.8 | +61.8 | +4.5 | +54.8 |
| GNP increase 7 versus 5 percent | | +53.7 | +59.5 | +3.8 | +53.7 |
| GNP increase 7 versus 3 percent | | +137.9 | +158.1 | +8.5 | +137.9 |
| | 3 | 22,217 | 0.580 | 26.09 | 3,818 |
| 2000 | 5 | 38,926 | 1.064 | 27.34 | 6,689 |
| | 7 | 68,311 | 1.879 | 27.51 | 11,738 |
| Percentage change | | | | | |
| GNP increase 5 versus 3 percent | | +75.2 | +83.4 | +4.8 | +75.2 |
| GNP increase 7 versus 5 percent | | +75.5 | +76.6 | +0.6 | +75.5 |
| GNP increase 7 versus 3 percent | | +207.5 | +324.0 | +5.4 | +207.5 |

the equilibrium solution for any particular target year exists and is unique and investigated the sensitivity of the solution to changes in the demand parameters.

While the model is relatively simple, it can nevertheless provide an important input for decisionmaking, because of its ability to examine policy issues for different postures and a variety of scenarios in the future and to assess the sensitivity of the solution to changes in economical and/or technological parameters at incredibly low computer cost and minimal input requirements. This capability has been demonstrated experimentally by running the model on a realistic system, resulting in rapid convergence to the equilibrium solution in very few iterations.

**Table 7–5.**  Equilibrium Solution as a Function of Change in Prices of Primary Energy Resources.

| Year | Rate of Increase in Primary Energy | Energy Produced (GWH) | Total Cost ($10⁹) | Equilibrium Price ($/MWH) | Max Load (MW) |
|------|-----------------------------------|----------------------|-------------------|---------------------------|---------------|
|      | Slow (A) | 21,086 | 0.538 | 25.52 | 3,623 |
|      | Moderate (B) | 20,270 | 0.589 | 29.06 | 3,483 |
|      | Accelerated (C) | 18,580 | 0.721 | 38.79 | 3,193 |
| 1990 |  |  |  |  |  |
|      | Percent change A to B | −3.9 | +9.5 | +13.9 | −3.9 |
|      | B to C | −8.3 | +22.4 | +33.5 | −8.3 |
|      | A to C | −11.9 | +34.0 | +52.0 | −11.9 |
|      | Slow (A) | 28,340 | 0.775 | 27.36 | 4,870 |
|      | Moderate (B) | 27,614 | 0.822 | 29.76 | 4,745 |
|      | Accelerated (C) | 25,088 | 1.029 | 41.02 | 4,311 |
| 1995 |  |  |  |  |  |
|      | Percent change A to B | −2.6 | +6.1 | +8.8 | −2.6 |
|      | B to C | −9.1 | +25.2 | +37.8 | −9.1 |
|      | A to C | −11.5 | +32.8 | +49.9 | −11.5 |
|      | Slow (A) | 39,189 | 1.048 | 26.75 | 6,734 |
|      | Moderate (B) | 38,926 | 1.064 | 27.34 | 6,689 |
|      | Accelerated (C) | 36,955 | 1.202 | 32.52 | 6,350 |
| 2000 |  |  |  |  |  |
|      | Percent change A to B | −0.7 | +1.5 | +2.2 | −0.7 |
|      | B to C | −5.1 | +13.0 | +18.9 | −5.1 |
|      | A to C | −5.7 | +14.7 | +21.6 | −5.7 |

## REFERENCES

Acton, J.P., and B.M. Mitchell. 1980. "Do Time-Of-Use Rates Change Load Curves?" The Rand Corporation, Rand Report; R-258-DWP/EPRI.

Anderson, D. 1972. "Models for Determining Least-Cost Investments in Electricity Supply." *The Bell Journal of Economics and Management Science* 3: 267–99.

Berndt, E.R., and D.O. Wood. 1975. "Technology, Prices and the Derived Demand for Energy." *Review of Economics and Statistics* 57: 259–68.

Brock, H.W., and D.M. Nesbitt. 1977. "Large-Scale Energy Planning Models: A Methodological Analysis." Prepared for the National Science Foundation, Office of Policy Research and Analysis.

Bullard, C.W., and A.V. Sebald. 1975. "A Model for Analyzing Energy Impact of Technological Change." Presented at the Summer Computer Simulation Conference, San Francisco.

Cazalet, E. 1977. "Generalized Equilibrium Modeling: The Methodology of the SRI-Gulf Energy Model." S.R.I. Draft Report to the Federal Energy Administration.

Cherniavsky, E.A. 1974. *Brookhaven Energy System Optimization Model*. Upton, New York: BNL #19569.

Connolly, T.G.; G.B. Dantzig; and S.C. Parikh. 1977. *The Stanford PILOT Energy/ Economy Model*. Technical Report SOL.77-19, Stanford: System Optimization Laboratory, Stanford University.

Day, R.H.; S. Morley; and K.R. Smith. 1974. "Myopic Optimizing and Rules of Thumb in a Micro-Model of Industrial Growth." *The American Economic Review* LXIV, (March): 11–23.

Electrical Power Research Institute (EPRI). 1979. *Review of Large Energy Models*. Report EA-968, Research Project 333-1. Boston, Massachusetts: Charles River Associates Inc.

Federal Energy Administration. 1974. *Project Independence Report*. Washington, D.C.: U.S. Government Printing Office.

Fuss, M.A. 1977. "The Demand for Energy in Canadian Manufacturing: An Example of the Estimation of Production Structures with Many Inputs." *Journal of Econometrics* 5: 89–116.

Halvorsen, R. 1978. *Econometric Models of U.S. Energy Demand*. Lexington, Massachusetts: Lexington Books.

Hnyilicza, E. 1975. "An Aggregate Model of Energy and Economic Growth." MIT Energy Laboratory Working Paper MIT-EL-75-010 WP.

Jorgenson, D.W., and E.A. Hudson. 1974. "U.S. Energy Policy and Economic Growth, 1975–2000." *The Bell Journal of Economics and Management Science* 5, (Autumn): 461–514.

Joskow, P.L., and M.L. Baughman. 1976. "The Future of the U.S. Nuclear Energy Industry." *The Bell Journal of Economics* 7 (Spring): 3–32.

Kydes, A.S., and J. Rabinowitz. 1979. "The Time-Stepped Energy System Optimization Model (TESOM)—Overview and Spacial Features." Upton, New York: BNL, August.

Levin, N.; A. Tishler, and J. Zahavi. 1980a. "An Electrical Energy Equilibrium Model: The Static Case." Research Report 29/80, The Israel Institute of Business Research, Faculty of Management, Tel Aviv University.

――――. 1980b. "An Electrical Energy Equilibrium Model: The Dynamic Case." Research Report 30/80, The Israel Institute of Business Research, Faculty of Management, Tel Aviv University.

――――. 1980c. "A Time-Step Equilibrium Model for the Energy Sector." Working Paper 663/80, Faculty of Management, Tel Aviv University, December.

_____. 1980d. "Capacity Expansion with Uncertainty in the Prices of Primary Energy Resources." Working Paper 654/80, Faculty of Management, Tel Aviv University.

_____. 1980e. "Loss Function Approach to Finding the Equilibrium Solution for the Electric Sector Under Uncertainty in the Prices of Primary Energy Resources." Working Paper, Faculty of Management, Tel Aviv University.

MacAvoy, P.W., and R.S. Pindyck. 1975. "The Economics of the National Gas Shortage (1960–1980)."Amsterdam: North Holland Publishing Co.

Maddala, G.S.; W.S. Chern; and G.S. Gill. 1978. *Econometric Studies in Energy Demand and Supply.* New York: Praeger.

Manne, A.S. 1977. "ETA-MACRO: A Model of Energy-Economy Interactions." Presented at ORSA/TIMS meeting, San Francisco, May.

Marcuse, W.; L. Bodin; E. Cherniavsky; and Y. Sanborn. 1976. "A Dynamic Time Dependent Model for the Analysis of Alternative Energy Policies." *Operational Research Quarterly,* pp. 647–67.

Modigliani, F., and F. Hohn. 1955. "Production Planning Over Time and the Nature of Expectation and Planning Horizon." *Econometrica* 23: 46–66.

Munasinghe, M. 1979. *The Economics of Power System Reliability and Planning.* Washington, D.C.: The World Bank.

Pindyck, R.S. 1979. "Interfuel Substitution and the Industrial Demand for Energy, An International Comparison." *Review of Economics and Statistics* 61: 169–97.

Phillips, D.; F.P. Jenkins; J.A.T. Pritchard; and K. Rybicki. 1969. "A Mathematical Model for Determining Generating Plant Mix." Central Electricity Generating Board, RD/C/N/337, June.

Preston, R.A. 1972. *The Wharton Annual and Industry Forecasting Model.* Philadelphia: Economic Research Unit, University of Pennsylvania.

Taylor, L.D. 1975. "The Demand for Electricity: A Survey." *The Bell Journal of Economics* 6: 74–110.

Stoughton, N.M.; R.C. Chen; and S.T. Lee. 1980. "Direct Construction of Optimal Generation Mix." *IEEE Transactions on Power Apparatus and Systems* PAS-99: 753–59.

Zimmerman, M.E. 1977. "Modelling Depletion in a Mineral Industry: The Case of Coal." *The Bell Journal of Economics* 8, no. 1 Spring: 47–65.

249-78

# 8 ISSUES IN MINERAL SUPPLY MODELING

William A. Vogely
Professor of Mineral Economics
The Pennsylvania State University

6322 ✓
Selected countries

## INTRODUCTION

This chapter reviews selected issues of mineral supply modeling. It was prepared and presented as a series of lectures at the International Seminar on Resource Policy Modeling in Herzlia, Israel, in December of 1980.

Mineral supply modeling must be undertaken within the constraints of the physical production function for minerals. This chapter discusses these constraints and relates them to the problems of supply modeling. In addition, the context in which supply modeling is used—namely, to predict industry performance and more importantly to address the issue of adequacy of mineral resources to sustain economic growth—is also discussed.

Most supply modeling in mineral resources has been of the type that assumes that mineral resources in the ground are a fixed stock and that this stock is exhausted through time. Thus, the idea of depletion of the mineral stock is fundamental to the mineral-supply-modeling technique. Unfortunately, the concept of depletion is poorly understood and is not consistent with the physical exhaustion of a fixed stock, which is the usual modeling approach. The first part of this chapter addresses the issue of depletion and draws the conclusion that depletion is fundamentally an economic concept within the constraints of a geological phenomenon. Adequacy as a supply and a demand concept is then discussed, followed by a description of the worldwide distribution of certain internationally traded materials for which world trade plays a major role. This nature of a world traded commodity

249

becomes significant within the context of the role of resource development in overall economic development.

Part two of the paper looks at the nature of materials supply functions. The generic structure of materials supply functions is discussed; the characteristics of metals markets are presented; and issues in modeling the supply of minerals are explored.

## MINERAL RESERVE AND RESOURCE CLASSIFICATION AND CONCEPTS

Materials and energy depletion and its ultimate result—the state of exhaustion—have been a continuing fear of mankind since the industrial revolution. Throughout the nineteenth and twentieth centuries, learned works have appeared that warn of the exhaustion of the materials and energy resources upon which society is based. The classical economists foresaw a steady state of no growth and labor at subsistence wages. Stanley Jevons (1866: vi) wrote in the preface to the second edition of *The Coal Question*: "Renewed reflection has convinced me that my main position is only too strong and true. It is simply that we cannot long progress as we are now doing—not only must we meet some limit within our own country, but we must witness the coal produce of other countries approximating it to our own and ultimately passing it ... our motion must be reduced to rest, and it is to this change my attention is directed." Jevons' words, in a different context, are echoed in the introduction to *The Limits To Growth* (Meadows et al. 1972: 29): "If the present growth trends ... continue unchanged, the limits to growth on this planet will be reached sometime within the next 100 years ... it is possible to alter these growth trends and to establish a condition of ecological and economic stability that is sustainable far into the future."

This part is organized into four sections. In the first section, the process of resource depletion and its dimensions are discussed. The second section examines resource adequacy. The third looks at the distribution of reserves worldwide. The fourth explores the relationship between resource production and economic development.

### The Process of Resource Depletion

Resource concepts are difficult to understand for a fundamentally semantic reason. The terminology used to describe resources is confused: The same words mean different things to different people. It is common to see in the literature life indexes of resources. These life indexes, which involve the division of some measure of resource stock by either annual or cumulative production based upon an annual rate of growth, measure the number of years to exhaustion. Such indexes misunderstand, perhaps deliberately, the nature of resource supply. In any case, whether presented with sophistication and understanding or presented in ignorance, the resource life indexes represent a fundamental misstatement of the problem of depletion. Resources flow into the economy: They are not an inventory to be used over time.

Depletion of a natural resource occurs at three distinct levels. Much of the misunderstanding about resource terminology has occurred because of the application of words derived from one of these levels to the other (Shantz 1975; McKelvey 1972). Resource depletion can be looked at at the level of a single deposit, the replacement of deposits in the production function, and the ultimate occurrence of the resource in the earth.

*Depletion of a resource deposit.*     Natural resources occur in nature in deposits that have unique chemical, physical, and locational characteristics. Deposits that have been found and are economic to produce with respect to the markets for their product may be developed into a producing site for the mineral resource. For solid resources such producing sites are called mines, and for liquid and gas resources they are called fields, reservoirs, or wells. A deposit that is known and is capable of being produced today is a reserve. These reserves will be produced through time from the deposit. The deposit may be extended through exploration and the reserves extended by additional capital investment. However, the material produced from that deposit will not be replaced in the deposit; this, the deposit will deplete as it is produced. Depletion of a deposit simply means that for every ton produced there is one ton less left to produce. However, as a single deposit depletes, the cost of production from that deposit will tend to increase. The deposit will be considered depleted when it is no longer economically attractive to continue production. The deposit will then be abandoned, and some would say it is exhausted.

It is important to note, however, that in virtually no case has physical exhaustion occurred. In the case of an oil field, upon abandonment, on average over 60 percent of the original oil in place still remains in the deposit. In the case of the nonfuel resources, mine sites will be abandoned because the additional ore does not justify further investment to develop it or replacement investment is not justified by the perceived amount of remaining ore. The fact that with high prices of gold, hundreds of abandoned mine sites in the West are being opened, and that with the increased price of oil, abandoned wells are being produced illustrates the point.

Reserves are determined and measured with respect to a specific deposit, and the abandonment of that deposit is an economic phenomenon. The content of the deposit with respect of the material at issue is not zero upon its abandonment or "exhaustion."

*Replacement of deposits.* Except in geologic time, the distribution of energy and materials in the earth's crust can be taken as fixed. In this distribution, there are deposits of all sizes, shapes, grades, and chemical characteristics. These deposits are discovered through exploration. The deposits that are profitable to develop become producing mines and contain reserves. As a specific deposit depletes in the terms described above, it is replaced by a new deposit that has been discovered by investment in exploration and will become a producing mine through further investment. The replacement of deposits is a function of exploration and of investment to develop the deposit. At any given time, there are deposits that have been discovered but have not been developed because the economic cost of so doing is not attractive given the markets for the commodities. Thus, deposits will be replaced either from discovery of a new deposit that has an attractive cost or with the discovery of new technologies that allow known deposits to be developed at an attractive price-cost ratio.

At this second level of consideration, depletion can be said to occur when the replacement deposits are of higher real cost per unit than the depleted deposits that they replace. This is the aspect of depletion that has been discussed most thoroughly in the literature. The path breaking book, *Scarcity and Growth* (Barnett and Morse 1963), tested the process of depletion of replacement deposits by positing that if it were occurring, the real costs or real price of materials should be rising through time. They were not able to prove this hypothesis and in fact found that such real costs were declining in the period of 1870 to the 1950s. Recent work by V. Kerry Smith and others has weakened that conclusion with respect to the period following the 1950s (Smith 1979). It is depletion in this sense, however, that underlies most of the literature with respect to resource exhaustion.

*Depletion of the resource base.* All of the elements that exist in the upper earth's crust, water, and atmosphere are considered the resource base. It is theoretically impossible to deplete these resources. Mankind is able only to redistribute, not destroy, them. In the case of the nonfuel resources, production concentrates them from their natural occurrence and, in a sense, creates new mines from which they can be reclaimed through recycling. In the case of the energy resources, use does reduce the energy potential contained in those resources and, in that sense, increases the entropy within the universe. Clearly the forces of geologic processes are to level the earth, and in time the energy flow will reach an equilibrium state of zero. However, the time spans for such events are well beyond the projected and possible survival of mankind.

In effect, from a global point of view, resource deposits that exist in nature can be ranked by their characteristics of cost of production under any given state of technology. Such a ranking, which it is impossible to quantify, would present a picture of a stepwise increase in cost as resources with different economic dimensions are used and in general will approach an "inexhaustible" supply of any given resource as the content of sea water or of common rocks is reached. The cost of availability, of course, of these ultimate resources for any given mineral element may be infinitely high, but nevertheless, in terms of the physical existence of the resource there is no exhaustion.

*Summary.*    The above discussion indicates, with Zimmerman (1964), that "resources are not, they become." Its principles underlie the current orthodox classification of resources along the double axis of economic availability and geologic identification. The current resource classification system used by the federal government, presented in Figure 8–1, illustrates these concepts. There are many variants on this basic idea of resource categorization, and of course, there is much discussion concerning what kind of numbers to put in the various boxes. The process of resource depletion is both an economic and a geological phenomenon. It is economic in the sense that any deposit will be abandoned when it is depleted so that continued production is no longer economic; the replacement of that depleted deposit depends on both the geological occurrence of deposits and the economics of additional capacity; and finally, the limit on further production is always an economic, not a geologic, phenomenon.

## The Concept of Adequacy

The concerns expressed by the authors quoted in the introduction relate not to exhaustion as a phenomenon but to the fact that a decline in resource availability to mankind will impose real limits to the quality of life of mankind. This concern, which broadens the scope of the analysis from the eco-

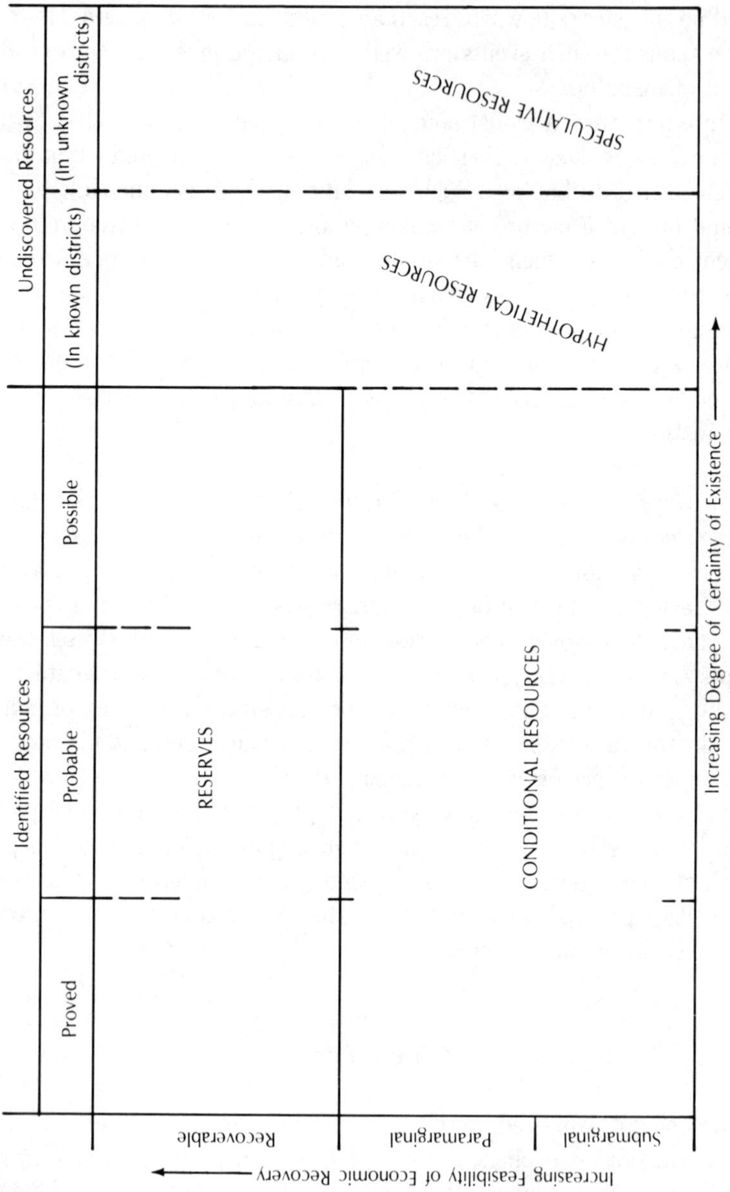


Fig. 8–1. Resource Classification Framework.

nomics and geology of resource deposits, raises the problem of resource adequacy. By definition, adequacy must be measured in terms of objectives. Thus, the subject of resource adequacy has both a supply and a use side. Several general measures of resource adequacy have been proposed—for example, Page (1977) proposes the test of resource adequacy consisting of constant costs of resource availability through time and Smith (1980) is reaching for a scarcity index. Others take a much narrower definition, such as resource adequacy for a three-year war that underlies government policy with respect to strategic stockpiles. Still others look at resource adequacy from the point of view of whether a given resource is adequate to allow society to undertake actions to replace its use with another, which is the current underpinning of energy policy with respect to liquid fuels. All of these concepts have a common analytical structure. They involve adequacy as measured by supply with respect to an objective or demand for the resource. Adequacy always has a supply and a demand side.

*The supply side of adequacy.*     Virtually all analysis of the supply side of adequacy start with some measurement of the size of the various resources categories shown in Figure 8–1. Recognizing that the transformation of resources to reserves is the fundamental issue from the supply side of resource adequacy, the determination of the amount of reserves that will be ultimately devleoped in terms of economic cost is the critical variable. It must be recognized that this is an attempt to quantify the unknown and, at the current state of man's knowledge, the unknowable. All attempts to estimate what Ridker and Watson (1980) call "prospective reserves" involve the application of the current state of mankind's knowledge to predict or project unknown quantities. There are three primary methodologies being used to make such estimates.

The most familiar methodology is that which relates the remaining volumes of prospective reserves to the rate with which reserves have historically been developed and used. These time rate methods flow from the pioneering work of King Hubbert (1969), and they indicate a limited prospective reserve category for oil and gas, uranium, and some other major mineral commodities. A second technique is to use a geologic or geographic analogy method, whereby the material and fuel content of a known geologic environment is assumed to be replicated in all such geologic environments in the earth's crust or, in a more general sense, the material and energy content of a given geographic area is assumed to be replicated in other equal in size areas. The third method is to ask the experts and develop a probability range around an estimate (Brobst 1979).

The usefulness and accuracy of each of these methods is, of course, open to sharp attack. This attack flows from the fact that there is no way to estimate a phenomenon when the basic scientific understanding of that phenomenon is flawed. At the beginning of the energy crisis, when it became very important to society that an understanding of the future availability of petroleum and natural gas in the United States be developed for public policy purposes, the Federal Energy Administration asked a group of distinguished statisticians to look at alternative methods for estimating the ultimate reserves or producibility of oil and gas in the United States. These statisticians, working independently, each arrived at the same conclusion that none of these estimating techniques were statistically reliable (Federal Energy Administration 1974). The U.S. Geological Survey has developed a model for the availability of petroleum that shows the absolute necessity of starting with a scientifically justified model of the occurrence of deposits by size distribution and other characteristics in the earth's crust. This has to be followed with knowledge of how many of these deposits can be discovered and at what cost through exploration and so on through the development and production stage (Sheldon 1975).

The import of the preceding paragraph is that there is now no possibility of developing a scientifically based model of future availability at whatever cost for any material or energy resource. The best that can be done is to take the first element of resource classification, reserves, as the minimum that will become available at, by definition, current real price. Beyond that, with decreased certainty, estimates of geologic discoveries and technological advances can be made. However, it must be understood that any such figure or range of figures so developed misstates the fundamental concept of the supply of resources. The supply of resources is, in fact, a flow of resources to the economy. It is not the exhaustion of a fixed stock. Whether or not resource depletion in the sense of rising costs occurs is a function of future technology in exploration and in production.

Knowledge of future supply side availability is very limited in time frame. The origin and real costs of supplies for the next decade are now known with very small margins of error. The margin of error consists primarily of the political availability of known resources—that is, cutoffs in supplies arising from political constraints, such as war or embargo. In addition, there is the unknown probability of major natural disasters. Finally, there is a small probability at the margin that major new deposits or technical advances could change the supply situation within the next decade. This is extremely unlikely, given the long lead times necessary to develop the productive capacity and infrastructure involved in major new material and energy projects. For many commodities, current reserves contain quantities that still will not be used before the end of the century. For others, current reserves will not, at current levels of demand, last this decade.

*Demand side of adequacy.*    The determinants of resource demand can be categorized into seven major variables:

1.  Demographic variables such as size, rate of growth, and age and sex distribution of population; number of households; and labor participation rates;
2.  Standard of living, usually represented by per capita gross product;
3.  Style of living, such as the pattern of preferences in consumer goods and transportation services;
4.  Geographic distribution of population between urban and rural;
5.  Technological structure—that is, the means by which goods are produced from resources;
6.  International trade relationships; and
7.  Institutions and policies—for example, environmental requirements (Vogely 1977).

These factors all affect the demand for total resources. The use of any single resource is the result of demands for final goods, the technology of production of each good, and relative prices.

It is clear that many of these variables are useless for projecting material demands, since their projection is difficult and the relationship between them and specific resource demands is very complex and uncertain. Most analyses of projected resource demands rest upon some simple assumptions of the relationship between specific resource demand, levels of production, and sometimes the price of the resource. The important point to be made here is that just as with the supply side of adequacy, the demand side of adequacy is also essentially unknown and unknowable, as it depends irrevocably upon the development of future technologies and price relationships.

*Recent studies of adequacy.*    Three major studies that attempted to measure in quantative terms the adequacy of materials and fuels resources published in 1979 and 1980. These were studies (Schurr et al. 1979; Landsberg et al 1979; and Ridker and Watson 1980) represent careful attempts to look at the evidence, make projections under what the authors consider to be conservative terms, and draw general conclusions. All three studies indicate that depletion, as measured by its economic dimension of increasing costs, does not present a challenge to resource adequacy for a minimum of three decades. The studies do conclude, however, in the energy area that society faces a transition from its current sources to alternative sources and that the question of resource depletion from the point of view of the quality of life rests upon the successful conduct of that transition.

*Summary of adequacy.*    The concept of adequacy rests upon the conjunction of material and energy supply with material and energy demand. The essential problem is whether or not quantities will be available at any given price level to meet requirements at that price level. The future characteristics of economic availability are unknown and, at the current state of knowledge, unknowable. Therefore, any projections of availability as a function of price through time for mineral resources is highly uncertain. The same can be said for the projection for the use of mineral resources—namely, the demand side. Both the supply function and the demand function are subject to extremely complex determination, and prediction of the factors determining each through the future is virtually impossible. The predictions progressively lose credibility as a function of future time. However, the situation is not as bleak as it seems. If the adequacy of resource availability is seen as a process rather than a point estimation, it is possible to develop strategies addressed to the process itself that have implications and viabilities beyond mankind's knowledge of the future outcomes.

## Worldwide Distribution of Reserves

Reserves are developed in response to economic incentives—that is, the prospects of returns from development of mineral resources. The factors that determine which deposits will be discovered and, after discovery, will be developed into reserves with an attached productive capacity involve calculations not only of the costs of developing the deposit itself but also of transportation and marketing of the output. A deposit of a given grade and cost of development will be more likely to be developed the closer it is to the marketplace. Deposits in remote areas must carry a substantial premium in the sense of economic rents to justify the transportation and infrastructure involved in their development.

It is not surprising, then, that mineral developments have been located near where industrial markets exist. The locational aspect of production is perhaps best illustrated by the steel industry, where location has been the result of the confluence of the basic raw materials, energy, and markets. In the United States, the original centers of production were in the Pittsburgh area, utilizing river transportation for the coal, iron ore, limestone, and other inputs to the process and serving the emerging industrial complex of Pennsylvania and Ohio. As the iron ore supply shifted northward to Minnesota, a second complex was generated along the shores of Lake Michigan, centered in Gary, Indiana. The Japanese steel industry takes full advantage of low cost ocean transportation for all of its raw materials and much of its product. It is the total cost of supplying a market that is critical in the location decision.

Of course, the location decision is affected by the geology of the mineral resource itself. Given, however, all other factors, exploration will tend to be concentrated in those areas where development, if a deposit is found, will be relatively easy. An example that is illustrative is the fact that an oil reservoir in Oklahoma that is a bonanza in offshore Nova Scotia may not be a commercial find.

Resources can be categorized with respect to the importance of the market and transportation systems in their location. For the construction materials that make up in total bulk most of the materials society uses, development is almost entirely market oriented. At the other extreme, the ferroalloy metals that are geologicaly scarce and whose use is measured in pounds rather than in tons are developed where they are found. Most major resources lie between these extremes.

It is commodities that are not produced near their markets that create international development implications. The major one, of course, is petroleum (not covered in this chapter), but others that are important are cobalt, chromium, platinum group metals, manganese, copper, and bauxite. Each of these is briefly discussed below.

*Cobalt.*    Over 40 percent of the world mine production of cobalt comes from Zaire, and Zaire has well over a third of the world reserve base. Cobalt has a variety of uses, but its most important use from the point of view of international security is that it is the material used for turbine engines in aircraft. It is produced as a by-product of copper, and the price is set by Zaire. Total world production is only about 35,000 tons of material.

*Chromium.*    Chromium is an essential ingredient for the making of stainless steel. Thirty-five percent of world production comes from the Republic of South Africa, and two-thirds of the world reserve base is in the Republic of South Africa.

*Platinum.*    Half of the world production and three-quarters of the world's reserve base for platinum group metals is in the Republic of South Africa. Virtually all of the remainder is in the USSR. A major use of platinum that raises international implications is as a catalyst in the refining of petroleum. It is also used for emission control in automobiles in the United States.

*Manganese.*    Manganese is an essential ingredient, under current technology, for the making of steel. The Republic of South Africa supplies a fifth of the world's mine production, but over 40 percent of free world production. South Africa contains three-quarters of the free world reserves and about a third of the world reserves of manganese.

*Copper.*    Copper reserves are much more broadly distributed than the other commodities listed above, but copper does enter into world trade in significant volumes. The largest producers are the United States, Chile, the USSR, Canada, and Zambia, in decreasing order. Approximately one-fifth of the reserves are held by Chile and another fifth by the United States, followed by Russia, Zambia, and Canada, each of whom has less than 10 percent.

*Bauxite.*    Bauxite is the ore for aluminum. Bauxite ores are widely distributed throughout the world, but it is a commodity in which the geographical separation between the ore producers and the metal producers is pronounced, and virtually all of the bauxite enters into foreign trade. The largest producer is Australia, which accounts for about 30 percent of the world's production. Guinea and Jamaica each produce about 15 percent, and individual countries drop off sharply from that level. On the reserve side, Guinea has approximately 30 percent and Australia 20 percent, followed by Brazil and Jamaica at about 10 percent each.

*Summary.*    Distribution of reserves and productive capacity within the world arises from geologic and economic factors. As indicated above, geology has played the most important role for some of the ferroalloy metals. For most other materials, the primary factor has been economics, not geology.


## Resources and Economic Development

The existence of rich natural resources has played a major role in the economic development of the nations of the world. At the time of the industrial revolution, the confluence of energy and material availability was a determining factor in the location of major industrial activities. Clearly, the emergence of Great Britain, Western Europe, the United States, and Japan as major industrial powers is based upon a natural endowment of energy and material resources or access to ocean transportation to permit their acquisition relatively cheaply.

The emerging world now looks upon resources as a major means to facilitate their economic development. The export earnings flowing to the oil producers, greatly enlarged by their cartel action, has provided a clear example of the transfer of wealth from the industrialized countries to the raw material producers. Copper has played a major role in Chile and Zambia and is looked to as a major contributor in such countries as Papua New Guinea and Panama. The Union of South Africa, which has a disproportionate endowment of manganese, chrome, and platinum group metals, has used these materials, plus gold and diamonds, as a major source of its wealth.

Among industrialized countries, the USSR is least dependent upon the international flow of goods for its mineral and energy supplies. This is due in part to resource endowment, but it is also due to deliberate government policies. For example, the USSR does use nonbauxitic sources for aluminum and thereby imposes substantial additional costs for the acquisition of aluminum metals. At the other extreme, Japan has virtually no natural resources and is therefore almost entirely dependent upon the rest of the world for imports of material and energy for her industrial production. Between these extremes, the United States lies closer to Russia, and Europe lies closer to Japan.

The nonindustrialized areas of the world depend upon raw material exports as their major earner of claims to goods and services, and the industrialized countries depend upon raw material imports to maintain their economy. This fact creates, in essence, a bilateral monopoly bargaining position between the raw material exporters and the industrialized countries of the West. The exporters have a strong bargaining chip in that the industrialized societies, certainly within short time spans, cannot operate without the materials and energy they produce. On the other hand, unless these materials and energy are sold to the industrialized countries, the exporters will not be able to enjoy the returns from them and will suffer dramatically in terms of wealth.

## THE NATURE OF MINERAL SUPPLY FUNCTIONS

In traditional microeconomic theory, supply functions representing the amount of goods that will be supplied relative to price can only be drawn for a competitive market—that is, where producers are price takers and the impact of their production does not affect price. This conception for minerals is trivial and applies, if at all, only to the trading of existing stocks of minerals as carried forth on such organized markets as the London Metal Exchange, the New York commodity exchanges, and the exchanges dealing with scrap or secondary materials. Therefore, the discussion of materials supplies has to depart from the traditional supply function and devote the analysis to a theory of production rather than a theory of supply. That is, it must be related to the cost of production and develop understandings of the nature of these costs, rather than trying to indicate the amount of goods actually supplied in response to a range of prices. Henceforth, when I am talking about supply, I am talking about the characteristics of the cost curves, not a supply response given a market structure.

The presentation is in five major sections. The first section discusses the generic structure of mineral supply and distinguishes the production functions for minerals from those of other commodities. Many of the issues involving supply modeling are based on the fundamental nature of the production function. The second section looks at Metals markets and discusses the nature of these markets and the implications for mineral supply and mineral supply modeling. The third section presents an integrated supply-side-modeling framework wherein a major issue—models of resource endowment and the associated exploration function—is identified and integrated into the analysis. The fourth section turns to the issue of resource endowment modeling, and the final section summarizes the discussion.

## Generic Structure of Minerals Production Functions

The production function for a mineral is multistaged and constrained by the facts of nature. Mineral deposits exist in nature and are distributed through the earth's crust. Each deposit is fixed in location both geographically and in three dimensional space and is also fixed in its chemical composition and in the physical characteristics of its deposition within the earth's crust. Before a mineral deposit can be produced it must be found; once found, it must be produced at the specific site where it exists.

The characteristics of the mineral body are such that normally the material, as it exists in nature, is not usable for the services for which it is desired. Usually the material must be beneficiated so that the waste can be eliminated and only the element desired is produced.

Once found, a production system must be designed to remove the mineral from its natural habitat and to transport it through further processing and refining. This stage, which is usually called development, requires in many cases the development of a specific technology, as each ore body is unique in its chemical and physical characteristics. Therefore, a uniquely designed mine and beneficiation process must be developed. This stage, like exploration, precedes any production or product.

In many cases, although not all, major investments may be required to bring the material to the market, usually via a dedicated transportation system. Natural gas on the north slope of Alaska cannot be brought to world markets without the construction of an extremely expensive pipeline. A copper deposit in central Africa cannot be marketed without the building of a dedicated transportation system to move the copper concentrate from the mine site to a smelter. Thus, the third stage, which may go on simultaneously with the previous investments, is the building of the transportation systems and other infrastructure that are required because of the fixed location of the mineral deposit. A fourth stage of production is the smelting and refining industry, which, unlike the earlier stages, is not fixed in location. Smelters and refineries are normally located close to the market for the primary good, and they are much closer to the traditional industrial plants in the economic characteristics involved in their construction and location. Finally, minerals are used as raw material inputs to other productive processes or, in some instances, are sold directly to consumers without further processing and become then indistinguishable from any other economic good in terms of theoretical discussions.

The problems in supply modeling that make the minerals industries unique are found in the first two stages of this generalized production function. In order to add to capacity to produce minerals, new deposits must be discovered. Thus, exploration for new deposits conducted within the constraints of nature generates very substantial uncertainty concerning the long-run shape of the cost curves for mineral commodities. The second characteristic—a fixed production site—also complicates the development of long-term production functions for these materials.

## Characteristics of Metals Markets

Mineral market organizations run the entire range of traditional market structures. Markets for existing supplies of certain refined metals, for example, are conducted in highly organized, highly competitive trading environments such as the London Metal Exchange. Other metals are produced primarily by single sources that dominate the market structures. In this section, I will discuss metals that illustrate the difficulty in supply side modeling for the mineral resources sectors.

*Metals.* The metal markets have a number of characteristics that control their behavior. The major ones, which apply in varying proportions to the different metals, are:

1. Highly inelastic supply functions in the short run;
2. Highly inelastic demand functions in the short run;
3. Highly elastic supply functions in the long run;
4. Highly elastic demand functions in the long run;
5. Very long lead times for the installation of additional capacity;
6. A wide variety of market organizations to mitigate the uncertainties caused by the above factors;
7. Some capacity controlled by national states, not private concerns; and
8. Wide swings in metal demand caused by changing economic conditions and the existence of the substantial discontinuities in the uses of metals over time.

The first four of these points reflect the underlying supply and demand situation of metals, which is rooted in the physical characteristics of their occurrence, production, and use.

*Metal Supply.* The short-run markets are characterized by inelasticity of supply for the variety of reasons rooted in physical production characteristics. The capacity to produce metals is normally limited by the capacity of the mill that beneficiates the ore at the mining stage and the capacity of the refinery at the final production stage. Both the mill and the refinery operate most efficiently on a twenty-four-hour day and a 365-day year. The producer will normally design his capacity, then, for full production, since the heavy capital cost involved places a premium upon utilization of capacity. Therefore, in response to higher prices, the producer is simply unable to increase output from any of his plants very significantly.

In order to increase output, substantial new capacity additions would be required. As indicated in point 5 above, the addition of new capacity is a long lead time item. The opening of a new mine involves an extensive exploration program to find the ore deposit and to delineate it, a lengthy development program to lay out an operating mine, and a considerable construction program to build the necessary facilities. The time lapse between a decision to increase capacity and the coming on stream of that capacity is normally at least five years and often may be ten. Thus, in the short run, the output expansion is limited in response to changing market conditions.

Since there is no shortage of mineral deposits in the world, active exploration programs will discover new deposits equivalent to those that we are producing today in large amounts. Thus, in the long term, substantial capacity expansions are possible at close to present cost. This situation is reflected in the highly elastic supply functions in the long term.

*Metal Demand.*    The situation is analogous to the demand side of the equation. Metals are not demanded as such by consumers, but they are used by manufacturers to produce products for consumption. Thus, the demand for metals is indirect, based upon the demand for the products that are produced from them. Manufacturers will normally design their production process around the engineering characteristics of a particular metal input. To change this input will require a substantial change in plant layout or production flow. Manufacturers are not likely to respond by substitution of other materials for metals because of short-run price fluctuations, but will only change when they are redesigning their production layout. The lead times here are not as long as those on the supply side of the equation, but they are substantial. Further, the metals input is normally a minor constituent in the final production price, and therefore, changes in metal prices are not likely to have a major impact on product demands. These considerations lead to the situation of highly inelastic demand functions in the short run.

Parallel to the supply situation, substitutions of one metal for another and between metals and other materials, such as plastics, are relatively easy at the design phase. Therefore, there will be very substantial elasticity of demand for a metal in the long term.

*Price Behavior.*    These supply and demand characteristics of the metal markets are clearly evident where there is an open market for trading of the metals. Such open markets exist, even though they are relatively thin, on the London Metal Exchange and the organized commodity markets in New York. If the producers maintain a more stable pricing structure, then production will vary to a greater extent.

*Market Organization.*    In response to the uncertainties caused by price variability, many metal markets have been organized by producers and consumers to stabilize prices. This organization usually takes the form of administered prices of some description. The actual organizations can range from the situation in tin, where an international council comprising both producers and consumers operates the market on a cartel-like basis, to the price leadership characteristics of the U.S. steel industry. The major metals—copper, lead, zinc, aluminum, and steel—are characterized in the United States by a producer-pricing system, with a relatively free market in secondary metals that reflects the current short-run supply-demand situation. Nickel and platinum are priced on world markets by producers or marketing agents that control a substantial portion of the supply and exhibit monopoly type market behavior. Thus, the underlying supply and demand situation has given rise to a wide variety of market organizations where the prices do not reflect current supply and demand conditions but are administered around some supposed long-term norm, to provide stability in price and some reduction in uncertainty in these markets.

The consequence of these organizations, however, is to cause periodic glut and shortage in actual availability of the metals. During periods of glut, where investment decisions made years ago are not in accord with current market demands, the actual prices of transactions will be discounted from the administered prices, often on a secret basis, and the market will not be signaling the current situation. On the other hand, in periods of shortage, where adequate investments were not made in previous time periods, producers will allocate metals to consumers at producer prices, and de facto rationing of supplies will occur. Manufacturers, in order to assure themselves of supplies, tend to enter into long-term arrangements with specific producers so that they can be on the preferred list for delivery during periods of shortage.

*Nationalization.*    The above complex situation is further exaggerated by the increasing trend toward nationalization of the primary ore industry. When this occurs, factors are built into the production and investment decisions that relate to political and social objectives and not solely to economics. We do not have long experience with major metal markets being affected by state-owned enterprises, but the existence of these enterprises in Chile, Zambia, and other underdeveloped nations is bringing new factors into these markets and will increase the uncertainties forced on the consumers of metals.

*Demand Shifts.*    The final point above generates two elements of uncertainty and complexity in these markets: First, because the demand for metal is derived from the sales of products using metals, demand will change rapidly with the general economic conditions. Minor fluctuations in total demand are magnified into major shifts in the demand for a specific metal. Such shifts accentuate the impact of inelasticity discussed above.

Second, consumers of metals, looking toward availability, are likely to make major shifts in metal use all at once. Perhaps an example would best illustrate the point. The automobile in the United States today is largely made of iron and steel. However, if the automobile industry becomes interested in lightweight materials and in long-term availability, a decision might be made to shift to aluminum blocks for motors and aluminum components for frames and transmissions. If this were done, it would not be done on a marginal basis: Entire product lines would be shifted at the end of a model year, resulting in a major shift in materials used at a single point in time, rather than a gradual shift through time as in a substitution function. These characteristics exist to a greater or lesser degree in most manufacturing operations, which places another element of uncertainty into these markets.

To measure the size and effects of market instability in metals, Dr. John Tilton and I have just completed a major study with the support of the U.S. Bureau of Mines (Tilton and Vogely 1981). Tables 8–1 through 8–5 indicate the results of that study, in which mine production, smelter production, refinery production, prices, and revenues are analyzed for copper, aluminum, tin, and iron and steel. It is clear from these data that instability is severe in these industries. At issue is the implications of this instability for modeling or understanding metal supply functions. As can be seen from the tables, the direct consequences of cyclical instability are fluctuations in price, output, revenues, and profits over the business cycles and periods of physical shortage where prices are not permitted to vary sufficiently to ensure that short-run supply and demand remain in balance. However, there are a number of other adverse effects beyond these direct consequences. During recessions, when metal markets are depressed, producing countries may experience severe unemployment in the mining and mineral-processing industries. This fact may be particularly severe in developing countries. During boom periods of the business cycle, the consuming countries face difficulties in the form of extremely high prices and limited physical availability of materials.

Perhaps more important from the point of few of our subject is the possibility that annual investment expenditures for exploration and for the development of new metal mines may be influenced by short-term market conditions rather than future market conditions. One of the findings of our study was that current conditions in the metal market do influence the level

**Table 8–1.** Instability Indices for Copper Production, Prices, and Revenues.[a]

A. *Mine Production*

|        | World[b] | United States | Canada | Chile | Peru | Zambia | Zaire |
|--------|--------|---------------|--------|-------|------|--------|-------|
| 1950–77 | 3.10 | 8.78 | 4.17 | 4.06 | 10.21 | 4.22 | 3.26 |
| 1950–59 | 3.29 | 6.66 | 3.62 | 5.88 | 11.78 | 5.26 | 2.98 |
| 1960–69 | 2.67 | 9.18 | 4.49 | 2.06 | 9.47 | 4.27 | 3.38 |
| 1970–77 | 3.39 | 10.94 | 4.46 | 4.30 | 9.18 | 2.86 | 3.46 |

B. *Smelter Production*

|        | World[b] | United States | Canada | Japan | Chile | Peru | Zambia | Zaire |
|--------|--------|---------------|--------|-------|-------|------|--------|-------|
| 1950–77 | 3.04 | 7.65 | 3.90 | 5.17 | 3.89 | 12.43 | 4.97 | 4.37 |
| 1950–59 | 3.18 | 6.91 | 4.13 | 4.88 | 5.99 | 16.21 | 6.12 | 2.94 |
| 1960–69 | 3.10 | 10.34 | 5.03 | 5.12 | 1.86 | 10.87 | 5.40 | 3.38 |
| 1970–77 | 2.81 | 5.21 | 2.21 | 5.60 | 3.80 | 9.67 | 3.00 | 7.39 |

C. *Refinery Production*

|        | World[b] | United States | Canada | Japan | Chile | Zambia |
|--------|--------|---------------|--------|-------|-------|--------|
| 1950–77 | 3.50 | 7.03 | 4.62 | 5.41 | 7.24 | 5.23 |
| 1950–59 | 3.38 | 6.38 | 5.18 | 5.04 | 11.92 | 7.87 |
| 1960–69 | 3.46 | 8.39 | 5.59 | 4.50 | 4.66 | 3.83 |
| 1970–77 | 3.69 | 6.15 | 2.70 | 7.01 | 4.61 | 3.68 |

D. *Prices[c]*

|        | LME | U. S. Producers |
|--------|-----|-----------------|
| 1950–77 | 15.21 | 11.18 |
| 1950–59 | 13.05 | 9.23 |
| 1960–69 | 14.64 | 7.07 |
| 1970–77 | 18.63 | 18.76 |

E. *Revenues[d]*

|        | World[b] | United States | Canada | Japan | Chile | Zambia |
|--------|--------|---------------|--------|-------|-------|--------|
| 1950–77 | 13.68 | 11.98 | 10.06 | 18.87 | 19.44 | 17.00 |
| 1950–59 | 11.51 | 13.23 | 14.19 | 16.43 | 24.89 | 14.73 |
| 1960–69 | 12.68 | 10.22 | 6.22 | 16.44 | 15.79 | 16.41 |
| 1970–77 | 17.62 | 12.61 | 9.70 | 24.96 | 17.19 | 20.56 |

[a]The instability index is defined as the absolute percentage deviation for each month from the centered five year main average, averaged for the period .

[b]World figures exclude centrally planned countries.

[c]Price indices are calculated from data indicating the average annual price in constant 1967 dollars per metric ton of copper.

[d]Annual revenues from copper sales are estimated by multiplying the average price for the year times refined copper output. The U.S. producers price is used for the United States and Canada, the LME price for other countries.

Source: Metallgesellschaft (various years).

**Table 8–2.**   Instability Indices for Copper Production, Prices, and Revenues after Eliminating the Effects of the 1967–1968 U.S. Copper Strike.[a]

A.   *Mine Production*

|  | World[b] | United States | Canada | Chile | Peru | Zambia | Zaire |
|---|---|---|---|---|---|---|---|
| 1950–77 | 2.50 | 6.17 | 4.17 | 4.06 | 10.21 | 4.22 | 3.26 |
| 1950–59 | 3.29 | 6.66 | 3.62 | 5.88 | 11.78 | 5.26 | 2.98 |
| 1960–69 | 1.11 | 2.30 | 4.49 | 2.06 | 9.47 | 4.27 | 3.38 |
| 1970–77 | 3.25 | 10.41 | 4.46 | 4.30 | 9.18 | 2.86 | 3.46 |

B.   *Smelter Production*

|  | World[b] | United States | Canada | Japan | Chile | Peru | Zambia | Zaire |
|---|---|---|---|---|---|---|---|---|
| 1950–77 | 2.38 | 4.65 | 3.90 | 5.17 | 3.89 | 12.43 | 4.97 | 4.37 |
| 1950–59 | 3.18 | 6.91 | 4.13 | 4.88 | 5.99 | 16.21 | 6.12 | 2.94 |
| 1960–69 | 1.34 | 2.31 | 5.03 | 5.12 | 1.89 | 10.87 | 5.40 | 3.38 |
| 1970–77 | 2.68 | 4.74 | 2.21 | 5.60 | 3.80 | 9.67 | 3.00 | 7.39 |

C.   *Refinery Production*

|  | World[b] | United States | Canada | Japan | Chile | Zambia |
|---|---|---|---|---|---|---|
| 1950–77 | 2.85 | 4.76 | 4.62 | 5.41 | 7.24 | 5.23 |
| 1950–59 | 3.38 | 6.38 | 5.18 | 5.04 | 11.92 | 7.87 |
| 1960–69 | 1.77 | 2.38 | 5.59 | 4.50 | 4.66 | 3.83 |
| 1970–77 | 3.54 | 5.70 | 2.70 | 7.01 | 4.61 | 3.63 |

D.   *Prices*[c]

|  | LME | U. S. Producers |
|---|---|---|
| 1950–77 | 15.21 | 11.18 |
| 1950–59 | 13.05 | 9.23 |
| 1960–69 | 14.64 | 7.07 |
| 1970–77 | 18.63 | 18.76 |

E.   *Revenues*[d]

|  | World[b] | United States | Canada | Japan | Chile | Zambia |
|---|---|---|---|---|---|---|
| 1950–77 | 13.00 | 9.69 | 10.06 | 18.87 | 19.44 | 17.00 |
| 1950–59 | 11.51 | 13.23 | 14.19 | 16.43 | 24.89 | 14.73 |
| 1960–69 | 10.90 | 4.18 | 6.22 | 16.44 | 15.79 | 16.41 |
| 1970–77 | 17.48 | 12.13 | 9.70 | 24.96 | 17.19 | 20.56 |

[a]The instability index is defined in Table 8-1. The effects of the 1967–1968 U.S. copper strike were eliminated by assuming U.S. production increased by equal quantities between 1966 and 1967, 1967 and 1968, and 1968 and 1969.

[b]World figures exclude centrally planned countries.

[c]Price indices are calculated from data indicating the average annual price in constant 1967 dollars per metric ton of copper.

[d]Annual revenues from copper sales are estimated by multiplying the average price for the year times refined copper output. The U.S. producers price is used for the United States and Canada, the LME price for other countries.

Source: Metallgesellschaft (various years).

**Table 8–3.**    Instability Indices for Aluminum Production, Prices, and Revenues.[a]

A.    *Bauxite Production*

|  | World[b] | United States | Australia | Guinea | Surinam | Guyana |
|---|---|---|---|---|---|---|
| 1950–77 | 4.57 | 8.74 | 27.29 | 20.42 | 6.38 | 8.02 |
| 1950–59 | 6.89 | 11.13 | 29.67 | 37.46 | 6.94 | 10.15 |
| 1960–69 | 3.63 | 8.81 | 43.35 | 10.38 | 4.37 | 7.60 |
| 1970–77 | 2.83 | 5.65 | 4.24 | 11.68 | 8.19 | 5.89 |

B.    *Aluminum Production*

|  | World[b] | United States | Canada | Japan | Germany | France | Norway |
|---|---|---|---|---|---|---|---|
| 1950–77 | 3.40 | 5.07 | 5.57 | 5.80 | 6.89 | 4.06 | 3.94 |
| 1950–59 | 3.75 | 6.05 | 3.82 | 6.32 | 10.79 | 6.97 | 4.71 |
| 1960–69 | 2.38 | 2.96 | 4.38 | 4.31 | 3.60 | 2.59 | 3.62 |
| 1970–77 | 4.25 | 6.49 | 9.23 | 7.00 | 6.12 | 2.26 | 3.38 |

C.    *Prices[c]*

|  | United States | United Kingdom | Germany |
|---|---|---|---|
| 1950–77 | 3.13 | 4.07 | 2.58 |
| 1950–59 | 1.73 | 4.88 | 2.76 |
| 1960–69 | 2.09 | 1.57 | 1.70 |
| 1970–77 | 6.19 | 6.18 | 3.46 |

D.    *Revenues[d]*

|  | World[d] | United States | Canada | Japan | Germany | France | Norway |
|---|---|---|---|---|---|---|---|
| 1950–77 | 5.24 | 6.40 | 8.47 | 7.58 | 8.18 | 7.25 | 5.34 |
| 1950–59 | 4.36 | 6.12 | 6.91 | 8.10 | 11.89 | 10.70 | 5.50 |
| 1960–69 | 3.04 | 3.86 | 4.84 | 4.81 | 3.84 | 3.55 | 3.44 |
| 1970–77 | 9.09 | 9.94 | 14.95 | 10.37 | 8.97 | 7.55 | 7.52 |

[a]The instability index is defined in Table 8-1.

[b]World figures exclude centrally planned countries.

[c]Price indices are calculated from data indicating the average annual price in constant 1967 dollars per metric ton of aluminum.

[d]Annual revenues are calculated by multiplying the average price for the year times aluminum production. The U.S. producers price has been used for U.S. production, Germany's price has been used for Germany's production, and the U.K. aluminum price has been used for the remaining countries. Revenue is in units of millions of dollars (constant 1967 dollars).

Source: Metallgesellschaft (various years).

**Table 8-4.** Instability Indices for Tin Production, Prices and Revenues.[a]

A. *Mine Production*

|  | World[b] | Indonesia | Malaysia | Thailand | United Kingdom | Japan | Bolivia |
|---|---|---|---|---|---|---|---|
| 1959–77 | 2.77 | 4.96 | 4.70 | 7.29 | 7.81 | 9.20 | 6.28 |
| 1950–59 | 4.97 | 3.38 | 8.28 | 11.28 | 6.86 | 10.19 | 7.29 |
| 1960–69 | 1.71 | 7.92 | 3.08 | 4.61 | 4.26 | 8.48 | 8.27 |
| 1970–77 | 1.33 | 3.22 | 2.24 | 5.65 | 13.44 | 8.86 | 2.52 |

B. *Smelter Production*

|  | World[b] | Indonesia | Malaysia | United Kingdom | Japan | Bolivia | United States |
|---|---|---|---|---|---|---|---|
| 1950–77 | 3.87 | 29.27 | 7.20 | 7.50 | 6.89 | 29.22[f] | 23.42 |
| 1950–59 | 6.00 | 54.72 | 10.72 | 6.01 | 7.91 | 24.79[g] | 26.19 |
| 1960–69 | 3.52 | 20.03 | 6.50 | 8.56 | 6.82 | 34.79 | 28.98 |
| 1970–77 | 1.62 | 9.01 | 3.66 | 8.05 | 5.69 | 25.79 | 13.01 |

C. *Prices[c]*

|  | United Kindgom | United States |
|---|---|---|
| 1950–77 | 9.27 | 8.83 |
| 1950–59 | 8.44 | 7.00 |
| 1960–69 | 6.78 | 6.73 |
| 1970–77 | 13.44 | 13.76 |

D. *Revenues[d]*

|  | World[b] | United States | Indonesia | Malaysia | United Kingdom | Japan | Bolivia |
|---|---|---|---|---|---|---|---|
| 1950–77 | 8.95 | 26.93 | 27.78 | 10.79 | 10.21 | 11.12 | 35.45[e] |
| 1950–59 | 8.80 | 24.98 | 49.88 | 15.33 | 10.66 | 11.98 | 29.72[f] |
| 1960–69 | 6.14 | 30.38 | 16.49 | 5.84 | 9.59 | 6.38 | 42.85 |
| 1970–77 | 12.66 | 25.04 | 14.28 | 11.30 | 10.43 | 15.98 | 31.21 |

[a]The instability index is described in Table 8-1.
[b]World figures exclude centrally planned economies.
[c]Price indices are calculated from data indicating the average annual price in constant 1967 dollars per metric ton of tin.
[d]Annual revenues are calculated by multiplying the average price for the year times tin production. The New York tin straits price is used for the United States. The London Metal Exchange price is used for the other countries. Revenue indices are calculated from data in units of millions of dollars (constant 1967 dollars).
[e]1953-1977
[f]1953–1959

Source: Metallgesellschaft (various years).

**Table 8–5.**     Instability Indices for Iron and Steel Production, Prices, and Revenues.[a]

A.    *Iron Ore Production*

| | World[b] | U.S. | U.K. | Germany | Japan | Canada | Australia |
|---|---|---|---|---|---|---|---|
| 1950–76 | 4.32 | 8.49 | 6.43 | 6.84 | 6.05 | 10.48 | 6.81 |
| 1950–59 | 6.04 | 12.93 | 4.89 | 5.65 | 6.80 | 17.25 | 3.57 |
| 1960–69 | 3.36 | 6.09 | 5.47 | 5.87 | 4.94 | 7.28 | 10.53 |
| 1970–76 | 3.22 | 5.58 | 9.98 | 9.93 | 6.55 | 7.31 | 6.13 |

B.    *Pig Iron Production*

| | World[b] | U.S. | U.K. | Germany | Japan | Canada | Australia |
|---|---|---|---|---|---|---|---|
| 1950–77 | 4.45 | 6.68 | 5.28 | 7.07 | 4.47 | 5.37 | 3.61 |
| 1950–59 | 5.80 | 9.48 | 3.63 | 6.98 | 5.81 | 9.16 | 5.21 |
| 1960–69 | 3.33 | 4.61 | 5.33 | 6.23 | 3.54 | 3.19 | 1.81 |
| 1970–77 | 4.17 | 5.76 | 7.29 | 8.11 | 3.95 | 3.35 | 3.88 |

C.    *Raw Steel Production*

| | World[b] | U.S. | U.K. | Germany | Japan | Canada |
|---|---|---|---|---|---|---|
| 1950–77 | 4.61 | 6.52 | 5.33 | 5.91 | 6.77 | 5.50 |
| 1950–59 | 5.60 | 8.87 | 3.45 | 4.68 | 7.24 | 9.02 |
| 1960–69 | 3.47 | 4.44 | 6.38 | 5.75 | 6.38 | 3.59 |
| 1970–77 | 4.79 | 6.20 | 6.37 | 7.66 | 6.67 | 3.48 |

D.    *Prices[c]*

| | Composite[d] Antwerp | U.S.[e] Finished Steel |
|---|---|---|
| 1952–74 | 12.53 | 1.25 |
| 1952–59 | 11.76 | 1.30 |
| 1960–69 | 7.41 | .88 |
| 1970–74 | 24.00 | 1.93 |

E.    *Revenues[f]*

| | World[b] | U.S. | U.K. | Germany | Japan | Canada |
|---|---|---|---|---|---|---|
| 1952–74 | 11.81 | 6.64 | 16.99 | 18.14 | 18.39 | 5.84 |
| 1950–59 | 10.69 | 9.54 | 14.22 | 15.73 | 16.18 | 10.10 |
| 1960–69 | 7.72 | 4.77 | 13.57 | 12.95 | 13.02 | 3.87 |
| 1970–74 | 21.76 | 5.74 | 28.26 | 32.36 | 32.65 | 2.96 |

[a]The instability index is defined in Table 8-1.
[b]World figures exclude centrally planned economies.
[c]Price indices are calculated from data indicating the average annual price in constant 1967 dollars per metric ton of steel.
[d]Composite f.o.b. Antwerp export price.
[e]Iron Age U.S. finished steel composite price.
[f]Annual revenues are calculated by multiplying the average price for the year times raw steel production. The Iron Age U.S. finished steel composite price is used for the United States and Canada. The composite f.o.b. Antwerp price is used for the other countries. Revenue indices are calculated from data in units of millions of dollars (constant 1967 dollars).

Sources: American Metal Market, *Metal Statistics*, (various issues).
Peter F. Marcus, 1978, "World Steel Dynamics," *World Steel Monitor*, Mitchell, Hutchin, Inc., Section A, A-14-3, A-14-4.
*Iron Age* (various issues).

of exploration activity as well as the number of investment projects started, delayed, and canceled. Thus, the market instability may create a situation where there is chronic underinvestment for meeting future demands if those demands are themselves growing. At the very least, the instabilities identified here make modeling of the long-term behavior of these markets from the supply side extremely difficult.

## Integrated Supply Side Modeling

To repeat, the production function for minerals is a complex one. It involves the application of exploration and search techniques to an existing resource endowment in the earth's crust. Upon discovery of a deposit, there are complex decisions that must be made with respect to whether or not the deposit is economically viable and whether it should be developed. The development process involves providing an infrastructure, as well as designing and developing the mine and mill. When the deposit reaches the production stage, the market for the material must be considered, and its use pattern in the economy must be understood. Finally, the flow of reclaimed material back into the economy must be considered.

This complex multistaged production function creates major demands upon an information system. The ideal information system can be sketched relatively simply in general terms, but implementation of such an information system may be extremely difficult both because of expense and because of fundamental gaps in knowledge concerning the subject.

To start at the beginning, the first element of the information system must be geological estimates of the resource endowments within a region. These estimates, which flow from the geological sciences, should be able to state the size of the resources occurring in the region and the distribution of these resources by deposit size. At this stage of the information system there are major difficulties with the state of the geological sciences. However, some work has been done in the United States and in Mexico on the estimate of the resource endowment of major areas. The U.S. Geological Survey is at the forefront of this effort, and the chief scholars attacking this problem are with the survey. In addition, the Department of Mineral Economics at the University of Arizona is also doing some pioneering work in the measurement and estimating of resource endowment (see Foose et al. 1980; Singer et al. 1980; Singer and DeYoung 1980).

The second stage of the information system involves search. Given the perceived distribution of deposits by size coming from the occurrence module, the number of these deposits that can be discovered is a function of the technology available for exploration and the economic calculation of how much exploration is efficient. Thus, this information module must contain information on price, cost, exploration technologies, and similar kinds of information. Flowing from the application of search techniques to the geologic area will be a resulting discovery function that is an estimate of the actual results of an exploration program.

The third stage arises after discovery. Here a wide-ranging set of information dealing with government policies, substitutions, world prices, markets, transportation systems—all of those things that are involved in the opening of a major new mine in any area of the world—is needed.

The fourth stage is the production decisions after the development of the capacity. This involves the standard kind of economic statistics with which you are all familiar. The fifth stage of the information system will involve the use of a material in the industrial economy. There will be a feedback to the production model from use because of recycling.

I have described here in very simple terms an extremely complex information system. This information system needs to be backed up by analytical models of all types. The occurrence module will rest upon models that predict the distribution of deposits in the earth. The discovery function will rest on exploration effort in response to economic and governmental stimuli and then predict findings from those efforts. The next module requires models to explain what deposits should be developed and the impact of infrastructure and of environmental, international, and governmental actions on the decision to develop. The production stage gets us close to standard economic theory—that is, a short-run supply model. At the consumption stage a short- and long-run demand model is required, and an interactive connection between all of these models is necessary to fully understand the feedback structure.

## Resource Endowment Modeling

The weak link in mineral supply modeling lies in the first two stages of the integrated supply system described in the preceding section. The problem is a twin one: First, we do not have a scientific basis for describing in physical terms the mineral resource endowment of an area or of the world as a whole. Second, we do not understand nor do we have an appropriate modeling procedure for exploration effort and the payout to exploration.

*Resource Endowment.*    The existing estimates of resource endowment are of the extremely general nature implied by the McKelvey classification of resources presented earlier in the chapter. There are estimates of the content of the various sections of the resource diagram expressed as single numbers (see also Berg and Corrillo 1980; and Davidoff 1980). These estimates are based upon very gross techniques. They are used in supply side modeling today as measures of stock, and the models exhaust the stock through time in ways prescribed by the modeling technique. There is no conception that the supply process is a flow, as indicated earlier, rather than a stock. The U.S. Geological Survey has developed an estimate of the prospective reserves yet to be discovered, and these estimates underly the examination of resource adequacy described earlier. From the point of view of supply modeling, however, such estimates are useless.

There is some interesting work going on in attempting to provide better information for supply side modeling of the geologic endowment. The only published example of this is that done in Alaska by Donald Singer and others from the U.S. Geological Survey, who attempt to predict the number and size of metal deposits within a region of Alaska (Singer and Overshine 1979). The beginning point was to apply the unit regional value concept, which compares the amount of mineral already mined in the region with the amount of mineral recovered from geologically similar regions. If this figure is low, then you may infer that there are large untapped endowments of minerals within the area. One way to estimate this is to proceed in a disagregate manner, involving the separate estimation of those variables related to the quality and quantity of mineralized area. These variables include grade and tonnage estimates; the physical, chemical, and mineral features of the rock; the geographical location; the geologic structure; hydraulic conditions; and the special distribution of mineralization and overburden. In the case of Alaska, the concentration was on mineral deposit types. By using deposit types, the resource assessment was performed in three basic steps. First, the areas are delineated according to the kinds of mineral deposits the known geologic character will permit. Second, the number of deposits within each area is estimated; and third, the amount of metal and the characteristics of ore in the deposits are estimated by means of models of grade and tonnages based upon similar deposits.

The work by geologists in developing usable models of resource endowment by size distribution of potential deposits is at its very infancy. There is no agreement with respect to the kind of physical models that should be applied to deposits—for example, a log normal distribution or a bimodal distribution—nor is there any agreement of how to evaluate differing geological structures with respect to the occurrence of deposits. Nevertheless, the work that is being undertaken here is of extreme importance in improving our ability to model the supply of mineral resources.

*Exploration Function.* The second major gap in our ability to model mineral supplies is our lack of understanding of the exploration function. In order to develop an intergrated supply model, we must have a discovery function by size and quality distribution of deposits related to exploration effort. Without knowledge of the geologic endowments, exploration is an art, not a science. In major studies done at The Pennsylvania State University on the process of investment in the mineral industries, it became clear that exploration investment is a matter of subjective judgments, not a matter of rational determination of optimum levels. Thus, this portion of the integrated supply-modeling system is very deficient. The existing models in the energy and in the nonfuels areas all assume either (1) that all deposits in the geologic stock assumed will be discovered or (2) that discovery will proceed to provide the resource for the required capacity that the model generates.

This lack of knowledge of the exploration function is extremely unfortunate, since many of the major public policy decisions affecting minerals have their initial impact on the exploration function. The closing of large amounts of land to exploration for preservation as wilderness within the United States, for example, certainly does not affect the resource endowment contained in these areas but it does affect the ability to discover these resources.

## Summary

The nature of the production function for minerals creates extremely difficult problems in modeling supply functions. Short-run supply functions are very inelastic and in combination with demand situations create highly unstable short-run market behavior. This instability in short-run markets hides or masks the long-term factors of resource cost that are at play and makes supply modeling based upon market observations extremely difficult. Supply modeling based upon cost is inhibited by the lack of fundamental knowledge of the first two stages of the production function—that is, the state of nature as incorporated in resource endowment and the modeling of the exploration function. Once a deposit is discovered and appraised, the entry of that deposit into the economic system as a source of supply much more closely parallels standard microeconomic theory, and so modeling problems at this stage do not create unusual difficulties.

## REFERENCES

Barnett, H. J., and C. Morse. 1963. *Scarcity and Growth*. Baltimore: The Johns Hopkins Press.

Berg, A.W., and F.V. Corrillo. 1980. *MILS: The Mineral Industry Location System of the Federal Bureau of Mines*. Washington, D.C.: U.S. Bureau of Mines IC8815.

Brobst, D.A. 1979. "Fundamental Concepts for the Analysis of Resource Availability." in V.K. Smith, ed., *Scarcity and Growth Reconsidered*. Baltimore: Johns Hopkins University Press.

Davidoff, R.L. 1980. *Supply Analysis Model (SAM): A Minerals Availability System Methodology*. Washington, D.C.: U.S. Bureau of Mines IC8820.

Federal Energy Administration. 1974. *Oil and Gas Resources, Reserves, and Production Capacities*. Washington, D.C.

Foose, M.P., et al. 1980. "The Distribution and Relationships of Grade and Tonnage Among Some Nickel Deposits." Washington, D.C.: Geological Survey Professional Paper 1160.

Hubbert, M.K. 1969. "Energy Resources." In *Resources and Man*. San Francisco: W.H. Freeman.

Jevons, W.S. 1866. *The Coal Question*. London: Macmillan.

Landsberg, H., et al. 1979. *Energy: The Next Twenty Years*. Cambridge, Mass.: Ballinger Publishing Company.

McKelvey, V. 1972. "Mineral Resource Estimates and Public Policy: United States Mineral Resources." Washington, D.C.: Geological Survey Professional Paper 820.

Meadows, D., et al. 1972. *The Limits to Growth*. New York: Universe Books.

Page, T. 1977. *Conservation and Economic Efficiency*. Baltimore: The Johns Hopkins University Press.

Ridker, R.G., and W.D. Watson. 1980. *To Choose a Future*. Baltimore: The Johns Hopkins University Press.

Schurr, S., et al. 1979. *Energy in America's Future*. Baltimore: The Johns Hopkins University Press.

Shantz, J.J. 1975. *Resource Terminology: An Examination of Concepts and Recommendations for Improvements*. EPRI 336. Palo Alto, California.

Sheldon, R.P. 1975. "Estimates of Undiscovered Petroleum Resources—A Perspective." In *U.S.G.S. Annual Report, 1975*, pp. 11–22. Washington, D.C.

Singer, D.A., and J.H. DeYoung, Jr. 1980. "What Can Grade-Tonnage Relations Really Tell Us?" Paris: Colloque C1, Mineral Resources. CIAM.

Singer, D.A., and A.T. Overshine. 1979. "Assessing Metallic Resources in Alaska." *American Scientist* 67, no. 5: 582–89.

Singer, D.A., et al. 1980. "Grade and Tonnage Data Used to Construct Models for the Regional Alaskan Resources Assessment Program." U.S.G.S. Open-File Report 80–799, Washington, D.C.

Smith, V.K., ed. 1979. *Scarcity and Growth Reconsidered.* Baltimore: The Johns Hopkins University Press.

———. 1980. "The Evaluation of Natural Resource Adequacy: Elusive Quest or Frontier of Economic Analysis?" *Land Economics,* 56, no. 3 (August): 257–98.

Tilton, J.E., and W.A. Vogely, eds. 1981. "Market Instability in the Metal Industries." *Materials and Society* 5, no. 3: 243–346.

Vogely, W.A. 1977. "Energy and Resources Planning—National and Worldwide." In *Air Pollution,* 3rd ed., pp. 293–353. New York: Academic Press.

Zimmerman, E.W. 1964. *Introduction to World Resources.* New York: Harper and Row.

279-304

# 9 ARE MINERALS COSTING MORE?

6322
6323
7230
OECD, LDC's

*Harold J. Barnett,*
*Washington University*
*Gerald M. van Muiswinkel,*
*International Institute for Applied Systems Analysis*
*and Mordecai Shechter*
*University of Haifa, Israel*

## INTRODUCTION

There is widespread belief that minerals become increasingly scarce during economic growth. Two elements of the concept are (1) that the physical endowments of mineral resources are a fixed total as compared to the increased demands from economic growth and (2) that we tend to use the best economic resources first. Like agriculture, minerals are conceived to be a decreasing returns or increasing cost industry; formal economic literature for agriculture goes back to Smith, Malthus, Ricardo, and Mill. In addition, the limited minerals resources are subject to depletion from use, and this is believed further to restrict returns. W.S. Jevons was one of the first to write on this, in 1863. A well-known Hotelling theorem treats minerals as a capital asset subject to withdrawals. Most resources writings of the past hundred years, ranging from early literature on *lebensraum* and colonialism to the new international economic order, affirm the theory of increasing economic scarcity of minerals related to physical limits.

This is an interim report in a continuing project, "Mineral Scarcity and Economic Change." The authors are happy to acknowledge the assistance of the U.S. National Academy of Sciences in a grant to IIASA. In addition, Professor Barnett is grateful to the U.S. National Science Foundation and Washington University, St. Louis, under grant #DAR78-15705. Professor Shechter is grateful for assistance from the Neaman Institute for Advanced Studies, Technion University, Israel.

A number of writings, however, have questioned its relevance in the modern world, in concept and in fact. With respect to the diminishing returns theory, it is static. It thus omits consideration of increases in knowledge; improvements in techniques of production, transportation, and use; discoveries of new resources and substitutes; growth in international trade; recycling; and other social-technical changes. With respect to the facts, a study from Resources for the Future discovered contrary evidence (Barnett and Morse 1963). In the United States, over a period of almost a century to

Figure 9–1.    U.S. Minerals: Labor Cost per Unit of Output 1870–1957.

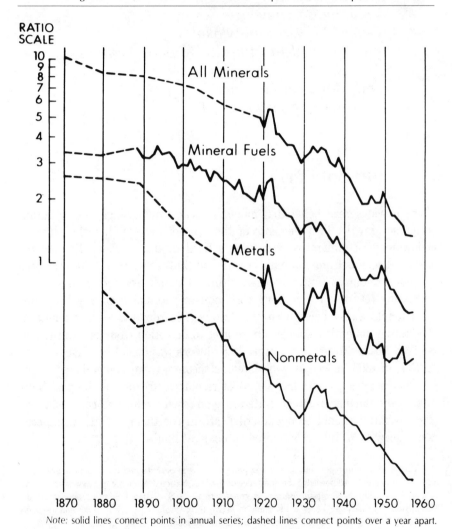

Note: solid lines connect points in annual series; dashed lines connect points over a year apart.

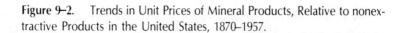

Figure 9–2. Trends in Unit Prices of Mineral Products, Relative to nonextractive Products in the United States, 1870–1957.

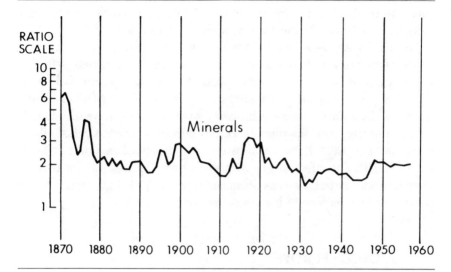

1957, minerals production was not subject to increasing costs either absolutely or relative to nonextractive goods. Figures 9–1 and 9–2 summarize the data. In Figure 9–1, we see that the opportunity cost of minerals in terms of man-days of labor to produce them has declined persistently. In Figure 9–2, we observe that the opportunity cost of units of minerals in terms of other goods foregone did not increase. Another recent study marshaled evidence from geology and technology on potential mineral supplies and substitutions to cast doubt on the concept of ineluctable, pervasive, increasing economic scarcity (Goeller and Weinberg 1978). However, public officials, the press, and book literature, as well as the general population, believe strongly in the doctrine of increasing economic scarcity of mineral resources, by a very large margin.

The matter is very important: The fact is that societies are making major decisions with belief in increasing economic scarcity of minerals as explicit or implicit premises. This is true, for example, in energy decisions of nations, international negotiations over ocean resources, and third world efforts to achieve a new international economic order.

The further simple fact, unfortunately, is that coherent evidence is lacking concerning the contemporaneous trend of costs of mineral resources in countries and regions. To a degree, societies are projecting future mineral costs without adequate understanding of their recent economic history. This chapter makes a step toward providing evidence, focusing primarily on Europe and its countries. Our purpose is to give evidence on trends in economic scarcity of imported minerals, expressed as the relative costs for regions and countries to obtain them. For discussion of various economic scarcity measures, see Smith (1979) and Barnett and van Muiswinkel (1980).

Our basic measure will be the trends of world market prices. In all cases unless otherwise explicitly stated, the mineral prices are deflated—that is, will be expressed relative to overall prices. For the European OECD countries as a group, our usual deflator is the price of GDP in OECD Europe (based on domestic currencies converted into dollars). When we turn to individual countries, the appropriate corrections for exchange rates will be made, and our usual deflator will be the country's wholesale price index or price of GDP. The effect will be that the corrected prices will not only express economic scarcity trends of minerals, but will also take into account the economic situations of individual countries.

## OECD—EUROPE

### Overall Minerals Price Index

The United Nations has constructed an index of mineral prices overall that includes the mineral fuels, ores, and crude fertilizers that are significantly involved in foreign trade.[1] The index unadjusted for inflation increased tenfold from 1950 to 1979. When deflated by the OECD price of GDP, the record is as given in Table 9–1.

The annual increases from 1950 to 1979 average about 1.4 percent compounded. We see, however, that there was a declining trend from 1950 to 1970. Then, in 1974, the minerals price index jumped sharply.

Table 9–1.    Overall Mineral Prices[1] (deflated). 1970 = 100

| | |
|---|---|
| 1950 | 188 |
| 1960 | 134 |
| 1970 | 100 |
| 1974 | 308 |
| 1979 | 287 |

1. Crude petroleum, coal, natural gas, iron ore, manganese ore, chrome ore, phosphate rock—weighted according to trade values.

The evidence suggests the following observations:

1. For this index, it is not useful to generalize about a trend for the *whole* period, when the pattern has reversed and changed so greatly since 1970.
2. The increase since 1970 does not represent a "trend." It was an abrupt change in 1974, reflecting oil price increases.
3. It is probably misleading to generalize about prices of minerals overall. Oil dominates the aggregate. In 1975, the oil statistical weight in the index was 85 percent, and in 1970 it was 61 percent.

For our purposes we abandon the overall index and turn to individual minerals and smaller groups.

### Fuel Minerals Prices

The U.N. fuel minerals index (petroleum, coal, and natural gas) is weighted by international trade values and thus is also dominated by petroleum. In 1975, petroleum was 90 percent of the index weight, and even in 1953 it was 70 percent. Again, it does not pay to look at the aggregate—it will move like petroleum. We look at petroleum directly, then at coal.

Deflated oil prices declined from 1950 to 1970. They then increased moderately for a few years, as individual countries and OPEC negotiated higher prices or pressured oil companies for higher royalties. Prices then trebled in 1974, when the governments of the producing countries and OPEC took full control, and have since moved sidewise. This is shown in Table 9–2.

The first column is a combined price of major oil exporters, and the second is Saudi Arabia alone, each deflated by the OECD-Europe price of GDP (see also Figure 9–3). From these data and other knowledge the following conclusions can be formed.

The first is that the decline in relative price of petroleum 1950 to 1970 represented increasing plenitude of the natural resource, oil. Much of the incremental oil supply cost as little as 10 cents a barrel to find, develop, and produce. Even today, such cost in the Middle East is less than $1 a barrel, as compared with a sale price of $30. The history of price statistics from 1950 to 1970 says that international oil supply from Middle East, Africa, Asia, and Latin America was becoming more plentiful and cheaper. This is why, of course, western nations rushed to invest in and develop and use it, in preference to their domestic sources and coal. The change in natural re-

**Table 9-2.**    Prices of Petroleum (deflated). 1970 = 100

|      | Major Exporting Countries | Saudia Arabia |
|------|---------------------------|---------------|
| 1950 | 238 | 315 |
| 1960 | 159 | 173 |
| 1970 | 100 | 100 |
| 1971 | 116 | 117 |
| 1972 | 117 | 117 |
| 1973 | 133 | 139 |
| 1974 | 407 | 459 |
| 1975 | 342 | 424 |
| 1976 | 366 | 460 |
| 1977 | 366 | 449 |
| 1978 | 308 | 387 |
| 1979 | 379 | 441 |

source availability and technological conditions of supply under competitive conditions was toward increased plenitude—namely, lower cost.

The second major conclusion has an opposite effect. Institutional parameters have changed. The increased economic and political cooperation of the major producers led to OPEC cartel controls that have been substituted for competition in supply. This is why relative prices rose in the 1970s, after an earlier period of plenitude. The OPEC claim that its price increases since 1974 have kept pace with inflation in industrialized countries is confirmed by the chart, to 1979. The world economic scarcity of oil in the 1970s is mainly or perhaps exclusively due to institutional restrictions and levies on supply by the governments in oil-producing countries—OPEC members and the non OPEC price followers in all other countries, among them the United States, the USSR, Norway, Mexico, Egypt, and so forth. A qualification is that the industrialized countries as a group have tried to find and develop their own petroleum resources, but have not been able to cover their own needs. Even if they could, it might require higher prices than we have today. On a world scale, without the current behavior of the main suppliers, however, it is likely that the pre-1970 trend would be closely followed, assuming ongoing efficiency improvements in finding and developing new resources.

We can draw a third conclusion if we look at the deflated prices of other fuels. Just as non-OPEC oil producers happily follow the higher prices in the cartel-controlled international oil market, so also gas, coal, and nuclear suppliers have tried to follow oil prices upward in the 1970s. Their ability to

Figure 9–3.   OECD–Europe, Prices of Imported Petroleum (deflated). 1970 = 100

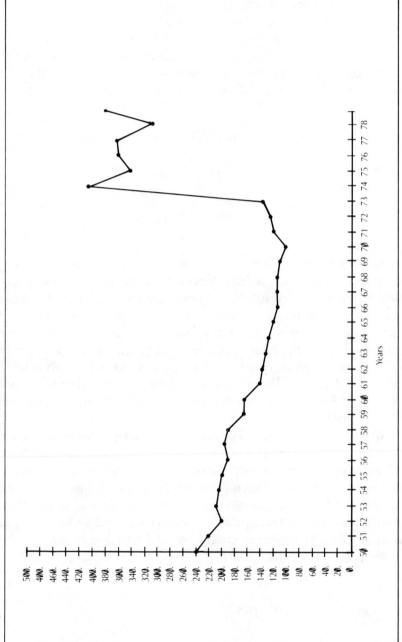

follow is, of course, subject to their characteristics and limitations—natural resources, technology, institutions, and changes in these.

Deflated coal prices in international trade declined or were roughly constant from 1950 to near 1970, as demand shifted to cheap foreign oils. Later, in the early 1970s and especially in 1974, coal rose in price because oil became expensive and nuclear fuel supply was restricted. Since 1974, when relative oil prices have stabilized, coal prices have declined. The statistical record is given in Table 9–3.

Table 9–3.    Coal Prices (OECD-Europe GDP deflator) 1970 = 100.

| | |
|---|---|
| 1950 | 141 |
| 1970 | 100 |
| 1974 | 162 |
| 1979 | 118 |

Is coal becoming increasingly scarce? Physically, coal reserves are very plentiful—hundreds and perhaps thousands of years of potential supply at present levels of use. Institutionally and technically, enlarged coal supplies are subject to enormous obstacles. These include safety regulations, pollution controls, transportation and manpower shortages, inadequate investment funds, and the threat of increased competition and capital loss from other energy suppliers. Whether coal supply becomes increasingly scarce and prices rise depend on the abilities of governments and industries to reduce these obstacles to coal production and use. Coal's present deflated price is close to the 1950 level.

We have only a few data on natural gas and no suitable data on nuclear. Natural gas prices tend to follow oil or sometimes coal, subject to the costs of gas transportation, the high value of imported LNG for peaking, and government regulations. A Dutch price series shows a 1979 index level of 130 relative to 1970. More generally, gas export prices, for example in Algerian efforts, have tended toward the btu price of oil. Nuclear fuel prices have been cartelized by producing governments and regulated by others at levels much higher than in the 1960s.

## Nonfuel Minerals

We now consider major nonfuel minerals. These are the metallic minerals and crude fertilizers. (We ignore building materials—sand, gravel, cement, etc. These are ubiquitous, unlimited resources and are not major in international trade.) As before, the essence of the question is whether we can discover increasing economic scarcity in evidence of deflated price trends. We consider first the following aggregate minerals indexes, published by the United Nations, the World Bank, and UNCTAD.

YA–(minerals, ores, metals), comprised of iron ore, manganese ore, phosphate, aluminium, copper, lead, zinc, tin, and tungsten

MM–(metals and minerals), comprised of the YA components plus nickel and bauxite (but we have this series only to 1978)

ANF–(nonferrous base metals), comprised of YA components plus nickel but excluding iron ore, manganese ore, tungsten, and phosphate

Has there been an increasing trend of deflated prices for nonfuel minerals groups from 1950 to 1979? The answer appears to be no. If the statistical data are valid, they are important evidence. They contradict widespread belief that these minerals like oil, have been becoming increasingly scarce and expensive.

Has there perhaps been an increasing trend in these deflated price series in recent years, even if not since 1950? The answer again appears to be no. The deflated prices of nonfuel minerals groups may have even declined slightly in the 1970s. The data are given in Table 9–4 (see also Figure 9–4).

There was a speculative mineral price boom in 1973–74, but this was reversed by later decline and the more general inflationary burst of the 1970s. The boom as such was not exceptional, because the same has happened with these nonfuel minerals in 1951, 1955, 1966 and 1969, as Figure 9–4 shows.

Another explanation for the general concern might be that prices of many agricultural raw materials showed a greater tendency to rise than the minerals. Deflated U.N. group indexes of prices of food and agricultural nonfood commodities illustrate this: The 1974 values relative to 1970 were 144 and 135 respectively. (Like nonfuel minerals, relative prices then fell: 1979 values were 97 and 99.)

## Individual Nonfuel Minerals

We have more than a dozen individual minerals and metals on which to present evidence and must try to simplify. We start this way. All declined or were approximately level in deflated price from 1950 to 1979 (see Table 9–5). In this respect, they give evidence against increasing economic scarcity of minerals. In some cases high peak values were reached, but these do

**Table 9–4.**    Nonfuel Mineral Prices (OECD-Europe GDP deflator). 1970 = 100

|        | YA  | MM  | ANF |
|--------|-----|-----|-----|
| 1950   | 121 | 137 | 114 |
| 1960   | 96  | 106 | 89  |
| 1970   | 100 | 100 | 100 |
| 1971   | 81  | 79  | 79  |
| 1972   | 70  | 68  | 69  |
| 1973   | 85  | 82  | 82  |
| 1974   | 107 | 102 | 93  |
| 1975   | 76  | 75  | 60  |
| 1976   | 76  | 74  | 66  |
| 1977   | 73  | 69  | 64  |
| 1978   | 66  | 59  | 58  |
| 1979   | 72  | –   | 65  |

Note:

YA—(minerals, ores, metals), comprised of iron ore, manganese ore, phosphate, aluminium, copper, lead, zinc, tin, and tungsten

MM—(metals and minerals), comprised of the YA components plus nickel and bauxite (but we have this series only to 1978)

ANF—(nonferrous base metals), comprised of YA components plus nickel but excluding iron ore, manganese ore, tungsten, and phosphate

not affect the general picture. Zinc and phosphate rock, for instance, re-acted strongly in 1974, but prices declined rapidly during the years following.

The question that remains is to detect whether there was a change in the trend in the 1970s toward increasing price. Three such possible cases—lead, tin, and bauxite—are presented in the lower portion of Table 9–5.

It is difficult to view the lead changes from 1970 to 1979 as a scarcity trend. The annual figures are volatile: seven of nine observations are below 100, and the 1979 terminal figure is an abrupt 44 percent higher than the preceding year.

The tin figures, on the other hand, indicate a degree of scarcity: Five of the nine figures following 1970 exceed 100, and the drift of the 1970s has been upward. Since 1956, the tin market has been influenced by the International Tin Council (ITC), by means of short-term buffer stock operations and export quotas in an effort to influence and stabilize prices. Although ITC quotas were in operation during short periods in 1973 and

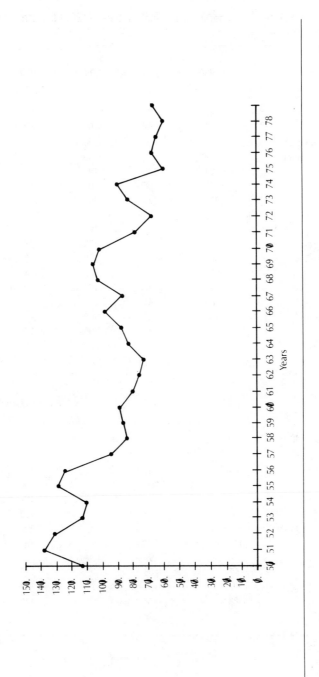

Figure 9-4. OECD–Europe, Deflated Price of Nonferrous Base Metals (ANF). 1970 = 100

**Table 9–5.**   Mineral and Metals Prices (OECD-Europe GDP deflator). 1970 = 100

|  | 1950 | 1960 | 1970 | 1974 | 1979 |
|---|---|---|---|---|---|
| Copper | 86 | 72 | 100 | 89 | 47 |
| Nickel | 81 | 87 | 100 | 83 | 79 |
| Bauxite (Guyana) | – | – | 100 | 103 | 117 |
| (Jamaica) | 149 | 93 | 100 | 118 | 113[b] |
| Aluminum | 124 | 135 | 100 | 75 | 82 |
| Lead | 225 | 98 | 100 | 114 | 127 |
| Zinc | 250 | 123 | 100 | 224 | 86 |
| Tin | 132 | 88 | 100 | 133 | 139 |
| Iron ore | 145 | 157 | 100 | 83 | 58 |
| Chrome ore | 140[a] | 128 | 100 | 78 | 105 |
| Manganese ore | 325 | 225 | 100 | 113 | 72 |
| Manganese | 555 | 239 | 100 | 126 | 85 |
| Mercury | 47 | 77 | 100 | 42 | 23 |
| Tungsten ore | 84[a] | 41 | 100 | 69 | 60 |
| Phosphate rock | 182 | 141 | 100 | 276 | 107 |
| Potash | 195[a] | 135 | 100 | 117 | 81 |

Prices (OECD-Europe GDP deflator). 1970 = 100

|  | Lead | Tin | Bauxite (Guyana) |
|---|---|---|---|
| 1950 | 225 | 132 | – |
| .... | ... | ... | ... |
| 1969 | 101 | 99 | 106 |
| 1970 | 100 | 100 | 100 |
| 1971 | 78 | 87 | 107 |
| 1972 | 80 | 82 | 100 |
| 1973 | 91 | 86 | 95 |
| 1974 | 114 | 133 | 103 |
| 1975 | 70 | 95 | 127 |
| 1976 | 77 | 108 | 143 |
| 1977 | 95 | 138 | 149 |
| 1978 | 88 | 138 | 129 |
| 1979 | 127 | 139 | 117 |

[a] 1955
[b] 1978

1975–76, it is unlikely that this consumer-producer forum (the ITC per se) caused the upward trend in the 1970s. This does not, however, exclude the possibility of institutional supply restrictions by individual producers and countries.

The bauxite trend in the 1970s, although weaker, also perhaps indicates scarcity. However, it is purely an institutional phenomenon. Bauxite and substitutes are extraordinarily plentiful resources. The individual producing countries have negotiated improved terms with the few oligopoly buyers. Improvements were overdue, but the methods of change were unfortunate in Jamaica and possibly elsewhere. The International Bauxite Association, however, has little effect as a cartel; it is unable to control quantities or prices (Barnett 1979).

With these two possible exceptions, all the evidence of the fifteen individual nonfuel minerals and metals series and three group series testifies against increasing scarcity. The significant ores, metals, and fertilizers have not had a rising price trend relative to the price of all goods and services in the OECD-Europe aggregation of nations.

## IMPACTS ON INDIVIDUAL COUNTRIES

The foregoing analysis has treated the mineral scarcity hypothesis—the supply price conditions for the Western European economy as a whole. We now consider what these have meant for the individual countries. To do this in full degree is beyond our capability. It would require that we compare the changes in the prices of mineral inputs with changes in the prices of other production inputs, then observe shifts in minerals use and factor proportions induced from changes in prices and technology, and then appraise a variety of macro and parameter change effects, leading to effects on income and output per capita.

At this time we can only do the first of these steps. We compare changes in prices of imported minerals with changes in wholesale prices (or prices of GDP) in individual countries. Since international mineral prices ($P_i$) are expressed in dollars and wholesale prices ($WHP$) in domestic currency, we make them comparable by employing a foreign exchange conversion factor ($FE$). This is the number of units of domestic currency per dollar in each year. Thus we can compare ($P_i \times FE$) with $WHP$. Alternatively, we can express the relationship as $P_i$ versus $FE/WHP$, and we can look at the real cost of minerals in terms of domestic wholesale goods generally by observing $P_i \times FE/WHP$.

## Petroleum

Almost all countries benefited from discovery and development of the remarkably cheap oil of Middle East, Africa, and other places during the two decades 1950 to 1970. During the worldwide gradual inflation of the period, petroleum prices in the consumers' own currency generally increased more slowly than wage rates or wholesale prices. Cheaper petroleum was substituted for other fuels and other factors of production, with attendant increases in the productivity of labor, capital, and other inputs.

In the decade of the 1970s, the process reversed. Every country without exception experienced increases in imported petroleum cost. The increases far outran increases in costs of other factors. Efforts have been made to substitute labor, capital, and other inputs for expensive petroleum, with inevitable losses in productivity.

The strength of the petroleum price movements in both periods was large. It was so dominant that the pattern of impact was common for all nations—significant decline in relative price in 1950–70; enormous increase in 1970–79.

Yet even so, the variability of effect on consuming nations was substantial. Table 9–6 arrays the relative impacts of petroleum price changes compared with wholesale price changes from 1950 to 1979 upon most of the OECD European countries.

We learn that when the actual mineral price change is very large (the petroleum dollar price rose elevenfold), the impact is clearly visible in the relative factor prices in each of the nations. But the impact is felt differently among nations for a variety of reasons. Among them is the relative strength of a nation's own economy as manifest in foreign exchange and domestic prices. Another main element in effect of the oil price rise is whether the country is an oil producer and thus somewhat shielded or even a net exporter.

## Nonfuel Minerals

In the case of nonfuel minerals, international mineral price increases expressed in dollars were far smaller than those for petroleum. The differences among countries in the multiplicative deflator index (*FE/WHP*) thus played a more substantial role in the calculations of deflated mineral prices than for petroleum.

**Table 9–6.**  Relative Prices of Imported Petroleum (1970 = 100).

| | Ratio: $P_{pet} \times FE/WHP$ | | | |
| | 1950 | 1970 | 1974 | 1979 |
|---|---|---|---|---|
| Austria | 159 | 100 | 376 | 373 |
| Belgium | 133 | 100 | 383 | 420 |
| Denmark | 154 | 100 | 357 | 368 |
| Finland | 132 | 100 | 361 | 401 |
| France | 136 | 100 | 365 | 432 |
| FRG | 160 | 100 | 364 | 367 |
| Greece | 115 | 100 | 375 | 418 |
| Ireland | 173 | 100 | 440 | 399 |
| Italy | 137 | 100 | 391 | 431 |
| Netherlands | 146[a] | 100 | 389 | 386 |
| Norway | 191 | 100 | 377 | 409 |
| Portugal | 143 | 100 | 377 | 417 |
| Spain | 168 | 100 | 374 | 383 |
| Sweden | 161 | 100 | 383 | 409 |
| Switzerland | 127 | 100 | 334 | 323 |
| United Kingdom | 158 | 100 | 452 | 401 |

[a]1953

Note: In Europe the largest and least relative impacts from the OPEC price rise from 1970 to 1979 were as follows (1970 = 100):

Ratio: $P_{pet} \times FE/WHP$

| Largest | | Least | |
|---|---|---|---|
| France | 432 | Switzerland | 323 |
| Italy | 431 | FRG | 367 |
| Belgium | 420 | Denmark | 368 |
| Greece | 418 | Austria | 373 |

How shall we present the information on relative price movements of individual minerals to the individual European consuming nations? We start with Figure 9–5 for Germany (FRG) that shows the trend of the nominal world market prices of nonfuel minerals. These prices are then adjusted by the rising value of the Deutschemark (DM) relative to the dollar, and then this price is further adjusted by the price of GDP in the FRG. The result is the price of the imported minerals relative to the price of all other economic goods in Germany, both expressed in DM and converted to index numbers.

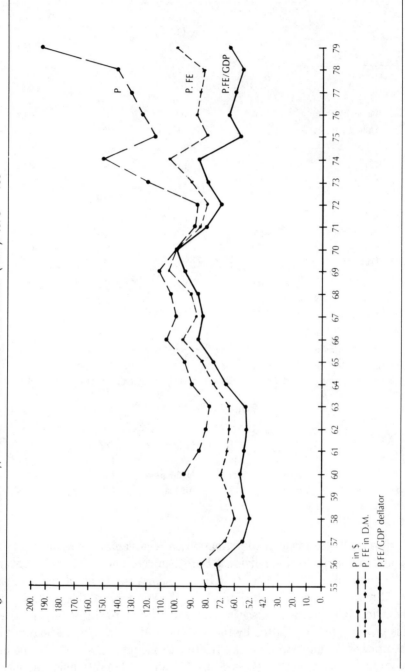

**Figure 9–5.** West Germany, Prices of Nonferrous Base Metals (ANF). 1970 = 100

However, with sixteen nations and price indexes for more than fifteen nonfuel minerals, the story would become repetitive and tedious. We try to avoid this by summarizing and simplifying in three ways. First, we remind the reader of the evidence presented earlier for the OECD group of nations as a whole: In only tin and perhaps bauxite among the nonfuel minerals, for only the 1970–79 subperiod, did we find what may be significant increases in relative prices. Second, we shall ignore declines or constancies or small increases in relative prices that characterize most of the minerals. We shall focus only on cases of possibly significant trends of price increase. We define these as increases that average 2 percent or more a year, compounded, for relevant periods. (For orientation: an average annual rate of 2 percent, compounded, doubles relative price in thirty-five years. Commodity prices fluctuate widely in short periods, sometimes 10 to 50 percent in a year or two.)

Third, we observe two patterns that typify the impacts of international mineral prices upon the price and foreign exchange systems of European countries. One group of countries is represented in this respect by, say, Austria. The other pattern is represented by, say, Belgium. The patterns are defined by the countries' multiplicative deflators ($FE/WHP$), which are applied to the common dollar international mineral prices. Table 9–7 presents these countries and information on the trends of their multiplicative deflators.

For the first group of countries, we find possibly increasing relative price trends for two nonfuel mineral commodites. These occur in the period 1970 to 1979 only. These commodities are tin (relative price rises about 3.5 percent a year) and lead (about 2.5 percent). This finding identifies as possibly scarce the same minerals as were identified earlier for OECD-Europe as a group, where the deflator was the price of GDP, except for bauxite (about 1.8 percent). The comments made there are applicable here as well—the period is short, only a decade; the annual lead changes are erratic; and revealed scarcity of tin is probably attributable to institutional influences rather than to natural resource limitations or technological conditions.

For the second group of OECD countries, we find (in addition to tin and lead) candidates for scarcity trends as given in Table 9–8.

To a degree, these scarcity effects—increase in relative prices of minerals in this group of countries—represent the individual country developments in trade and domestic economic affairs. This is why bauxite, nickel, chrome, tungsten, and phosphates appear here and not in the first group of countries as well and why the rates of increases in the prices of tin and lead are higher.

**Table 9–7.** Average Annual Compound Rates of Decline in *FE/WHP* (percent).

|  | 1950–79 | 1970–79 |
|---|---|---|
| **Group 1** | | |
| Norway | 5.5 | 10.7 |
| Ireland | 5.4 | 10.9 |
| Spain | 5.4 | 11.3 |
| FRG | 5.4 | 11.8 |
| Austria | 5.3 | 11.6 |
| Denmark | 5.3 | 11.7 |
| Netherlands | 5.2 | 11.2 |
| United Kingdom | 5.0 | 10.9 |
| Switzerland | 5.0 | 13.0 |
| **Group 2** | | |
| Finland | 4.6 | 10.9 |
| Portugal | 4.6 | 10.4 |
| Belgium | 4.3 | 10.2 |
| Italy | 4.3 | 10.4 |
| France | 4.3 | 10.2 |
| Greece | 3.8 | 10.4 |

**Table 9–8.** Relative Price Increase Per Year (percent).

| Mineral | 1950–79 | 1970–79 |
|---|---|---|
| Tin | 2.6 | 5.2 |
| Lead | 0.4 | 4.2 |
| Bauxite | 1.6 | 3.4 |
| Nickel | 2.4 | −1.1 |
| Chrome ore | 1.7 | 2.0 |
| Tungsten ore | 2.6 | −2.0 |
| Phosphates | 0.5 | 2.2 |

Second, concerning the additional minerals, there are unanswered questions:

- Nickel and tungsten—what accounts for the change in direction of movement only since 1970? It is not consistent with the idea of a persistent, long-term scarcity trend.

- Phosphates—We have an alternative price series, also for Morocco phosphates, that shows decline in relative price 1950 to 1979 and increases of only 1.5 percent a year in 1970–79.
- Chrome—the increasing price in each period and its acceleration in 1970–79 tend to support the increasing scarcity hypothesis in mild degree.

Finally, we conclude as follows concerning nonfuel minerals: There is very little support for Malthusian or Ricardian hypotheses of increasing mineral scarcity. Most of the individual minerals and also the nonfuel minerals group indexes have declined or been constant in relative price. The few instances of evidence of scarcity in supply can be more readily related to the institutional phenomena of governmental interventions than to natural resource deposits or technological conditions. In addition, in a number of Western European economies, several international minerals are costing more in terms of foreign exchange and domestic goods. This is an increase in unit value of imported minerals because of deflator change. It is due to decline in the international value of domestic goods and is not related to technology, costs, or institutional conditions of foreign mineral supply.

## PRICE IMPACTS ON DEVELOPING COUNTRIES

It is apparent that changes in international mineral supply prices have varied impacts upon the price and cost systems of the consuming countries. We just analyzed and discussed this with respect to Western European countries. We now want to observe the differential impact of changes in international oil and coal prices in the 1970s upon developing countries. We want to compare them with changes in prices of other factors. As before, we do this by examining deflated mineral prices, $P_i \times FE/WHP$. For orientation, we also show the impacts on Austria and Belgium. The data appear in Table 9–9.

In general, the impact of the petroleum price rises of the 1970s was substantially greater in a sample of developing countries than in developed Western European nations. The cost of energy relative to domestic goods and foreign exchange went up more sharply in less-developed countries. The price pressure to substitute away from the imported energy commodities and the tendency for factor productivity to fall were stronger. One unhappy choice was to reduce even more greatly energy inputs in productive activity, thereby reducing productivity of labor and other factors and growth of GNP. Another was to maintain such energy use and pay for it by exporting

**Table 9–9.**  Deflated Prices of Oil and Coal ($P_i \times FE/WHP$) in 1979 (1970 = 100).

|  | Petroleum | Coal |
|---|---|---|
| Pakistan | 780 | 242 |
| India | 589 | 183 |
| Zambia | 566 | 176 |
| Brazil | 553 | 172 |
| Thailand | 481 | 149 |
| Korea | 455 | 141 |
| Malaysia (GDP deflator) | 440 | 137 |
| Colombia | 387 | 120 |
| Phillipines | 359 | 112 |
| Argentina | 328 | 102 |
| .... | ... | ... |
| Austria | 373 | 116 |
| Belgium | 425 | 131 |

more at lower prices (thereby reducing growth of real GDP) or by borrowing more foreign exchange.

Beyond these adversities there were dislocations and disruptions. Even in advanced economies like the United States and Europe, with developed, more efficient market and public decision institutions, the economic losses merely from adjusting to the sharp price changes were large. Developing countries are far less robust in economic efficiency mechanisms. Energy supply catastrophes in these countries have been averted only by extreme extensions of credit from the developed countries. These are unlikely to be repaid or properly serviced and risk widespread financial catastrophes. The evidence here, which includes domestic price trends, supports the observation that developing countries that do not export oil have experienced greater balance of payments problems from OPEC prices than developed nations.

## SUMMARY AND QUALIFICATIONS

Since World War II, natural resource and technological change conditions for all minerals have tended to result in improved supply, and thus declining or constant prices, relative to the overall price level in OECD-Europe.

However, in the last decade the development of institutional innovations has restricted the supply of oil. The powerful OPEC cartel has engendered scarcity and substantially increased prices of petroleum. This has tended to increase prices of other fuel minerals. Also, in this decade, but in lesser degree, governments have fostered stabilization or moderate increases in tin and bauxite prices. Thus, in the decade of the 1970s, OECD-Europe has experienced increasing economic scarcity of fuels and of two other minerals of the group considered.

The scarcities have institutional causes. European industrialized countries depend substantially on minerals supply from developing countries and have invested and produced in them under favorable conditions in the past. This situation, however, has been changing in recent years. Developing countries have been increasing control over the exploitation and exports of their natural resources. In some cases this results in higher prices and thereby increased economic scarcity of the minerals.

The impacts of mineral price changes on individual countries differ substantially. Different trends in exchange rates and domestic price levels caused relative prices of some imported minerals to indicate increasing economic scarcity in certain countries, where increasing plenitude was registered in other countries. Especially the developing countries are confronted with severe impacts from rising energy prices.

These findings rest upon the validity of the price indexes of the commodities and of the OECD-Europe price indexes. The sources are respectable—the United Nations, the World Bank, OECD, the London Metal Exchange, and the like. In addition, we have compiled data on more than one index for most of the individual commodities and groups, and they give roughly the same results as those we reported above. It is also useful to observe that the statistical trend results are similar in both group and individual commodity data. But we are at an early stage of a long-term study, and it would be desirable to identify still other worthy indexes and to see whether these give the same results. Also, data series are being extended to 1980.

Explicit consideration should also be given to several major influences on minerals prices and deflators in the 1970s. Increases in oil prices have directly pushed up costs and prices of minerals, transportation, and other goods generally. Also, increased governmental interventions on social legislation, environmental pollution, safety, and energy conservation have reduced productivity advances and increased prices. On the other hand, reduced economic growth rates have tended to depress demand for and prices of minerals in the world economy. These several influences have obviously influenced both numerators and denominators of our measures of relative prices.

## APPENDIX A
## PRICES OF IMPORTED PETROLEUM RELATIVE
## TO PRICES OF LABOR

A strong form of the classical concept of increasing natural resources scarcity is that their prices will rise relative to price (wage rate) of labor during economic growth. Contemporary economic growth theory holds, on the contrary, that labor is the factor that becomes increasingly scarce; and because of productivity advance, its price will rise relative to natural resources. It is useful to look at the evidence on relative scarcity of labor and petroleum during the 1970s, following OPEC's entrance into control of oil markets. We look at the ratios of imported petroleum prices per barrel to the wage rates in the consuming countries, adjusted for foreign exchange ratios—$P_{pet} \times FE/WR$.

Table 9–10 shows that imported petroleum has become very scarce relative to labor in European countries since 1970. In 1979, the increase in petroleum price was about 2.3 to 4.2 times the increase in wage rate in the countries in OECD-Europe.

We may suggest the significance of these large relative price increases of petroleum. In these Western market economies, factor proportions and relative marginal productivities of factors tend to be adjusted to the ratios of their prices. Such large price ratio changes of oil relative to labor would call for substantial efforts to change factor proportions. So doing would significantly affect factor productivities and in particular would slow productivity advances of labor. In fact, advances of labor productivity have slowed greatly in the 1970s, and some part of this is the effect of the great rise in petroleum prices. (See Jorgenson's recent econometric analyses of the effects of increased energy prices in slowing productivity gains in the 1970's.)

## APPENDIX B
## SOURCES OF DATA

### Commodity Price Indexes

*Description*                                                                                        *Source*

- Minerals overall: fuels (94 percent: petroleum, coal,          UN
  gas); iron ore (3.5 percent); manganese ore (0.3
  percent); chrome ore (0.2 percent); crude fertilizers (1.5
  percent)

Table 9–10.    Relative Prices of Imported Petroleum (1970 = 100).

| | $P_{pet} \times FE/WR^a$ | | |
|---|---|---|---|
| | 1970 | 1974 | 1979 |
| Austria | 100 | 290 | 233 |
| Belgium | 100 | 274 | 227 |
| Denmark | 100 | 303 | – |
| Finland | 100 | 318 | 302 |
| France | 100 | 321 | 251 |
| FRG | 100 | 314 | 272 |
| Greece | 100 | 380 | 276 |
| Ireland | 100 | 349 | – |
| Italy | 100 | 363 | 290 |
| Netherlands | 100 | 295 | 255 |
| Norway | 100 | 326 | 291 |
| Portugal | 100 | 235 | – |
| Spain | 100 | 278 | – |
| Sweden | 100 | 381 | 419 |
| Switzerland | 100 | 309 | 242 |
| United Kingdom | 100 | 405 | 340 |

$P_{pet} \times FE/WR$ in 1979 (1970 = 100)

| Largest | | Least | |
|---|---|---|---|
| Sweden | 419 | Belgium | 227 |
| United Kingdom | 340 | Austria | 233 |
| Finland | 302 | Switzerland | 242 |
| Norway | 291 | France | 251 |

<sup>a</sup>Wage rates refer in most cases to hourly earnings.

- Petroleum, major exporters: Saudi Arabia, fob Ras-    UN
  Taruna (37 percent); Iran, fob Kharg Island (19
  percent); Iraq, fob Khar al Amaya (10 percent); and
  others

- Petroleum Saudi Arabia: Ras Taruna    IFS

- Coal: U.S. coking coal c.i.f. North Sea (66 percent);    UN
  FRG hard coal ex-mine (34 percent)

- Minerals, ores, metals (YA): phosphate rock (11 percent), manganese ore (2 percent), iron ore (21 percent), aluminium (13 percent), copper (33 percent), lead (2 percent), zinc (4 percent), tin (12 percent), tungsten (1 percent)    UNCTAD

- Metals and Minerals (MM): copper (London Metals Exchange), tin (London Metals Exchange), nickel (Canada), aluminum (New York), lead (London Metals Exchange), zinc (London Metals Exchange), iron ore (Brazil), bauxite (U.S., Jamaica), manganese ore (India); weighted by 1974–76 developing countries export values    WB

- Nonferrous base metals (ANF): copper (44 percent), nickel (10 percent), aluminium (28 percent), lead (4 percent), zinc (8 percent), tin (7 percent)    UN

- Copper: U.S. f.o.b. Atlantic (9 percent); London Metals Exchange wirebar (91 percent)    UN

- Nickel: Canada producer price f.o.b.    UN

- Bauxite: U.S. imports Jamaica    WB
  U.S. imports Guyana    IFS

- Aluminium: U.S. producer (18 percent); Canada del. U.K. (82 percent)    UN

- Lead: U.K., London Metals Exchange (86 percent); Canada (14 percent)    UN

- Zinc: U.K., London Metals Exchange (73 percent); Canada (27 percent)    UN

- Tin: Malaysia, ex-works Penang (73 percent); U.K., London Metals Exchange (27 percent)    UN

- Iron ore: Brazil (45 prcent); Canada (25 percent); Sweden (18 percent); Liberia (11 percent)    UN

- Chrome ore: Turkey, c.i.f. euroports    UN

- Manganese ore: India, c.i.f. euroports    UN

- Manganese: India, U.S. ports    IFS

- Mercury: Spain                                           EMJ

- Tungsten: c.i.f. Europe                              UNCTAD

- Phosphate rock: f.a.s. Casablanca                        UN

- Potash: Canada                                          IFS

The prices on price indexes are from five different sources. All series have been transferred into indexes with 1970 = 100 and are based on U.S. dollar prices. They can be found in:

- "Methods used in compiling the U.N. indexes for basic commodities in international trade," U.N. Statistical Papers, Series M, No. 29, Rev. 2 of 1979. These series have been updated with the "U.N. Monthly Bulletin of Statistics" of July 1980. Weighting patterns are adjusted every five years (latest 1975) and are based on trade patterns.
- "International Financial Statistics" of the IMF, Yearbook 1979 and Aguust 1980 issue
- "Commodity Price Forecasts," World Bank, May 1979.
- "Monthly Commodity Price Bulletin," Special Supplement and Handbook, UNCTAD, Geneva.
- *Engineering and Mining Journal,* March 1980.

### Exchange Rates

Used were "International Financial Statistics"(IMF) quotations of the period averages (yearly) of par rate/market rates (line rf). For countries that express dollars in local currency, reciprocals were taken. All exchange rates were converted into index numbers with 1970 = 100.

### Wage Rates

Sources are the ILO Yearbooks 1975 and 1979 and the most recent ILO Quarterly Bulletins and Supplements. The wages are for manufacturing (all industries), expressed either as earnings or as rates per month, week, hour, or day. The data are annual averages except for some of the 1979 values, where the latest monthly data were taken. All wage rates were converted into indexes with 1970 = 100.

## Wholesale Price Indexes

Sources are IFS volumes, country pages, line 63. They differ in coverage, which might complicate country comparisons. The series have been rebased on $1970 = 100$.

## Implicit GDP Deflators

These deflators are from the U.N. Yearbook of National Account Statistics 1977, table 8A. For the years 1976–79, the deflators are based on IFS series, by dividing GDP (line 99b) by GDP in 1975 prices (line 99bp). These series were rebased to $1970 = 100$ and linked to the U.N. data. The OECD-Europe GDP deflator was computed from OECD "Main Economic Indicators."

## Growth Rates

The growth rates are compound interest rates or the $i$ from $X_n = X_0 (1+i)^n$, where $X_n$ and $X_0$ are the latest and first value for the period . . . $n$.

## REFERENCES

Barnett, H.J. 1979. "The Bauxite Cartel in the New International Economic Order." In *Advances in the Economics of Energy and Resources,* vol. II, ed. R.S. Pindyck. JAI Press.

Barnett, H.J., and C. Morse. 1963. *Scarcity and Growth.* Baltimore: Johns Hopkins University Press.

Barnett, H.J., and G. van Muiswinkel. 1980. "Minerals Scarcity and Economic Change: Design and Discussion." WP-80-100. Laxenburg, Austria: IIASA.

Goeller, H.E., and A.M. Weinberg. 1978. "The Age of Substitutability." *American Economic Review* V, no. 68:6.

Smith, V.K., ed. 1979. *Scarcity and Growth Reconsidered.* Baltimore: Johns Hopkins University Press.

$72\frac{30}{322}$

$6\frac{3}{6}\frac{2}{190}$

$US$

# 10  A METHODOLOGY FOR ANALYZING THE IMPACT OF REGULATIONS ON THE COAL INDUSTRY

*Raphael H. Amit,*
*Susan E. Martin,*
*and Michael C. Naughton*
*Data Resources, Inc.*

## INTRODUCTION

The purpose of this chapter is to test a methodology for measuring the effects of coal-related regulations on regional coal production, distribution, and prices. This methodology must measure the direct and indirect economic effects of these regulations on producers and consumers first by measuring the impacts over time on where, when, and how much coal will be produced and then by identifying the additional costs to coal consumers that result from this altered production and distribution scenario.

The methodology to be tested utilizes a spatial optimization linear programming model to represent mathematically the economic trade-offs implied by a specific regulation. The approach is first to simulate the model while assuming the implementation of all coal-related regulations and then to simulate the model while excluding any or all of the regulations. Comparison of the resultant simulations yields the effects of these regulations on prices, production, and distribution. Application of this methodology to the coal industry will lead to a better understanding of the impacts of the complex set of coal-related government regulations.

Government coal policy has two main—although sometimes conflicting—objectives. One is to increase the production and use of coal; the other is aimed at tightening environmental, health, and safety controls. These policies, which are carried out through various pieces of legislation

305

passed by the U.S. Congress, impose restrictions on both coal supply and coal demand.

The significant number of federal regulations on coal extraction and use is a relatively recent development, beginning in 1969 with the Federal Coal Mine Health and Safety Act. This act was amended in 1970 and 1977 as part of a continuing effort to improve mining conditions. The enforcement of this act is the major reason for the sharp decline in deep-mining productivity observed over the last decade, particularly in the East, and it has also contributed to the increase in the cost of mining coal in the United States.

There are many other pieces of legislation that have been enacted over the last decade. The most well-known are the Surface Mining Control and Reclamation Act of 1977; the Clean Air Act and its 1977 amendments; and most recently, the Fuel Use Act (FUA). These and other pieces of legislation, as well as regulations issued by as many as twenty-one different federal departments and agencies, span all segments of the industry. In most cases, the issuing agency performs a study in which it investigates the implications of a particular regulation. However, the potential conflict with other existing or proposed legislation is often overlooked. Some critics of federal coal policy argue that the industry is over regulated; others contend that more regulations are needed because of conflicts or gaps between the mandates of the various agencies with coal-related responsibility. These gaps preclude the existence of a coherent national coal policy, and no comprehensive quantification of the full impact of all coal-related regulations on the costs of producing and using coal has been made to date. Our hypothesis is that the combined effects of all regulations are different from the individual implications of each separate regulation.

In the section that follows, we present in detail our methodology for measuring quantitatively the implications over time of government regulations. In section three we apply our methodology to two pieces of legislation, thereby providing a quantitative analysis of their impact on production and prices. In section four we discuss the implications of this technique on measuring the private sector cost associated with complying with the government regulations. We conclude with a discussion of the ramifications of this study on other industries.

## METHODOLOGY

In general, the idea is to represent mathematically the economic trade-offs implied by a specific regulation and/or to add to production costs the estimate of the additional expenditures incurred in order to comply with any particular rule. This information is used by a demand-driven policy simulation model for coal production, prices, and interregional coal flows in the following manner: The model is simulated first while assuming the existence and implementation of all regulations and is simulated a second time while excluding any or all of the regulations. Comparing the two simulations allows us to examine over time the implication of any given regulation for where coal will be produced, when it will be produced, what the markets are for various coals, and to what extent the competitive market position of coal in any supply region changes due to that regulation. Also, the comparison of the two simulations yields the effect on both mine-mouth and delivered prices of any regulation. Finally, by comparing coal expenditure patterns of consumers, we are able to capture the financial implications of government regulations. As will be discussed later in the chapter, the interactions between the regulations may cause expenditures to vary so that cost associated with any particular regulation may not be the appropriate measure for estimating the full cost of the regulations, since the sum of the individual regulations may be less than the total cost of all regulations.

The tool that is used for quantitative economic evaluation of the regulation is the DRI/Zimmerman Coal Model. In what follows, we provide a specific overview of this model and its relationship to other models.[1] As Figure 10–1 illustrates, the coal model draws upon and feeds into an overall energy demand model, which allows it to capture the potential interfuel substitu-

1. The coal model has been developed in collaboration with Martin Zimmerman, who is the author of the coal supply model—one lement of the DRI/Zimmerman Coal Model. The energy model and the macroeconomic model have been developed by various staff members of DRI.

**Figure 10–1.** Comprehensive Planning Framework for Coal Analysis.

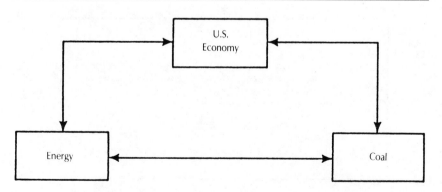

tions resulting from any set of regulations. The coal model is further related to the macroeconomic model of the U.S. economy, allowing us to examine the evolution of the coal industry while considering the interrelationships between the behavior and performance of the economy, energy consumption, and coal production and prices.

Figure 10–2 illustrates the technical structure of the model, which is annual and can be solved sequentially out to the year 2010. For each year that is being simulated, regional and sectorial coal demands, which are derived from DRI's overall energy demand model, are fed into the distribution submodel. In addition, exogenous variables (referred to as parameters) used in

**Figure 10–2.** DRI/Zimmerman Coal Model.

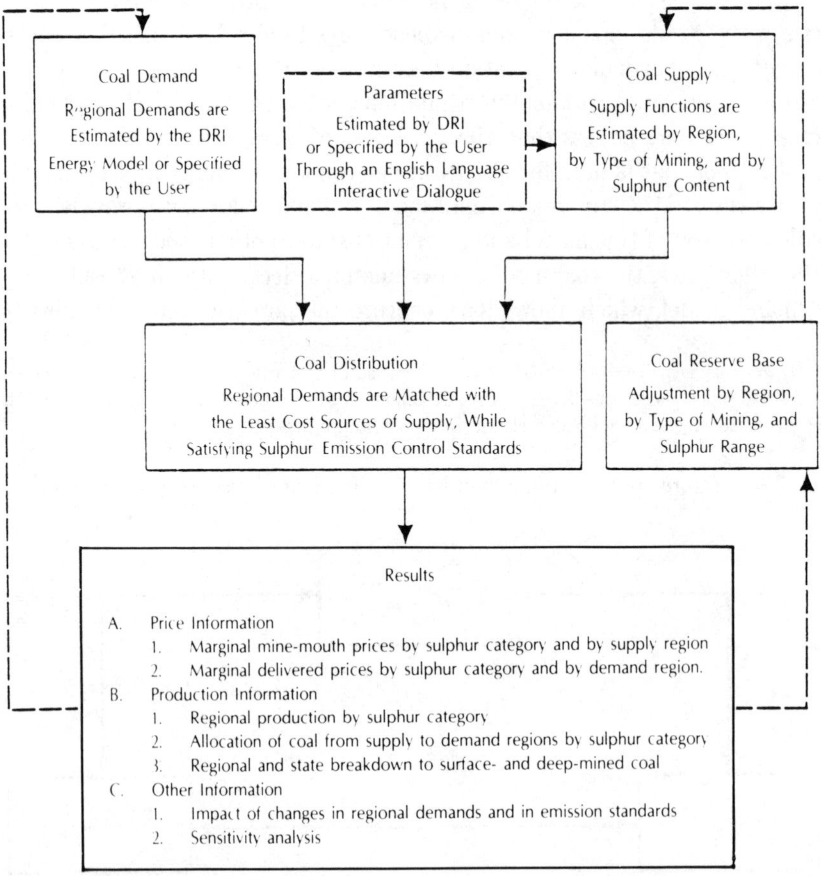

the simulation are specified. These include key factors affecting the cost of producing coal as well as transportation costs, regional sulphur emission standards, taxes, and other variables. For each year simulated, some of the parameters are fed into the supply model, which estimates the long-run cost of mining as a function of cumulative production. These cost estimates, for each of six supply regions and each of six sulphur ranges, are fed into the distribution submodel together with the rest of the parameters. In the distribution submodel, the regional demands are matched with the least cost sources of supply. This process results in regional production estimates and price forecasts, both mine mouth and delivered. The production estimates obtained for each year simulated are used to adjust the coal reserve base. This is important, since the cost of producing coal is related to the remaining stock of reserves. Following this adjustment, the next year may be simulated.

As Figure 10–2 suggests, there are three main elements to the model—demand, supply, and distribution. Each of these elements is explained briefly below. The detailed mathematical formulations of the various elements of the model can be found in DRI (1977, 1979), DOI (1978), and Zimmerman (1977). In this chapter we chose to provide a general overview of these three elements.

The model considers thirteen coal demand regions, as shown in Figure 10–3. The model further considers eighteen coal-producing states aggregated into six regions, as shown in Figure 10–4; two types of mining; and six types of coal in each of the producing states.

## Coal Demand

The coal model draws upon the DRI U.S. Energy Model for demand forecasts for coal. Eight coal-consuming sectors are considered. The largest (73 percent of total production in 1978) is the electric utility sector. Regional electric utility coal demand forecasts are derived from a structural econometric model. This model accounts for existing and planned generating capacity by fuel type, plant capacity factors, fuel prices, and assumptions on the rate of return.

The other consuming sectors considered are the metallurgical, industrial, household-commercial, export, and synthetic fuel sectors. Also accounted for are imports and changes in stock. Coal consumed for producing coke (metallurgical coal) is forecast in the energy model as a function of industrial output in the iron and steel sector. Industrial noncoking coal and household

**Figure 10–3.**    Energy Demand Regions.

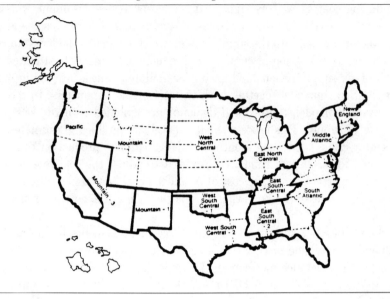

**Figure 10–4.**    Coal Supply Regions.

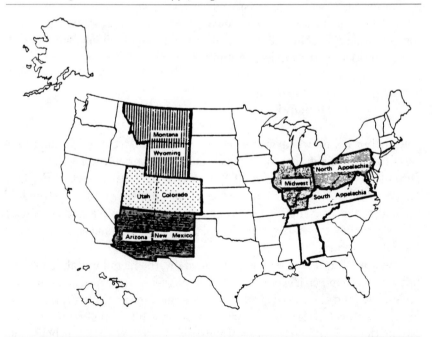

and commercial coal use are forecast using structural demand equations in which industrial output (by sector), relative energy prices, and other variables are included in the formulation. The energy model provides national annual demand forecasts for these sectors. The figures are regionalized by using weights obtained from historical distribution patterns. Finally, total regional coal demands are obtained by summing the regional demands of all sectors.

The regional aggregate approach used in the demand model allows explicit treatment of price elasticities among fuels, simulating the interfuel substitution effects that occur over time as relative prices change. Regulations that affect these choices can be easily overlaid to analyze their impact on choices that would otherwise be made on an economic basis. However, by looking at aggregate demand by region, decisions by individual consumers, which are in large part determined by site-specific fuel availabilities, emission regulations, capital costs, and fuel transportation availabilities, are not evaluated. This is particularly true in the industrial sector, but because the utility sector so dominates coal consumption, the approach works well in forecasting aggregate demand for coal. Capacities, generation plans, and fuel-switching capabilities are well documented in the utility sector, providing a basis for strong analysis.

The majority of coal consumed in 1978 was either purchased through previously signed contracts or came from captive mines (i.e., user-owned coal mines). Therefore, the actual distribution of coal may not be optimal as long as old contracts are in effect and as long as captive mines are productive. The distribution process accounts for these constrained coal movements and allocates only unconstrained coal.

Metallurgical coal demands and coal exports are allocated to supply regions and sulphur category based on historical distribution trends. This allows the optimization model to consider domestic steam coal demands and to require those demands to meet sulphur emission standards.


## Coal Supply


The costs of producing coal are estimated by the supply submodel. This model derives supply functions by state, type of mining, and sulphur content for the major bituminous and subbituminous producing areas of the United States. This disaggregation allows consideration of changing economic and regulatory conditions. The supply curves are estimated by combining an analysis of coal mining costs and reserve data. In essence, a cost function is estimated that relates the geology of the coal deposit to the cost of mining. Data on coal reserves and the characteristics of the deposits are then combined with cost functions to establish the amount of coal available at any given level of cost.

The cost functions are estimated separately for deep- and surface-mined coal. For deep mining, the production costs are related to the thickness of the coal seam, an index of the geological conditions, and the cumulative quantity produced. For surface-mined coal, costs are related to the overburden ratio, an index of other geological characteristics, and the quantity mined. These cost functions are estimated using an engineering-based model of mining that provides a flexible framework for dealing with changes in key parameters affecting costs, such as changes in surface- and deep-mining productivity or in factor prices. For both deep and surface mining, production costs are related to the remaining coal reserves, so that the marginal costs of production increase as the remaining reserves decrease.

The equations have been estimated using U.S. Geological Survey and U.S. Bureau of Mines reserves and cost information as well as data from some of the large coal-producing states. Investment costs for new mines, labor costs, equipment expenditures, reclamation costs, and federal and state taxes are each identified in the model and influence the shape of the supply curve. For future years, these costs are projected using DRI's estimates.

For each supply curve, it is assumed that in the long run, the large new mine will set the price of coal or be the marginal supplier. Because past mining operations extracted coal from the most accessible, easy to extract, least cost sources, the new operation will have to contend with poorer quality reserves, which translates to a higher per ton extraction cost.

A three-step process provides the estimation of the marginal cost of coal production. Productivity equations are estimated that determine the relationship between the capital, labor, and materials requirements and the output and geological characteristics of the reserve. The poorer the quality of the reserve, the more inputs will be required to extract a ton of coal. Second, expenditure functions are estimated for each of the factor inputs in coal production. These are then combined or substituted into the productivity relationship estimated in the first step to derive a relationship between the cost of production and the geological characteristics. Step 3 combines this estimated relationship with a distribution relationship that describes the quantity of coal available by characteristic.

Since these characteristics determine the cost of production, it is then possible to determine what quantity of coal is available at a given level of cost. Least cost resources are extracted first, and as coal reserves are depleted, production costs escalate due to the requirement of more factor inputs per ton of production.

## Coal Distribution

The interaction between the cost of producing coal in various regions, as estimated by the supply submodel; the cost of moving coal, possibly using various modes of transportation; the demand for coal; and government restrictions on using coal will determine the delivered price of coal. The analysis system combines all of these factors in a logically consistent manner by formulating a mathematical program that matches regional demands with the least cost sources of supply while satisfying several constraint sets.

A linear programming framework is utilized for this optimization process. The objective is to minimize the cost of producing six types of coal (distinguished by sulphur content) in six supply regions and of delivering it to thirteen demand regions. The endogenous variables in the optimization model are the forecast of coal produced in each region by sulphur type and the optimal amount of coal that should be shipped from supply to demand regions by sulphur range. The model takes into consideration existing contracts and captive coal movements and optimizes coal flows for uncommitted production only.

The minimization of cost is subject to constraint sets that assure that coal shipments satisfy the appropriate emission control standards, both regional and national. The choice of purchasing low sulphur coal or employing desulphurization techniques to comply with emission ceilings is incorporated in the analysis except where scrubbing of coal is required by law. In this case, an additional constraint insures that coal satisfying demand subject to the "best available control technology" portion of the Clean Air Act Amendments is scrubbed.

Two additional constraints—on regional incremental production and on interregional coal flows—may be incorporated to reflect production capacity constraints or transportation capacity constraints, respectively. The optimization model is solved for each year that is simulated. It has a recursive nature, since each year's solution depends on the results obtained in previous years.

It may seem surprising that a cost-based supply model and a cost minimization distribution model are used to examine the case of an exhaustible resource. Economic rents, however, are not considered to be a factor in the theory of regional coal pricing, at least over the forecast term of this model. The coal industry is highly competitive, with over 6,000 mines in operation in the United States and with very low concentration among the largest producers. Coal is a relatively substitutable good by supplying region when technological adjustments such as boiler configuration, sulphur reduction equipment, and particulate control equipment are added in. The supply curves faced by western coal producers, particularly in the Powder River Basin of Montana and Wyoming, are so elastic, even over the long term, that pricing coal at its substitute level (generally residual fuel oil) would bring so many entrants into the industry as to cause large excesses of supply. This is already a concern of western coal producers as they look out to the late 1980s.

Transportation companies or state governments are actually in a better, although still not commanding, position to collect economic rents from the consumption of coal. The transportation of coal is currently confined to either railroads or barges, with trucks used only locally. The barriers to entry in the rail industry are enormous, and water transport is only available in limited areas. Competition from slurry pipelines may hold down rail rates in the future, but currently the railroads are in a reasonable position to garner some piece of the economic pie. State governments operate in the coal industry by levying severance taxes on the production of coal. Montana and Wyoming currently have the highest taxes of this kind in the country, at 30 and 17 percent, respectively. Other states are considering implementing or raising taxes. All of these issues will affect future prices of coal but are not expected to raise them to the level of oil prices.

The coal model is a resource-based tool for analyzing regulatory and other issues in coal consumption, production, prices, and distribution. In what follows, we attempt to utilize this tool to quantitatively assess the economic ramifications of two major pieces of legislation while focusing on the implications of the interactions between the regulations.

## APPLICATIONS

To illustrate the application of the methodology of mathematically representing the economic trade-offs implied by government regulations, we will look in this section at the effects on regional coal production and prices for two sets of regulations. The first relates to the final revised new source performance standards (NSPS) issued by the Environmental Protection

Agency (EPA) in May of 1979, and the second relates to the Surface Mining Control and Reclamation Act (SMCRA).

The revised NSPS passed in May 1979 modifies the plant-by-plant emission ceiling of 1.2 lbs. $SO_2$/MMbtu of heat input established by the Clean Air Act of 1970. Although the revised NSPS maintains the ceiling, with the addition of a thirty-day rolling average, it additionally imposes a minimum 70 percent reduction in potential sulphur dioxide emissions. Previously, a coal consumer was allowed to choose between mechanical sulphur emission reduction, or "scrubbing," and the use of low sulphur coal in order to meet the emission ceiling. The choices are reduced by the revision to the regulation. In order to be able to take advantage of less than "full" 90 percent scrubbing, controlled emissions must meet a tighter ceiling of 0.6 lbs. $SO_2$/MMbtu; otherwise, 90 percent scrubbing is required. Therefore, partial scrubbing is a viable economic choice only if the cost of more expensive, lower sulphur coal with partial scrubbing is less expensive than full scrubbing of a higher sulphur coal that would meet the 1.2 lbs. $SO_2$ ceiling. This economic choice is explicitly incorporated into the framework of the DRI Coal Model.

The Surface Mining Control and Reclamation Act of 1977 (SMCRA) contains several specific performance standards and design criteria, with the goal of returning mined land to its original contour and to the capability of sustaining its original use. These rules govern not only the postmining period but also the mining period itself. The major impact of these reclamation regulations is to increase the costs of surface-mining production in the various coal-producing regions. This will affect the competitiveness of surface-mined coal produced in states such as Ohio and Pennsylvania, where compliance with the regulation will be much more costly than in states such as Indiana or western Kentucky.

Four cases are identified in order to examine the impacts of these sets of regulations. The first, or base, case looks at the regulations as they currently stand—with scrubbing required for demand subject to the revised NSPS and higher estimates of surface-mining reclamation costs due to the SMCRA. The second case looks at a scenario with regional reclamation costs as estimated prior to the passage of the SMCRA. These two sets of reclamation costs, for the base and no SMCRA cases, are shown in Table 10–1.

The third case, no RNSPS, isolates the impact of not requiring flue gas desulphurization for all new coal-fired capacity, contrary to what was outlined in the regulations issued in May 1979. In this case, all coal consumers are free to evaluate the economic costs of all levels of scrubbing effectiveness and all available sulphur qualities of coal. The final simulation, no SM-

Table 10–1.     Reclamation Cost Comparison (dollars per ton).

| Supply Region | Base | No SMCRA[a] |
|---|---|---|
| N. Appalachia | 7.04 | 4.54 |
| S. Appalachia | 7.04 | 4.54 |
| Midwest | 5.70 | 3.40 |
| Montana–Wyoming | 0.77 | 0.22 |
| Colorado–Utah | 0.96 | 0.26 |
| Arizona–New Mexico · | 0.74 | 0.19 |

[a]SMCRA: Surface Mining Control and Reclamation Act

CRA/RNSPS, looks at the interacting impacts of omitting both sets of regulations.


## Production

Revised NSPS demand first appears in 1983. To summarize the trends shown in this application, it is useful to consider three different time periods—1979–83, 1984–90, and 1991–2000 (shown in Table 10–2). Before the advent of demand subject to the revised NSPS, the base and no RNSPS scenarios are identical. The impact of the removal of the SMCRA is shown in the following ways: (1) North and South Appalachia production is higher and Midwest production lower, resulting in overall higher eastern production. (2) Montana-Wyoming and Colorado-Utah production is lower, and Arizona-New Mexico production is nearly the same, resulting in lower western production levels. This is due to the greater capacity for eastern coal production to shift between mining methods, relative to that in the West.

Between 1984–90, the following observations may be made: (1) The no SMCRA case with lower reclamation costs still favors North and South Appalachia and disfavors the Midwest, with higher overall eastern production forecasts. (2) The lack of revised NSPS required scrubbing has very little impact on expected production levels in Appalachia but a significant negative impact on expected midwestern production. (3) With both regulations omitted, eastern production is lower than in the base case, driven by the larger impacts of no RNSPS on midwestern production. In the West, (1) Arizona-New Mexico production is still nearly the same in all four cases; (2) the impact of no RNSPS is felt in higher production for Montana-Wyoming

Table 10–2.  Average Annual Production by Region (million tons).

| Supply Region | 1979–83 | | | | 1984–90 | | | | 1991–2000 | | | |
|---|---|---|---|---|---|---|---|---|---|---|---|---|
| | Base Case | No SMCRA[a] | No RNSPS[b] | No SMCRA/ RNSPS | Base Case | No SMCRA | No RNSPS | No SMCRA/ RNSPS | Base Case | No SMCRA | No RNSPS | No SMCRA/ RNSPS |
| N. Appalachia | 173.9 | 178.1 | 173.9 | 178.1 | 210.9 | 215.6 | 208.3 | 211.1 | 337.8 | 314.6 | 335.6 | 315.2 |
| S. Appalachia | 232.6 | 234.9 | 232.6 | 234.9 | 277.2 | 288.3 | 278.4 | 286.8 | 273.8 | 300.8 | 277.6 | 302.5 |
| Midwest | 132.3 | 127.9 | 132.4 | 127.6 | 191.0 | 177.8 | 180.5 | 168.6 | 276.6 | 267.5 | 259.8 | 255.9 |
| Total East | 538.8 | 540.9 | 538.9 | 540.6 | 679.2 | 681.7 | 667.1 | 666.5 | 888.1 | 883.0 | 873.0 | 873.6 |
| Montana–Wyoming | 131.7 | 128.9 | 131.7 | 128.9 | 272.4 | 272.4 | 281.8 | 285.9 | 495.7 | 515.5 | 514.6 | 513.2 |
| Colorado–Utah | 29.9 | 28.8 | 29.8 | 29.5 | 78.2 | 73.4 | 81.4 | 77.1 | 93.1 | 79.3 | 101.0 | 98.5 |
| Arizona–New Mexico | 34.2 | 34.8 | 34.1 | 34.3 | 62.9 | 64.0 | 64.8 | 65.6 | 97.3 | 101.2 | 89.0 | 92.2 |
| Total West | 195.8 | 192.5 | 195.6 | 192.7 | 413.5 | 409.7 | 428.0 | 428.6 | 686.1 | 695.9 | 704.6 | 703.9 |
| Total Model | 734.6 | 733.4 | 734.6 | 733.4 | 1,092.7 | 1,091.5 | 1,095.1 | 1,095.1 | 1,574.2 | 1,578.9 | 1,577.5 | 1,577.5 |

[a]SMCRA: Surface Mining Control and Reclamation Act
[b]RNSPS: Revised New Source Performance Standards

and Colorado-Utah, resulting from greater penetration of the East North Central demand region; and (3) overall western production is nearly the same when both regulations are omitted as when only RNSPS is omitted, due to slightly higher Montana-Wyoming production and slightly lower Colorado-Utah production balancing out.

After 1990, depletion effects begin to be felt in Appalachia in the no SMCRA case because of this case's higher production levels in earlier years. This results in a switch of advantage to the West under the lack of enforcement of the SMCRA. Montana-Wyoming particularly benefits. Montana-Wyoming also shows strong benefits from the lack of required scrubbing in the no RNSPS case, as does Colorado-Utah at the expense of Arizona-New Mexico. When both regulations are omitted, the West still benefits, particularly Montana-Wyoming, but to no greater degree than under the asumption of omission of either of the regulations individually. This is because annual allowable production increases in Montana-Wyoming are already being met, and although the combined favorable effects would in theory induce even greater production in Montana-Wyoming, expansion is already occurring at the maximum pace. Colorado-Utah is probably the principal beneficiary of this phenomenon. Also, the Midwest might be hurt more than is displayed in the no SMCRA/RNSPS case if Montana-Wyoming production increases were unlimited.

The impacts on coal production by regulation may be summarized as follows. The absence of the cost impacts of the SMCRA have only a minor impact before the mid-1980s. This is partly due to the fact that a significant amount of coal is committed under long-term contracts in the earlier portion of the forecast interval. Over the decade of the 1980s, the absence of the SMCRA favors greater production of North and South Appalachia coal, at the expense of midwestern and Montana-Wyoming coal. These eastern regions produce greater shares of their coal from deep mineable reserves and have greater flexibility than western regions. After 1990, however, Appalachian coal prices begin to rise at faster rates than the cost of factor inputs due to the effects of depletion. As a result, coal from North Appalachia becomes less competitive, and production is lower in the no SMCRA case than in the base case. Montana-Wyoming, however, with its vast reserves, begins to show higher production levels in the no SMCRA case, a reversal of the trend seen in the early 1980s. Within the West, additionally, the competition between Colorado-Utah and Arizona-New Mexico favors the latter in the absence of the SMCRA.

Revised NSPS regulations, requiring mechanical flue gas desulphurization, were lobbied for by eastern and midwestern coal producers in an effort to protect the markets for their high sulphur coal. This analysis indicates that expected Appalachian coal production levels are nearly the same across the entire interval regardless of the required scrubbing regulation. Both of these regions serve the eastern seaboard demand regions of New England and the Mid and South Atlantic states to the exclusion of other supply regions because of large transportation costs, and all of these demand regions choose to use scrubbing for a large portion of coal delivered to them. Scrubbing high or medium sulphur coal serves as a least cost method of compliance with emission control regulations even in the absence of required scrubbing. The Midwest, however, is not so insensitive to the structure of this regulation, due to the direct competition between its high sulphur product and low sulphur coal from Montana-Wyoming. In the absence of the revised NSPS, production is significantly lower in the Midwest and higher in Montana-Wyoming. A smaller scale version of this competition occurs between Colorado-Utah, which benefits in the absence of required scrubbing and Arizona-New Mexico, whose slightly higher sulphur coal is more economically attractive when scrubbing is required.

When both regulations are omitted, western production, particularly in Montana-Wyoming and Colorado-Utah, is favored. But the increases seen are no greater than the increase seen in either of the other scenarios because of limitations on how quickly these regions can expand production. When the combined effects of both the revised NSPS and the SMCRA are examined, the analysis indicates that if each regulation separately favors a particular supply region, the combined impact will be less than the sum of the individual impacts. Besides being due in part to limitations on the rate of production expansion in each supply region, other economic factors, such as transportation costs or the costs of depletion, are a factor in causing the observed shift, at the margin, to equal the shift caused by a single regulation.

The swing between East and West production levels over the decade of the 1990s across all four scenarios is less than 15 million tons per year. Greater divergence occurs for individual regions, however, indicating the importance of a detailed, yet consistent examination of the impact of these issues. Production levels vary within a range of 22–25 million tons per year across scenarios in all three eastern supply regions and 11–22 million tons per year across scenarios in the West. These variances in forecast production levels are a good measure of the sensitivity of a forecast to the structure of regulations imposed upon market decisions.

## Prices

Prices of coal, both mine mouth and delivered, represent another area in which the specific structure of a set of regulations has a measurable impact. When examining mine-mouth prices, one must remember that an additional impact, representing the change in price due to differing levels of cumulative coal production, must be accounted for within the analysis.

Table 10–3 presents mine-mouth prices in 1990 and 2000 under the four sets of assumptions. In 1990, when the production forecasts show relatively less variation across scenarios, the differences in prices can be attributed most directly to the impacts of reclamation cost estimates. In the two scenarios in which the lower estimates are used, no SMCRA and no SMCRA/ RNSPS, it may be seen that lower mine-mouth prices are forecast, as would be expected.

By the year 2000, it is interesting to note that a similar pattern of mine-mouth prices is evident—lower in the absence of the SMCRA and higher when it is enforced, despite differing regional production forecasts across scenarios. For instance, coal production in South Appalachia is higher in the absence of the SMCRA, and yet prices are lower at the mine, indicating that the effects of depletion over the range of production forecasts presented do not offset the price impacts of higher reclamation costs. It is this interaction of relative regional impacts of regulations and relative regional rates of coal depletion by coal quality that the model is able to evaluate within a consistent analytical framework. In the West, where reclamation costs are substantially lower and the depletion effects are much less pronounced due to the greater supply elasticity, prices at the mine vary less across these two scenarios than they do in the East.

Changes in mine-mouth prices in the no RNSPS case versus the base case should represent only the changes due to different levels of regional production, since none of the actual costs of mining have been changed. Only the effects of depletion are in evidence. Very small differences in the mine-mouth prices are seen in the absence of required scrubbing, particularly in eastern producing regions. An interesting phenomenon occurs in Colorado-Utah and Arizona-New Mexico, however. Mine-mouth prices in the year 2000 for low and medium sulphur coal exactly reflect the shifts in coal production. In the absence of required scrubbing, more low sulphur Colorado-Utah coal is consumed, driving up its mine-mouth price relative to the base case, and less Arizona-New Mexico medium sulphur coal is demanded in the no RNSPS case, resulting in a lower mine-mouth price. So despite the impact of depletion on prices, the Colorado-Utah low sulphur coal is a more competitive method of compliance with the emission ceiling, particularly in the West South Central 2 region.

Delivered prices of coal, shown in Table 10–4, show the greatest divergence between the base case and the no SMCRA/RNSPS case, as would be expected. On a national scale, it can be concluded that the revised NSPS regulations have a smaller impact on the delivered price of coal than the regulations and cost increases resulting from the SMCRA.

As would be expected, all demand regions experience lower delivered coal prices when the regulations of the SMCRA are relaxed. The regions that benefit the most are the eastern seaboard demand regions, since they consume Appalachian coal almost exclusively; it will be in these coal-producing regions that SMCRA's impact will be felt most strongly. On a national level, the delivered price of coal averages 1.5 percent lower in the year 2000 without the SMCRA, not a significant figure on a per btu basis.

On a per btu basis, the absence of required scrubbing has even less impact on the nationally averaged delivered price of coal—only 0.1 percent in the year 2000. Many demand regions are able to switch among sulphur qualities of coal or among sources of coal supply when scrubbing is required, thereby offsetting some of the impact of this environmental regulation.

Several regions show the interesting result that delivered prices of coal are actually higher in the absence of required scrubbing. This is due to the interaction of the bounds on the maximum annual percentage increase in allowed coal production and to the shifting preferences of coal consumers under alternative sets of regulations on how emission ceilings must be met. The bounds on yearly coal production increases apply to each sulphur category; therefore, a shift in demand for a given sulphur quality of coal may not be able to be satisfied within the production increases allowed to the model.

A second factor that causes this phenomenon is the manner in which the model decides which demand regions are entitled to get which quality coal from which supply regions. An example will illustrate the point. In the no RNSPS case, the East North Central demand region incurs no savings in the absence of the revised NSPS. In fact, their delivered price of coal, including scrubbing costs, is higher than in the base case. The West North Central demand region, which purchases all of its coal from Montana-Wyoming, chooses scrubbing of coal only when it is required by regulation. If scrubbing is required, however, this region chooses some coal of the lowest sulphur category and some of second and third lowest sulphur categories from Montana-Wyoming, this being the least cost method of complying with the emission regulations.

**Table 10-3.** Mine-mouth Prices of Coal (dollars per ton).

| Supply Region Sulphur Type | 1990 | | | | 2000 | | | |
|---|---|---|---|---|---|---|---|---|
| | Base Case | No SMCRA[a] | No RNSPS[b] | No SMCRA/RNSPS | Base Case | No SMCRA | No RNSPS | No SMCRA/RNSPS |
| N. Appalachia | | | | | | | | |
| Low sulphur | 114.80 | 113.80 | 114.90 | 113.80 | 230.40 | 226.40 | 231.70 | 228.30 |
| Medium sulphur | 97.15 | 94.81 | 96.58 | 94.55 | 210.10 | 203.70 | 208.30 | 204.00 |
| High sulphur | 79.91 | 79.61 | 80.11 | 79.29 | 166.70 | 162.50 | 166.60 | 163.10 |
| S. Appalachia | | | | | | | | |
| Low sulphur | 121.80 | 120.30 | 126.00 | 120.50 | 255.40 | 245.40 | 255.80 | 246.00 |
| Medium sulphur | 109.10 | 105.90 | 109.30 | 106.20 | 232.50 | 220.20 | 233.50 | 221.10 |
| High sulphur | 94.15 | 91.75 | 94.15 | 91.39 | 202.00 | 200.20 | 203.10 | 198.30 |
| Midwest | | | | | | | | |
| Low sulphur | 104.70 | 102.50 | 104.70 | 102.50 | N.A. | 195.70 | N.A. | 195.70 |
| Medium sulphur | 89.96 | 89.19 | 89.96 | 88.96 | 194.00 | 185.00 | 193.00 | 184.50 |
| High sulphur | 70.66 | 71.36 | 70.27 | 69.88 | 134.30 | 134.30 | 135.00 | 134.30 |

| | | | | | | | | |
|---|---|---|---|---|---|---|---|---|
| Montana–Wyoming | | | | | | | | |
| Low sulphur | 22.58 | 21.99 | 22.61 | 22.03 | 42.24 | 41.04 | 42.29 | 41.07 |
| Medium sulphur | 21.99 | 21.44 | 21.97 | 21.43 | 37.90 | 36.89 | 37.90 | 36.89 |
| High sulphur | 21.84 | 21.29 | 21.84 | 21.29 | 37.59 | 36.60 | 37.59 | 36.60 |
| Colorado–Utah | | | | | | | | |
| Low sulphur | 58.60 | 58.35 | 58.73 | 58.54 | 114.40 | 113.20 | 121.30 | 119.90 |
| Medium sulphur | 54.06 | 53.82 | 54.06 | 53.01 | 102.40 | 101.90 | 96.76 | 96.32 |
| High sulphur | 52.39 | 52.15 | 52.39 | 52.15 | 94.17 | 93.73 | 94.17 | 93.73 |
| Arizona–New Mexico | | | | | | | | |
| Low sulphur | 55.13 | 54.17 | 57.33 | 57.84 | 132.60 | 129.70 | 135.90 | 134.50 |
| Medium sulphur | 48.18 | 47.22 | 48.13 | 47.17 | 98.20 | 97.61 | 87.97 | 85.51 |
| High sulphur | 47.77 | 46.81 | 47.77 | 46.81 | 84.23 | 82.50 | 84.23 | 82.50 |

Note: Low sulphur is coal with up to 1.04 percent sulphur. Medium sulphur is coal with from 1.05 to 2.24 percent sulphur. High sulphur is coal with 2.25 percent or more sulphur.

[a]SMCRA: Surface Mining Control and Reclamation Act
[b]RNSPS: Revised New Source Performance Standards

**Table 10-4.** Delivered Prices of Coal Including Scrubbing Costs (dollars per million btu).

| Demand Region | 1990 Base Case | No SMCRA[a] | No RNSPS[b] | No SMCRA/RNSPS | 2000 Base Case | No SMCRA | No RNSPS | No SMCRA/RNSPS |
|---|---|---|---|---|---|---|---|---|
| NENG | 5.93 | 5.87 | 5.95 | 5.86 | 12.10 | 11.90 | 12.67 | 12.58 |
| MATL | 5.36 | 5.32 | 5.37 | 5.32 | 11.28 | 11.10 | 11.07 | 11.22 |
| SATL | 5.82 | 5.74 | 5.83 | 5.74 | 11.99 | 11.87 | 12.10 | 11.81 |
| ENC | 4.89 | 4.87 | 4.97 | 4.94 | 10.32 | 10.01 | 10.38 | 10.02 |
| WNC | 3.91 | 3.83 | 3.70 | 3.67 | 8.16 | 8.13 | 7.78 | 7.72 |
| ESC1 | 5.14 | 5.08 | 5.10 | 5.12 | 10.12 | 10.01 | 10.12 | 10.10 |
| ESC2 | 5.36 | 5.62 | 5.39 | 5.31 | 10.58 | 10.54 | 11.02 | 10.75 |
| WSC1 | 4.60 | 4.53 | 4.53 | 4.49 | 9.67 | 9.65 | 9.31 | 9.28 |
| WSC2 | 5.09 | 5.05 | 4.95 | 5.11 | 11.08 | 11.03 | 10.70 | 10.60 |
| MTN1 | 3.50 | 3.45 | 3.50 | 3.48 | 8.29 | 8.29 | 7.09 | 7.03 |
| MTN2 | 3.08 | 3.09 | 2.81 | 2.78 | 6.24 | 6.17 | 5.78 | 5.71 |
| MTN3 | 3.98 | 3.93 | 4.04 | 3.94 | 8.94 | 8.91 | 9.59 | 9.77 |
| PAC | 4.97 | 4.95 | 4.81 | 4.76 | 10.45 | 10.43 | 10.09 | 10.07 |
| U.S. | 4.94 | 4.90 | 4.92 | 4.87 | 10.26 | 10.11 | 10.20 | 10.04 |

[a]SMCRA: Surface Mining Control and Reclamation Act
[b]RNSPS: Revised New Source Performance Standards

In the absence of required scrubbing, the West North Central region purchases almost all of its coal in the lowest sulphur category from Montana-Wyoming, pushing the bound on the year-to-year production increase allowed for this sulphur category (10 percent increase is allowed in all sulphur categories in all regions). This leaves the East North Central region with fewer supply choices, given the production constraints. The model allocates more of the very low sulphur Montana-Wyoming coal to the West North Central region rather than to the East North Central, because the overall cost savings are greater to the West North Central region than to the East North Central region.

Other demand regions show similar behavior, where either production bounds in the supply regions or larger impacts of depletion in a particular sulphur quality result in certain areas paying higher delivered prices for coal when scrubbing is not required. New England, for example, purchases lower sulphur coal from North Appalachia in the no RNSPS case, at higher cost, since Middle Atlantic increases its use of high sulphur North Appalachia coal, which New England had been using in the base case, scrubbing it at a 90 percent effectiveness level. Less intensive scrubbing is employed in New England in the no RNSPS case, but the net result is slightly higher costs.

The Mountain 3 demand regions shows the very interesting result that the delivered price of coal is higher in the case where both regulations are omitted (no SMCRA/RNSPS) than in any of the other three cases. This region, Nevada-Arizona, gets all of its coal from the Arizona-New Mexico supply region in all four scenarios. In the absence of required scrubbing (the no RNSPS case), several other demand regions that consume Arizona-New Mexico coal (Mountain 1 and West South Central 1) increase their consumption of the region's medium sulphur coal relative to their use of low sulphur coal from Arizona-New Mexico. This change in sulphur quality decreases delivered coal prices significantly in these two regions.

As a result, the choices open for Mountain 3 are affected in two ways—greater demand for medium sulphur coal results in higher prices due to depletion of these reserves and in the production increase limit being reached in the medium sulphur categories in Arizona-New Mexico. The medium sulphur coal results in greater cost savings to Mountain 1 and West South Central 1, relative to Mountain 3; therefore, it is more "valuable" there. The Mountain 3 region moves to its next best choice, low sulphur Arizona-New Mexico coal at a slightly higher price. Relaxation of reclamation regulations makes Arizona-New Mexico coal even more attractive to demand regions other than Mountain 3, and therefore for the same reasons, the delivered price of coal in Mountain 3 is even higher in the no SMCRA/ RNSPS case.

In summary, very few differences due to these regulations are seen before 1984. After that time, the absence of the SMCRA increases Appalachian and Montana-Wyoming coal production and lessens the forecast of midwestern and Colorado-Utah production. Mine-mouth and delivered prices are lower in all regions. The absence of required scrubbing has much more complicated impacts, as coal consumers alter their compliance strategies by switching among both sources and qualities of coal. Appalachian production is nearly unchanged, although shifts occur by sulphur quality. In the competition between the Midwest and Montana-Wyoming, the Midwest loses out without required scrubbing. Delivered prices show the interesting result that although most demand regions benefit by the absence of required scrubbing, several are forced by market conditions to pay higher delivered prices for coal. These market conditions represent, in part, greater demand for certain coal qualities whose year-to-year production increase is limited and, in part, the cost impacts of depletion of certain coal qualities in heavily demanded coal qualities.

## COSTS OF COAL-RELATED REGULATIONS

Beyond measuring the effects of government regulations on regional production and prices, a second aspect of our methodology is that it can translate these effects into a quantification of the additional costs to coal consumers that result from the imposition of these regulations. The methodology implemented for quantitatively assessing the total costs of regulatory activities is to compute the increased total expenditures on delivered coal, including the costs of complying with the environmental regulations due to each rule or regulation. Therefore, in this context, the annual total costs of a given regulation are defined as the increased expenditures on delivered coal, including scrubbing costs, that are caused by the given regulation. This approach of analyzing the total costs of each regulation is followed because the goal is to define the flow of all private funds diverted to each regulation activity.

The base case forecast incorporates all the regulations that are quantitatively assessed in this study. It therefore serves as a benchmark for computing the total costs of specific regulations. For each year over the forecast period (1979–2000), total U.S. coal production in trillion btu is computed. This time series is then multiplied by forecasts of delivered prices that include production costs, transportaiton costs, and scrubbing costs. By the above calculation, the total expenditures on coal are derived for the base case.

For each regulation that is quantitatively assessed, another forecast is generated that incorporate exactly the same assumptions as in the base case forecast except that the specific regulation under study is assumed to be nonexistent. In the case of the revised NSPS, demands subject to these regulations are set to zero. However, both the new source performance standards and the state implementation plans' regulations are assumed to be met. In the case of the Surface Mining Control and Reclamation Act, the incremental costs of the regulations pertaining to this act are set to zero. However, state reclamation regulations in existence previous to the act's passage are assumed to be met. The procedure outlined above for computing the total expenditures on coal is repeated for each alternative case. By comparing the annual expenditures on coal in the base case and each alternative case, we obtain the total cost of the regulation in current dollars for each year over the twenty-one-year forecast period. This time series is transformed to real 1979 dollars, and the cumulative cost of the regulation over the forecast period is presented in both nominal and real dollars. A final forecast is performed that excludes both the regulations that are quantitatively assessed in order to examine the cumulative total costs of both the regulations. This final forecast is performed because the sum of the individual impacts of the regulations may not be equal to the cumulative costs of both regulations analyzed together due to the interactive impacts of these regulations on coal production, distribution, and prices.

A few notes on the appropriateness of the above methodology are in order. First, from a practical point of view, the computation of the total cost of a regulation as described above is preferred to the use of the loss in consumer surplus as a measurement of cost. This is because the computation of total costs, as described above, provides an appropriate measurement of the opportunity costs of the loss of the private flow of funds diverted to regulatory activities. Second, under each regulatory activity quantitatively assessed, the demand for coal, on a btu basis, is assumed to be the same. Although this is not a totally adequate depiction of reality, the differences in demand for coal under each forecast will in reality be minor. Also, this assumption serves the purpose of enhancing the comparability of total expenditures under each forecast.

Finally, the total expenditures in each case considered may be biased slightly upward. This is because the total expenditures for each year are computed by multiplying the U.S. total quantity produced by the weighted average of the marginal delivered prices for each demand region, as opposed to the weighted average of the average delivered price for each demand region. The marginal delivered price for a given demand region represents the weighted average of the delivered price for the last deliveries from each sulphur category and supply region to the given demand region. Because these last deliveries come from new mines that would not have opened unless they could cover their long-run marginal costs, which include variable (operating) and fixed (capital) costs, the delivered prices for the last deliveries may be higher than the delivered prices from old (existing) mines. This is because in the short run, old mines will continue to operate as long as they can cover their minimum average variable costs (the costs of operating the mine). Also, it is expected that the most profitable mines in a given sulphur category and supply region will open first and that therefore old mines may tend to have lower average costs if the impacts of depletion on these old mines have not been strong. However, any upward bias in delivered prices that does exist will decrease over time as the percentage of deliveries originating from new mines increases. In addition, this upward bias will tend to be small, since the delivered prices of coal to a given demand region from new and old mines in a given sulphur category and supply region will tend to be equal at the margin. If coal from new mines can receive a price equal to its long-run marginal delivered cost, then there is no reason why coal from old mines in the same sulphur category and supply region cannot receive the same price for a delivery to a given demand region. Therefore, the delivered prices for all coal from a given sulphur category and supply region and to a given demand region will approach the marginal delivered costs of the coal from the new mines; and the pure profits on the old mines will be in the form of an economic rent that will accrue to the coal mine owners, the laborers, or the transportation system owners. In conclusion, the marginal delivered prices will be higher than average delivered prices only when the old coal is delivered under a long-term contract in which the escalation factors do not take into account the changing market conditions.

The measurements of costs incorporated with this analysis are on a national level. It shoud be noted that the costs vary significantly among regions; an analysis that explicitly examines the regional variations in costs could be performed in the future.

## Surface-Mining Control and Reclamation

In order to estimate the incremental private sector costs of federal reclamation regulations, a coal model forecast (no SMCRA case) was performed with the same assumptions as the base case forecast except that the incremental costs of the federal reclamation regulations were excluded. The incremental costs of these regulations are the costs imposed over and above the costs of state programs that were in existence before the act's passage (see Table 10–1). The total expeditures on coal in both the base case and the no SMCRA case forecasts are presented in Table 10–5 and 10–6. The annual percentage growth in total expenditures on coal, in current dollars, between 1979 and 2000 is 14.61 percent in the no SMCRA case, while it is 14.5 percent in the base case. Expenditures increase at a slower rate in the base case because the impacts of the federal reclamation regulations are larger in the earlier years. As production shifts to western coal over the forecast period, the impacts of reclamation become less severe, because the costs of reclamation are less in the western producing regions.

Tables 10–7 and 10–8 present the total costs of reclamation regulations. These costs are found by taking the difference between the total expenditures in the base case and in the no SMCRA case. The percentage increase represents the percentage increase in the total expenditures in the base case with respect to the no SMCRA case. The increase in costs due to reclamation is 3.73 percent in 1979, and this percentage tends to decrease over time as the relative importance of the western producing regions increases. The cumulative costs of federal reclamation regulations between 1979 and 2000 are $45.343 billion in nominal dollars and $17.918 billion in real 1979 dollars. The costs of complying with the federal reclamations regulations, averaged over 1979 to 2000, represent 1.25 and 1.28 percent of the total expenditures on coal in nominal and real dollars, respectively.

Although the cumulative costs of federal reclamation regulations over the forecast period are significant, more important is the fact that the relative burden these regulations impose on the coal industry decreases over the forecast interval. As mentioned above, one reason for this decreasing impact is the shift to western coal production over time. Another reason is that the delivered price of coal is forecast to increase in real terms as a result of many other factors, and these other factors will tend to reduce the relative burden that federal reclamation regulations impose on the delivered price of coal. Two main factors that will cause the price of coal to increase in real terms are the impact of reserve depletion and the impact of other federal regulations, particularly those pertaining to the Clean Air Act. The impacts of reserve depletion will be felt because they will cause production to shift to more costly coal reserves, particularly in the Appalachian producing regions, thereby causing the delivered price of coal to increase in real terms. The impacts of the Clean Air Act on the delivered price of coal, in real

**Table 10-5.** Total Expenditures on Delivered Coal Including Scrubbing Costs (billions of current dollars).

| | Years | | | | | | | | | | Percent Growth | | |
|---|---|---|---|---|---|---|---|---|---|---|---|---|---|
| | 1979 | 1980 | 1981 | 1982 | 1983 | 1984 | 1985 | 1990 | 2000 | 1979–85 | 1985–90 | 1990–2000 |
| No SMCRA[a] Case | 23.68 | 25.16 | 27.37 | 31.83 | 35.24 | 38.27 | 44.61 | 64.39 | 108.20 | 11.1 | 7.6 | 5.3 |
| No RNSPS[b] Case | 24.56 | 25.91 | 28.00 | 32.39 | 35.70 | 38.68 | 45.04 | 64.58 | 109.19 | 10.6 | 7.5 | 5.4 |
| No SMCRA/RNSPS Case | 23.68 | 25.16 | 27.37 | 31.83 | 35.20 | 38.15 | 44.44 | 63.98 | 107.49 | 11.1 | 7.6 | 5.3 |
| Base Case | 24.56 | 25.91 | 28.00 | 32.39 | 35.75 | 38.80 | 45.19 | 64.87 | 109.80 | 10.7 | 7.5 | 5.4 |

[a]SMCRA: Surface Mining Control and Reclamation Act
[b]RNSPS: Revised New Source Performance Standards

**Table 10-6.** Total Expenditures on Delivered Coal Including Scrubbing Costs (billions of 1979 dollars).

| | Years | | | | | | | | | Percent Growth | | |
|---|---|---|---|---|---|---|---|---|---|---|---|---|
| | 1979 | 1980 | 1981 | 1982 | 1983 | 1984 | 1985 | 1990 | 2000 | 1979–85 | 1985–90 | 1990–2000 |
| No SMCRA[a] Case | 23.68 | 27.34 | 32.34 | 40.70 | 48.52 | 56.68 | 70.97 | 140.83 | 415.32 | 20.1 | 14.7 | 11.4 |
| No RNSPS[b] Case | 24.56 | 28.16 | 33.08 | 41.41 | 49.15 | 57.29 | 71.64 | 141.22 | 419.08 | 19.5 | 14.5 | 11.5 |
| No SMCRA/RNSPS Case | 23.68 | 27.34 | 32.34 | 40.70 | 48.47 | 56.51 | 70.68 | 139.91 | 412.58 | 20.0 | 14.6 | 11.4 |
| Base Case | 24.56 | 28.16 | 33.08 | 41.41 | 49.22 | 57.47 | 71.89 | 141.87 | 421.45 | 19.6 | 14.6 | 11.5 |

[a] SMCRA: Surface Mining Control and Reclamation Act
[b] RNSPS: Revised New Source Performance Standards

**Table 10–7.** Total Cost of Regulations (billions of current dollars).

| | YEARS | | | | | | | | |
|---|---|---|---|---|---|---|---|---|---|
| | 1979 | 1980 | 1981 | 1982 | 1983 | 1984 | 1985 | 1990 | 2000 |
| SMCRA[a] | | | | | | | | | |
| Total Cost | 0.88 | 0.82 | 0.75 | 0.71 | 0.69 | 0.79 | 0.92 | 1.05 | 6.13 |
| Percent increase | 3.73 | 3.01 | 2.31 | 1.75 | 1.43 | 1.39 | 1.30 | 0.74 | 1.48 |
| Revised NSPS[b] | | | | | | | | | |
| Total cost | 0.00 | 0.00 | 0.00 | 0.00 | 0.07 | 0.18 | 0.25 | 0.65 | 2.37 |
| Percent increase | 0.00 | 0.00 | 0.00 | 0.00 | 0.13 | 0.31 | 0.35 | 0.46 | 0.56 |
| SMCRA and revised NSPS | | | | | | | | | |
| Total cost | 0.88 | 0.82 | 0.75 | 0.71 | 0.75 | 0.96 | 1.21 | 1.96 | 8.87 |
| Percent increase | 3.73 | 3.00 | 2.31 | 1.75 | 1.54 | 1.70 | 1.71 | 1.40 | 2.15 |

Note: Total cost is found by taking the difference between the total expenditures on delivered coal in the base case and in the case that does not include the given regulation. Percentage increase is the percentage increase in the total expenditures on delivered coal in the base case with respect to the case that does not include the regulation.

[a]SMCRA: Surface Mining Control and Reclamation Act
[b]NSPS: New Source Performance Standards

**Table 10–8.** Total Cost of Regulations (billions of 1979 dollars).

| | YEARS | | | | | | | | |
|---|---|---|---|---|---|---|---|---|---|
| | 1979 | 1980 | 1981 | 1982 | 1983 | 1984 | 1985 | 1990 | 2000 |
| SMCRA[a] | | | | | | | | | |
| Total cost | 0.88 | 0.76 | 0.63 | 0.56 | 0.50 | 0.53 | 0.58 | 0.48 | 1.60 |
| Percent increase | 3.73 | 3.01 | 2.31 | 1.75 | 1.43 | 1.39 | 1.30 | 0.74 | 1.48 |
| Revised NSPS[b] | | | | | | | | | |
| Total cost | 0.00 | 0.00 | 0.00 | 0.00 | 0.05 | 0.12 | 0.16 | 0.30 | 0.62 |
| Percent increase | 0.00 | 0.00 | 0.00 | 0.00 | 0.13 | 0.31 | 0.35 | 0.46 | 0.56 |
| SMCRA and revised NSPS | | | | | | | | | |
| Total cost | 0.88 | 0.76 | 0.63 | 0.56 | 0.54 | 0.65 | 0.76 | 0.90 | 2.31 |
| Percent increase | 3.73 | 3.00 | 2.31 | 1.75 | 1.54 | 1.70 | 1.71 | 1.40 | 2.15 |

Note: Total cost is found by taking the difference between the total expenditures on delivered coal in the base case and in the case that does not include the given regulation. Percentage increase is the percentage increase in the total expenditures on delivered coal in the base case with respect to the case that does not include the regulation.

[a]SMCRA: Surface Mining Control and Reclamation Act
[b]NSPS: New Source Performance Standards

terms, will increase as the regulations pertaining to this act become more stringent over time and as more consumers become subject to these regulations.

## Revised NSPS

In order to quantify the total costs of the revised NSPS resulting from the 1977 Clean Air Act amendments, a coal model forecast (no RNSPS case) was performed with the same assumptions as the base case forecast except that demands subject to the revised NSPS were set to zero. Tables 10–5 and 10–6 present the total expenditures on coal in this forecast. The annual percentage growth in total expenditures on coal in nominal dollars between 1979 and 2000 is 14.46 percent in this case, while it is 14.5 percent in the base case. Prices increase at a faster rate in the base case, due to the fact that the percentage of demand subject to the revised NSPS increases over time.

Tables 10–7 and 10–8 present the total costs of the revised NSPS. As can be seen, these standards impose no costs on the private sector until 1983. This is because the law applies only to steam electric power plants beginning construction after September 18, 1978, and in 1983 the first of these new plants are expected to come on line. In 1983 the increase in costs due to the revised NSPS is 0.13 percent, and this percentage increase in costs increases over time as the percentage of consumption subject to the revised NSPS grows. The cumulative costs of these standards are $11.462 billion nominal dollars of $4.297 billion real 1979 dollars. The costs of complying with the NSPS, averaged over the forecast period, represent 0.32 and 0.31 percent of the total expenditures on coal in nominal and real dollars, respectively.

The impact of the revised NSPS on the total costs of delivered coal is significantly less than the impact of the federal reclamation regulations on these costs. However, unlike the federal reclamation regulations, the relative impact of the revised NSPS increases over time as the percentage of demand subject to these regulations increases, as mentioned above. The percentage of demands subject to the revised NSPS is forecast to be 0.63 percent in 1983 and increases to 16.8 percent in 1990 and 25.4 percent in 2000. Also, although the impact of the revised NSPS on the delivered price of coal is relatively moderate as compared to that of the federal reclamation regulations, the impacts of the revised NSPS on regional coal production and distribution are significant, as discussed in a previous section.

## Surface-mining Control and Reclamation and
## Revised NSPS: Cumulative Impacts

In order to quantify the cumulative impacts of both the revised NSPS and the SMCRA, a forecast was performed (no SMCRA/RNSPS case) that excludes both of these regulations. The total expenditures on coal under this forecast are presented in Tables 10–5 and 10–6. The annual percentage growth in total expenditures on coal, in nominal dollars from 1979 to 2000, is 14.58 percent in this case, while it is 14.5 percent in the base case. Expenditures increase at a slower rate in the base case due to the fact that the impacts of the federal reclamation regulations are larger in the earlier years, as stated previously.

Tables 10–7 and 10–8 and Figures 10–5 present the annual private sector costs of both of the above regulations, as derived through the no SMCRA/RNSPS case forecast. The costs of complying with both of these regulations, averaged over 1979 to 2000, represent 1.62 and 1.63 percent of the total expenditures on coal in nominal and real dollars, respectively. It is interesting to note that the cumulative private sector costs of the two regulations, as derived through the above forecast, are greater than the sum of the individual cumulative private sector costs of the regulations, as derived

Figure 10–5.    Total Costs of the Revised NSPS and SMCRA (Billions of current dollars).

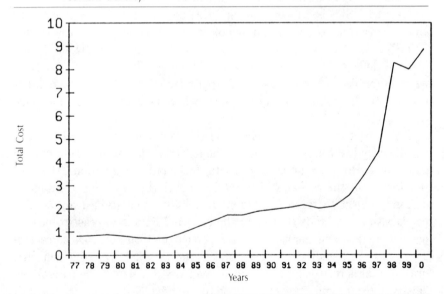

through the no SMCRA case and the no RNSPS case forecasts. The cumulative private sector costs of both regulations, as derived through the no SMCRA/RNSPS case forecast, are $58.743 billion nominal dollars ($22.820 billion real 1979 dollars), and the sum of the individual cumulative costs of the regulations is $56.805 billion nominal dollars ($22.215 billion real 1979 dollars).

This result is due to the fact that when the cumulative costs are measured individually, through the no SMCRA and no RNSPS case forecasts, some double counting of these costs occurs. In the no RNSPS case there is a greater shift to western coal production than in the base case after 1983. This is due to the fact that coal scrubbing is not required in the no RNSPS case, and therefore low sulphur western coal becomes a more competitive means of meeting the clean air regulations. In the no SMCRA case there is also a greater shift to western production than in the base case in the 1990s. This is due to the fact that the elimination of the federal reclamation regulations in the no SMCRA case causes an increase in eastern coal production in the earlier years, as compared to the base case, which in turn causes eastern coal reserves to deplete at a faster rate, thereby making western coal more competitive in the later years. Both of these shifts to western coal result in reduced expenditures on delivered coal as compared to the base case. However, when analyzed together, in the no SMCRA/RNSPS case, the savings due to this shift to western coal are only counted once, and therefore the cumulative costs of the two regulations, as measured in this forecast, are greater than the sum of the cumulative costs of the two regulations, as measured separately in the no SMCRA case and the no RNSPS case forecasts.

## CONCLUSION

The piecemeal legislative approach to promoting the use of coal, while at the same time requiring that coal must be mined and burned in a manner that minimizes the negative environmental effects, will obviously lead to conflicts. This chapter has presented and tested a methodology for comprehensively analyzing the impacts of sometimes conflicting coal-related regulations on production, price, and expenditure patterns.

We have tested this methodology by assessing quantitatively two pieces of regulation, the SMCRA and the revised new source performance standards. This examination revealed that these regulations have significant impact on coal production, distribution, and prices. Very few differences due to these regulations are seen before 1984. After that time, the absence of the SMCRA increases Appalachian and Montana-Wyoming coal production and lessens the forecast of midwestern and Colorado-Utah production. Mine-mouth and delivered prices are lower in all regions. The absence of required scrubbing has much more complicated impacts, as coal consumers alter their compliance strategies by switching both among sources of coal and among qualities of coal. In terms of the costs that these regulations impose on the coal industry, it was found that the cumulative costs of both the regulations, when analyzed together, are greater than the sum of the individual cumulative costs of the regulations analyzed separately. This result is due to the fact that when the regulations are analyzed together, their interactive impacts on the coal industry may be assessed.

This methodology for analyzing the impacts of government regulations on the coal industry has ramifications for other mineral industries where a comprehensive policy does not exist. We believe that the observations made in this chapter would have been revealed if a similar application of our methodology to the oil and gas industry had been performed. At a time in which the country is developing new energy-related industries such as the synthetic fuels industry and the solar industry, it is of utmost importance to have a comprehensive and consistent policy that would lead to creating a set of well-defined national goals.

## REFERENCES

Department of Interior, Office of Surface Mining Reclamation and Enforcement. 1978. "Final Environmental Impact Statement, Permanent Regulatory Program Implementing Section 50(b) of the SMCRA of 1977."

――――. 1979. "The Data Resources Coal Reference Manual." 5th ed. Lexington, Massachusetts, December. Unpublished.

Data Resources, Inc. (DRI). 1977. "The Data Resources Coal Model." Lexington, Massachusetts, December. Unpublished.

Federal Register. Various issues.

Zimmerman M. 1977. "Modeling Depletion in a Mineral Industry: The Case of Coal." Bell Journal of Economics. (Spring)

337-63

7230

7230

# 11 A METHODOLOGY FOR THE FORMULATION AND EVALUATION OF ENERGY GOALS AND POLICY ALTERNATIVES FOR ISRAEL

*Julius Aronofsky*
*School of Business Administration, Southern Methodist University*
*Reuven Karni*
*Faculty of Industrial Engineering and Management, Technion*
*William Marcuse*
*Brookhaven National Laboratory*

## INTRODUCTION

The continuation and exacerbation of the "energy crisis" has forced realization that "technological fixes" will not provide short- or medium-term solutions to the problem. Thus, more attention is being paid to social and behavioral aspects of energy supply and demand, and recourse is being made to decision sciences, policy analysis, goal formulation techniques, and other such disciplines in order to come to grips with the energy issue.

In the last few years, several reports and studies have dealt with aspects other than technology—goals and objectives, methods by which these goals may be achieved, governmental and nongovernmental bodies involved in implementation, the role of information and propaganda, and in particular, the postulation of a series or "catalogue" of possible actions that could be

This research was sponsored by the Samuel Neaman Institute for Advanced Studies in Science and Technology

337

taken and from which a rational and consistent energy policy could be developed. Such reports, dealing with the subject at the national level, have been put out in Israel (Ministry of Energy 1980), Greece (Ministry of Coordination 1977), Switzerland (Federal Commission 1978), South Africa (Energy Research Institute 1980), and Australia (Diesendorf 1979), among others. In this connection, we also mention the CONAES (1980) series of papers, which in addition to considering alternative energy systems, describe the necessary accompanying actions, policies, and R&D programs for implementing these systems.

This chapter describes the conceptual foundations of a methodology for formulating energy goals and policy alternatives, within a general research effort in national policymaking being carried out under the auspices of the Samuel Neaman Institute for Advanced Studies in Science and Technology. The methodology has especially benefited from fruitful interactions with other groups dealing with water policy and urban planning policy.

Figure 11–1 presents a general scheme for goal-directed policymaking—that is the definition of the issue involved and the formulation of policies as related to goals. The process may be described as follows:

1. An issue emerges that is of concern to the policymakers.
2. Together with a policy analyst, the policymakers formulate a generalized set of goals to be aimed for in response to the problems raised by the issue.
3. The policymaker selects a specific subset of these goals, to be achieved wholly or partially over some period of time. This subset we refer to as the policymaker's objectives.
4. Together with the policy analyst, policymakers develop a set of measures or criteria to enable the level of attainments of the objectives to be determined.
5. In parallel, spurred on by ideas from policymakers, analysts, experts, and other stakeholders, a series of solutions is generated. The impact of each solution is expressed by the same measures as the objectives intended to be achieved by the solution.
6. Each solution is evaluated in terms of its contribution to objective attainment; a series of solutions may be required in order to achieve the set of objectives.
7. The results of the evaluation are passed to the policymaker for his or her decision as to which set of solutions best satisfy his objectives.
8. The solutions are implemented.

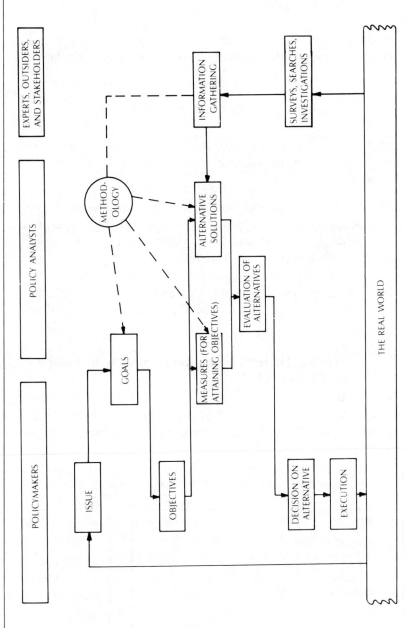

**Figure 11-1.**     General Scheme for Goal-Directed Policymaking.

## FORMULATING ENERGY GOALS AND POLICY ALTERNATIVES

We now particularize the scheme described above to the energy issue, although, in principle, the approach is applicable to other similar issues.

### Relating Energy Goals to Societal Goals

Virtually every action undertaken to attain fulfillment of societal goals generates a requirement for a service related to energy (see Figure 11–2), where we define:

- Social goal hierarchy—A structured ensemble of entities that presents specific national goals and subgoals that are central to the political, economic, and Judaic viability of Israel as a modern state.
- Energy-related service—The useful or desired product of an activity that requires an energy service as one of its inputs.
- Energy service—The useful or desired product from an activity that consumes energy with the aid of an energy conversion device.

### Relating Energy Service Requirements to Energy Goals and Policies

Demands for energy services lead to goals relating to the provision of such services and policies for attaining these goals (see Figure 11–3), where we define:

Figure 11–2. Energy Services for Societal Goals.

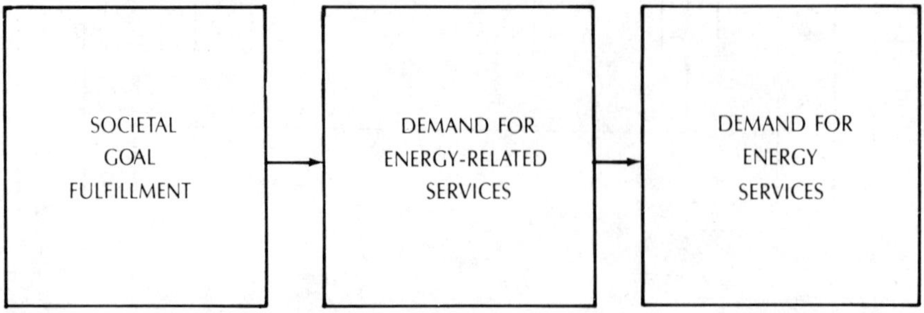

- Energy goal hierarchy—A structured ensemble of entities detailing goals, subgoals, and policy activities in the energy sector whose achievement affects the fulfillment of the society's national goals. The level of achievement and mix of societal goals are directly affected by the demand for energy-related services as expressed in the energy goal hierarchy.
- Energy policy—Any combination of one or more energy policy actions directed toward the achievement or maintenance of a specific set of goals or objectives.

## Relating Energy Policies to Alternative Sets of Solutions or Policy Actions

Formulation of energy policy requires the availability of sets of actions, preferably alternative sets, that can be implemented. A set of such actions constitutes the concretization of the policy (see Figure 11–4), where we define:

- Energy policy alternatives—Alternative sets of policy actions, directed toward the achievement or maintenance of the same set of goals or objectives.
- Energy policy action—A specific measure directed to manipulating one or more aspects of the energy system with the intent of encouraging system modification.

**Figure 11–3.**    Energy Policies for Energy Services.

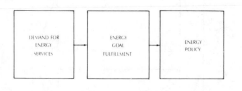

**Figure 11–4.**    Energy Policy Actions Make Up Energy Policy.

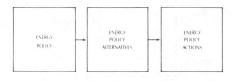

## Deriving Those Characteristics of Policy Actions
## By Which Goal Attainment May Be Measured

Energy policy actions are proposed, combined, evaluated, and selected for implementation on the basis of their ability to contribute to the achievement of desired goals (see Figure 11-5), where we define:

- Energy policy action impact—The (measurable) result or effect of implementing a given energy policy action. Internal impact relates to the effects on energy goals; external impact relates to the effects on societal goals.
- Energy policy action effectuation—The means or process whereby a given energy policy action can be realized—or thwarted—by modifying the energy system (internal effectuator) or any other related system (external effectuator).

Characteristics of energy policy actions are enlarged upon in a subsequent section.

Figure 11-5.    Energy Policy Actions Contribute to Goal Fulfillment.

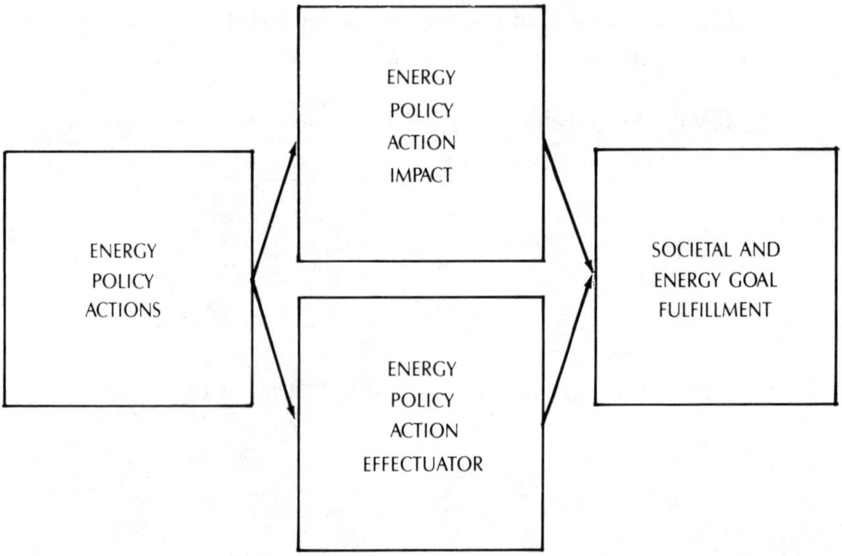

## Deriving a Multicriterion Scoring System for Evaluating the Combined Worth of a Set of Energy Policy Actions

An energy policy is comprised of a set of actions, each with its own attributes. The aggregate attributes of the policy are derived, via a suitable multicriterion scoring system, from those of the constituent actions. In principle, with fully quantified attributes and a proper set of weightings, one should be able to evaluate and select a preferred policy. At this stage, the current research has not yet dealt with this aspect of the process.

### Formulating Objectives

Within a generalized set of goals, the policymaker will select those particular goals and define for each one the level of achievement he would want to attain. These particularized goals then constitute the specific objectives of the policy to be formulated, (as shown in Figure 11–6), where we define:

- Goal—An aspiration or ideal expected to be achieved or maintained in the long run and expressed in qualitative, nonmeasurable terms.
- Objective—A quantified expression of the desired level and timing of attainment of a specific goal.

### Formulating Policies

Within a collection or "catalogue" of possible policy actions, a set will be selected that must be implemented in order to achieve the stated objectives.

**Figure 11–6.**    Selection of Goals to be Attained.

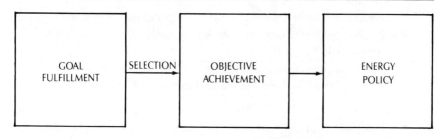

There are several approaches by which alternative policies—sets of policy actions—may be generated.

1. A set of actions may be selected "arbitrarily," using expert opinion, the participation of policymakers, and the judgment of the policy analyst. The worth of each selection would then be evaluated using the aggregation methods referred to above.
2. A "filter" would be applied to each policy action to see whether it can contribute potentially to the objective. If so, it would be compared with current policy; if not incorporated in such policy, then the quantifiers would be reexamined for bias. If they pass this test, they would become candidates for future government policy actions.
3. A more formal approach would utilize the aggregate worth values of policies and the desired level of achievement of the objective. This would utilize techniques of goal seeking in order to eliminate undesirable policies (or actions) and try to find the best policy in the circumstances.

The scheme described above is portrayed in Figure 11–7. Two main stages are delineated—(1) developing goal hierarchies, a catalogue of policy actions, and the structural relations and attributes of these goals and actions; and (2) formulating objectives and policy alternatives, leading to a decision by the policymaker of the course he would prefer to follow.

## AN INFORMATION SYSTEM FOR THE POLICYMAKING PROCESS

The complex nature of the policymaking process calls for a computer-based information system to support the process. In particular, the system would have to support the following characteristics:

1. Hierarchies
   - Handling relationships between goals, subgoals, and actions;
   - Enabling interactions between sets of goals and sets of actions to be studied;
   - Enabling goals, actions and relationships to be added or changed in accordance with the dynamic nature of the issue being analyzed.

2. Data
   - Handling "current" and "future" data corresponding to the time period involved;

- Handling descriptions of goals and actions at varying levels of detail;
- Handling attribute data expressed in different ways—numerical (approximate or exact values), magnitude (low, medium, or high impact), direction (negative, no, or positive impact), descriptive (effectuators).

3. Manipulative Rules
- For combining data of different structures;
- For comparing data of different structures;
- For tracing relationships along the hierarchies;
- For summarizing relationships along the hierarchies.

Thus, the information system may be considered as being built up from three basic components:

1. Entities—Goals, policy actions, impacts and effectuators—the four categories that comprise the "objects" of the national-plus energy system to be analyzed.
2. Relations—Goal to subgoal, goal to action, action to impact, impact to goal, effectuator to action—the linkages making up the national-plus energy system hierarchy.
3. Aggregations—Those rules whereby impacts and effectuators may be grouped or combined when passing upward through the hierarchy of goals and subgoals to create information at various levels of the hierarchy.

The conceptual structure of the information system is shown in Figure 11–8. Particular stress may be laid upon the types of relationships to be handled:

1. Hierarchical relates a goal to another, higher level goal. From these relationships the national and energy goal hierarchies are formed.
2. Action impact relates a policy action to its various impacts by defining the amount (numerical, directional, or range level) of each impact afforded by the action.
3. Goal impact—Defines which impacts relate to a specific goal (i.e., how the achievement of the goal is to be measured). Note that a policy action may impact several goals, each in a different way (i.e., with a different impact) so that those impacts relating to the goal have to be defined explicitly.

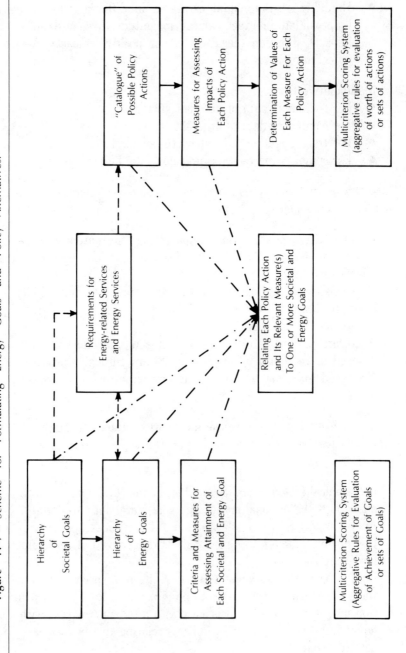

**Figure 11–7** Scheme for Formulating Energy Goals and Policy Alternatives.

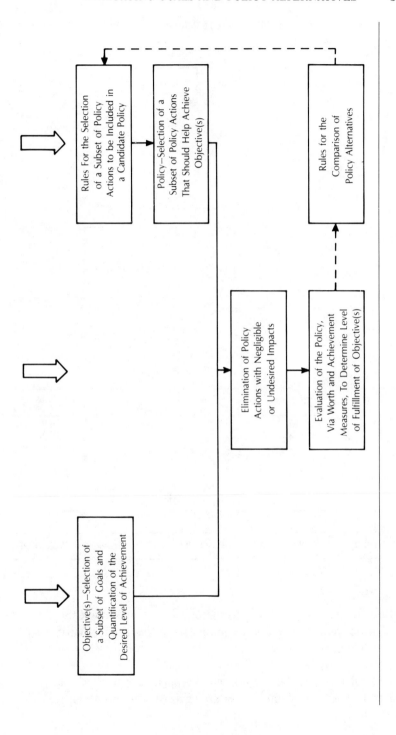

**Figure 11–8.**    Entities    and    Relationships–General,    Hierarchies,    and
Aggregations.

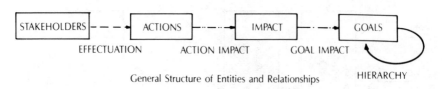

General Structure of Entities and Relationships

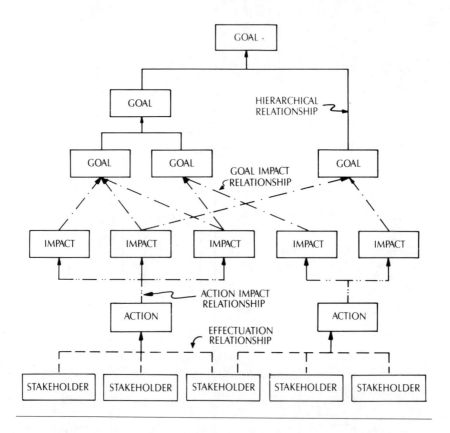

4.    Effectuation–Relates an effectuator to a policy action. Several relationships may be required to link all the relevant effectuators to a specific action.

Examples of these relations are given in Appendix F of this chapter.
Several types of system outputs are envisaged at this stage:

1. Goal hierarchy (all social goals; all energy goals; from any given goal downwards—that is, all the subgoals of any goal)
2. Policy actions, with or without impacts, by impact type (grouping all actions contributing to that impact type); goal (grouping all actions affecting that goal and its subgoals); effectuator (grouping all actions associated with that effectuator).
3. Effectuators by policy action (grouping all effectuators associated with the action); goal (grouping all effectuators associated with the goal via the policy actions affecting that goal).
4. Action impacts or impact vectors by policy action (grouping all impacts of the given policy); goal (aggregating the impacts of all actions affecting that goal; only those action impacts identical to the relevant goal impacts are considered).

## IDEAS FOR POLICY ACTIONS AND GOALS

So far, emphasis has been placed on the structural aspects of the methodology—goals, actions, attributes, and the relationships between them. One of the tenets of our approach has been openness to the inclusion of goals and actions from any source—policymakers, experts, analysts, and stakeholders in general. Nevertheless, the question arises as to whether some systematic methods exist, in addition to interviewing and brainstorming, for generating ideas for policy actions and goals. In the course of this research, three approaches were found to be of use.

### Energy Axioms

A study may be made of the assumptions, or axioms, underlying the way in which the energy issue is to be approached. These are expressed as (currently) factual statements describing the physical, sociological, and environmental characteristics of energy-related activities. Such statements are intended to lead to goals and actions logically implied by them and encompass such aspects as

- The current and future state of the art in the technological sphere;
- Physical realities and limitations on technological ability, capability, and freedom of choice;

- Political realities and limitations on freedom of action, independence of action, and maneueverability;
- Degree of interaction-independence between the issue and other issues;
- The ways in which different groups can, should, and will work together in order to resolve the issues and problems involved.

A list of energy axioms is given in Appendix E of this chapter, encompassing energy conversion and devices, energy availability, and the pervasiveness of the energy issue.

### Energy Services and Energy-Related Services

A catalogue of energy services or energy-related services provides a large number of leads to develop energy goals, to incorporate related societal goals, to suggest policy actions related to current services, and to suggest policy actions related to improving, modifying, or eliminating services.

### The Societal and Energy Goal Hierarchies

Fully developed goal hierarchies serve a number of important functions, including a source of ideas for policy actions, a checklist on the comprehensiveness of the policy action catalogue, a possible taxonomy for classifying policy actions, and a means of checking both the internal (energy system) and external (societal and other systems) impacts of policy actions.

### GOAL HIERARCHIES AND POLICY ACTION CATALOGUE

At this stage, a fairly detailed hierarchy of societal and energy goals has been built up, and the start of an energy policy action catalogue has been made (Marcuse 1980; Aronofsky, Karni, and Tankin 1980). Examples of the goal charts and catalogue are presented in Appendixes A and B to this chapter, respectively.

The societal goal hierarchy is laid out as follows. Overall societal goals lead to economic goals, environmental goals, security goals, and settlement goals. These in turn culminate in a comprehensive set of resource-related subgoals, requiring certain services—amongst them, energy services—as "supergoals" for each resource type.

The overall energy goal—to provide energy services required to attain higher level societal goals—is in turn broken out into subgoals:

- To decrease fuel requirements (retrofit, more efficient equipment, conservation practices, decreased demands);
- To secure regular energy supplies (diversification, substitution, local production);
- To assure energy requirements in times of crisis (military, nonmilitary, stockpiling, rationing).

At the lowest level of this hierarchy of energy subgoals one can construct one or more specific policy actions to meet these goals. Thus, the catalogue of actions is closely coupled to the energy goal hierarchy and, via the hierarchy and also directly, to the societal goal hierarchy.

## ATTRIBUTES: CHARACTERISTICS OF POLICY ACTIONS AND GOALS

In order to accommodate the technological, physical, societal, and behavioral aspects of the energy issue, we cannot take too narrow a view of the "measure" of a policy action or the goal affected by that action. Quantitative, qualitative, behavioral, and operational characteristics of any action have to be considered, in order that the feasibility of an action and level of achievement of a goal may be fully appreciated.

As stated previously, we categorize attributes into two types—impacts and effectuators. Impacts cover changes in energy consumption patterns, financial ramifications, uncertainty, time horizon, security, and quality of life. Effectuators include economic measures, technological means, administrative and legislative actions, behavioral means, effectuating institutions, vested interest groups, and political interactions. A detailed list of attributes is given in Appendixes C and D of this chapter.

We place particular emphasis on the effectuators, as the means by which a government agency or any other body may wish to implement a proposed policy action will have a decisive effect on the degree of success achieved. Most policy actions will have a dominant effectuator, but none will rely on a single means. Gasoline conservation, for example, may be undertaken by drastic price increases or strict allocation. By themselves, such effectuators may be successful in reducing consumption. However, public understanding, participation, and support are also necessary if a conservation campaign is to reach all sectors and to be of lasting duration. In addition, we must consider the acceptability of any step taken. Thus, a full description of the characteristics of a policy action or goal must include all those factors that provide a realistic and comprehensive picture of the action and its implementation.

## DISCUSSION

A methodology has been described for supporting the energy policymaking process. The approach is based upon the principle that no single aim or single solution will help alleviate the energy crisis, but rather a series of aims achieved by a series of solutions. The solutions are characterized by a spectrum of attributes encompassing the effects of each solution and the means by which it may be carried out.

Traditionally, transformation models have been used to determine the impacts of policy activity in many types of systems. With regard to energy, such a model would portray the manner in which energy resources are explored, exploited, and processed into fuels, the subsequent distribution of those fuels to various energy sectors to be used in conversion equipment, and the use of various types of conversion equipment to deliver a variety of services to society. Such a model thus allows someone interested in energy policy to examine how a given input works its way through the energy system and how it affects the total system and/or specific parts of the system. Implicitly, the model includes "all" the effects to be studied.

As opposed to this approach, the use of linked social and energy goal hierarchies to drive policy provides a wider opportunity to understand how actions and policies in the energy sector affect the ability of the energy system to provide the necessary services to achieve societal goals. In other words, it provides the mechanism to go beyond the energy system.

A more effective achievement is that energy policy analysis is explicitly regarded as an interdisciplinary effort and that contributions are deliberately sought from government officials, social scientists, physical scientists, engineers, and other stakeholders in order to formulate and execute effective policies. In this sense, the process described is "open"—it does not claim a priori that all goals and all actions have been accounted for; whatever the policymaker or policy analyst deems relevant will be incorporated and analyzed. Naturally, the larger the scope, the less chance that a significant item will be overlooked and omitted.

# APPENDIX A
# HIERARCHY OF SOCIAL AND ENERGY GOALS

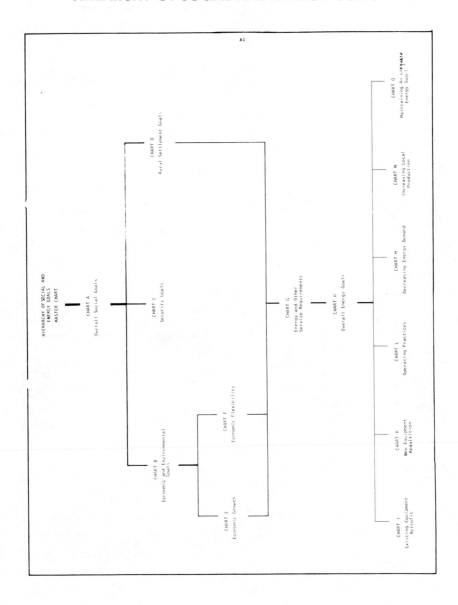

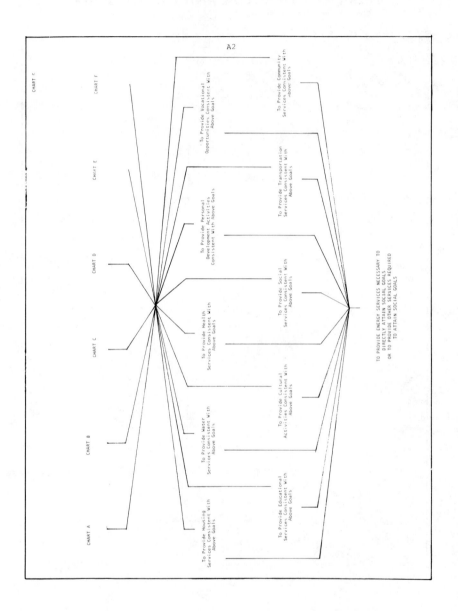

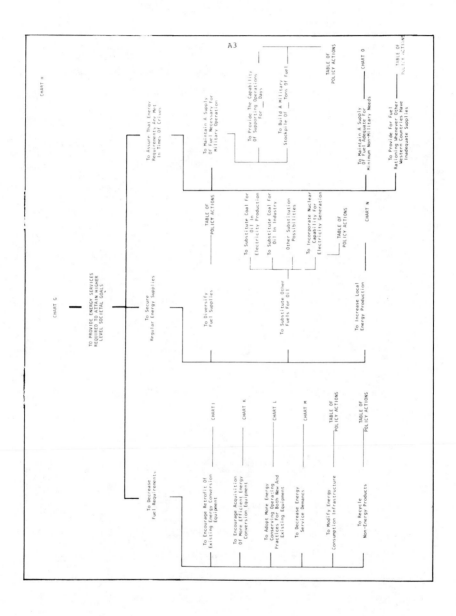

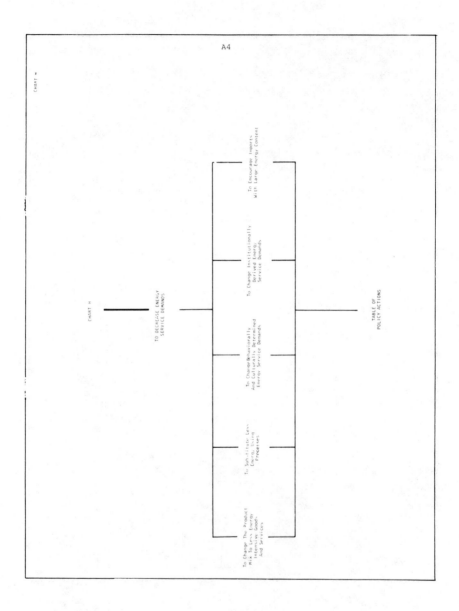

# APPENDIX B
# ENERGY POLICY ACTION CATALOGUE

| *Energy Goal Number and Description* | *Energy Policy Action* |
| --- | --- |
| #208 To Modify Energy Consumption Infrastructure | Control fuel choice through import controls, refining controls, distribution, and supply.<br><br>Control and/or influence fuel use. |
| #209 To Recycle Nonenergy Products | Discourage the use of high energy disposable products.<br><br>Develop a practical recycle technology and industry for plastics.<br><br>Stimulate public and commercial use of recycled products. |
| #210 To Diversity Fuel Suppliers | Identify and use reliable foreign suppliers.<br><br>Purchase from the spot market.<br><br>Stimulate domestic exploration and exploitation. |
| #213 To Substitute Coal for Oil in Electricity Production | Stimulate initial change in fuel preference.<br><br>Make equipment changes in old plants.<br><br>Construct new plants where necessary.<br><br>Establish reliable coal suppliers.<br><br>Establish sufficient coal stockpiles. |
| #214 To Substitute Coal for Oil in Industry | Stimulate initial change in fuel preference.<br><br>Make equipment changes and/or add new equipment.<br><br>Ensure adequate coal supplies to industry. |
| #216 To Incorporate Nuclear Energy for Electricity Generation | Plan and select site of reactor.<br><br>Construct plant and infrastructure.<br><br>Secure adequate fuel supplies.<br><br>Develop operation and security procedures.<br><br>Develop secure waste control procedures.<br><br>Encourage public acceptance. |

#303 To Increase Decentralized Generation Equipment

Encourage utility purchase of interface electricity from windmills.

Encourage utility purchase of interface electricity from co-generation.

Encourage utility electricity back up for solar.

#304 To Decrease Waste Heat Losses

#305 To Utilize Waste Heat

Encourage demand for low energy steam from power plants.

Construct co-generation power plants.

#306 To Adopt More Energy-conserving Operating Practices for Transportation

Stagger work and production hours and adjust the work week to increase mass transit efficiency and reduce congestion.

Improve equipment mix by utilizing appropriate vehicles for given distance and capacity.

Shift mode from private vehicles to mass transit via (1) automobile bans and parking prohibitions in specific areas and specific hours, (2) improved bus and rail transit services and equipment, (3) shuttle services between transportation modes.

Shift mode from private vehicles to car pools.

Shift mode from private vehicles to company-sponsored transit or car pools.

Shift freight transport from truck to rail for long distance hauls.

Improve passenger and vehicle routing by optimizing the use of buses and taxis with regard to distances and capacity.

#330 To Improve the Seasonal Load Duration Curve

Require thermostats on all heating and cooling equipment.

Stimulate the use of more efficient heating and cooling devices (e.g., heatpumps).

Encourage residential use during off-peak hours.

Limit the use of air conditioning in private residences and office buildings.

Close shops and offices from 12:00 to 7:00 during the summer.

#333 To Change Product Mix to Less Energy-intensive Goods and Services

#334 To Substitute Less-energy-using Processes

Shift to more energy-efficient equipment.

Utilize materials requiring less energy.

Develop more efficient production processes; attempt to combine processes for several products.

#335 To Behaviorally and Culturally Change Energy Service Demands

Reduce the use of private automobiles for commuting.

Encourage public and institutional conservation of energy.

Introduce Daylight Savings Time for one hour per day from May 1 through September 30.

Stimulate improved mass transit and increased participation.

Encourage greater consumer selectivity in purchasing appliances.

Stimulate greater family and group leisure activities.

Discourage the use of disposable products.

Reduce the extensive use of the private automobile.

## APPENDIX C
## IMPACTS

Changes in energy consumption patterns

    Substitution of oil (products) by coal

    Substitution of oil (products) by electricity

    Reduction of primary fuel (oil products) requirement

    Reduction of secondary fuel (electricity) requirement

Financial ramifications

    Reduction of the import bill

    Cost of implementation

    Addition and/or reduction of tax revenue

Uncertainties

    Degree of technical risk

    Degree of implementation risk

    Degree of behavior modification required

    Degree of public acceptance

    Degree of institutional acceptance

    Degree of political acceptance

Effective time horizon

    Short term

    Medium term

    Long term

Security

    Impact on short-term security

    Impact on long-term security

Quality of life

    Impact on freedom of choice

    Impact on civil rights

    Impact on environment and ecology

## APPENDIX D
## EFFECTUATIONS

Economic measures
 Pricing of energy products
 Pricing of nonenergy products (related to energy services)
 Subsidies
 Taxes
 Tax rebates
 Government participation in investment

Technological means
 Technological demonstration
 Research and development
 Technological information

Administrative actions
 Allocation
 Rationing

Legislative actions
 Enactments
 Regulations
 Standards

Behavioral means
 Changes in lifestyle
 Conscientiousness ("energy awareness")
 Public information campaigns
 Improved energy services
 Improved energy-related services

Effectuating institutions
 Central and local government bodies
 Public (government-owned) and private enterprise
 Agricultural enterprise
 Public interest groups
 Media and educational systems

## APPENDIX E
## ENERGY AXIOMS

Energy conversion

Energy users desire energy only for the services it provides.

Energy services are provided by fuels in combination with conversion devices.

Energy conversion devices are being acquired every day, and unless modified, each acquisition determines an energy use for from five to fifty years.

The total collection of energy-producing and consuming devices—the capital stock of energy conversion equipment—determines both fuel type and fuel efficiency during its useful life.

No single or small set of conversion devices and uses or producing sectors represents a large enough portion of all energy consumption to have a substantial effect by itself.

At this stage, no single breakthrough is envisaged that would substantially affect energy production or consumption patterns.

Energy availability

Oil, supplied by hostile—or at most indifferent—and unreliable suppliers comprises virtually all of Israel's energy imports.

Israel is almost totally dependent upon imports for primary energy.

The international energy supply environment is not within Israel's control, and Israel's requirements do not constitute a significant fraction of the world's energy requirement.

Energy pervasiveness

The energy sector interacts with all aspects of economic, social, and political activity.

An energy program may therefore conflict with economic goals, social goals, security goals, and environmental goals.

## APPENDIX F
## EXAMPLES OF POLICY RELATIONSHIPS (a to b)

Hierarchal
  (a)  Encourage acquisition of energy efficient appliances.
  (b)  Encourage acquisition of more efficient energy conversion equipment.
Action Impact
  (a)  Double the number of solar collectors for hot water.
  (b)  Tons oil displaced per annum ($1 \times 10^5$).
  (b)  Import savings per annum ($22.2 million).
  (b)  Risk level (negligible).
Goal Impact
  (a)  Encourage acquisition of energy efficient appliances.
  (b)  Tons oil displaced per annum.
Effectuation
  (a)  Double the number of solar collectors for hot water.
  (b)  Private consumers.
  (b)  Private enterprise.
  (b)  Ministry of Energy and Infrastructure.
  (b)  Ministry of Housing.
  (b)  Ministry of Interior.

## REFERENCES

Aronofsky, J.; R. Karni; and H. Tankin. 1980. "A Methodology for the Formulation and Evaluation of Energy Goals and Policy Alternatives for Israel." Samuel Neaman Institute Report No. 02/102/80.

Committee on Nuclear and Alternative Energy Systems. 1980. "Energy in Transition 1985–2010," National Research Council. San Francisco: W. H. Freeman.

Diesendorf, M. ed. 1979. "Energy and People: Social Implications of Different Energy Futures." Canberra: Society for Social Responsibility in Science.

Energy Research Institute. 1980. "Energy 1980–An Energy Policy Discussion Document." Report No. 24/01/05. Capetown.

Federal Commission for the Formulation of an Energy Concept for Switzerland. 1978. December. Berne, Switzerland.

Marcuse, W. "Energy Goals and Policy Actions for Israel." 1980. Samuel Neaman Institute Report No. 01/102/80.

Ministry of Coordination and Planning. 1977. "Report on the Energy Policy of Greece." National Energy Council, December.

Ministry of Energy and Infrastructure. 1980. "Energy Policy for Israel." Jerusalem, Israel: Department of Planning and Policy.

7230

# 12 PERSPECTIVES ON WORLD OIL
## Modeling in a Context

Martin Greenberger
Department of Mathematical Sciences
Johns Hopkins University

The price shock by oil-exporting countries in 1973–74 and 1978–79, together with the concurrent institutional changes in the world oil market, have left most experts convinced that crude oil prices are on an inevitable upward course. The uncommon concurrence among forecasters on this point is reflected in the conclusions of the sixth study of the Energy Modeling Forum (EMF), a comparative modeling analysis of the supply, demand, and price of world oil.[1] Ten models run in the EMF study by modelers from several organizations and countries represented a number of different methodologies and research approaches. Despite the basic differences, the models almost all projected systematically higher real oil prices in the next forty years under a wide range of futures, including some optimistic scenarios that might have been expected to produce lower oil prices.

The experts may be right in their projections. But they also could be wrong, uniformly, and it would not be the first time.[2] Simulations of the

Based on a presentation to the International Seminar on Resource Policy Modeling, Herzlia, Israel, December 28–31, 1980. Thanks are due the many people who cooperated patiently and with good cheer in completing the questionnaires, some on two occasions.

1. Material on the work of the EMF may be obtained by writing to: Energy Modeling Forum, Terman Hall, Stanford University, Stanford, CA, 94305, U.S.A. Prior studies of the Forum include Energy and the Economy, Coal in Transition, Electric Load Forecasting, Demand Elasticities, and Domestic Oil and Gas.

2. For an interesting commentary on energy forecasting and the influence of the *Zeitgeist* or spirit of the time, see Franssen (1978).

future naturally reflect conventional wisdom and the context of contemporary conditions. Policy models run in a "surprise-free" environment do not try to anticipate or incorporate the hypothetical effects of the major disruptions and political actions that often rule future policy outcomes. If they did, matters could soon get out of hand. For the most part, modeling exercises are forward projections of the way things are—or seem to be—rather than how they might loom in some soothsayer's crystal ball. It is thus not surprising for different modelers, in exploring a variety of possibilities starting from the same base point with the same preconceptions, to reach fundamentally similar conclusions.

We should not surmise from this, however, that modelers either think the same or think differently as a group from nonmodelers. The thought process of modelers is subject matter for some interesting research. The informal study outlined here is a start.

We have approached the problem by designing a questionnaire for experts on world oil. The questionnaire explores attitudes about the factors affecting the behavior of the world oil market—factors both of the type that are customarily embodied in models and those that generally are not. We gave the questionnaire to the EMF group, and we also gave it to a control group of managers and senior staff of a large American oil company. We administered it to each of these groups on two separate occasions, spaced a year apart. In addition, we gave the questionnaire to participants in an Israeli seminar on resource policy modeling. Though our procedure did not conform to customary social-scientific traditions and did not employ standard statistical tests, the results are interesting and suggestive.

What the findings imply is that the perspectives of modelers as a group are not that different from other experts as a group, even though they vary widely from one other. Although they seem less affected by popular opinion than nonmodelers, and therefore may be less likely to get caught up in the mood of the times, modelers do reach conclusions that reflect currently accepted assumptions.

It is fairly clear from the results of the questionnaire that the attitudes of modelers and other experts are affected by professional and organizational affiliations. Yet there is evidence that this influence can be tempered and in some measure outweighed by the impact of world events. It seems the views of experts, shattered by the 1973–74 oil price shock, are tending to drift back together with the passage of time and the broadening of outlooks. We find extreme opinions moderating over time and regressing toward a mean that reflects the middle ground of an emerging world view. This world view, right or wrong, will form the basis for future policy actions.

## INTRODUCTION

It is testimony to the continuing importance of world oil as an economic and political issue that within a ten-day period in December 1980, at the time of an OPEC ministerial meeting in Bali, Indonesia (over seven years after OPEC first made headlines), there were at least five major editorials and stories on the subject in a single major newspaper. The first was a December 9 editorial by an MIT economist who argued that the protracted cutoff of oil exports because of the war between Iraq and Iran might lead to a price rise of about 37 percent—but no more (Pindyck 1980). Two news articles eight days later, after the OPEC meeting, reported that the organization had agreed to let oil climb to a new $41 per barrel ceiling and pointed out that this action had come in spite of worldwide oil demand running below 1979 levels and oil supplies being relatively abundant (Hollie 1980; Martin 1980a). The following day, Saudi Arabian oil minister Yamani was quoted as having warned Western nations that prices could rise to $50 a barrel by spring (Martin 1980b). Finally, on December 19, Exxon Corporation previewed its new World Energy Outlook in which it predicted a 50 percent increase in the real price of energy by the year 2000 (Martin 1980c).[3]

The general outlook on oil prices represented by these accounts was one then shared by most analysts and commentators. It was radically different from the outlook in 1970. But despite the similarity among conclusions reached, the bases for the respective views were seemingly very different. The MIT economist, for example, posed a simple model of demand elasticities: "Conservatively, a 5 percent price rise would lead to about a 1 percent reduction in demand." Thus, a 7.5 percent drop in production resulting from a permanent cutoff in Iraqi and Iranian oil "would lead to a 37 percent increase in the average price" (Pindyck 1980).

Sheik Yamani's warnings, by way of contrast, were not based on economic deductions but on political considerations. His remarks were said to have been "intended to persuade Western nations to use oil they are keeping in storage, to reduce pressure on the oil market. This is a refrain of the OPEC nations, which tend to believe also that their power is enhanced if consuming nations are more dependent on them" (Martin 1980b).

Exxon addressed the long-term prospects for the oil market by stressing the supply side of the energy equation. "Since production cannot increase

---

3. In the aftermath, sustained Saudi production in excess of 10 million barrels a day contributed to a world oil glut. Heavy downward pressure on the market brought spot prices from $40 for a barrel of Arabian light crude in November of 1980 to under $35 by May of 1981.

368 PERSPECTIVES ON RESOURCE POLICY MODELING

indefinitely in the face of declining discovered reserves, it seems reasonable to expect that conventional oil production will reach a plateau some time shortly after the turn of the century.... Supplies will increasingly come from sources other than oil" (Martin 1980c).

The stark truth is that there are a welter of economic, political, geological, institutional, and regulatory factors that affect the supply and price of world oil. Any one person is naturally going to concentrate on a small set of these factors in his or her reasoning and explanations, just as any one model is going to emphasize certain of the factors to the exclusion of others in its calculations. It is a strenuous and necessary exercise in parsimony to model the world oil market.

We would like to understand better the cognitive process that determines which arguments and considerations get selected and highlighted in this competition among alternative explanations. We would like to explore the thinking of modelers relative to other experts on world oil and examine their views on the factors that do and do not get included in their models. As a start, we have composed and administered a questionnaire for experts on world oil.

## THE QUESTIONNAIRE

We designed the questionnaire to elicit information on how respondents regard and weight factors contributing to movements in world oil prices. We administered the questionnaire twice—first in December 1979 and a second time a year later, in December 1980. During the interval between the two trials, the world oil market had both softened and tightened as a consequence of aggressive stockpiling by buyers, economic recession, and the outbreak of hostilities between Iraq and Iran. The second time we gave it, we simplified and slightly modified the questionnaire. The revised version is shown in the chapter appendix.

Although we gave the questionnaire both times to the same two groups, we did not give it to precisely the same people, since the composition of the groups changed somewhat during the intervening year. The first (control) group consisted of a cross-section of management and professional staff from a large American oil company. They included senior executives, engineers, economists, financial specialists, political scientists, oil buyers, accountants, and government relations personnel. The second group, consisting largely of economists and policy analysts participating in the EMF study of world oil, came from a wide variety of universities, research organizations, government agencies, and energy companies. Almost all the members of this latter group had either built, used, or maintained formal models.

We also gave the questionnaire to participants in a seminar on resource policy modeling held in Israel at the end of December 1980. Although most of this group were Israelis, there were a few people from the United States, England, France, and some other countries among them. Many of the Israelis attending the seminar were connected with energy activities in their government. The non-Israelis were mostly energy policy analysts.

## FIRST SET OF RESULTS

The outcome of the first round of the questionnaire showed surprising overall consistency between the two groups, despite the differences in the composition of these groups. Although there was wide divergence among individual responses—both within and between groups—there was remarkable similarity between the group averages (Greenberger 1980).

Most of the people in the control group felt that the factors affecting the price of world oil had undergone a shift around 1978 or, at the very least, had changed in importance at that time. About half of the EMF group agreed. Among those who did not were several well-known developers of models of world oil who might be swayed by their faith in the timelessness and robustness of their modeling structures. A year later, their view prevailed.

"Institutional factors" and the "growing demand for energy relative to available supply" were considered to be the major influences in the pre-1978 period by both groups. The control group thought "institutional factors" had become somewhat less important after 1978, as did the EMF group, although the EMF group generally tended to put less weight on these factors. Most believed that demand had become more of a factor since 1978. The EMF group placed more emphasis on this shift than did the control group. Neither group considered "geological factors" to be of much significance before 1978, but both groups saw these factors assuming much more importance since then, especially when viewed ahead in the long term.

Both groups accorded a major increase in importance since 1978 to "other economic factors"—namely, "revenue requirements of producing countries, changing perception about the value of oil in the ground versus the value of the dollar, inflation, and the terms of trade." Hardly anyone appears to have regarded these factors as having been decisive before 1978, but many did for the subsequent period.

Rated about equally with "other economic factors" were "political factors," including U.S.–Saudi relations, Arab solidarity, Arab-Israeli problems, Iran, and the third world. Interestingly, only a few members of either group called "U.S. government actions" a decisive influence on the world price of oil either before or after 1978. "U.S. government actions" include the "oil import program, price regulation, and tax policy."

With respect to more specific factors cited on the questionnaire, the one pointed to as most decisive both before and after 1978 by each of the groups was the "total level of international demand for oil relative to supply," hardly surprising, since this factor has the power of economic doctrine on its side and is so broad in scope as to include many of the other factors listed. It is also, incidentally, the factor most easily and often modeled.

In second place for the period after 1978 was a factor regarded as relatively insignificant before 1978: the "cost and availability of alternative energy sources." Both groups cited this factor as having a major effect on world oil prices after 1978. The higher prices go, the more the cost of alternatives becomes limiting. Among other factors that both groups agreed were clearly influential were the "rate of new oil finds"; the "oil production capacity of Saudi Arabia and other OPEC countries" (which the EMF group felt had become especially significant since 1978); "revenue needs, import prices, and trade balances of oil-exporting countries"; and "Mideast internal politics." Of these factors, oil production capacity was regarded as having greatest importance at the present time.

Both groups concurred that the "effect of rising oil price on demand and energy conservation" was now very influential, whereas before 1978 it had not been. A similar opinion to a somewhat lesser degree was held with respect to the "effect of rising oil price on the development of new reserves."

Both groups saw the "threat of economic or military reprisal and Saudi defense concerns" as growing greatly in importance since 1978, although still not ranking with the other factors cited. Many members of the control group felt that the "degree of U.S. energy self-sufficiency" had become decisive, a view not as strongly held by the EMF group.

In reflecting on the significance of the Iranian crisis, 61 percent of the control group and 45 percent of the EMF group said that the "game is being played differently" now. A sharper divergence occurred in answers to the question of why "OPEC has lasted longer than the typical cartel." Many more persons from the control than from the EMF group cited the fact that OPEC "is so profitable for its members" and "has great flexibility in controlling production." According to the EMF group, "oil prices had to increase anyway," and "OPEC is not a cartel." Whereas 19 percent of the control group assigned significance to OPEC's having "taken over from the international oil companies," none of the members of the outside group seemed to have that opinion.

In general, the control group showed a greater tendency to attribute meaning to the actions and interests of OPEC, while the EMF group was more inclined to attach importance to conventional market forces. Economists, of course, are first and foremost students and modelers of the market, and there were many such in the EMF group. Members of the control group, on the other hand, as representatives of the oil industry, are more likely to see Mideast events in power and institutional terms. For example, over 80 percent of the control group (as compared to about half of the EMF group) felt that "the fourfold increase in oil prices in 1973–4 was due essentially to the power play by OPEC." Conversely, 60 percent of the EMF group (again compared to about half of the other group) thought that the price hike was "understandable based on market forces." Since many respondents checked both of these reasons, however, it would be incorrect to characterize the control group as "institutionalists" and the EMF group as "economists," although there are noticeable leanings in those directions.

On the all-important question of what will happen to the real price of world oil, the majority of the control group believed prices would "show modest and gradual increase" over the next ten years. Less than 30 percent of the EMF group shared this opinion. EMF participants tended to expect higher price rises, in general, than did members of the control group. Many of them felt that prices would double in this period, whereas estimates in the control group ranged closer to a 50 percent price rise over the same time frame.

Greater than 40 percent of all respondents expected future price to "display great turbulence and instability," no matter what the overall change. This pessimism was expressed somewhat more by members of the EMF group than by those from the control group.

Of special interest was the fact that almost no one believed that future prices would descend from present levels, a very different picture than six years earlier, when some prominent economists were predicting the cartel would collapse and world prices would soon tumble.

In summary, answers to the questionnaire on the first round showed a wide divergence of opinion among respondents but, given this, surprising similarity between group averages. Members of the EMF group were more attuned to market forces, whereas members of the control group were more

impressed with the roles of institutions such as OPEC and the oil companies. There was general agreement overall on the major influence of growing
demand relative to accessible supply and also on the increasing importance
since 1978 of perceptions of resource limitations, the value of oil in the
ground, energy conservation, and the cost and availability of alternative energy sources. EMF participants expected higher price rises and somewhat
more turbulence than did members of the control group. Whereas this difference between groups became more pronounced in the second round of
testing, other differences narrowed.

## SECOND ROUND

The second administration of the questionnaire took place a year after the
first. We gave the questionnaire to the same two groups as before, but since
there was a partial changeover in the composition of these groups, not to
precisely the same people. The results were striking. The control group,
which in the first round had assigned great meaning to the role of OPEC in
the price rises, was now considerably less impressed by the OPEC "power
play." Only 38 percent saw OPEC as responsible for the 1973–74 fourfold
increase in oil prices, whereas the year before the number had been 81 percent. Furthermore, 63 percent, as opposed to the earlier 35 percent, now said
that "oil prices had to increase anyway." Finally, 29 percent now agreed
that "Opec is not a cartel"—the same number that held this view in the
EMF group (down from 39 percent the year before). We might conjecture
that events of a year in which OPEC had demonstrated increasing divisive-
ness from the military confrontation between two of its principal members
had changed some minds about the potency and cohesiveness of the Organization of Petroleum Exporting Countries.

It was as though the "institutionalists" were conceding that maybe the
"economists" had been right. But members of the EMF group also under-
went a change of views. The proportion who believed the fourfold price rise
was understandable based on market forces fell from 61 to 40 percent (as
compared to the control group where it stayed relatively constant from 52
to 50 percent). In addition, there was a general decline in the importance
EMF respondents attached to growing demand for energy, to geological factors (especially in the post-1978 period), and to the importance of OPEC
production capacity and price effects. One might sense a tendency in this
group to move away from purely economic explanations during a year in

which political events in the Mideast dominated the news and oil prices continued to rise despite the fact that importers had abundant oil stocks.

The Israeli group differed most from the others in the low rating it gave to the effect of rising oil price on demand and conservation. A country whose general price level more than doubled in one year—where indexing is widely applied—might be getting a bit cynical about the influence of price (albeit real price) on consumption. The Israeli group also put less weight than the other two groups on growing demand, and on oil finds, as explanations for the price rises.

The most significant result from the second administration of the questionnaire was a sharp decline in the belief that since the 1978–79 Iranian revolution, the game was "being played differently." The percentage was down markedly, from 61 to 38 percent in the control group and from 45 to 18 percent in the EMF group. Correspondingly, larger numbers of respondents believed that "nothing much has changed" since 1979 and that "the real shift was in 1973–4." This had been the viewpoint of the modelers from the start.

This shift in the beliefs and perspectives of nonmodeling respondents is understandable. It suggests that the Iranian revolution, fresh in their minds at the time of the first administration of the questionnaire, had made quite an impact then, but that the impact had been softened by the lapse of time. There may have developed over the year an increasing awareness that the effect of the revolution on the world oil market could equally well have followed from any of a variety of other political occurrences in the Mideast. People may be getting inured to the inevitability of such events in the future.

As a matter of peripheral interest, a new question was added in the second administration of the questionnaire. It is question 5, having to do with the reasons for deterioration of Western influence in the Mideast. A wide difference of opinion was expressed on whether Great Britain's withdrawal from the Persian Gulf at the end of 1971 "began a policy of abandonment and appeasement that has led to a dangerous power vacuum in the Middle East." In the control group, 54 percent felt it had. In the Israeli group, only 17 percent did. (The EMF group was in the middle.) The disparity may reflect the contrary perspectives of the colonizer and the colonized—the powerful versus the vulnerable.

As for the final item on the questionnaire, once again there was general concurrence that oil prices will continue to rise. Almost none of the respondents believed that prices would fall, and very few saw them as likely even to remain level in real terms. A larger number, 61 percent of the EMF group (up from 45 percent) now anticipated price turbulence and instability. (That conclusion was consistent with the outcome of many EMF computer runs during the year). Most interestingly, the differences between groups on price expectations widened. Only 38 percent of the control group now expected price turbulence and instability (down from 42 percent). On the other hand, 67 percent of this group believed prices would show modest and gradual increase, as opposed to only 32 percent of the EMF group (compared to 52 and 29 percent, respectively, the first time).

Overall, the conviction that real prices would stay on the upward slope was at least as pronounced in the second administration of the questionnaire as in the first. But the size of the expected rise diminished. Whereas many of the earlier respondents anticipated a doubling of prices in a ten-year period, respondents in the second round expected increases more in the range of 25 to 50 percent over the next ten years (Greenberger 1980).

## CONCLUSION

As part of our analysis, we segregated the responses of the modelers from those of other respondents and made a comparison. There was little evidence to support the contention that modelers are a breed apart in their outlooks or in the factors to which they attached importance (Greenberger, Crenson, & Crissey 1976). Modelers did appear to favor economic rather than political, regulatory, or institutional explanations; and the tendency to downplay institutional factors found in the EMF group for the pre-1978 period was especially noticeable among modelers, but their difference in this respect from other respondents was one largely of degree. The place where modelers clearly distinguished themselves the most from others was in the high level of significance they accorded the oil production capacity of Saudi Arabia and other OPEC countries, especially in the period since 1978. OPEC production capacity plays a key role in many world oil models.

In checking the second year's results with the first, the influence of international events was apparent—and pronounced—even when seen against such clearly biasing personal characteristics as organization and professional affiliation. The differences attributed to political events might be considered spurious because of the variations in samples between successive administrations of the questionnaire, except that a set of matched pairs removed from the samples exhibited similar differences. There was a definite diminution over the course of the year in the power assigned to OPEC and a very decided shift away from the initial view that the Iranian revolution was a turning point in the world oil market.

The propensity of the models to project higher world oil prices under a variety of scenarios was reinforced and perhaps partially explained by the consistency shown in the results of the questionnaire on this issue. Almost all respondents expressed the belief that real prices would continue to increase; a growing number of EMF respondents expected continued price turbulence as well.

A study like this raises far more questions than it answers. The subject is ripe for investigation, and there are good reasons for more systematic, carefully designed research. A better understanding of the part played both by personal attitudes in determining the outcome of modeling projections, and by projections in changing perspectives, could improve the meaningfulness of modeling analysis for future policy applications.[4]

# APPENDIX
## THE REVISED QUESTIONNAIRE

1.  Influences on the price of world oil fall into several general categories. Which of the categories below do you feel include (or will include) the primary causes of change in the world price of oil? Rate 3 for "decisive," 2 for "significant," 1 for "of dubious importance," and 0 for "no opinion." Star the category you consider most critical in each of the two time periods considered.

    *pre-1978   post-1978*

    A.  Institutional factors (changing role of producing countries, actions of multinationals and independents, performance of OPEC)
    B.  Geological factors (resource limitations, rate of new finds)
    C.  Growing demand for energy relative to available supply (use patterns in industrialized world, needs of developing countries)
    D.  Other economic factors (revenue requirements of producing countries, changing perception about

4. A full version of this paper that includes tables summarizing the results of the analysis is available from the OR Group Office, 206 Ames Hall, The Johns Hopkins University, Baltimore, MD 21218.

value of oil in the ground versus value of dollar, inflation, terms of trade)

E. Political factors (U.S.–Saudi relations, Arab solidarity, Arab–Israeli problems, Iran, third world)

F. U.S. government actions (oil import program price regulation, tax policy)

2. Moving from the general to the more specific, and using the same rating system as in question 1, how important were (and will be) each of the following factors in influencing the world price of oil? Star the ones you consider most critical. You can add to the list.

*pre-1978    post-1978*

A. Total level of international demand for oil relative to supply

B. Rate of new oil finds considering location, quality, and lifting cost

C. Market competition and level of oil imports of the United States vis-à-vis other oil-consuming nations

D. Cost and availability of alternative energy sources

E. Oil production capacity of Saudi Arabia and other OPEC countries

F. Degree of U.S. energy self-sufficiency

G. Problems in the development of nuclear energy

H. U.S. price controls stimulating world demand for oil

I. Dependence of GNP and economic growth on energy consumption

J. Size of OPEC's increasing profit margin

K. Cost and difficulty of importing nation's storing oil

L. Revenue needs, import prices, and trade balances of oil-exporting countries

M. Mideast internal politics, desire for Arab solidarity, and Arab-Israeli problems

N. World economic conditions and problems of inflation

O.  Importer-exporter interdependencies and OPEC investment opportunities

P.  Threat of economic or military reprisal and Saudi defense concerns

Q.  Third world concerns and World Bank financing of risky oil exploration

R.  Effect of rising oil price on the development of new reserves

S.  Effect of rising oil price on demand and energy conservation

T.  Elimination of fixed parity among international currencies,

U.  Declining confidence in the dollar and its role as a medium of exchange in oil transactions;

V.  Possibility of major new oil finds or other causes of a break in the world price of oil

W.  U.S. politics, taxes, and regulatory policy

X.  U.S. foreign policy, Russia, and U.S. relations with Saudi-Arabia and Iran;

Y.  Changing property rights of owners of oil resources and changing replacement costs

Z.  IEA and other international arrangements among consuming countries

For the following questions, check as many blanks as seem appropriate.

3.  With respect to the factors outlined in questions 1 and 2, since the 1978–79 Iranian crisis

> The game is being played differently _____
> Nothing much has changed _____
> The real shift was in 1973–74 _____
> No opinion _____, or other point _____

4.  OPEC has lasted longer than the typical cartel because

> It is so profitable for its members _____
> It has great flexibility in controlling production _____
> It took over from the international oil companies _____
> Oil prices had to increase anyway _____
> It is not a cartel _____
> No opinion _____, or other point _____

5.  Great Britain's withdrawal from the Persian Gulf at the end of 1971

    Began a policy of abandonment and appeasement by the West that
    has led to a dangerous power vacuum in the Middle East _____
    Threw oil-importing countries to the mercy of OPEC _____
    Signaled acquiescence to repeated rises in the price of crude _____
    Was unavoidable with the dismantling of Europe's overseas em-
    pires _____
    Has had little meaning to the price of crude _____
    No opinion _____, or other point _____

6.  The fourfold increase in oil prices in 1973–74 was

    Due essentially to the power play by OPEC _____
    Understandable based on market forces _____
    Instrumental in determining present price levels _____
    Overdue and exaggerated in significance _____
    No opinion _____, or other point _____

7.  Discounting the effect of inflation on prices, the "real" price of world
    oil (in 1980 dollars) will in the next ten years

    Stay relatively constant _____
    Fall from present levels _____
    Show modest and gradual increase _____
    Rise by _____ (fill in) percent _____
    Display great turbulence and instability _____
    No opinion _____, or other point _____

## REFERENCES

Franssen, Herman T. 1978. *Energy: An Uncertain Future.* An Analysis of the U.S.
    and World Energy Projections through 1990. Publication No. 95–157. Prepared for
    U.S. Senate Committee on Energy and Natural Resources. December.
Greenberger, Martin. 1980. "Results from a Questionnaire on World Oil." March.
Greenberger, Martin; Matthew A. Crenson; and Brian L. Crissey. 1976. *Models in the
    Policy Process.* New York: Russell Sage Foundation.
Hollie, Pamela G. 1980. "OPEC Price Accord Will Let Oil Climb to New $41 Ceiling."
    *The New York Times,* December 17.
Martin, Douglas. 1980a. "OPEC's Broad Move Leaves Questions." *The New York
    Times,* December 17.

———. 1980b. "Yamani Warns of New Oil Rise to $50." *The New York Times,* December 18.

———. 1980c. "Exxon Foresees 'Real' Energy Price Up 50% by 2000." *The New York Times,* December 19.

Pindyck, Robert S. 1980. "The War, and Oil Prices." *The New York Times,* December 9.

381-91

7230

# 13 ENERGY POLICY MODELING AND DECISIONMAKERS

*Jona Bargur*
*Director of Planning and Policy Division*
*Ministry of Energy and Infrastructure, Israel*

## PREFACE

I have been involved in modeling for planning and policymaking for the last ten years. I had faith in the contribution of empirical, yet rigorous, models to the decisionmaking process. I was sure that systematic modeling was a prerequisite for systematic planning, that even if point solutions of specific models cannot be considered a reflection of reality, they are a major input to the evaluation of trade-offs between avenues of public policies. In time, sensitivity analyses became the more important by-product of the planning model. In short, I enjoyed building and applying models; I believed in their significance and was confident that appropriate models and correct applications could close a gap between professional planners, in the broad sense of planning, and responsible decisionmakers.

Now I have changed my position, literally, and I am now on the receiving end—that is models and their results, formulated by professionals, are forwarded for application to us, the decisionmaking staff. Gradually, a change of mind—although to present not of heart—has evolved. My strong confidence has been replaced by a kind of disillusionment, which in turn has currently been modified to a more realistic attitude—that expectations should be reduced and the efforts of model builders redirected to what is needed and can be applied, rather than to promote and deliver heroic, universal models. If this process of mutual modifications prevails, useful mod-

381

els, currently the exceptions, will regain their rightful status within the policymaking community.

## EXPECTATIONS: THE POINT OF VIEW OF THE DECISIONMAKER

The role of energy models in the decisionmaking process followed, in an accelerated manner, the history of general economic and econometric models in the service of government. The initial phase of suspicion and skepticism that was based on ignorance was followed by a phase of overconfidence and expectations for universalism. This period, which only very recently has come to an end, was reflected by the general phenomena of "public officials which increasingly fell back on the computer model as their ultimate authority." Juan Cameron, writing in *Fortune* has summarized this situation as follows: "When the history of economic policy-making in the turbulent late 1970's is written, an important part of the story will be about the ever widening impact of econometric models on federal policy decisions. The wondrous computerized models—and the economists who run them—have become new rages on the Washington scene" (Cameron 1978).

Confidence was placed not only in the validity of the results, but extended to something of a myth: Models have been expected to be of universal value, to be able to provide answers to any question, to be not the tool for making up our minds, but the oracle itself. Model builders and economists fell easily into this trap and have become captives of their own skill; they extended their readiness to deliver goods that they actually could not deliver. Mathematical rigor replaced empirical validity, and this resulted in the third phase of mutual relationship between decisionmakers and model builders—disillusionment.

Disillusionment was actually the natural outcome of overconfidence on the one hand and of the actual turmoil of the world energy scene on the other. The predictive power of the various models was not sufficient to be of empirical value in the light of events. Hence, with expectations that high and performance that questionable, disillusionment was unavoidable.

This is where we stand now: There remains a lot of distrust in ever-expanding comprehensive models that are supposed to simulate all techno- and socioeconomic interrelationships combined with some hope for reassurance of their credibility. What we, policy analysts and decisionmakers, are required to do is to be more realistic in our expectations, more to the point in formulating out terms of references from the models, thus realizing the necessity of classifying in a one-to-one manner the relationship between types of models and the types of answers we expect to have at our disposal.

In order to clarify the ongoing expectations with respect to the model's effects two classes of policy models related to energy planning and management may be distinguished—comprehensive planning models and specific-problem-solving models. These two classes of models, which may, among themselves, be distinguished in terms of the methodology used (heuristic models, simulation models, and optimization models), could be classified in terms of their objectives in the analysis and planning process—namely, general orientation objectives and prediction of definitive futures. Again, these objectives may be realized in either deterministic or probabilistic terms, with associated sensitivity analyses to account for the range of valid assumptions.

Combining model classifications with the objectives of application may be represented as in Figure 13–1.

Further elaboration of Figure 13–1 is given by Table 13–1.

Whether resource planning in general and energy planning and management in particular can be handled in terms of a comprehensive prediction domain is still open to question. However, most of the efforts are made and most of the expectations are directed to this domain (quadrant 2), and hence, frustration of significant proportion is experienced. Only a redirection of expectations to quadrants 1 and 4 will bring to a more fruitful interaction between the decisionmakers and the model builders in their capacity of policy analysts.

Figure 13–1.   Model Classification by Objectives.

| Objectives / Models | General Orientation | Prediction |
|---|---|---|
| Comprehensive models | 1 | 2 |
| Specific-problem-solving models | 3 | 4 |

**Table 13–1.**   Model Applications by Type and Class.

| Quadrant | Type of Models | Type of Output |
|---|---|---|
| 1 | Multi sector, macro models | Trend analysis |
| 2 | Large scale, multi sector models | Point solutions and detailed forecasts |
| 3 | – | – |
| 4 | Problem oriented models | Specific answers to specific questions |

## ACCEPTABILITY OF MODELS: ASSUMPTIONS, CONVENTIONS AND LIMITATIONS

The concept of model is conceived to mean "a representation of some phenomenon or observable system in the real world. Thus the model builder must seek to balance his or her model between two extremes. It must be complex enough to be a reasonable representation of the phenomenon, but it must also be simple enough to be constructed and used" (Weinberg 1979).

The five simplifying assumptions listed in *Energy Future* (Stobaugh and Yergin 1979) as limitations on the model, may be recalled as reflecting

- Exclusion—Omitting factors of assumed unimportance.
- Aggregation—reduction of the model to a manageable size.
- Range—Range of validity for extrapolation.
- Reversibility—The notion that investment and disinvestment, growth and contraction, and energy input and output are symmetrical operations.
- Trade-off between time and energy—Investment of time versus conservation of energy.

It is worthwhile to add to these limitations the following intrinsic limits.

First, many of the economic models constructed for public policy analysis dwell on the convention of a "Pareto optimum," which underlies the free competitive market models. This optimum is defined as the situation in which no one can be made better off without making someone else worse off. When we look at the broad range of public policy decisions, this turns out to be essentially trivial. Most of the decisions that would make someone better off without making anyone else worse off are made without centralized intervention. Usually they are not in the domain of government action.

Attempts to increase welfare by government activities by means of compensations from those who gain to those who lose (Kaldor Hicks optimum) require interpersonal decisions that represent an array of goals. These are public policy problems. They are probably far too complex to permit reducing the multiple goals of the many individuals or interest groups to a single one inherent to most optimization models.

The most representative problem of this kind in the energy management field is that of energy conservation. As Stobaugh and Yergin (1979) state "The decentralized character of energy consumption means that decisions to conserve, unlike decisions to produce energy, have to be made by millions and millions of often poorly informed people." Now, how can our currently available models provide us with estimates of how much conservation we can achieve by a given policy—generally meaning pricing policy?

The use of price and income elasticities of demand have been employed by many econometricians in various countries. The poor data, the short period of validity of the statistical significant time series, and the necessity to distinguish between short-run and long-run elasticities seem to make the results, if not meaningless, then certainly doubtful. The direct result of the uncertainty of such behavioral changes involving decisions of millions of individuals is the failure of the analysts to convince the decisionmakers of the validity of their behavioral predictive models. This in turn leads usually to only one conclusion on behalf of the decisionmakers: They opt for a technological fix in terms of consumption patterns and downplay price-induced conservation in favor of increased energy production, mainly oil substitutes.

We may even go one step further, from uncertainty to undecidability. The quality of undecidability implies that a sociopolitical phenomenon formulated by a system of nonlinear equations can depend discontinuously on the initial conditions, so that an infinitesimal change in an initial condition can lead to entirely different long-term regimes. This situation may be best examplified by following the nominal or even real oil prices since 1973.

The seesaw character of recent price history makes any prediction highly dependent on the initial condition of the analysis, whether it is a high or low price in real terms and whether we are on an upward or downward trend of real prices. It is not the uniqueness of the outcome that is questionable, but the uniqueness of the initial input data, which may determine the validity of the model's predictive value.

Finally, can energy analysts argue in clear conscience on behalf of the validity of mathematical functionality to reflect what really happens in the world oil scene? Is mathematical modeling proficient enough to capture "rare" events (a term suggested by Weinberg 1979)?

How can we ever predict in light of unforeseen events? Even if they do not completely defy economic rational, they are triggered by political aspirations and by individual desires, social behavior, and preferences that may hardly be subjected to systematic categorization and treatment by formal mathematical models.

## EXCEPTIONS: COMPREHENSIVENESS VERSUS SPECIFICITY; PREDICTION VERSUS FUTURE ORIENTATION

Expressing criticism on both sides of the spectrum—being critical of over-expectations and hence the resulting disillusionment of decisionmakers, as well as denying the overenthusiasm and preparedness of analysts and model builders to sell their goods either as a prerequisite to successful decision-making process or as an antidote to ill conceived process—I should make room for the exceptions. These exceptions, as I conceive of them and have experienced them, can be singled out from the four-way combination matrix developed in Figure 13-1, superimposed on the interactions between the decisionmaker and the model builder (see Figure 13-2).

Figure 13–2.    Four-way Model Classification Matrix.

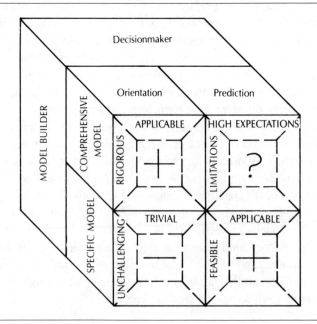

The trouble that we actually confront in the interaction between model builder and decisionmaker is that both parties are committed to the comprehensive prediction quadrant of the domain of interactions. Due to the high expectations and the inherent limitations, it often slips to the specific orientation quadrant. It actually provides only trivial answers with respect to the decisionmaker, and it becomes most unchallenging on behalf of the model builder.

Thus, if we accept this representation, there is an extended area within this domain that currently reflects the exceptions but that may very well (and it seems to me it should) become, with mutual consent, the main line of activity. The decisionmaker distinguishes between orientation and prediction outputs, while the model builders are faced with the choice of application of comprehensive models versus specific-problem-solving models. The exceptions of successful application of models result from mutual consent between the model builders and the decisionmakers to concentrate on quadrants 1 and 4, the comprehensive orientation models, and the specific prediction models.

## Comments: Empirical Demonstrations from the Modeling–Planning Experience in Israel

It is not the purpose of this chapter to serve as a discussion on some of the papers of the Israeli energy-modeling efforts as presented by the OMER study (see Chapter 3) and the time step equilibrium model (see Chapter 7). However, since these papers constitute the major contribution of modelers to the planning and policy analysis efforts in Israel and were initiated and subsequently presented to government agencies as inputs in the ongoing decisionmaking purpose, I will attempt to substantiate some of the preceding remarks with references to these models.

*Basic assumptions and input data: sophisticated integration of superficial estimates.* The tendency of modelers is not to bother with those issues that sometimes are referred to as "exogeneous inputs." In both studies mentioned above, the annual rate of change of real world oil prices is proposed to be used in three somewhat subjective levels—slow, moderate, and high. The common recommendation is: We'll give you the results under these scenarios, you make your own choice. Where does this leave us? What we need is either a thorough study of this issue, which will be anyway questionable, or at least an approach that will result in the indication of those near-term decisions (investments or others) that are insensitive to these assumptions.

The OMER model is quite insensitive to energy prices to the consumer. But even the Levin-Tishler-Zahavi model, where a serious attempt was made by the investigators to estimate sectoral demand functions, is not sufficient, as was proven by the authors themselves. Following their demand studies, with highly questionable interfuel substitutions (electricity versus direct use of fuels as well), they come up with aggregate price elasticities. But it seems that they have not enough confidence in these aggregate elasticities, so they run the model for various other ones. Finally, incorporating point estimates of unit investments for new technologies with relatively minor engineering backup is another source of possible errors. Hence, as with much more rough estimates, results may be definitely different. Where does this leave the decisionmaker?

*Naive versus Sophisticated Models.*    Inherent to input-output studies are the proportionality and fixed technology assumptions. Using demand functions with an income elasticity coefficient is one way of introducing the demand patterns. However, in both cases, this implies the acceptance of the historical linkage between energy consumption and economic growth. Both approaches do not "catch" the option of reducing energy consumption without a major impact on the GNP by change of consumption patterns, by change of lifestyles, or by substituting other economic goods in place of energy (Hitch 1977). Some relevant examples may be (1) insulation in homes, (2) increased use of heat pumps and of co-generation within industry, and (3) the use of diesels to replace gasoline fuelled engines in automobiles (Hitch 1977).

If these options are not captured in the more comprehensive models, maybe the naive approach of scaling the energy–GDP ratio along the time horizon will not necessarily be much less accurate.

*Calibration versus Validation.*    All worthwhile models are calibrated to a reference case base year. Most models do not attempt to validate their empirical value for the decisionmaking process by means of reconstructing a much earlier reference case, calibrated as well, and demonstrating their usefulness if they would have been available at that time. Current models for electricity generation expansion plans are suggesting a program for the next ten to fifteen years. Would these models, with the same methodology, be able to propose our electricity generation plan for 1984–85 if constructed in the year 1970?

*Positive versus Normative Planning Context.*    A major energy-planning concept in Israel is related to the question of intensification of electricity use. With most of the alternative energy supply options being available in the electricity sector—coal, nuclear, solar—it seems reasonable to promote the additional uses of electricity—domestic, industrial, and even for transportation. This optional shift requires infrastructural investments of significant magnitude and change in the patterns of demand.

These development strategies are hardly, if at all, captured by the two models. Both extrapolate demand patterns from the past to the future, and the share of electricity remains relatively stable.

Is this the right and perferred future?

*Operational Considerations.*    The mix of base load, intermediate, and peak load electricity generation units dictates the future fuel mix of the national electricity system and in turn the fuel mix (or energy resources mix) of the country. The justification for introducing new technologies (coal, nuclear, hydro, solar, and others) lies in the aggregate cost benefit ratios, even if not introduced in this form explicitly. A time schedule is thus derived for these technologies.

However, operational considerations of startup and shutdown for base units, two-shift operations that are common to operational practices, are not and cannot easily be considered. Hence, the mix may vary, the capital investment costs may differ, and the expansion program will have to be altered.

In addition, the continuous linear character of the models does not account for indivisibilities. The immediate problem before the decisionmakers is to weigh between the advancement or delay of investment in either generating units or petroleum-cracking systems for one or two years. These are the real issues!

*Comprehensiveness versus specificity.*    This discussion brings us back to the main argument with respect to the advantages of large-scale, multi-issue-oriented models. Investment decisions and the corresponding timing in the electricity systems will not be made subject to either of the models. An input-output study without the introduction of the technological options of diesel automobiles will not have an impact on the decision of additional cracking capacity in the refineries. However, an input-output model to analyze trade balance problems and impact on economic growth and employment rates subject to specific energy scenarios of a highly aggregated nature will be most beneficial.

Effects of forced curtailment of oil imports on the economy on a sectoral basis may be very well derived, as has actually been done. The impact of changes in relative prices of energy services in a controlled economy on the various macroeconomic indices (consumer price index, industrial input cost index and so forth) can only be made by means of such a model, due to the direct and indirect impacts inherent to an input/output model.

Similarly, the economic analysis of demand for electricity, in a context of an equilibrium model such as the Levin-Tishler-Zahavi model, is an improvement on the naive extrapolations. But investment decisions will not be derived from the model. If done exogeneously, by other means, their impact on the demand side can be tested.

In light of these reservations, it should be mentioned that we experienced most favorably the applications of even complex models oriented to specific issues, such as to derive time of day marginal costs of electricity for peak-load-pricing purposes; mathematical programming model for refineries; and the application of the above-mentioned models on methodologies to specific issues as specified above.

Hence, I would advocate in a most general manner a hierarchy of studies and models for policy analysis in the resources field as given in Figure 13–3.

**Figure 13–3.**    Hierarchy of Models.

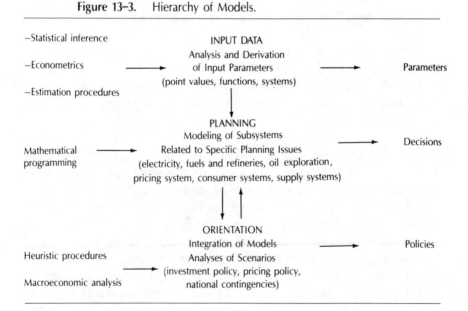

## CONCLUDING REMARKS

It is not my intention to advocate the abandonment of modeling efforts as inputs to the decisionmaking process. I believe that models and modelers should adopt a more issue-oriented approach. I will advocate, as well, to my colleagues in government not to expect any precision model that will predict the future accurately. With these models we may be able to understand better the interdependence of various factors—both those that are within our control and those that are not. We may realize the sensitivity of interactions of the various forces within the energy scene and hence benefit from this information in the decisionmaking process.

However, we all—modelers, policy analysts and decisionmakers—should remember that "ultimately all policies are made and all weapon systems are chosen on the basis of judgements. There is no other way and there never will be. The question is whether these judgements have to be made in the fog of inadequate and inaccurate data, unclear and undefined issues and a welter of conflicting personal opinions, or whether they can be made on the basis of adequate, reliable information, relevant experience and clearly known issues" (Alain C. Enthoven, at that time Assistant Secretary of Defence, System Analysis).

## REFERENCES

Cameron, Juan. 1978. "The Economic Modelers Vie for Washington's Ear." *Fortune*, November 20.

De Neufville, Judith Innes and Karen Stromme Christensen. 1980. "Is Optimizing Really Best?" *Policy Studies Journal* 8 (Special Issue 3) no. 7.

Fisher, Glenn W. 1980 "Introduction" (to the Section of Optimizing). *Policy Studies Journal* 8 (Special Issue 3), no. 7.

Georgescu-Roegen, Nicholas. 1976. "Dynamic Models and Economic Growth in Energy and Economic Myths". Institutional and Analytical Economic Essays. Pergamon Press.

Hitch, Charles J., ed. 1977. "Modeling Energy-Economy Interactions: Five Approaches." Research paper R-S. Washington D.C.: Resources for the Future.

Stobaugh, R. and D. Yergin. 1979. *Energy Future*. New York: Random House.

Weinberg, Alvin M. 1979. "Limits to Energy Modeling." Institute for Energy Analysis, Oak Ridge Associated Universities, ORAU/IEA-79-16(0) Occasional Paper. September.

393-414

NA to and

# 14 THE ROLE OF RESOURCE POLICY MODELS IN THE DECISIONMAKING PROCESS

*Panel Discussion*

## Members of the Panel

Nathan Arad, Consultant; former Director General, National Energy Authority, Israel

Mordecai Avriel, Professor of Industrial Engineering and Management, Technion-Israel Institute of Technology, Israel

James M. Griffin, Professor of Economics, University of Houston

Amos Horev, President, Technion-Israel Institute of Technology, Israel

Dale W. Jorgenson, Professor of Economics, Harvard University (Panel Coordinator)

William A. Vogely, Professor of Mineral Economics, Pennsylvania State University

Edited for publication by M. Avriel

**D. W. Jorgenson:** The all but final subject for our seminar here is a panel discussion on The Role of Resource Policy Models in the Decisionmaking Process. First, members of the panel will make short opening statements. After that, the floor will be open to the audience for discussion. With that in mind, I will turn to members of the panel in alphabetical order and begin with Dr. Nathan Arad:

**N. Arad:** Addressing ourselves to the question of the role of resource policy models in the decisionmaking process, I would like to relate my comments to three categories of models. Since I have been involved in the planning and policymaking as well as in the operational aspects of both water and energy, it is obvious that my comments will relate to management and policymaking for these two resources. The first type of model that in my judgement has not been dealt with sufficiently is what I would call the partial or subsectorial model. By this I mean models that assist the decisionmaker in deciding upon planning and operational aspects of the system involved. Examples are the operation of underground water reservoirs, optimum mix of water resources, development of brackish water desalting capacity, models to determine the real marginal cost of electricity, or models to determine the optimum mix of crude oil supply to refineries to yield needed distillate and residue mix. The second type is integrated resource supply-demand equilibrium models such as modelers and decisionmakers would have liked to have at their disposal for repeated operation regarding policy issues for adequate exploitation, supply, and consumption of the resource, be it water, energy, or others. The third type is what I call policy issue models or objective models, where various policy action alternatives are weighed against the objectives of the system, be it in the water system or energy system in this case, and appropriate indexes measure the impact of each alternative on the national economy and the neighboring systems.

In weighing the adequacy of each of the types of models detailed above, as a tool for arriving at appropriate policy actions, we have to address ourselves to the complexity of the model as well as to the multitude of the issues to be resolved. In striving for adequacy, one has to face issues, most of them linked to the real world, such as the availability of data, institutional and legal complexities, politics, environmental constraints, and ability to forecast supply or demand that in turn are linked to variables such as the standard of living, lifestyle, international prices, elasticities, geopolitical issues, and technological impact and last but not least to the risks involved both in terms of economics and, especially in the case of energy, in terms of national security.

The first type of model that is aimed at providing a solution, and in many cases an optimal solution, to a subsector of the economy involves in most cases just a few of the complex issues mentioned above and therefore could be handled by modelers and provide a reliable link in the decision-making process. Several models of this type exist. The art of their building and utilization is progressing all the time both in water resources and in energy management, and I see here an important contribution of the model-er to the decisionmaking process.

On the other hand, models aimed at providing the decisionmaker with the tool for policymaking on a level of integrated supply-demand equilibri-um is usually bogged down with many of the complex issues that I enumer-ated above, issues that might be very difficult to deal with. The use of these models is therefore questionable. Let us take as an example the role of OPEC in energy modeling. Is OPEC as a group or is each individual mem-ber country going to act rationally? How do we include in a forecasting model the upheaval of Khomeini or the Iran-Iraq war? We have to remem-ber when discussing this that these two events, which so greatly influenced the energy world, occurred within the last two years.

Yet we need some analytical and objective tools to assist the poli-cymaker, so what do we do? In this regard I suggest withdrawing a little bit from the ambitious type of models and concentrating efforts on what I call the policy issue model, or objective model, where various policy action alter-natives are weighed against the objectives of the system and appropriate indexes measure the impact of each alternative on the national economy or in a neighboring system, such as the effect of water policy on agriculture or of energy policy on inflation or on national security. This type of model presented by Karni in Chapter 11 is by all means less sophisticated, but provides a systematic and objective analysis of the issues involved and with an appropriate interaction with the decisionmaker may provide an impor-tant link in the decisionmaking process. Let me just make a last comment here that I definitely tend to agree with the comment made by Professor Vogely [see Chapter 8] when he stated that despite the drawbacks and com-plexity in most sophisticated types of models, the effort should continue toward resolving many of these problems and complexities.

**D. W. Jorgenson:** Thank you very much. The next panelist is Professor Avriel.

**Mordecai Avriel:** I would like to reflect in my opening remarks on my experience with models and decisionmakers in Israel in the last few years. I am involved in modeling in the energy area, and when I think about the similarities and differences of my problems as a modeler and the decisionmakers' problems in government, I can see some very great differences between the energy sector in Israel and the energy sectors of most other industrialized countries.

The main difference is that the decisionmakers in the Israeli energy sector can be regarded as officials of an "energy enterprise." It is not as rich and complex as say, a multinational oil company, but it is quite complex. Its role in the Israeli economy is vary large, and it works under interesting economic conditions. All of its raw materials right now are imported—that is, they are not controlled by the enterprise—yet it controls all the market.

Now if you look at the headquarters of this enterprise—and I refer to the Ministry of Energy and Infrastructure—and if you try to compare it with the headquarters of similar companies in the world, you find some striking differences. For example, take the Policy and Planning Division in the ministry and just count the number of people who work in this division. I think there are two or three, maybe four, people there at most. Is this an indication of the importance attached to policymaking and planning in the ministry? I have no doubt that the importance of this group in this "energy enterprise" should be much greater than it is now. As a simple example, take the case of energy conservation. It is infinitely easier to achieve some result in energy conservation by a right decision made by this group of two, three, or four people than to get the cooperation of tens of thousands of customers. In other words, if you have a decision on energy conservation made by a very few people on the supply side that controls the whole market, it is then much easier to carry out the policy than asking or requiring the demand side to enforce conservation. Because of the unique position of the ministry in the Israeli energy sector, most of the planning and policy actions should have been done in this division. I am not sure that this is the way it is done now.

I received research contracts from this division during the last three or four years. My research focused mainly on quantitative methods and energy modeling, and it was quite interesting to interact with the people who work in this division. They all have an excellent quantitative background. They understand quantitative methods, and they understand models. Some or all of them were modelers in the past, so there was no difficulty communicating with this group about models. However, I cannot say that we have worked out an ideal relationship.

The trouble was that both sides wanted to choose the easy route. What I mean is that for a modeler it is very convenient to present the decisionmaker some policy alternatives—say in the form of three scenarios, a "base case," a "low case," and a "high case"—without recommending clear conclusions. When this happens, the decisionmaker looks at the result presented to him and says: What should I do? You have three cases, but which one is the right scenario to use for planning? But the modeler actually has finished his work; he has presented policy alternatives. This is an easy route that leaves the decisionmaker with the dilemma of choosing the right decision from the model. The decisionmaker also wants the easy route. He is really looking for a single answer from the modeler and not for alternatives. I think neither approach is correct. Rather, both sides should approach each other. The modeler should make a more serious effort to present more than just alternatives on one hand, and the decisionmaker must make some effort to come toward the modeler to discuss his problems in using the models or the quantitative methods and to arrive together perhaps at a single or some reasonable small number of decisions. So I think in this respect, we were both wrong.

As it happens, more is needed in order to improve the working relations between decisionmakers and modelers. I think modelers are always willing to incorporate decisionmakers in the modeling process. They are open to discuss models; they are open for suggestions, discussion, critique, and so on. In my experience I had no difficulty involving decisionmakers in the formulation and actual building of models. But I think the process should also be reversed. First of all, analysts must be given full information. I must say that in my work I did not always have complete information about the subject of my model. In other words, decisions that were already taken, or those that were considered, were not told to me. Maybe I was not supposed to know about them, but it is certainly difficult and quite frustrating to model a real situation like the energy system in Israel without having the complete information. So when I talk about getting together analysts and decisionmakers, I mean both involving the decisionmaker in the modeling process and having the analyst involved a little more in the decisionmaking process.

**D. W. Jorgenson:** Thank you very much, Professor Avriel. The next panelist will be Professor Griffin.

**J. M. Griffin:** Having spent about three years working for two oil companies and being involved in their planning activities before entering academia, I would like to share with you some reflections that I gained from that experience. Essentially this work involved petroleum refining, where decisions had to be made with regard to capacity expansions. This required the use of econometric techniques in forecasting the demands into the future. In addition, there was the requirement you needed to use optimization tools to select optimal capacity configurations.

I think my experience from this work has convinced me that modeling really did have a role to play in the world, and models were indeed used in the decisionmaking process. This modeling activity was very successful, and the question you have to then ask yourself is, Why was it successful? I think one reason was that there was very close contact between the modelers and the decisionmakers, and there was a continuing dialogue between the two. The second ingredient for success was that the objective that we were trying to maximize was very clear. I think this was an important difference when one is looking at decisions in the public sector versus those in the private sector. A third factor was a minimum of political constraints that would prevent the decisions from being implemented.

When one turns to examining what role models have played in the public sector as far as energy policy is concerned in the United States, the record is not nearly so good. I would like to distinguish here between two types of what I call economic education. One type of economic education is what I would call the public perception of what the economic realities are. I say public perception because the perception and reality may not be the same, but nevertheless, the question is, What does the general public assume are the economic realities? The second type of economic education is the use of models to quantify exact responses to different policies. If you look at U.S. energy policy over the decade of the 1970s you can ask yourself, Did economic education play any role in those sets of policies? What were those policies? The major features were price controls on oil and natural gas; environmental limitations that prevented substitution of coal and nuclear power; and a variety of nonprice methods for promoting conservation. Given those realities, you might conclude that economic education played no role at all.

However, I think that the first type, the public perception of economic realities, did indeed play a role over this period, because early in this period an influential book appeared, an energy policy project report entitled *A Time to Choose*, and there was a general feeling that the demand for oil and that for energy in general are extremely price inelastic in both the short and the long run. A second perception was that there was really not much additional domestic oil or gas to be found and that the environmental cost of finding it would be likely to be very high. Thus, you take these public perceptions, continue them with a set of political constraints that were definitely labeled proconsumer and anti–oil companies, and out of that you get a system of oil price controls. And then you may conclude that the first type of public perception of economic realities really did play some role.

But how about energy models? Here the story is that energy models were completely ineffective both in shaping public perception of economic realities and in affecting the course of policies. The reason is that if you look at the models that were developed over these periods, they all showed considerable responsiveness to prices both on the supply and the demand sides; and if we were going to deal with using models in the public sector, I think that modelers are not only going to have to be concerned with trying to see that their results are imparted to high level decisionmakers but that they may also want to focus on trying to affect or shape public perceptions of economic realities. I think that modelers have a role in the education process that has not been played in the past; and I think that that may be important in the future if modelers are really going to shape public policy.

**D. W. Jorgenson:** Thank you very much. The next panelist is President Horev.

**A. Horev:** First of all, I would like to tell you a little bit about my experience with the role of models in the decisionmaking process. My experience was that there are cases where you cannot really accumulate enough information to assist you in decisionmaking without a model. But the model that you have to rely on must be limited in scope to answer exactly the question that you have stated before the analyst, making very sure that he is not being carried out of this limit to try and encompass more and more factors and variables into the model itself. I do not recall that I have ever succeeded when the modeler tried to encompass the whole problem issue in one single model. It became so complicated, in a way so insensitive to changes, that it did not serve its role at all. So the question is really a matter of proportions. The model can serve as one of the inputs into the decisionmaking process, if it deals with a matter that could be really modeled. Of course, there are some difficulties with questions of trade-offs that are based on policy values when one wants to encompass the model in a greater system. As an example, How much is independence in the energy area worth to our country? When I say independence, this term must be defined. How long, for example, can a country like Israel be independent of energy brought from outside? For a period of a year, two years, or three years? How much is it worth to the policymaker, if he wants to look at a solution that includes a certain amount of investment? When you put a question like this to the government, it is very difficult to get an answer that can be included in a model.

Let me tell you now about a problem I am working on presently. The issue of nuclear energy was already brought up in Israel twenty years ago. Twenty or twenty-five years ago, it was thought that Israel would probably be one of the first countries to install nuclear power plants in order to achieve energy independence, because we realized that we are short of oil resources, we are short of water that could enable us to develop hydropower, and the only way we can generate enough power independent of outside sources would be nuclear power. The issue was investigated periodically, and there were enough reasons then not to take the first step toward the construction of a nuclear power plant. Since 1973 the question of energy became more crucial, and the question of nuclear power was again brought up for a government decision.

A few months ago the minister of energy, probably as a result of public pressure and because there were so many controversial opinions about nuclear power in Israel, decided that he is going to look into the problem. He thought of bringing together all the information available and then to try to convey enough information to the government for it to once and for all make a definite decision either to go ahead and introduce nuclear power to Israel or to abandon the idea. Since 1973, people in the media or in government circles used to blame the previous government and the present one for the mistake of not introducing nuclear power long ago and for the fact that we are so dependent today on energy from outside. This dependence, by the way, is so crucial that one can look at it as the most dangerous single problem that we have to live with.

I took upon myself to be the chairman of the committee whose role is to accumulate information and to prepare it in a way that the government will be able to arrive at a decision. We have started accumulating all the available information related to the issue of nuclear power and have looked at various mathematical models that have to do mostly with the question of future energy demand linked with the economic growth of the country or with the standard of living. But those models do not take into consideration military problems, energy independence, and so forth, so their use for us is limited. The first thing that I did was try to get all the parties involved around one table. The reason is that I was not looking for the lowest common denominator, but for getting the conflicting ideas together and trying to look at the problem from as many angles as possible, so as to arrive at a final report that will represent a consensus of the various groups that are connected with this problem. Even if the process of convincing each other will take a little longer, if we end up with a report that is acceptable by the electric power company, the Atomic Energy Commission, the Ministry of Finance, and representatives of industry and other organizations, the effect of this report certainly will be much larger.

What are the questions that we have to look into if we are to give the government a comprehensive report? First, we certainly need a demand forecast of electric power to the year 2000. Like any forecast, it is very difficult thing to obtain, and as you realize, it is uncertain, too, but what we need is a minimum and maximum demand curve, which is important for us if we want to look into the future development of electric production capability in the country (not talking yet about what kind of power plant we are going to install) and whether we should continue with the present development of relying on coal or whether a move to nuclear power should be justified. There does not exist in Israel today a widely accepted demand forecast, and it seems to me that for our report, we certainly need some demand forecast—perhaps not one but at least a range, a minimum and maximum demand forecast. In this respect, we looked at various types of mathematical models that have to do mostly with the question of future energy demand linked with economic growth and standard of living. Some of these models were presented in the seminar [see Chapter 3], and you are familiar with them.

The next issue that we have to study is the economic one. The question one may ask is simple: What will be the cost of a kilowatt hour produced in the various technologies—oil, coal, and nuclear—because in the recommendations we certainly have to take into consideration the economic aspects of the development of nuclear capability in the country. We certainly do not know enough about costs of technologies that do not exist at present in Israel, like those based on coal and nuclear energy. We have to learn from other countries with experience in these technologies and then superimpose on their cost estimates the unique problems of our country. If we had models to help us in this respect, we could have done a better job.

Then we have to look into entirely different issues that a country like ours must study in great detail. There can be two extreme situations. One is what we call "blue and white"—or purely Israeli-designed and made nuclear power plants without help from outside—and the other extreme is a fully "turnkey" purchased plant. There are many points between these two extreme situations that are also feasible. These intermediate points of feasibility should be studied. What parts of a nuclear power plant could be made in Israel, what must be brought from outside, what is the relative dependence on know-how from outside—without talking yet about political implications of the various degrees of self-sufficiency in the development, production, and so on? I do not believe models can help us in this issue. We certainly have to study the unique political situation of Israel, the size of the country, and the meaning of a nuclear disaster in case of war. For the last issue, scenarios should be submitted to the committee by the appropriate authorities. A very important problem area is the possible sites that take into consideration the same issues, and we have to remember that this country is quite small and to think in terms of what will happen when a political agreement may change the present boundaries of the country, a decision that may affect the selection of sites.

I did mention the question of relative independence. I say relative independence because it is a matter of how long and how much you are ready to pay for it. As an example, if our liquid fuel consumption, say, is about 8 million tons a year and if we could store in this country 40, 50, or 100 million tons of oil (if economically or technologically it was feasible), we certainly would have gained a long period of relative independence by not relying on political situations subject to embargo or war. It is a government policy that must be defined—whether we are looking for independence only in case of an emergency like war, or if we are looking for relative independence. Certainly this is a problem that has to be looked at. One has to compare the various solution alternatives with regard to oil, coal, and nuclear power. It makes sense that you can reach a higher degree of relative independence with nuclear power than with coal. If, say, a certain 500 megawatt nuclear power plant uses 50 pounds of natural uranium a year and if we need, say, 5,000 megawatts installed capacity that uses 500 tons of natural uranium a year, then in terms of twenty year's stock of fuel, it is possible to store the necessary quantity, moneywise and logistically, provided you can purchase that amount of uranium. So we need a method that would give us the value of the relative independence in terms of money or in any other terms that will enable us to evaluate the various alternatives and present them or recommend one or more to the government for their decision. In this aspect policy analysts, and perhaps models, can be of great value.

One can make the work of the committee impossible, because we know that there are always additional issues involved that we do not consider. Everything we deal with may affect something else in the system, and unless we decide that we will limit ourselves to a well-defined issue, we will never be able to complete our work. There are various depths that we can go into in each of the subjects, and we have decided that we are going to work at first not too much in depth to be able to provide a preliminary report. This preliminary report will have to justify in a way the continuation of our work in order to do a more comprehensive work to present the final report. The reason is that we may find during our preliminary work that some of the issues are clear, that the answer to them is just negative or positive, and that it does not make sense to continue studying them.

In summary, I do not think that elaborate, fully encompassing types of models can be constructed for the type of problems I am involved in now, and even if they were feasible to build, they would not have given us the answers we are looking for, because the system is far too complex. Second, in order to have a chance to affect decisionmakers, we must come out with a report that will be supported by all the parties involved in the issue, and models are not capable of doing this. However, specific and simple models would be of tremendous help in our work.

**D. W. Jorgenson:** Thank you. Our next panelist is Professor Vogely.

**W. A. Vogely:** I would like to offer some free advice that is worth what you are paying for it. I have been involved in all stages of decisionmaking systems. I was assistant director of the Bureau of Mines, where I was in charge of an information system on minerals and energy. I was advisor to the secretary of interior, where I was involved in giving policy analysis to a decisionmaker. For a period of time, I exercised the responsibility of an assistant secretary of interior, where I was involved in receiving policy analyses; and I have now joined the academic area, where I am giving free advice. It seems to me that one has to structure information and analysis very carefully, because information and analysis are extremely expensive goods and their existence is extremely scarce. It seems to me that one can structure an ideal system in which there is at one end a source of unbiased information, which is accepted as reliable and which is used by all parties in the decision structure. This does not exist, for example, in the United States. One of our basic problems in energy policy is that portions of the community will not believe information. They will not believe scientists who say nuclear power is safe. They will not believe oil companies who tell them about reserves. They will not believe anybody. And so you are not working with an information source that is accepted. This is absolutely essential. If you develop policy analysis on differing information bases, then you are coming up with a comparison of apples and oranges, and you get nowhere.

Second, it is clear to me that a policy analyst must be attached to a decisionmaker—that is, he must be making analysis that is useful to a decisionmaker at the level that the decisionmaker is making his analysis. This means that in any issue that involves conflict between environment, economic goals, energy goals, or whatever, there will be many decisionmakers involved, and each of these decisionmakers will have his own policy analysis directed at his objectives. This implies that there has to be at the final level of decision an analysis group that can reconcile, that can take the policy analysis from the environmentalists, from the conservationists, from the energy technologists, and so forth and reconcile them and then communicate to the final decisionmaker the issues and the trade-offs and the directions in terms of the objectives of the final decisionmaker.

Now this is a very simplified statement of a very complex system. Involved in that system are three components: One, there should be a very large effort devoted to modeling to understand the system: In other words, models like the Hudson-Jorgenson model, which is directed toward understanding the trade-offs between labor, capital, and industry, are fundamental to making good decisions. Second, there need to be much simpler models to look at alternatives. Here the model cannot comprise all of the effects, all of the complexities. It must be simplified down to the major trade-offs, the major instruments, and the effect of the major instruments on the major trade-offs. Third, after you do that, you have to communicate the modeling or the analysis and to justify to the constituency the decision that is made. I think all three of these are very distinct, all three of these have very distinct characteristics, and I urge you to have an information system and to have modeling to understand, modeling to decide, and modeling to justify and not to try to do it all in one stage.

**D. W. Jorgenson:** Thank you very much. This concludes the first part of the discussion. I would like to open the floor to the audience, but first we had one paper earlier [Chapter 13] that focused specifically on problems in Israel, and that was by Dr. Jona Bargur. It may be that some of you have lost the essence of that, and I wonder, Jona, if you would like to give us just a brief summary of your conclusions so that we can use that as a starting point and then go on from here.

**Jona Bargur** (Ministry of Energy and Infrastructure, Israel): Some of the comments made by the panel members reflect to a major extent the spirit of my ideas which I tried to convey in my presentation yesterday morning: First, there are the high expectations of those decisionmakers or those who are involved with government who would like to see models or analysis that can give them immediate and accurate results on lots of issues and on each issue at once. On the other hand, there are modelers who to some extent are ready to encompass in large-scale models a lot of issues, and I feel that between these two groups we are losing the direction in which we would like to proceed in making our decisions. I thought it would be important to scale down to some extent the expectations of the decisionmakers and to redirect their efforts to more specific issues rather than to try to promote large-scale universal models.

If you allow me, I would like to comment on some of the points raised in the panel discussion here. One of the most important issues is that government is working in "real time" and that this is a major limitation on using models or any kind of policy analysis that takes a long time. It often happens that the issues that are presented to the modelers become obsolete by the time they present an analysis. I think that to some extent the decisionmakers have the responsibility to try to prepare issues, problems, and ideas ahead of time and to let analysts work on them, so that their analysis is available when it is requested.

The second comment I want to make, and it was exemplified in this seminar, is that modeling to us means mainly quantitative models. They all use the same basic assumptions, such as economics principles and mathematical programming. And I think that we should promote somewhat conceptual models, like the one presented earlier by Karni, before we go ahead with quantitative models.

Finally, I would like to address myself to what Professor Avriel said, and I would say that here in Israel we have an advantage. We are quite small. I mean the community that is involved in energy issues—the government, modelers, academicians, and utilities—is really a quite small group, and if we had good and effective models, and realistic ones, I believe we could easily implement them.

**D. W. Jorgenson:** Thank you very much. At this point, I would like to throw the floor open for discussion.

**A. Nir** (Weizmann Institute, Israel): I have experience with environmental models, and I would like to quote some of our experiences, which you may consider relevant here. I would like to paraphrase the statement of one of the best environmental modelists at one of our conferences, when he summed up the advances in the field. He said: "Summing up, we know more and more about the behavior of models, but we don't know more about the environment...." And that was a very good consensus of opinion. On the other hand, our feeling was that by understanding more of models, we are making a better contribution to the decisionmaker. My impression of this seminar was that we know more and more about energy, mineral, and economic models, but not necessarily about the energy or mineral problems facing us.

**A. Levanon** (Ministry of Finance, Israel): I think there is an important issue that can be dealt with by models. I refer to a good prediction of trends of energy prices. Regarding equilibrium models that were presented here, casual observation can group them into three categories—those that concentrate on the demand side; others that concentrate on the supply side; and the third category, concentrating on the interaction and equilibrium process. Now it appears to me that the outcomes or results of the third type of models—interaction models—concentrate more on the structure of the economics of the market or the whole economy involved. Among the other two groups, those models that concentrate on the demand side predict that the price of energy or the price of oil will increase at a certain rate of growth—2 percent, 5 percent, and so on—and the decisionmaker can take it or leave it and start from there. Models that concentrate on the supply side predict different conclusions—namely, that the price of energy should decrease because supply is unlimited or very price elastic and so forth. My question is, with respect to energy prices, is there one side, demand or supply, that is more important than the other and should be emphasized in a model?

**D. W. Jorgenson:** Maybe Professor Avriel would like to respond now?

**M. Avriel:** I would like to respond to some of the issues that were raised here. First of all, the question of comprehensive models versus specific models. I agree with everyone who said that it is impossible to capture all the features of a system or to address every issue by a single model. There must be a hierarchy of models. Reuven Karni [Chapter 11] presented a conceptual framework for models and decisionmaking, and he had one block there that said "The Impact of Policy Issues on Goals." I think this is very important. Certainly, if you want to address a specific issue and want to get quantitative answers, and you build a model, then the model should address that specific issue and should give you answers to that specific issue. But then if you take policy action on that particular issue and that policy action has an impact on other parts of the system, it is very easy to make mistakes, because systems are usually interrelated, and there is always the impact of one policy action on all of the system. Policy action in any important issue has a great impact on other parts of the economy, the society, security, and so on. So to solve a particular issue in the energy sector, you may need a model for that specific issue; but to assess the impact of a decision on that issue, on the rest of the economy, on the rest of the society, you need something else. You may need another model that addresses more general issues and that can evaluate the feasibility and desirability of one policy action with respect to other parts of the system.

Now to answer Professor Nir, I do not think we came here to understand the energy problems of Israel or any other country. I think we came here mainly to understand some models. The purpose of this seminar, at least partially, is to understand models, to expose an Israeli audience to models that exist in other countries, to expose our guests from abroad to the Israeli models, and to try to get some indications on how to proceed in the future with regard to policy models.

**W. Vogely:** I would like to address myself to the question asked by Mr. Levanon. Essentially, the prediction of price of anything is impossible. And if you are waiting for a prediction of the price of oil in the year 2000 before you decide whether or not you are going to build a nuclear plant, then I say you are waiting in vain. You must make that decision on the basis of some other thing. Now, there are a couple of ways to get at it. In the multinational metals industry in the United States, I can tell you that the companies no longer use price at all. They simply see whether or not their project is within the supply schedule in terms of cost with other projects that are being built and with other projects that are on line; and they assume that if their costs are competitive with those, then the project will be good because the price will eventually have to cover it. And so you are not going to get predictions of price, you are not going to get predictions of supply, you are not going to get predictions of demand that mean anything.

To understand this, simply go back to all of the major studies that have been done in the past thirty years, and you find that all of them are dead wrong—none of them are right. So that should not be the basis for decision-making. However, if you understand how the system works, you know that prices are going to have to cover those costs, and therefore we do not have to know what the price is. All we have to know is what the cost is—and we can make decisions. You have to be sure that the implications of your decision do not have extreme, unintended consequences and that the decision in a sense does not foreclose a lot of flexibility and a lot of options. On the nuclear issue, for example, if you feel it forecloses a whole set of other strategies, then you should be much more careful about it than if you feel it is complementary to a whole set of other strategies. And so I urge you not to look at models to predict outcomes but to look at models to predict directions of outcomes and to predict interrelationships.

**N. Arad:** We were indeed introduced in this seminar to models and their capabilities—and also to their limitations. But in fact, our interest in models lies in the various links in the problem-solving process. I listened carefully to what Mr. Horev had to say here about the role of models. Let us take the example mentioned by Mr. Horev: The minister of energy called upon a group of people and put Mr. Horev in charge of them, and now they have to go through the process to arrive at a solution or to give alternate solutions and probably point out a most favorable solution in a given aspect. I also listened carefully to the list of agencies that are represented in this group. And we also listened to the fact that he wanted not to get to the lowest common denominator but rather to get a consensus among the people. I also noticed that he did not mention the people from the Department of the Interior that are in charge of the Environmental Protection Agency. Suppose that the environmentalists arrive at some recommendations concerning nuclear power different from Mr. Horev's committee. Then Mr. Horev's recommendations will not be accepted because of the environmentalists, and eventually either the whole issue will be sent back to the committee or a revision will be taken to the proposed decision.

I want to stress here the fact that to my judgment, there is nothing holy about analytic models; that whenever we are getting into very complex problems, there are other means of arriving at, say, optimal solutions; and that I am very careful in saying that, because it seems to me that nobody can prove that arriving at solutions in this fashion is not optimal. Now it seems to me that whenever we have to address ourselves to a very complex issue and we bring together all the people involved and really interact between modelers and specific models and specific issues and decisionmakers, I think that we are most likely to arrive at the most favorable solution.

**M. Greenberger** (Johns Hopkins University): I will also reflect on a number of issues that were raised. As far as Mr. Horev's effort, I agree with Dr. Arad that the omission of the environmentalists in the committee may be of serious consequence regarding the acceptability of their future recommendations.

The second point that Mr. Horev made was about the situation being too complex to model in Israel, and that may well be. It is just that there are a lot of people in the United States who do not recognize that difficulty. There are a great number of modeling efforts underway in the United States at the present time to determine what they call the import premium, which I think is quite akin to what your interest is. It essentially is a measure of how important it is to reduce vulnerability, to reduce dependence on imports, and of course Israel has that concern even more acutely than the United States. With the United States, it is a more relative degree of gaining independence than you are suggesting in your investigation. And these are modeling efforts trying to put specific numbers on the value of gaining this kind of self-sufficiency and invulnerability.

On Jim Griffin's remarks, I think you would be interested to know that some people take the same data that he was remarking on and come up with exactly opposite conclusions. What I am referring to is the remarks made about models not influencing public perception and the fact that they were not used during the policy discussions and decisions made in the middle 1970s, even though they were suggesting a very important supply response and demand response. For those who are not familiar with what that means, the modelers were saying that if we raise the prices of energy, demand will be curtailed, and there will be new finds, new sources of energy, so both sides of the balance will be improved, and the shortages will eventually work their way through.

In fact there are people—and I will just cite one case, the Harvard Business School study—who were very critical of modelers for making just that point. And they suggest—I'm not saying I agree with this—that the public, and in particular Congress and the decisionmakers in Washington, were very much influenced by these modelers and were lulled into a state of complacency because they thought everything would take care of itself. And as a result, they did not take policy initiatives, they did not invest in alternative sources of energy and push nuclear and synthetics and all the rest (and of course in the Harvard Business School study, it is not synthetics and nuclear they want to push, it is rather more initiative toward solar and in particular conservation, more measures to reduce energy consumption). So they find fault with the modelers on that count.

Finally, I'll just mention one other thing that occurred to me while I was listening to the panelists. In Bill Vogely's comment, I got the impression at one point that there was an ultimate decisionmaker who needed a forum, a way of reconciling all the analyses that were done by the special interests that impinge on his decision. In fact (and I am sure Bill would be the first one to tell us this), in the United States certainly, and I think in Israel too, the decisions are not made by single decisionmakers. They are made in a political negotiation, with many people pulling in many directions and using analysis to support their cases; and so the final resolution of all these analyses comes not from one master analysis that sort of weighs all the separate analyses and comes up with the consensus result. Rather it is made in the political process itself.

**B. Avi Itzhak** (Technion-Israel Institute of Technology): From my experience of quite a few years of modeling, mostly micro models, but in the last three or four years macro modeling, I reached some conclusions that other modelers may not find to agree with their experience. But it seems to me that when you talk about macro models, models for public policymaking, we try to capture lots of features for a very large system. It happens very often that by the time the model is complete, it is already obsolete; and this is of course relevant to the comments made earlier about real-time decisions, where the policymakers say, I need the model today. I do not need it in a year from today or in five years from today. And there is a kind of a vicious circle. You start to make the model. It is very, very complex, because you deal with a total economy. By the time you finish building it and the model runs, the decisionmaker is already several steps ahead in his problems. So the modeler adjusts the model, and the same thing goes on again and again. Well, at some point it probably catches up with real life, but in order for this to happen, there is a need for very large resources; and it takes more and more resources and continuous effort to catch up with the issues so that the model will be a real-time model or at least a model that can give updated answers very quickly.

This raises another point: For such an "ideal" situation to happen, the model becomes dependent on government resources, because such large resources come usually from government sources. And, at least in a country like Israel, I do not see any hope for developing such a model unless it is government supported. And there is another question: Is this model any good anyway? Since it becomes the "servant" of government, it actually tends to reflect what government wants to do. But maybe one would like to have an alternative model that is not the government's servant, that does not have to give answers only to the government but may give answers to the public. This is a very important question, and I do not see the answer—in Israel certainly not. In the United States the situation is better, because there are several rich institutions that can support such models, although I can still say that most large models in the United States are strongly government dependent.

**D. W. Jorgenson:** I would like to make a few closing comments and try to sum up the discussion here in the panel. I think the starting point for an attempt at a consensus—we're not going to sit here and see if everybody agrees, so this is a little different than the problem of arriving at a committee report. But if I were to try to look at a consensus view of what has been said here, I guess I would put it in the following way—that there is a great deal of confidence in modeling at the level of the individual enterprise or the individual establishment, which is based on the development of the discipline of applied operations research over the last twenty or twenty-five years; and as Jim Griffin has said, by now this is a success story, and the initial stages of the developments were very closely analogous in some respects, involving exaggerated expectations, lowered expectations, and finally, realistic expectations about what modeling could actually achieve. Modes of operation have been established, the discipline has made advances, more complicated problems are comprehended, and we have an ongoing process that is not any subject for public concern at least.

On the other hand, the use of models in the public sector involves problems that are similar in some respects and different in others. As I understand it from what has been said here, it is very important for people coming from outside Israel to focus on the fact that many of the problems of energy policy for the Israeli government are essentially problems at the enterprise level. We are talking, after all, about managing the capacity expansion of the electric utility or the configuration of the refinery industry or the management of the fuel supply and so on—all of which are things that are amenable to applied operations research techniques that are well established both abroad and here in Israel and can be applied to these problems and of course are being applied to these problems. When we think about the application, though, to public sector problems in general, then we see that there is something of a fundamentally different character that could be characterized and has been characterized here on this panel as essentially the partial equilibrium versus the general equilibrium point of view. That is to say that there are some problems that involve substantial spillovers from one sector to another, spillover say from the management of energy to the way in which the water supply is managed or vice versa; and then there are also problems of spillover from problems in a given sector to the economy as a whole and beyond that to the environment in which the economy actually exists, so that in order to comprehend those effects, we have a new range of problems to deal with.

Now, of course, the situation in that respect is very similar in the United States and any other country where people have attempted to confront the implications of the higher energy prices. The initial attempts in the United States, I would say, were based on a fairly naive extrapolation of experience from the private sector and the belief that it was possible to take the type of model that Jim Griffin described as growing out of the experience in the private sector at the enterprise level to the national level. In fact, some of the firms that produced the most sophisticated, say, refinery models, were precisely the firms that were called upon as consultants to the national government to construct the first national energy-planning models. The same software was used, the same analysis was used, and so on. That turned out to result in this problem in differences in expectations, because it turned out that when these techniques were applied at the national level, it was discovered that the models did not match the problem very well and that even though some aspects of the problem were fairly well treated—and especially those that could be reduced—engineering considerations were pretty well handled by techniques that had been developed in the private sector, extrapolated to the economy as a whole—that there were whole ranges of problems that we have discussed here at great length in this panel and in the seminar that simply were left out of account.

On the one hand, you have the modelers selling the product, so to speak, either at the scientific level or as a policy analysis device, who did make exaggerated claims; and you had analysts who accepted these claims first at face value, in the hope that faced by this new range of problems they could at least find some way of dealing with them. That lead to an agreed upon set of expectations temporarily—until the work was done, the contract was complete—that then turned out to be completely unrealistic. In other words, the models really held out a great deal more promise than they were able to deliver. A period of disillusionment set in, and I would say that in the United States at least we are just beginning to recover from that period; and that kind of experience seems to be something that in a different way is taking place here in Israel. That is to say, what we have had here is both the development of an indigenous technology for modeling and the technology transfer of modeling techniques and approaches that are developed elsewhere, adapted to the Israeli scene, and used here. And without any malevolent intent on anybody's part, there has been this same problem of expectations that are at first agreed upon, then turn out to be unrealistic; and then dissonance follows and disagreements and mistrust. And that, I think, is an inevitable part of the process. So that I do not want to hold out an overly optimistic view, but I do feel that it is the case that the developments are sufficiently parallel that we can see that some of the solutions that have been discussed here in the conference for applying models to policy may in fact be helpful in suggesting directions for the evolving discussion here in Israel and, vice versa, that the discussion that has taken place here may be very helpful to those of us who are not from Israel in understanding and gaining a perspective on the discussions in our own countries.

In any case, I think that what is added to all of that which is specific to models is the following—that there is a very important role in the decisionmaking process of policy analysis for problem formulation or for what operations researchers tend to refer to as decision analysis. Again, this is the type of thing that was discussed in Reuven Karni's paper [Chapter 11] and is simply a way of formalizing what any military decisionmaker would do, I think, in laying out the alternatives, trying to understand what the objectives are, and then trying to relate the objectives to the alternatives—all before appearing before any kind of computerized framework.

Then the problem is, as Mr. Horev suggested, to try to find out which of these are really interesting problems to investigate. Some of them may in fact be relatively easy problems to answer and make it possible to focus on this question that Bill Vogely raised, which is that at this level, one of the most important things that we have to keep in mind is that there is a vast cost in terms of the time of the decisionmakers; of ourselves, for that matter, attending a conference like this; and of policy analysts in doing this kind of work—putting the information together, doing the modeling, analyzing the results—and this in itself is something that has to be regarded as an important resource management problem. But I think this seems to be something that all of us agree on, and it is certainly reassuring to find that despite the enormous differences in the sizes of, say, the United States, which most of the outside people here represent, and Israel, as a small country, there are in fact striking parallels that are extremely informative.

Needless to say, we have not answered all of the questions that people have raised about modeling and its potential role. I do not have any doubt that there is going to be a lot more modeling in Israel, and there is certainly going to be a lot more modeling in the United States. There are very important problems in managing this modeling that I think decisionmakers should be conscious of when they set their policy analysts out to interact with the scientific community that supplies the modeling services. And I think that what Dr. Bargur said about the necessity for interchange of roles—at least hypothetically if not actually, although actually would be even better—so that people can move back and forth among these various roles would be a valuable part of this resource management project, because it is the people after all who do the analysis, it is the decisionmakers, the policy analysts, and so on. The quality of those people and their character really determine the outcome and the quality of the results, and that is probably the most important lesson of all.

Before I turn the floor over to Raffi Amit for closing this seminar, I would like, perhaps presumptuously, to add a few remarks of my own on a different subject. On behalf of the participants, I would like to thank our hosts for an extremely stimulating conference. Anybody who has spent any time in Israel, as I have previously, knows of course that an Israeli conference is going to be very exhausting. The discussions are going to be lengthy and exhausting, and they are going to go very deeply into the subject matter. It is always, of course, a matter of continuous surprise that the scientific level in Israel is so incredibly high; that it is possible to learn from a conference like this, which after all is focused primarily on Israeli problems, so much that is of scientific value; and that we will be able to take home with us, in addition, a great deal of information that our hosts have generally shared with us.

# NAME INDEX

415

# SUBJECT INDEX

419

# ABOUT THE EDITORS

**RAPHAEL AMIT** specializes in energy modeling as well as in private and public policy analysis. He holds B.A. and M.A. degrees in economics from the Hebrew University of Jerusalem, and a Ph.D. degree in managerial economics and decision sciences from Northwestern University. During the last three years with Data Resources Inc., he has been leading the development of DRI's modeling, forecasting, and analysis work related to the U.S. coal industry, and has published numerous policy evaluation studies related to energy and coal. Recently he joined the Faculty of Industrial Engineering and Management at Technion—Israel Institute of Technology.

**MORDECAI AVRIEL** is professor of operations research in the Faculty of Industrial Engineering and Management at Technion—Israel Institute of Technology. During the last five years he has worked in energy modeling in the United States and Israel and is presently directing a research project on energy policy for Israel in Technion's S. Neaman Institute of Advanced Research in Science and Technology. Professor Avriel is the author of *Nonlinear Programming: Analysis and Methods,* the editor of *Advances in Geometric Programing,* and co-editor of *Optimization and Design,* and *Engineering Optimization.* He has published numerous articles in leading journals of mathematical programing, optimization and operations research.

# LIST OF CONTRIBUTORS

Raphael Amit
Faculty of Industrial Engineerings and Management
Technion—Israel Institute of Technology

Nathan Arad
MAOT LTD.
Consulting Engineers

Julius Aronofsky
School of Business Administration
Southern Methodist University

Mordecai Avriel
Faculty of Industrial Engineering and Management
Technion—Israel Institute of Technology

Jona Bargur
Ministry of Energy, Israel

Harold Barnett
Department of Economics
Washington University

Gail R. Blattenberger
Department of Economics
University of Utah

Avishai Breiner
Faculty of Industrial Engineering and Management
Technion–Israel Institute of Technology

J.D. Fuller
Department of Management Science
University of Waterloo

Martin Greenberger
Department of Mathematical Sciences
Johns Hopkins University

James M. Griffin
Department of Economics
University of Houston

Amos Horev
Technion–Israel Institute of Technology

Dale W. Jorgenson
Department of Economics
Harvard University

Reuven Karni
Faculty of Industrial Engineering and Management
Technion–Israel Institute of Technology

Nisan Levin
Faculty of Management
Tel Aviv University

William Marcuse
Economic Division
Brookhaven National Laboratory

Susan E. Martin
Data Resources, Inc.
Lexington, Massachusetts

Gerald M. van Muiswinkel
International Institute for Applied Systems Analysis
Laxenburg, Austria

Mohan Munasinghe
Energy Department
The World Bank

Michael C. Naughton
Data Resources, Inc.
Lexington, Massachusetts

Robert K. Rennhack
Yale University

S. L. Schwartz
Management Science Department
University of British Columbia

Mordecai Shechter
Department of Economics
University of Haifa, Israel

Lestor Taylor
Department of Economics
University of Arizona

Asher Tishler
Faculty of Management and Department of Economics
Tel Aviv University

William A. Vogely
Department of Mineral Economics
Pennsylvania State University

Jacob Zahavi
Faculty of Management
Tel Aviv University

William T. Ziemba
Management Science Department
University of British Columbia